Success in Academic Surgery

Series Editors

Lillian Kao
McGovern School
The University of Texas Health Science Centre
Houston, TX
USA

Herbert Chen
Department of Surgery
University of Alabama at Birmingham
Birmingham, AL
USA

All of the intended volume editors are highly successful academic surgeons with expertise in the respective fields of basic science, clinical trials, health services research, and surgical education research. They are all also leaders within the Association for Academic Surgery (AAS). The previous AAS book, Success in Academic Surgery: Part I provided an overview with regards to the different types of surgical research, beginning one's academic career, and balancing work and life commitments. The aims and scopes of this series of books will be to provide specifics with regards to becoming successful academic surgeons with focuses on the different types of research and academic careers (basic science, clinical trials, health services research, and surgical education). These books will provide information beyond that in the introductory book and even beyond that provided in the Fall and International Courses. The target audience would be medical students, surgical residents, and young surgical faculty. We would promote bulk sales at the Association for Academic Surgery (AAS) Fall Courses (www.aasurg.org) which take place prior to the American College of Surgeons meeting in October, as well as the AAS International Courses which take place year-round in Australasia, Colombia, West Africa, and France. Courses are also planned for India, Italy, and Germany and potentially in the United Kingdom and Saudi Arabia. As the AAS expands the course into other parts of the world, there is a greater need for an accompanying series of textbooks. The AAS has already received requests for translation of the book into Italian. These books would be closely linked with the course content and be sold as part of the registration. In 2011, there were 270 participants in the Fall Courses. In addition, we would anticipate several hundred participants combined per year at all of the international courses.

More information about this series at http://www.springer.com/series/11216

Eugene Kim • Brenessa Lindeman

Editors

Wellbeing

 Springer

Editors
Eugene Kim
USC Keck School of Medicine
Children's Hospital Los Angeles
Los Angeles
CA
USA

Brenessa Lindeman
Division of Surgical Oncology
University of Alabama at Birmingham
Birmingham
AL
USA

ISSN 2194-7481   ISSN 2194-749X   (electronic)
Success in Academic Surgery
ISBN 978-3-030-29469-4   ISBN 978-3-030-29470-0   (eBook)
https://doi.org/10.1007/978-3-030-29470-0

This Springer imprint is published by the registered company Springer Nature Switzerland AG
The registered company address is: Gewerbestrasse 11, 6330 Cham, Switzerland

Contents

Part I
Introduction

Chapter 1
What Is Wellbeing?

Denny Scaria, Mary L. Brandt, Eugene Kim, and Brenessa Lindeman

What is wellbeing? The Oxford English Dictionary informs us that "wellness first appeared in written English in 1654 and, "like adding "ness" to "ill" to make "illness" it was a way to designate the state of being well (i.e. absence of disease)" [1] Despite its' early origins, the concept of "wellness" fell out of favor and the word is hardly found in any publication from the 1800s until the 1960s. If and when it was used, it was used only in the context of the absence of disease.

The modern understanding of the term wellness originated with Halbert L. Dunn in 1961. Dr. Dunn, chief of the National Office of Vital Statistics, was "looking for new terminology to convey the positive aspects of health that people could achieve, beyond simply avoiding sickness" [1]. His ideas led to the slow growth of a movement concerned with optimizing health rather than just preventing disease. The wellness movement gained momentum over the next two decades, reflected by the first publications in the medical literature concerning "wellness" in the early 1980s. "Wellness," intoned Dan Rather in November 1979, introducing a "60 Minutes" segment on a new health movement known by that name. "There's a word you don't

D. Scaria
Department of Surgery, Baylor College of Medicine, Houston, TX, USA
e-mail: Denny.Scaria@bcm.edu

M. L. Brandt
Division of Pediatric Surgery, Baylor College of Medicine, Texas Children's Hospital,
Houston, TX, USA
e-mail: mlbrandt@texaschildrens.org

E. Kim
Division of Pediatric Surgery, USC Keck School of Medicine,
Children's Hospital Los Angeles, Los Angeles, CA, USA
e-mail: eugeneskim@chla.usc.edu

B. Lindeman (✉)
Department of Surgery, University of Alabama School of Medicine,
Birmingham, AL, USA
e-mail: blindeman@uabmc.edu

© Springer Nature Switzerland AG 2020
E. Kim, B. Lindeman (eds.), *Wellbeing*, Success in Academic Surgery,
https://doi.org/10.1007/978-3-030-29470-0_1

hear every day" [1]. A PubMed search bears this out. The first article on physician wellness, published in 1980, was entitled "Physician Survival: Should the Doctor Come First?", and explored difficult doctor-patient relationships and the effect they had on the physician (and, as a result, on the patient) [2]. The first articles in PubMed on physician burnout were published in 1981: "Burnout: A current problem in Pediatrics" [3] and "Physician burnout: When the healer is wounded" [4].

The concept of burnout first appeared in 1974 in a publication by Herbert Freudenberger who developed the term "to describe the consequences of severe or prolonged stress and anxiety experienced by people working in the "healing professions" [5]. Burnout is defined by Merriam-Webster as "exhaustion of physical or emotional strength or motivation usually as a result of prolonged stress or frustration" [6]. In the medical literature, burnout is defined by the presence of one or more of three cardinal "symptoms" of burnout: "losing enthusiasm for work (emotional exhaustion), viewing and/or treating patients and colleagues as objects (depersonalization) and feeling others could do your job better than you (low personal achievement)" [7]. And too often, the surgical literature which addresses physician wellbeing is in fact addressing burnout. This may be because of the assumption that reduction in burnout leads to greater wellbeing. And as such, it is important to be reminded that although burnout is often used as a surrogate for lack of physician wellbeing, it is not the opposite of wellbeing. The opposite of wellbeing is the distress that results when one is not able to appropriately respond to the stresses that result from caring for others.

1.1 Origin of Wellbeing Concepts

Wellbeing is not just a modern concept, but it was addressed thousands of years ago, starting with Plato, Socrates, Epicurus and Aristotle. Two distinct schools of thought about wellbeing have been described in the literature: hedonistic and eudaimonistic [8]. The hedonistic view argues that the good life consists of a life with more positive than negative pleasures. On the other hand, eudaimonism argues that the good life consists of the life that is worth seeking or living.

For a surgeon, wellbeing through a hedonistic lens may consist of greater positive pleasures, such as going through a great surgical case, getting manuscripts published, being praised by colleagues, going on vacation to a favorite destination, being loved by significant others, and enjoying favorite foods and drinks. Negative experiences may include the arduous nature of the work, being called to see inappropriate consults, a nurse or resident reporting mistreatment, and the coding department constantly filling an inbox with inquiries. However, if the positive pleasures outweigh the negative pleasures, then the hedonistic approach to wellbeing is sustainable.

In contrast, the good life may look quite different to those ascribing to the eudaimonistic view. The writings of Ryff et al. offer a framework of components of the good life referred to collectively as psychological wellbeing [9, 10]. These include self-acceptance, personal growth, relatedness, autonomy, relationships, environmental mastery and purpose in life. Let us look at the wellbeing of the above surgeon from a eudaimonistic perspective. Surgeons are living the good life if they are happy with who they are and the choices they made in the past. They are glad to be assistant program director and that they spent time traveling during research years in residency. They have a strong group of friends at work that they trust and can confide in. They are satisfied with relationships they have with family. They have set reasonable standards for themselves, and they are content with where they are in their careers. Even though their colleagues may be publishing more and may be more academic, they believe that they are putting their efforts into what they truly believe in and are happy with that. They may work at a county hospital where they and the staff have a high degree of mutual respect. They can get the most out of a team to care for patients. With regards to long-term goals, they find meaning in their work as they help those less fortunate through the county hospital and are grateful for being able to be physicians. Moreover, they continuously feel challenged as trauma surgeons and look back at how much they have grown over the years as human beings and as surgeons. If you ascribed to the eudaimonistic view of a good life, you would argue that this surgeon, regardless of the negative pleasures he may be experiencing day to day, is living the good life and has wellbeing. He has "eudaimon" or he would be described as "flourishing."

1.2   Concept of Wellbeing

Despite consideration of a definition of wellbeing and descriptions of the good life from the hedonistic and eudaimonistic perspectives, we must also consider how it has been used in the literature. While some have argued that wellbeing is a construct, something that is dependent on the existence of a mind, Dodge et al. posit that it is not a construct and suggest that it can be measured [11, 12]. However, this level of granularity is seldom seen in the literature on wellbeing in surgeons and surgery residents.

One of the landmark studies about surgeon burnout was published in 2009 and surveyed approximately 25,000 surgeons through the American College of Surgeons [13]. Around 8000 recipients responded, making it one of the largest studies done at the time and perhaps to this day, on evaluating the perceptions of surgeons on burnout and career satisfaction. In this study, 40 percent of respondents met criteria for burnout, 30% screened positive for depression, and significant percentages had a mental or physical quality of life more than one half of the standard deviation lower compared to the general population. Moreover, only 74% would choose a career in surgery again. In their discussion of the findings, the authors call for increased efforts to improve the physical and emotional health of surgeons, but they do not define these terms or wellbeing specifically.

Similar patterns emerge upon examination of the literature on residents. A survey of US general surgery residents in 2014 collected surveys from 753 general surgery residents, and 69 percent of these residents met criteria for burnout, with 44 percent having considered dropping out and 44 percent indicating that they would not pursue general surgery again if given the option [14]. Among the respondents, female residents and those working more hours were more likely to be burned out. Following this, a systematic review of wellbeing in residents from all specialties suggests sleep, exercise, family interactions, religious activity and missing significant life events as wellbeing markers, all of which were reduced in training, but goes further to describe that there is no consensus yet on how wellbeing should be measured [15]. The author goes on to note that the included studies touch upon aspects of wellbeing that have been put forth in the psychology literature such as autonomy, competence and relatedness.

While the studies above measured burnout, others have attempted to measure psychological wellbeing. A 2004 study of residents in North Carolina assessed their psychological wellbeing, which they only defined as the absence of psychological distress, using the Symptom Checklist-90 and Perceived Stress Scale, finding that more than a third of the residents met criteria for clinical psychologic distress [16]. Moreover, a study by Salles et al. used the short grit scale to determine the association between grit and psychological wellbeing, finding the two were positively correlated. However, as we have pointed out above, this may only approach one aspect of the different components of a person's wellbeing [17]. Multiple groups have also studied the association between emotional intelligence and psychological wellbeing, finding that those with higher emotional intelligence were less likely to be burned out [18–20]. Therefore, although studies conducted in surgery to date may be attempting to assess wellbeing, what is measured most often is the absence of negative experiences such as burnout rather than true wellbeing.

Therefore, what is wellbeing and how do we measure it? Merriam Webster defines wellbeing as "the state of being happy, healthy, or prosperous" [21] which they differentiate from wellness: "the quality or state of being in good health especially as an actively sought goal" [22]. However, Dodge et al. studied this question at length, stating "As interest in the measurement of wellbeing grows, there is a greater necessity to be clear about what is being measured, and how the resulting data should be interpreted, in order to undertake a fair and valid assessment" [11]. They argued that defining wellbeing is fundamental to measuring it, and went further to propose a new conceptual framework for wellbeing, shown in Fig. 1.1:

"The balance point between an individual's resource pool and the challenges faced."

In a follow up paper the authors propose a multidimensional framework (Fig. 1.2) to measure wellbeing that incorporates both the challenges and resources from the model above [12].

This framework is similar to the Job Demands-Resources (JD-R) theory initially proposed by Bakker et al. [23]. This posits that all jobs are characterized by a set of job demands, those aspects of the job that that require physical and/or cognitive

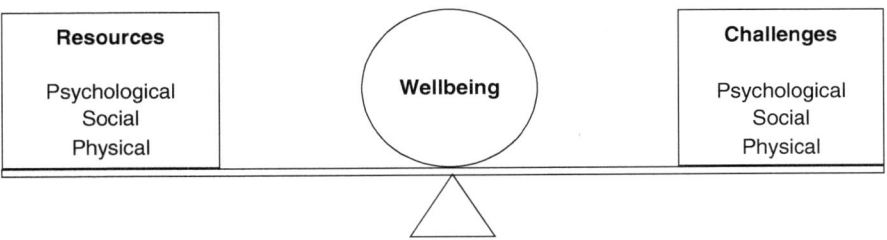

Fig. 1.1 Wellbeing can be viewed as a see-saw balance between psychological, social and physical resources versus psychological, social and physical challenges [11]

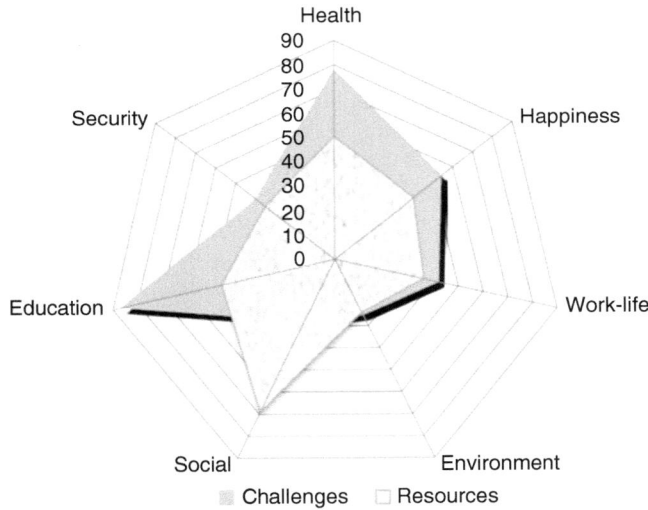

Fig. 1.2 Wellbeing can be further analyzed as a multidimensional balance between challenges and resources. Factors that contribute to wellbeing, such as physical health, happiness, work-life balance, work environment, social support, education, and security, each are faced with balancing reousrces and challenges. Some areas have greater resources than challenges, while other areas are the opposite. It is important to consider wellbeing as a multidimensional concept [12]

engagement, and resources, both personal and work-related facets that can stimulate personal growth and help employees to achieve work-related goals. According to JD-R theory, work engagement is fostered and individuals perform well when the work environment poses high job demands in combination with sufficient job and personal resources to meet those demands [24]. One study identified that more positive perceptions of job resources were related to lower levels of burnout in surgical trainees [25]. Thus interventions that strive to optimize individuals' job demands and increase both their personal and professional resources should be targeted [26].

1.3 Definition of Wellbeing

Clear definitions lead to clear thinking and, in that spirit, we would like to propose an alternate definition of "physician wellbeing", as physician wellbeing is more than the above definition applied to physicians. We are in need of a definition to guide our discussions, strategies and research. We propose to define physician wellbeing as:

The ability to appropriately respond to expected and unexpected stresses in order to be healthy, happy and prosperous in work and in life.

Since prosperity is often misinterpreted as being only about money, it is important to understand the meaning of that word as well: Prosperity is "the condition of being successful or thriving" [27]. If we were to rephrase the definition with this in mind, it might look like this: Physician wellbeing is the ability to appropriately respond to expected and unexpected stresses in order to thrive in a healthy, happy and successful manner in work and in life. This definition also has the advantage of including the concept of resilience within the definition of wellbeing instead of considering it separately. Resilience, which has taken on a deserved and important role in discussions of physician wellbeing is defined as "1. the capability of a strained body to recover its size and shape after deformation caused especially by compressive stress and 2. an ability to recover from or adjust easily to misfortune or change" [28]. Resilience is innate to human beings, and is especially innate in physicians. Resilience by definition has two variables that cannot be separated – the force on the system and the system's response, or put a different way, the stresses of our work and our ability to respond.

Therefore, while most studies which describe interventions to improve wellbeing focus on reducing burnout, this may not be the best or only way to improve wellbeing. Wellbeing for a surgeon, thereby, may assume a state of balance between opposing forces. On one end there are the psychological, social and physical challenges. Psychological challenges may include burnout, social challenges may refer to the work environment, and physical challenges to the physical health of the surgeon. On the other end, resources could include psychological parameters such as grit, social resources may include support systems such as family, colleagues and friends, and lastly physical resources may again be state of good health. Therefore, rather than adopting a eudaimonisitc or a hedonistic view, wellbeing must be assessed in a customized manner for the individuals who are being assessed. Wellbeing for an attending surgeon and a surgical resident may not necessarily be able to be measured with the same tool. Although wellbeing in and of itself refers to a state of balance between resources and challenging demands, according to Wassell and Dodge, tools to measure wellbeing and the interventions to improve wellbeing should be customized to the group to which it is applicable [12]. We suggest that there may be a need for a tool developed in a multidisciplinary fashion to evaluate wellbeing designed for physicians and perhaps for surgeons specifically. Truly, the imperative underlying discussions of physician burnout is the common desire to ensure the safest and best care for our patients, a goal not entirely possible without a workforce whose wellbeing remains a critical component.

References

1. Zimmer B. Wellness. The New York Times. https://www.nytimes.com/2010/04/18/magazine/18FOB-onlanguage-t.html. Accessed 24 Feb 2019.
2. Evans CE. Physician survival: should the doctor come first? Can Fam Physician. 1980;26:856–9.
3. Pines A. Burnout: a current problem in pediatrics. Curr Probl Pediatr. 1981;11:3–32.
4. Golin M. Physician burnout: when the healer is wounded. Am Med News. 1981;24(29):1–2.
5. Rothenberger DA. Physician burnout and Well-being: a systematic review and framework for action. Dis Colon Rectum. 2017;60:567–76.
6. Merriam Webster Dictionary. Burnout. https://www.merriam-webster.com/dictionary/burnout.
7. Brandt M. Sustaining a career in surgery. Am J Surg. 2017;214:707–14.
8. Deci EL, Ryan RM. Hedonia, eudaimonia, and Well-being: an introduction. J Happiness Stud. 2008;9(1):1–11. https://doi.org/10.1007/s10902-006-9018-1.
9. Ryff CD. Happiness is everything, or is it? Explorations on the meaning of psychological Well-being. J Pers Soc Psychol. 1989;57(6):1069–81. http://coursedelivery.org/write/wp-content/uploads/2015/02/2-Happiness-is-everything-or-is-it.pdf
10. Ryff CD, Keyes CLM. The Structure of Psychological Well-Being Revisited. 1995;69(4):719–727.
11. Dodge R, Daly A, Huyton J, Sanders L. The challenge of defining wellbeing. Int J Wellbeing. 2012;2(3):222–35. https://doi.org/10.5502/ijw.v2i3.4.
12. Wassell E, Dodge R. A multidisciplinary framework for measuring and improving wellbeing. Int J Sci Basic Appl Research. 2015;21(2):97.
13. Shanafelt TD, Balch CM, Bechamps GJ, et al. Burnout and career satisfaction among american surgeons. Ann Surg. 2009;250(3):463–70. https://doi.org/10.1097/SLA.0b013e3181ac4dfd.
14. Elmore LC, Jeffe DB, Jin L, Awad MM, Turnbull IR. National Survey of burnout among US general surgery residents. J Am Coll Surg. 2016;223(3):440–51. https://doi.org/10.1016/j.jamcollsurg.2016.05.014.
15. Raj KS. Well-being in residency: a systematic review. J Grad Med Educ. 2016;8(5):674–84. https://doi.org/10.4300/JGME-D-15-00764.1.
16. Zaré SM, Galanko J, Behrns KE, et al. Psychological Well-being of surgery residents before the 80-hour work week: a multiinstitutional study. J Am Coll Surg. 2004;198(4):633–40. https://doi.org/10.1016/j.jamcollsurg.2003.10.006.
17. Salles A, Cohen GL, Mueller CM. The relationship between grit and resident Well-being. Am J Surg. 2014;207(2):251–4. https://doi.org/10.1016/j.amjsurg.2013.09.006.
18. Lin DT, Liebert CA, Tran J, Lau JN. Emotional intelligence as a predictor of resident Well-being. J Am Coll Surg. 2016;223(2):352–8. https://doi.org/10.1016/j.jamcollsurg.2016.04.044.
19. West CP, Dyrbye LN, Erwin PJ, Shanafelt TD. Interventions to prevent and reduce physician burnout: a systematic review and meta-analysis. Lancet. 2016;388(10057):2272–81. https://doi.org/10.1016/S0140-6736(16)31279-X.
20. Wall J. Millennium Generation Poses New Implications for Surgical Resident Education. American College of Surgeons. https://www.facs.org/education/resources/rap/millennium-generation-poses-new-implications-for-surgical-resident-education. Published 2012.
21. Merriam Webster Dictionary. Definition of Well-Being. https://www.merriam-webster.com/dictionary/well-being. Accessed 24 Feb 2019.
22. Merriam Webster Dictionary. Definition of Wellness. https://www.merriam-webster.com/dictionary/wellness. Accessed 24 Feb 2019.
23. Schaufeli WB, Bakker AB. Job demands, job resources, and their relationship with burnout and engagement: a multi-sample study. J Org Behavior. 2004;25:293–315.
24. Bakker AB, Demerouti E, Sanz-Vergel AI. Burnout and work engagement: the JD-R approach. Ann Rev Org Psychol Org Behavior. 2014;1:389–411.

25. Lindeman B, Petrusa E, McKinley S, Hashimoto DA, et al. Association of burnout with emotional intelligence and personality in surgical residents: can we predict who is most at risk? J Surg Educ. 2017;74(6):e22–30.
26. Wingerden V, Bakker D. A test of a job demands-resources intervention. J Manag Psychol. 2016;31(3):686–701.
27. Merriam Webster Dictionary. Definition of Prosperity. https://www.merriam-webster.com/dictionary/prosperity. Accessed 24 Feb 2019.
28. Merram Webster. Resilience. https://www.merriam-webster.com/dictionary/resilience.

Chapter 2
Why Focus on Wellbeing?

Mary L. Brandt

The primary reason to focus on our own wellbeing and that of our colleagues is to prevent losses associated with living in a state of chronic and/or severe distress. These losses are known to all who practice medicine and include declining personal health, loss of relationships, loss of employment and even loss of life. In addition to these personal losses, physician distress also leads to profound losses for institutions. These institutional losses can be measured in dollars, patient satisfaction and institutional prestige, losses that are therefore persuasive to organizational leadership. And finally, and perhaps most importantly, chronic distress, particularly if it is the result of misalignment of core values, results in loss of meaning and purpose, or, put a different way, loss of a life well-lived.

2.1 Personal Losses

The personal losses experienced by physicians, PAs/NPs, nurses and other medical providers who are suffering from work-related distress include impaired physical health, impaired mental health, loss of relationships, loss of employment and loss of life.

M. L. Brandt (✉)
Division of Pediatric Surgery, Baylor College of Medicine, Texas Children's Hospital, Houston, TX, USA
e-mail: mary.brandt@bcm.edu

2.1.1 Loss of Physical Health

It is not surprising that physicians experience impaired physical health; we are terrible at practicing what we preach when it comes to routine health care. According to a large survey performed by the American College of Surgeons, 25% of surgeons did not undergo recommended screening for colon cancer, heart disease or prostate cancer" [1]. "This pattern starts during residency; in a recent study of surgical residents, 56% did not have a primary care provider, 37% had not seen a dentist in 2 years and 29% did not have a current prescription for glasses or contacts" [1]. Research will determine whether age appropriate screening and routine dental and eye exams will be a metric that might serve as a surrogate for the ability of individuals and institutions to focus on self-care. This is not trivial; burnout correlates with an increased incidence of cardiovascular disease and short life expectancy [2]. Another area for institutional focus in terms of physical health is ergonomic injury. Although this is more acute, and often severe, for surgeons, ergonomic issues are found in all hospitals and clinics, and for everyone who works there. In institutional terms, significant ergonomic injury results in personnel unable to work. For this physician, this means loss of employment but also a loss of things that might bring one joy such as golf, tennis, hiking and other physical activities [3–5].

2.1.2 Loss of a Healthy Lifestyle

Most of us who work in health care would choose a healthy lifestyle with attention to diet, hydration, exercise, and sleep when possible. Often our working conditions and schedules interfere with choices we might otherwise make, a loss which also contributes to loss of personal health.

Hippocrates recognized the importance of a good diet 2400 years ago when he said, "Let food be thy medicine and medicine be thy food." For physicians who understand the importance of a healthy diet of "real" food, there are barriers at work that make it almost impossible to achieve a healthy diet without bringing all food from home [6]. It is a sad reality that our hospitals provide food that, in general, meets the sub-standard expectations of the American public, often without other, healthier choices. This is a financial "necessity" according to the hospitals, but it must be recognized and discussed as a decision that is financially based, but that is in opposition to what is requested by physicians and supported by data. The deleterious effects of a diet high in fat, high in sugar and consisting mostly of processed foods are well known, and physicians routinely counsel patients to avoid these food, while partaking of the morning donut at Grand Rounds, on-call pizza and "free" junk food that is available in many hospitals [7, 8]. Although all of us occasionally indulge in foods like this (and there is nothing wrong with that!) , most of us would also choose healthy, well-prepared food if it were available. In a nutshell, eating healthy is a choice that requires additional energy. If we are to prevent a "default" to poor eating habits, we (both individuals and institutions) have to create environments and habits that make it easy to choose healthy food over poor food. Appropriate nutrition is an important part of good patient care; "The acute effects of caloric intake on cognition are well understood, but unfortunately, many physicians routinely skip meals, consume food too rapidly, or consume food with poor nutritional value" [9]. Good food not only provided optimal nutrition, as Lemaire points out, "good food also improves a sense of wellbeing" [1, 10]. A part of good nutrition that deserves more focus is hydration. Along with not eating properly, physicians are notorious for not staying hydrated during the working day and/or when on call [8]. "One study of clinicians completing 150 shifts in the UK revealed that significant portions started (36%) and ended (45%) their shifts clinically dehydrated" [9]. From the individuals point of view, you are likely to be dehydrated (not just hypohydrated) if your urine is darker than normal and you are thirsty [11].

Like diet, many physicians and other healthcare providers would choose to maintain physical fitness with regular exercise but feel that they are not able to do so because of the time constraints and demands of their jobs. In time-constrained settings, choices have to be made… do I spend time with my family, prepare my healthy meal for tonight or go for a run? Often the "return on investment" for tired, stressed physicians is less for exercise than for other aspects of self-care. This is reflected in the data; "…in several surveys of US surgeons, only 50% met the CDC guidelines for aerobic exercise and only 33% met the requirements for resistance (weight) training" [1]. When one considers that, apart from the small percentage of compulsive (or almost compulsive) exercisers, exercise is often sacrificed for other aspects of self-care, it becomes apparent that this may be a particularly important marker of institutional success in promoting healthy behaviors.

Physicians and other health care providers must be present and providing care 24/7 in the hospital setting. For that reason, sleep restriction (chronic, low-grade sleep deprivation) and sleep deprivation (a sleepless night on call) are the norm, not the exception for many practitioners. The negative effects of sleep deprivation and chronic sleep restriction on health is well known [12]. With the exception of a very small percentage of people who need 7 or 9 h of sleep, adults need 8 h of sleep per night, "60% of surgeons reported an average of less than 6 hours of sleep per night, resulting in chronic sleep restriction" [1]. As more information becomes available about sleep, call schedules may have to be adjusted. For example, there is evidence that combining sleep deprivation with being awake from midnight to dawn is additive in its deleterious effect [1].

Thinking about physical health as the number of women in medicine grows extends beyond our own physical health. New mothers who are practicing physicians are ironically disadvantaged compared to other women in the workforce when it comes to breastfeeding their newborns. This is truly a "walk the walk" issue for health care institutions since the data is clear that breast milk, when it is possible to provide it, is key in promoting optimal health in the newborn. Although it may not directly affect the health of the provider in question, it is truly shameful that many medical institutions have relegated breast pumping to bathrooms and other public spaces.

2.1.3   Loss of Mental Health

The incidence of mental health issues in medical students is no different at baseline than the general population. However, with time in training and time practicing, the incidence of depression and its horrific endpoint, suicide, increases to well above that of the general population. In terms of a summary of the issues that create psychological stress for physicians (and everyone else in medicine), I can't do better than this summary, published in 2005 by BA Harms: "Once entering medical practice, additional stressors include shift work, long workdays, high case loads, time pressures, poor sleep habits and high performance expectations, challenging patients, personal fears regarding competency, and changing roles in the workplace. In addition, physicians and trainees regularly face suffering, fear, failures, and death, as well as difficult interactions with patients, families and other medical personnel" [13]. Added to the stressful nature of our work, there are two additional stressors that warrant mentioning here, the second victim syndrome and a sense of not being safe at work.

The second victim syndrome occurs in response to medical errors, adverse outcomes and malpractice lawsuits [14]. Due to the emotional trauma these events create, the physicians who find themselves experiencing them inevitably become a "second victim" [15]. This is not an uncommon situation since physicians will experience errors and adverse outcomes in their careers. 42% of all US physicians will be sued during their career, a number that increases to 90% for surgeons [14]. Because we are human, all of us will make mistakes and will experience adverse outcomes that had nothing to do with our actions - and these events will deeply hurt us. The culture of medicine is to hide our emotions after these events, to pretend that all is right. As a result, institutions need to recognize the need for support of any physician who finds themselves in the position of being a second victim and create the infrastructure necessary to provide that support.

Safety at work is increasingly a problem, both in the sense of personal safety and job security. Even a minor sense of not being safe can "wholly dominate" the world of a physician [9]. The issue of physical safety is relatively minor for most physicians, as institutions usually have a mature security system in place. However, job security has become a major concern for many physicians. As the finances and culture of medicine have shifted to a more "corporate" model, more and more physicians experience the feeling that their positions at work are somehow not as safe as they once perceived them to be. As Shapiro has pointed out, "Job insecurity is a threat to wellness for physicians in downsizing or struggling systems…Managing patients while simultaneously feeling insecure about one's employment is challenging" [9]. This feeling of being unsafe is often exacerbated by a sense that they are not respected or supported by leadership. This perception is important; Shanafelt has demonstrated that in physicians who are burnt out, "11% of the variation in burnout and 47% of the variation in satisfaction with the organization was explained by the leadership rating of the division/department chairperson" [2]. This is also supported by a large study of over 20,000 workers performed by Christine Porath.

In her study, she found that those "who feel respected by immediate supervisors, report 56% better health and wellbeing, 89% greater enjoyment and satisfaction with their jobs, and are significantly more likely to stay" [9].

2.1.4 Loss of Relationships

It is well known that there is a high rate of divorce in medicine [16]. Although there are no published data, there is also much anecdotal evidence of friendships and other family relationships that have suffered as the result of work related stress. In addition to the loss of these important relationships, the current medical care environment has led to loss of other important relationships - the relationships we have with our patients. One of the key findings of the MEMO (Minimizing Error, Maximizing Outcome) study performed by Linzer et al. in 2005 was "that physician satisfaction was derived primarily from patient relationships..." [17, 18].

2.1.5 Loss of Employment

Not all behaviors or transgressions that result in being fired, "pushed out" or "laid off" from medical employment are due to physician stress or burnout... but many of them are. A meta-analysis of 47 studies performed by Pangiotti showed that burnout "is associated with 2-fold increased odds for unsafe care, unprofessional behaviors, and low patient satisfaction" [19]. Alcohol and other substance abuse, is common in physicians, with almost 13% of men and 21% of women meeting criteria for alcohol abuse or dependence, numbers that are higher than the general population. This increased use of alcohol and other substances may represent attempts to self-medicate to numb the effects of distress.

2.1.6 Loss of Life

The increased incidence of physician suicide, almost 2.5 times that of the general population, is well recognized [9]. Suicidality, or thoughts of committing suicide occurs in 6.3% of all surgeons [20]. Tragically, suicide is now the most common cause of death for all male residents and the second most common cause of death for female residents [9]. The tragedy of physician suicide, if anything, is underappreciated as the statistics represent only known suicides. If one includes unexpected deaths in young physicians, such as single car accidents, the number would be much higher.

2.2   Institutional Losses

The role of the institution in improving physician wellbeing is critical. The environment of the workplace contributes substantially to the stresses that can become distress and lead to burnout. According to Shanafelt and Noseworthy, "the local work environment is a major factor in determining whether physicians are likely to develop burnout or, alternatively, to become fully engaged and dedicated to their work [18]. For the institution, investment in preventing physician distress and burnout is key, as the institutional losses related to these disorders are significant. These losses include loss of employees, loss of productivity, as well as decreased patient safety and patient satisfaction.

2.2.1   Loss of Employees

Physicians who are suffering will leave, unless there are family or other constraints that keep them from leaving, in which case they will continue to work in a depleted state. The rate of turnover for physicians who meet the criteria for burnout is double that of peers who are not burnt out [2]. Replacing physicians costs money in recruitment and lost revenue during the transition to a new hire, a cost that has been estimated as 2–3 times the annual salary of the physician being replaced [1, 2]. If the physician who leaves is in a specialty with significant physician shortages, the cost will be even higher [2]. For the institution, preventing and/or treating physician burnout is a smart business plan. As Shanafelt has pointed out - "If the organization [hypothetical with 450 MDs] believed that it had identified an organizational intervention that cost $1 million/y that could reduce the prevalence of burnout from 50% to 40% (a 20% relative risk reduction), the intervention would be expected to reduce turnover by 0.5% (a 20% reduction in the 2.5% turnover attributable to burnout). The associated organizational cost savings would be $1.125 million per year (ROI, 12.5%)" [2].

In addition to the financial burden of losing a physician, a high rate of turnover will affect the reputation of the organization [2]. Most organizations run "lean" without much redundancy in staffing. Losing a physician places a significant burden on the remaining team members, risking their wellbeing, and increasing the risk that additional physicians will leave the organization. There is another, long-term issue that is not often discussed, but is a looming crisis - the future recruitment of physicians. It is a telling and very worrisome finding that 40% of young physicians would not choose a career in medicine again if they had the choice [21]. As Cohen pointed out in his paper entitled "Productivity, Meet Burnout", "We are approaching a tipping point in which the rewards of being a radiologist and the conduct of other valuable work (e.g., research and educating trainees) are being overwhelmed by the pressures of an increasingly demanding clinical workday" [22]. Medicine is a profoundly rewarding career, but with 50% of physicians meeting the criteria for burnout, we risk losing an entire generation of potential physicians who are not willing to sacrifice their wellbeing, and the wellbeing of their families for a career in medicine, unless we develop strategies to turn this crisis around.

2.2.2 Loss of Productivity

High quality institutions value their team members and want them to be happy, but in case that is not enough motivation, there are clear financial implications for an institution when physicians are burnt out. Although it is difficult to quantify, there is little doubt that a physician who is in distress will be less productive than physicians who experience wellbeing at work [2]. In a meta-analysis, Dewa et al. used surrogate measures of productivity which included number of sick leave days, intent to continue practicing, intent to change jobs, and work ability to ask the question "Does burnout decrease productivity?". In the five high-quality papers they were able to study, the answer was "yes" in all five studies [23]. For institutions, it is also important to realize that burnout is "contagious", the implication being that as more team members begin to suffer distress and even burnout, that productivity will decrease [2].

2.2.3 Loss of Patient Satisfaction, Quality and Safety

In addition to financial losses, there are other important institutional losses associated with burnout. The data are clear that burnout is associated with increased medical errors, increased malpractice suits, more unprofessional behavior and decreased patient satisfaction [1, 19]. Physician satisfaction at work may be a good surrogate metric for these issues as it is "strongly linked" to patient satisfaction. [21]

2.3 Societal Losses

As stated so well by Jager et al., "At a societal level, the public benefits from having a group of individuals who are motivated to do work that goes beyond satisfying personal self-interest" [24]. Loss of talented physicians who leave practice early is a societal loss. Perhaps more importantly, there is now concern about the future of medicine – who we will be able to recruit and whether we will be able to maintain the same high quality of students in our medical school classes. As noted above, 40% of young physicians would not choose a career in medicine again if given the choice. In surgery, 60% of surgeons would retire if they could and there are all a large number of surgeons leaving practice early [25]. As bright college students consider their future careers, these data, and other similar data, will almost certainly play a role in whether or not they choose medicine as their career.

2.4   Loss of Meaning and Purpose

How to live a "good" life has been the work of philosophers and theologians since humans began to ponder these important questions. In that context, there is a philosophical, or for some, a spiritual loss associated with physician distress and burnout. The need for meaning is not often articulated in the workplace, but it is well recognized; "The importance of spirituality is recognized by surgeons. Along with protected time for relationships, surgeons rank meaning in work and "focusing on what is most important in life" as the most essential strategies to promote wellness" [1]. In addition to the many losses discussed above, physician burnout adversely affects physicians' "professionalism, altruism, and sense of calling" [2, 24]. This "sense of calling", which is the source of an intrinsic motivation for work, is a characteristic of service professions, and results in being more engaged in work [24]. Intrinsic motivation, no matter its source, is important for institutions to nurture and support; "Decades of social psychological and organizational behavior research have found that intrinsically motivated individuals perform better (especially over the long term) because they are more task focused and persistent" [24].

When we talk about the philosophical or spiritual losses associated with physician distress, what we are really talking about is not being able to live in a way that allows us to "realize our true potential", i.e. Maslow's highest hierarchy of need [9]. As Maslow stated, "A musician must make music, an artist must paint, a poet must write, if he is to be ultimately happy. What a man can be, he must be. This need we may call self-actualization. This tendency might be phrased as the desire to become more and more what one is, to become everything that one is capable of becoming" [9]. For example, most physicians today point to the marked increase in clerical work due to EMRs as taking away from patient care and, therefore, keeping them from patient care. Burnout, as concluded by Maslach after 20 years of research on the subject, arises "when there is a major mismatch between the nature of the job and the nature of the person who does the job." Loss of purpose and meaning may be more important than the physical and emotional factors that contribute to physician distress and burnout since what we are fundamentally talking about when we talk about physician wellbeing is the ability to be whole.

2.5   Conclusion

Wellbeing, in the context of this book, means focusing on effecting means to prevent distress and, when that fails, to heal ourselves, our colleagues and our profession in order to further our mission of high quality and compassionate patient care. At its core, promoting physician wellbeing means a personal commitment to promoting wellness of body and soul - and an institutional commitment to sustain work practices and an environment that allows physicians to achieve and celebrate our potential as healers.

References

1. Brandt M. Sustaining a career in surgery. Am J Surg. 2017;214:707–14.
2. Shanafelt T, Goh J, Sinsky C. The business case for investing in physician wellbeing. JAMA Intern Med. 2017;177:1826–32.
3. Park A, Lee G, Seagull FJ, et al. Patients benefit while surgeons suffer: an impending epidemic. J Am Coll Surg. 2010;210:306–13.
4. Berguer R. Ergonomics in the operating room. Am J Surg. 1996;171:385–6.
5. Rosenblatt PL, McKinney J, Adams SR. Ergonomics in the operating room: protecting the surgeon. J Minim Invasive Gynecol. 2013;20:744.
6. Brandt ML. The Claude organ memorial lecture: the practice of surgery: surgery as practice. Am J Surg. 2009;198:742–7.
7. Kim H, Hu EA, Rebholz CM. Ultra-processed food intake and mortality in the USA: results from the third National Health and nutrition examination survey (NHANES III, 1988–1994). Public Health Nutr. 2019:1–9.
8. Hamidi MS, Boggild MK, Cheung AM. Running on empty: a review of nutrition and physicians' wellbeing. Postgrad Med J. 2016;92:478–81.
9. Shapiro DE, Duquette C, Abbott LM, et al. Beyond burnout: a physician wellness hierarchy designed to prioritize interventions at the systems level. Am J Med Epub. 2018;13 https://doi.org/10.1016/j.amjmed.2018.11.028.
10. Lemaire JB, Wallace JE, Dinsmore K, et al. Physician nutrition and cognition during work hours: effect of a nutrition based intervention. BMC Health Serv Res. 2010;10:241.
11. Cheuvront SN, Kenefick RW. Am I drinking enough? Yes, no, and maybe. J Am Coll Nutr. 2016;35:185–92.
12. Bianchi MT. Sleep deprivation and disease. New York: Springer; 2014.
13. Harms BA, Heise CP, Gould JC, et al. A 25-year single institution analysis of health, practice, and fate of general surgeons. Ann Surg. 2005;242:520–6; discussion 526-9
14. Balch CM, Oreskovich MR, Dyrbye LN, et al. Personal consequences of malpractice lawsuits on American surgeons. J Am Coll Surg. 2011;213:657–67.
15. Marmon LM, Heiss K. Improving surgeon wellness: the second victim syndrome and quality of care. Semin Pediatr Surg. 2015;24:315–8.
16. Daily JA. Divorce among physicians and medical trainees. J Am Coll Cardiol. 2019;73:521–4.
17. Linzer M, Baier Manwell L, Mundt M, et al. Organizational climate, stress, and error in primary care: the MEMO study. In: Henriksen K, Battles JB, Marks ES, et al., eds. Advances in patient safety: from research to implementation (Volume 1: Research Findings). Rockville, MD: Agency for Healthcare Research and Quality (US). http://www.ncbi.nlm.nih.gov/books/NBK20448/. 2005. Accessed 19 Mar 2019.
18. Rothenberger DA. Physician burnout and Well-being: a systematic review and framework for action. Dis Colon Rectum. 2017;60:567–76.
19. Panagioti M, Geraghty K, Johnson J, et al. Association between physician burnout and patient safety, professionalism, and patient satisfaction: a systematic review and meta-analysis. JAMA Intern Med. 2018;178:1317–30.
20. Balch CM, Freischlag JA, Shanafelt TD. Stress and burnout among surgeons: understanding and managing the syndrome and avoiding the adverse consequences. Arch Surg. 2009;144:371–6.
21. Brown S, Gunderman RB. Viewpoint: enhancing the professional fulfillment of physicians. Acad Med. 2006;81:577–82.
22. Cohan RH, Davenport MS. Productivity, meet burnout. Acad Radiol. 2018;25:1513–4.
23. Dewa CS, Loong D, Bonato S, et al. How does burnout affect physician productivity? A systematic literature review. BMC Health Serv Res. 2014;14:325.
24. Jager AJ, Tutty MA, Kao AC. Association between physician burnout and identification with medicine as a calling. Mayo Clin Proc. 2017;92:415–22.
25. Shanafelt T, Sloan J, Satele D, et al. Why do surgeons consider leaving practice? J Am Coll Surg. 2011;212:421–2.

Part II
Maintaining Wellbeing as a Surgeon

Chapter 3
Important Terms in Wellbeing

Jason C. Pradarelli, Naomi Shimizu, and Douglas S. Smink

3.1 Introduction

To create positive change for the wellbeing of surgeons, we must first acquire a thorough understanding of its components. Wellbeing for surgeons has been described by the National Academy of Medicine as a state of personal fulfillment and engagement that leads to joy in one's practice and a connection to why one entered health care and surgery as a profession in the first place [1]. In this chapter, we define important terms in wellbeing specific to surgeons and surgical practice. This list of wellbeing terms is not exhaustive but covers a range of key topics, from instinctual stereotypes to lesser-known and poorly-characterized concepts. Each term is defined, and an example is provided to give the term context in surgery. Our goal is to help the audience develop a common language for discussing complex issues related to surgeons' wellbeing throughout this book and in the real world.

J. C. Pradarelli · D. S. Smink (✉)
Department of Surgery, Brigham and Women's Hospital, Harvard Medical School, Boston, MA, USA

Ariadne Labs at Brigham and Women's Hospital and the Harvard T.H. Chan School of Public Health, Boston, MA, USA
e-mail: jpradarelli@partners.org; dsmink@bwh.harvard.edu

N. Shimizu
Department of Surgery, Brigham and Women's Hospital, Harvard Medical School, Boston, MA, USA
e-mail: nshimizu2@bwh.harvard.edu

© Springer Nature Switzerland AG 2020
E. Kim, B. Lindeman (eds.), *Wellbeing*, Success in Academic Surgery, https://doi.org/10.1007/978-3-030-29470-0_3

3.2 Factors Positively Associated with Wellbeing

To characterize surgeons' wellbeing, we must introduce a vocabulary that surgeons can use to support their own wellbeing and the wellbeing of others. First, we describe general terms that are positively associated with personal wellbeing.

Viewing wellbeing as the opposite of burnout and depression would be an incomplete definition. **Wellbeing** is more than merely the absence of burnout; it is characterized by positivity and content with one's life, including their work life [1]. Surgeons who experience wellbeing are not immune from stress or pressure in the workplace; rather, they feel equipped to take on the challenges of the surgical environment with joy and curiosity. *Example*: While reaching the end of a shift on-call, a surgeon receives a late afternoon consult from the medicine service. Instead of reacting with anger and bitterness about a mundane consult from a lazy or incapable physician, a surgeon who has achieved wellbeing might view the consult as an opportunity to care for a new patient, to improve that patient's current care, and to help a fellow physician in a different specialty.

Wellness encompasses similar principles as wellbeing but with a more narrowed focus on an individual's health [2]. Whereas wellbeing is a holistic state of being that an individual may reach, wellness focuses on good health that an organization can help to cultivate. Wellness depends on an organization's culture; it represents the priorities of a group of individuals to support physically, mentally, and spiritually healthy connections with their work. *Example*: In a surgical residency program, one resident unfortunately experiences the loss of a family member. A program that prioritizes wellness immediately arranges for coverage on that resident's service to allow the resident to return home and be present with family, without portraying a sense of inconvenience to the program. Although coverage could be arranged even without a culture of wellness, a wellness-oriented program protects mental wellness by *encouraging* the resident to take the necessary time with family and by not inducing guilt in the resident.

Work fulfillment refers to a sense of satisfaction and content with one's job. It is a component of an individual's wellbeing and is particularly relevant for individuals such as surgeons who spend a large portion of their day in a work setting [3]. *Example*: A transplant surgeon feels excitement and happiness when called in at midnight for a transplant case on a patient that has been on the waiting list for months, despite the hour of the day or the opportunity cost of not spending time at home resting or with family.

Work engagement characterizes the level to which a person feels invested in and has influence over the processes and outcomes that occur in their workplace [4]. *Example*: Surgeons with a high level of work engagement willingly participate in committees within their division, department, or group, because they are invested in making decisions that shape the culture of their work environment. In contrast, surgeons with a low level of work engagement may focus solely on seeing their own patients at work and abstain from participating in any extra-clinical activities, thus effectively disengaging themselves from the work environment around them.

Autonomy in the workplace refers to the level of independence that an individual has in making decisions that directly affect their work and/or work environment. Autonomy is also described as control over one's practice [1]. *Example*: A highly autonomous surgical practice might be characterized by the ability of a surgeon to decide how many patients they see in clinic without being pressured to meet a quota of clinical productivity enforced by others. An autonomous practice might also allow a surgeon to take a half-day off to attend their child's school play. On the other hand, a surgeon with a low level of autonomy at work might feel as if they have no control over the number of patients they see in clinic or whether they can decide to take a half-day off for family events—that is, somebody else makes the decisions, and the individual surgeon may feel like a "cog in the wheel."

Health is a broad concept but includes physical, mental, and spiritual health, among others. Physical health includes eating a balanced diet consistently, maintaining wakefulness by getting adequate sleep, and ensuring physical fitness with regular exercise. Mental health spans the issues of anxiety and depression all the way to substance abuse and addiction, including avoidance of these mental health stressors and treatment if they do occur. Spiritual health may differ for each person, but generally refers to a belief that one is connected to something greater than oneself. Spiritual connection may be as structured as religion or as free-form as yoga or meditation. *Example*: A surgeon might ensure they practice 30 minutes of yoga on most days of the week, because even though they are not directly providing patient care or advancing their academic agenda, they feel more energy, creativity, and physical strength for their surgical career when they maintain their personal health this way.

3.3 Factors Negatively Associated with Wellbeing

In reading this next section, it is important to be open and straightforward with the current state of wellbeing in surgery. Here, we describe several factors that directly threaten wellbeing for surgeons.

Burnout has been defined as a syndrome of emotional exhaustion, depersonalization, and reduced personal accomplishment, particularly among individuals who work with other people in some capacity [5]. Physicians are known to be at higher risk for burnout than the general U.S. population [6]. Reported burnout rates vary widely among surgeons, ranging from 40 to 60%, depending on the surgical subspecialty [6, 7]. Burnout has many manifestations in surgery, spanning its three major domains—emotional exhaustion, depersonalization, and reduced sense of personal accomplishment—which are defined below.

Emotional exhaustion refers to the phenomenon that as emotional resources are depleted, individuals feel they are no longer able to give of themselves at a psychological level [5]. *Example*: Surgeons may experience emotional exhaustion during or after caring for a dying patient, including the numerous end-of-life conversations with the patient, family members, and others on the care team.

Depersonalization is a calloused and dehumanized perception of others [5]. For surgeons, depersonalization typically refers to negative and cynical feelings toward one's patients, although these feelings could also be directed toward one's colleagues or family members. *Example*: Surgeons experiencing depersonalization may be more likely to view a noncompliant patient as *deserving* of their suffering and less likely to demonstrate empathy in patient care. Depersonalization may also manifest for surgeons in the absence of an empathetic attitude toward patients, viewing the next patient in the emergency department as just another "case" or a note to write.

Reduced sense of personal accomplishment, in contrast to depersonalization, refers to negative evaluations about one's *self* in relation to their work achievements [5]. These pessimistic feelings are directed inwardly and are characterized by exaggerated criticisms of oneself. *Example*: One surgeon may feel personally unhappy and dissatisfied with their clinical accomplishments despite seeing 30 patients in one clinic session and helping to reassure many patients and families about their health concerns. Other surgeons may criticize or punish themselves for receiving suboptimal grant scores despite the numerous prior awards and publications they have already accumulated.

Depression is different from, yet intricately linked with, burnout. Depression is a clinical mood disorder with defined diagnostic criteria. A diagnosis of depression requires that an individual experience a collection of symptoms (such as depressed mood and loss of interest in activities, among others) over a two-week period and that these symptoms cause the individual significant distress or impairment in daily functioning [8]. Depression differs from sadness in that sadness is usually caused by a specific situation, person, or event. On the other hand, depression does not require a trigger; a depressed person feels sad or hopeless about everything [8]. Burnout is closely linked with depression. Prolonged burnout may result in depression; conversely, untreated major depressive disorder could contribute to an individual experiencing the syndrome of burnout. *Example*: Depression may have a range of manifestations for surgeons. On one end of the spectrum, a surgeon might mutter a comment in their office within earshot of a colleague that they want to kill themselves. On the other end, a surgeon may be more discreet and appear perfectly content in the presence of colleagues at work, yet at home they may self-medicate with alcohol.

3.4 Individual Characteristics to Combat Burnout and Support Wellbeing

In this next section, we define terms that relate to an individual's ability to support their own wellbeing. These are personal skills that some individuals possess naturally, but that all can learn to adopt and improve.

Emotional intelligence (EI) is defined as an individual's ability to detect, understand, and respond to their own emotions and the emotions of others [9]. It allows an individual to manage their internal emotional stressors and to navigate external relationships with others. EI encompasses behavioral skills such as empathy in addition to communication skills such as active listening and questioning. *Example*: An emotionally intelligent surgeon notices when their administrative assistant is upset and frustrated, takes a few minutes to acknowledge the assistant's emotions and inquires about why they feel that way. This action gives their assistant the opportunity to express concerns they had with the surgeon's conflicting schedule, thus relieving the assistant's angst. Here, the surgeon mitigates a problem that could have stifled an effective work partnership, thus sparing the surgeon burdensome administrative tasks.

Resilience is a less well-characterized concept that refers to an individual's ability to recover from distress and is thought to be protective of burnout [10]. Related to "grit," resilience enables an individual to withstand adverse events and subsequently to continue moving forward [11]. Resilience is often used to describe successful surgical residents when they demonstrate clinical or academic productivity after initial failed attempts, all while advancing through long work hours and rigorous training requirements. Despite this notion, resilience is a trait that is useful for surgeons throughout their careers to maintain and improve their wellbeing. *Example*: A junior faculty surgeon whose major grant proposal was rejected at six funding agencies attends a grant-writing course, downsizes the scope of their proposal, and resubmits to a young investigator award, which then gets funded to conduct a pilot study.

Mindfulness refers to an individual's ability to be present in the moment and to pay attention to one's thoughts, emotions, and experiences in a non-reactive way [12]. Mindfulness can be achieved through guided reflection and meditation practices and is correlated with reductions in individuals' stress levels, including for surgical residents [12]. *Example*: Imagine an obese, smoking patient in clinic is yelling at staff for having to wait too long for their appointment, and then accuses the surgeon of poor patient care when they recommend against a surgery for an asymptomatic inguinal hernia. A surgeon who attains a state of mindfulness recognizes that the patient's anger is likely multifactorial and not directed personally at them, which better equips the surgeon to diffuse the patient's anger and regain control of their clinic's tempo.

3.5 External Strategies to Promote Wellbeing

Beyond the personal and interpersonal skills that an individual can use to support their own wellbeing, several external factors may also promote an individual's wellbeing. These external factors can be viewed as strategies that groups or organizations can implement to foster wellbeing among their individual constituents.

Mentorship is a dynamic relationship between two individuals in which the mentor imparts perspective, skills, and guidance to the mentee [13]. Although both parties are responsible for sustaining the relationship, a mentor tends to hold the power, authority, and expertise, while the mentee seeks guidance and advice [14].

The relationship between a mentor and mentee is reciprocal and aimed at promoting the careers of both [15]. Mentoring relationships have been associated with reduced rates of burnout, particularly among surgical residents [16]. *Example*: When looking to advance their career position, a junior faculty surgeon may tap into an experienced mentor's advice to better understand the challenges and opportunities of leaving their current institution for a new one. The mentee surgeon may feel relief in having the mentor's advice, thus boosting their confidence and positively contributing to their wellbeing.

Sponsorship is similar to mentorship but entails a relationship that is more outwardly visible to third parties. Like a mentor, a sponsor is also committed to the development of a particular project or individual. However, a sponsor typically spends less time with a mentee than does a mentor; instead, a sponsor uses their influence in a field to vouch for a mentee and to make them more visible [15]. Sponsors may not directly promote an individual's wellbeing but are critically important for an individual's career advancement, which is linked to work fulfillment and wellbeing for high-functioning professionals. *Example*: A sponsor may use their social capital and political influence to recommend that a junior faculty surgeon deliver an important presentation at a national meeting instead of the sponsor. Another sponsor may promote a surgical resident's career by calling the program director of the resident's top fellowship choice.

Similarly, **coaching** is another form of professional development that may promote an individual's wellbeing. A coach helps an individual target improvements in a particular skill or subject [15, 17]. Coaching is different from mentoring, however, as coaching focuses on performance related to a specific issue rather than overall growth in multiple dimensions [15]. Although coaching has not been studied for burnout among surgeons specifically, early results of a professional development program for internal medicine residents indicate that positive psychology coaching is associated with lower burnout rates [18, 19]. In another high-performing professional context, the business community has embraced the use of coaching for addressing burnout among executives and entrepreneurs [20]. *Example*: Focusing on intraoperative performance, a surgeon who wants to continue improving with a procedure may ask a colleague to observe them in the operating room and give direct feedback, thus lowering their anxiety about the procedure and helping them to feel more competent. In an academic context, a surgeon seeking to write their first book may look to a gifted writer as a coach, to help them specifically develop their writing skills, which may subsequently enhance their work fulfillment.

Moving beyond one-on-one relationships, the **learning and practice environment** also has an important influence on surgeons' wellbeing. The learning and practice environment refers to the physical space and intangible culture that permeates where learners are taught and where surgical care is delivered. Numerous factors influence the learning and practice environment itself, including workplace safety and violence, psychological safety, and the physical conditions of the hospital or clinic rooms [1]. Student affairs policies, formal mentoring programs, and electronic health record (EHR) systems all contribute to an individual's learning and practice environment. *Example*: A medical record that is divided among several EHR systems and paper charts may present a major challenge to a surgeon in a busy clinic, whereas an integrated single EHR could support the wellbeing of the surgical practice by easing the surgeon's ability to access patient records, review labs, and enter orders all in one place. Additionally, medical scribes may support surgeons' practice environments by reducing their burden of documentation.

As burnout among surgeons becomes more visible and surgeons' wellbeing becomes a greater priority, several institutions have implemented wellness interventions to combat physician burnout. These interventions may be categorized either as systematic or patchwork interventions. **Systematic wellness interventions** involve programmatic changes that upend the infrastructure and/or culture of an institution to support physician wellbeing. *Example*: The Southern California Permanente Medical Group (SCPMG) implemented the Complete Care initiative in 2004 to redesign its primary care services with the goal of improving patient outcomes and physician satisfaction [21]. It focused on sharing accountability of clinical primary care with specialist colleagues, delegating responsibilities to non-physician providers (e.g. medical assistants, licensed vocational nurses) to relieve physicians' task burden, and leveraging technology to better interface with patients. These were system-wide changes in clinical care delivery that intended to support physicians' wellbeing by improving their work fulfillment and engagement and reducing burnout and emotional exhaustion.

In contrast, **patchwork wellness interventions** take on a piecemeal approach that offer physicians certain services or benefits but do not often address the underlying institutional culture. *Example*: Residency programs that offer financial stipends to offset the cost of living in expensive cities in the U.S. may alleviate some of the financial stress for residents, but these isolated benefits may ignore an underlying culture of work hour violations and would do little to reduce the overall stress load leading to burnout in residents.

In conclusion, we provide a vocabulary for surgeons to use when discussing important issues around surgeons' wellbeing. By using a common language to characterize threats to and promoters of individuals' wellbeing, we are better positioned to design and implement interventions that combat burnout and support wellbeing. While other terms not mentioned here may also influence wellbeing, this list of key concepts teaches fundamental tools to help the audience build a thorough understanding of the range of topics related to surgeons' wellbeing presented in the rest of this book.

References

1. Brigham T, Barden C, Legreid Dopp A, Hengerer A, Kaplan J, Malone B, et al. A journey to construct an all-encompassing conceptual model of factors affecting clinician Well-being and resilience. NAM Perspect National Academy of Medicine. 2018;8
2. Definition of wellness [Internet]. Merriam-Webster Dictionary. 2019. https://www.merriam-webster.com/dictionary/wellness. Accessed 9 Feb 2019.

3. Shanafelt TD, Oreskovich MR, Dyrbye LN, Satele DV, Hanks JB, Sloan J, et al. Avoiding burnout: the personal health habits and wellness practices of US surgeons. Ann Surg. 2012;255(4):625–33.
4. Kutney-Lee A, Germack H, Hatfield L, Kelly S, Maguire P, Dierkes A, et al. Nurse engagement in shared governance and patient and nurse outcomes. J Nurs Adm. 2016;46(11):605–12.
5. Maslach C, Jackson SE, Leiter MP. The Maslach burnout inventory manual. 3rd ed. Palo Alto, CA: Consulting Psychologists Press; 1996.
6. Shanafelt TD, Boone S, Tan L, Dyrbye LN, Sotile W, Satele D, et al. Burnout and satisfaction with work-life balance among US physicians relative to the general US population. Arch Intern Med. 2012;172(18):1377–85.
7. Shanafelt TD, Hasan O, Dyrbye LN, Sinsky C, Satele D, Sloan J, et al. Changes in burnout and satisfaction with work-life balance in physicians and the general US working population between 2011 and 2014. Mayo Clin Proc Elsevier Inc. 2015;90(12):1600–13.
8. Diagnostic and Statistical Manual of Mental Disorders (DSM-5). 5th ed. American Psychiatric Association; 2013.
9. Lin DT, Liebert CA, Tran J, Lau JN, Salles A. Emotional intelligence as a predictor of resident Well-being. J Am Coll Surg American College of Surgeons. 2016;223(2):352–8.
10. Dyrbye LN, Power DV, Stanford Massie F, Eacker A, Harper W, Thomas MR, et al. Factors associated with resilience to and recovery from burnout: a prospective, multi-institutional study of US medical students. Med Educ. 2010;44(10):1016–26.
11. Lechner T. Resilience and grit: how to develop a growth mindset [internet]. The Chopra center. 2019. https://chopra.com/articles/resilience-and-grit-how-to-develop-a-growth-mindset. Accessed 9 Feb 2019.
12. Lebares CC, Guvva EV, Ascher NL, O'Sullivan PS, Harris HW, Epel ES. Burnout and stress among US surgery residents: psychological distress and resilience. J Am Coll Surg. American College of Surgeons. 2018;226(1):80–90.
13. Waljee JF, Chopra V, Saint S. Mentoring millennials. JAMA. 2018;319(15):1547–8.
14. Saint S, Chopra V. How doctors can be better mentors [internet]. Harvard Business Review. 2018. https://hbr.org/2018/10/how-doctors-can-be-better-mentors
15. Chopra V, Safety P, Program E, Ann VA, Healthcare A, Arbor A, et al. Will you be my mentor ?— four archetypes to help mentees succeed in academic medicine. JAMA Intern Med. 2018;178(2):175–6.
16. Elmore LC, Jeffe DB, Jin L, Awad MM. National Survey of burnout among US general surgery residents. J Am Coll Surg. 2016;223(3):440–51.
17. Greenberg CC, Ghousseini HN, Quamme SRP, Beasley HL, Wiegmann DA. Surgical coaching for individual performance improvement. Ann Surg. 2015;261(1):32–4.
18. Palamara K, Kauffman C, Stone VE, Bazari H, Donelan K. Promoting success: a professional development coaching Program for interns in medicine. J Grad Med Educ. 2015;7(4):630–7.
19. Palamara K, Kauffman C, Chang Y, Barreto EA, Yu L, Bazari H, et al. Professional development coaching for residents: results of a 3-year positive psychology coaching intervention. J Gen Intern Med. 2018;33(11):1842–4.
20. Council FC. 15 Ways to Identify and Overcome Workplace Burnout [Internet]. Forbes CommunityVoice. 2018. https://www.forbes.com/sites/forbescoachescouncil/2018/05/01/15-ways-to-identify-and-overcome-workplace-burnout/#6206838bd812. Accessed 8 Feb 2019.
21. Arabadjis S, Sullivan EE. How one California medical group is decreasing physician burnout [internet]. Vol. June, Harv Bus Rev 2017. https://hbr.org/2017/06/how-one-medical-group-is-decreasing-physician-burnout. Accessed 8 Feb 2019.

Chapter 4
Conceptual Framework for Wellbeing

Arghavan Salles, Jennifer Yu, Carol Bernstein, and Charlee Alexander

4.1 The National Academy of Medicine Action Collaborative on Clinician Wellbeing and Resilience

Following the suicides of two medical interns in New York City in the summer of 2014, the Board of Directors of the Accreditation Council for Graduate Medical Education (ACGME) had an extensive discussion regarding the status of physician mental health and ultimately formed a working group to hold a symposium for invited stakeholders in medical education in November of 2015. Subsequently, Darrell Kirch, MD, President and CEO of the Association of American Medical Colleges, and Thomas Nasca, MD, President and CEO of the ACGME, approached National Academy of Medicine (NAM) president, Victor Dzau, MD, to determine if there was a role for the NAM to convene the many organizations working on the issue of clinician burnout. During a meeting in July of 2016 with 30 professional health care organizations, participants assessed the parameters of clinician burnout, considered the opportunities underway to address challenges to clinician wellbeing, and explored opportunities for collaborative engagement. Participants agreed that

A. Salles (✉)
Stanford University School of Medicine, Stanford, CA, USA
e-mail: arghavan@alumni.stanford.edu

J. Yu
Department of Surgery, Washington University in St. Louis, St. Louis, MO, USA
e-mail: yuj@wudosis.wustl.edu

C. Bernstein
Department of Psychiatry and Neurology, NYU School of Medicine, New York, NY, USA

C. Alexander
National Academy of Medicine, Washington, DC, USA
e-mail: cmalexander@nas.edu

© Springer Nature Switzerland AG 2020
E. Kim, B. Lindeman (eds.), *Wellbeing*, Success in Academic Surgery,
https://doi.org/10.1007/978-3-030-29470-0_4

the NAM would form a collaborative structure to address these issues with the belief that collective action was necessary to address an issue of such magnitude.

The NAM Action Collaborative on Clinician Wellbeing and Resilience (Clinician Wellbeing Collaborative) formally launched in January 2017 with three key goals[1]:

- Raise visibility of clinician stress, burnout, depression, and suicide
- Improve baseline understanding of challenges to clinician wellbeing
- Advance evidence-based, multidisciplinary solutions that will improve patient care by caring for the caregiver

As stated in a commentary published by Drs. Dzau, Kirch, and Nasca, the chair and co-chairs of the collaborative, "Through collective action and targeted investment, we can not only reduce burnout and promote wellbeing, but also help clinicians carry out the sacred mission that drew them to the healing professions – providing the very best care to patients" [1].

Efforts are needed at all levels—individual, institutional, and systemic—but especially at the systemic level. The Clinician Wellbeing Collaborative operates from the perspective that the system in which individuals learn and practice is primarily responsible for the epidemic of burnout among health care professionals. The efforts of the Clinician Wellbeing Collaborative are focused on promoting institutional, systemic, and culture change while remaining mindful of individual factors that contribute to resilience.

4.2 Conceptual Model of the Factors Affecting Clinician Wellbeing and Resilience

Although there are widely used definitions of wellbeing and burnout, there has been no agreed-upon conceptual model of the underlying contributing factors to burnout, making it difficult to identify solutions to promote wellbeing and reduce burnout. Therefore, an early priority for the Clinician Wellbeing Collaborative was to create a conceptual model that depicts the factors associated with burnout and wellbeing, applies them across all health care professions and career stages, and identifies the connection between clinician wellbeing and outcomes for clinicians, patients, and the health system [2]. In developing the model, the group deliberated on many challenging questions, included in Box 4.1. The model, finalized in December 2018 is presented in Fig. 4.1.

The conceptual model includes three components: the nucleus, external factors, and individual factors. The nucleus of the conceptual model, in green, is composed of three distinct but related elements. The outermost ring is **clinician wellbeing**, which has cascading effects on the clinician-patient relationship and patient wellbeing. If a clinician is well, the clinician-patient relationship is more likely to flourish, and patient wellbeing can improve. Conversely, clinicians cannot do their best work for others if they, themselves, are unwell. The relational aspect of caregiving has

---

[1] For more information on the NAM Action Collaborative on Clinician Well-Being and Resilience, please visit https://nam.edu/initiatives/clinician-resilience-and-well-being/

Box 4.1 Challenging Questions Discussed in Creation of the NAM Conceptual Model of Factors Affecting Clinician Wellbeing and Resilience

- Who or what should be at the center of the model?
- How should the model represent the external, institutional, systemic and cultural drivers and internal, individual factors affecting wellbeing, and the interrelationship among the factors?
- How should the model convey that burnout exists at all stages of the clinician's life cycle, from student to early career clinician to nearing retirement?
- What is the most effective way to articulate that factors and solutions will differ among the clinical disciplines and may depend upon the learning and practice environment (e.g., academic, community, inpatient, or outpatient settings)?

Source: Brigham et al. [2]

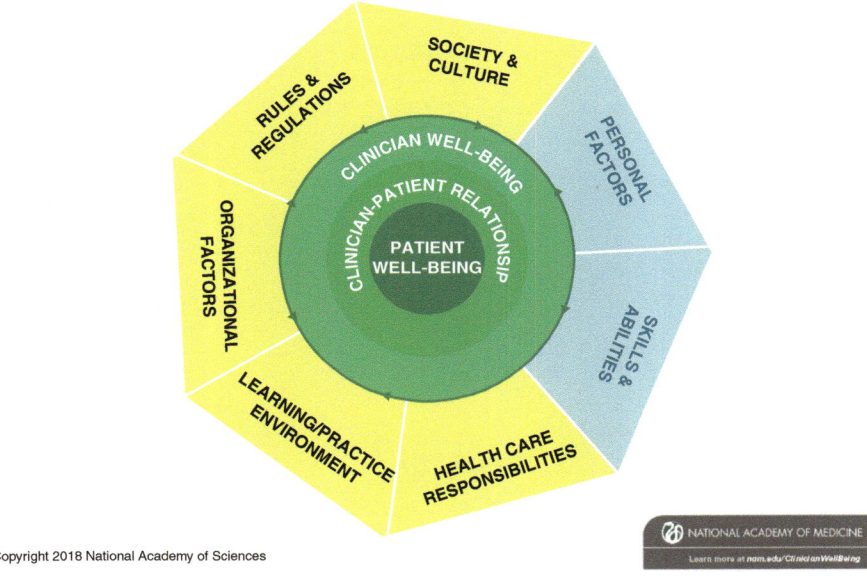

Fig. 4.1 Factors affecting clinician wellbeing and resilience. Note: The model should be used to understand the factors affecting clinician wellbeing and resilience. It is not a diagnostic or assessment tool. (Reprinted with permission from A Journey to Construct an All-Encompassing Conceptual Model of Factors Affecting Clinician Wellbeing and Resilience, 2018 by the National Academy of Sciences, Courtesy of the National Academies Press, Washington, D.C.)

effects on both clinician wellbeing and patient wellbeing. The **clinician-patient relationship** is the bridge between these two areas and represents the quality of care and communication between clinicians and the people they care for. **Patient wellbeing** is the core of the conceptual model. Careful consideration was given to placing patient wellbeing at the center of the model to highlight clinicians' primary objective: to provide quality care for patients. Encircling the nucleus are external factors, in yellow, and individual factors, in blue, that affect clinician wellbeing and resilience. Among the external factors are Society and Culture; Rules and Regulations; Organizational Factors; the Learning/Practice Environment; and Health Care Responsibilities. Individual contributing factors are Personal Factors and Skills and Abilities. The arrows around the nucleus convey the interconnectivity and fluidity of the factors that affect wellbeing.

Figure 4.2 demonstrates that each domain is further sub-divided into specific aspects affecting clinician wellbeing. In recognition of the complexity of clinician wellbeing, these sub-factors are presented in alphabetical order to avoid prescribing a hierarchy. Instead, users of the model will determine the importance of the ele-

EXTERNAL FACTORS

SOCIETY & CULTURE
- Alignment of societal expectations and clinician's role
- Culture of safety and transparency
- Discrimination and overt and unconscious bias
- Media portrayal
- Patient behaviours and expectations
- Political and economic climates
- Social determinants of health
- Stigmatization of mental illness

RULES & REGULATIONS
- Accreditation, high-stakes assessments, and publicized quality ratings
- Documentation and reporting requirements
- HR policies and compensation issues
- Initial licensure and certification
- Insurance company policies
- Litigation risk
- Maintenance of licensure and certification
- National and state policies and practices
- Reimbursement structure
- Shifting systems of care and administrative requirements

ORGANIZATIONAL FACTORS
- Bureaucracy
- Congruent organizational mission and values
- Culture, leadership, and staff engagement
- Data collection requirements
- Diversity and inclusion
- Harassment and discrimination
- Level of support for all healthcare team members
- Power dynamics
- Professional development opportunities
- Scope of practice
- Workload, performance, compensation, and value attributed to work elements

LEARNING/PRACTICE ENVIRONMENT
- Autonomy
- Collaborative vs. competitive environment
- Curriculum
- Health IT interoperability and usability/Electronic health records
- Learning and practice setting
- Mentorship program
- Physical learning and practice conditions
- Professional relationships
- Student affairs policies
- Student-centered and patient-centered focus
- Team structures and functionality
- Workplace safety and violence

HEALTH CARE RESPONSIBILITIES
- Administrative responsibilities
- Alignment of responsibility and authority
- Clinical responsibilities
- Learning/career stage
- Patient population
- Specialty related issues
- Student/trainee responsibilities
- Teaching and research responsibilities

INDIVIDUAL FACTORS

PERSONAL FACTORS
- Access to a personal mentor
- Inclusion and connectivity
- Family dynamics
- Financial stressors/economic vitality
- Flexibility and ability to respond to change
- Level of engagement/connection to meaning and purpose in work
- Personality traits
- Personal values, ethics and morals
- Physical, mental, and spiritual well-being
- Relationships and social support
- Sense of meaning
- Work-life integration

SKILLS & ABILITIES
- Clinical Competency level/experience
- Communication skills
- Coping skills
- Delegation
- Empathy
- Management and leadership
- Mastering new technologies or proficient use of technology
- Optimizing work flow
- Organizational skills
- Resilience skills/practices
- Teamwork skills

Fig. 4.2 Sub-factors affecting clinician wellbeing and resilience. Note: The model should be used to understand the factors affecting clinician wellbeing and resilience. It is not a diagnostic or assessment tool. (Reprinted with permission from A Journey to Construct an All-Encompassing Conceptual Model of Factors Affecting Clinician Wellbeing and Resilience, 2018 by the National Academy of Sciences, Courtesy of the National Academies Press, Washington, D.C.)

ments based on their unique context and available resources. This integrated approach creates an opportunity to identify potential leverage points and generate solutions at the institutional, systemic, and cultural levels. Based on this model, more granular models can be developed for particular specialties and environments.

This model captures the magnitude and urgency of challenges to clinician wellbeing by considering the relationship between the clinician and the patient, which is central to improving the wellbeing of both parties. Second, the model accounts for the external and individual factors that contribute to wellbeing [3] and depicts the interconnectivity of the factors. Third, by including more external factors than individual factors, the model illustrates that external factors have a larger effect on clinician wellbeing than individual factors [4].

4.3   Intervening on Physician Wellbeing

The work of the NAM Clinician Wellbeing Collaborative provides a framework for individual physicians and institutions to understand and counter the current physician wellbeing crisis, taking into account all of the relevant and various factors. However, it can be challenging to apply theory in the field. One example is how the Stanford Health Care General Surgery Residency Program developed a wellbeing program for its surgical residents, following the suicide of one of their former residents [5]. The program became known as Balance in Life and consists of multiple facets covering social, psychological, professional, and physical wellbeing. Figure 4.3 shows the specific programs that were developed in each of these four areas.

After a few years, we began to investigate the efficacy of the program [6] and have since undertaken a qualitative evaluation from the residents about their experience with the program. To be sure, there have been challenges along the way. The *After Hours Guide*, designed to help trainees identify physicians, dentists,

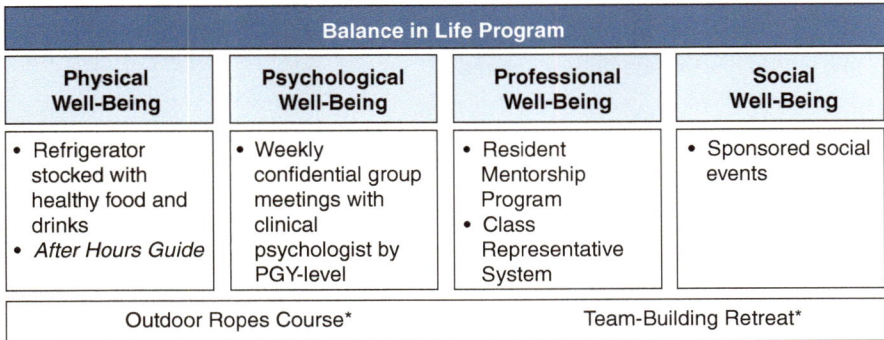

Fig. 4.3 Components of Balance in Life. *Components added to the Balance in Life program after completion of study. (Figure used with permission from Arghavan Salles, Perceived Value of a Program to Promote Surgical Resident Well-being. Journal of Surgical Education;74 (6):921–927. Elsevier, 2017)

gyms, and outdoor activities in the area, was underutilized as it was not widely publicized. A Resident Mentorship Program had mixed results, with some pairs having difficulty finding time to meet. Scheduling leadership retreats, including providing coverage for inpatients and surgery schedules, has created administrative challenges and concerns. The Balance in Life program is not perfect, but it continues to be re-evaluated and adjusted to meet the needs of the residency program. We are reassured by the fact that residents continue to appreciate the wellbeing program. Its existence is in and of itself evidence that residents' wellbeing is valued.

The Balance in Life program began before the NAM Clinician Wellbeing Collaborative. Within this framework for wellbeing, the Balance in Life program addresses aspects of both external (Society & Culture, Organizational Factors, Learning/Practice Environment, Health Care Responsibilities) and individual factors (Personal Factors, Skills and Abilities). The program does not explicitly address Rules and Regulations. Table 4.1 shows which elements of the Balance in Life program are relevant to each of the factors in the NAM framework.

There has been more attention to physician wellbeing in recent years. Initially, wellbeing researchers focused on individual characteristics of physicians and how those relate to wellbeing. For example, we have examined grit, self-efficacy, and sense of belonging as predictors of both wellbeing and risk of attrition for surgical residents [7–10]. More recently, people have become very interested in how to foster resilience or select for resilient individuals [11–16]. However, there is now a growing recognition that grit, resilience, and similar factors cannot overcome systemic challenges to physician wellbeing [3, 17, 18]. For example, the pressures of productivity increasing the pace of work [19], the increasing demands of electronic health records [20], and fighting for access [21] to care for patients are all systemic problems that place undue stress on physicians.

Mindfulness and yoga are unlikely to change the course [21] of the current wellbeing crisis. Ultimately systems must change. Some data suggest, for example, that hiring scribes for physicians increased physicians' satisfaction and was associated with less burnout [22–24]. In addition, institutions should value physicians for what they are: highly trained, compassionate, intelligent humans. Rather than treating physicians like exchangeable worker bees, processes that maintain physician autonomy, within reason, should be explored.

Table 4.1 Balance in Life program in terms of NAM framework

NAM factor	BIL element(s)
Society & culture	Psychology sessions
Organizational factors	Involving program directors in asking about dental and health visits, class representation, after hours guide
Learning/practice environment	Resident mentorship program, social events
Health care responsibilities	Leadership retreat (ropes course)
Personal factors	Social events, psychology sessions, refrigerator
Skills and abilities	Class representation, resident mentorship program, team-building
Rules and regulations	–

References

1. Dzau VJ, Kirch DG, Nasca TJ. To care is human - collectively confronting the clinician-burnout crisis. NEJM. 2018;378(4):312–4.
2. Brigham TB, Dopp C, Hengerer AL, Kaplan A, Malone J, Martin B, McHugh C, Nora M, LM. A journey to construct an all-encompassing conceptual model of factors affecting clinician well-being and resilience. NAM perspectives; 2018. https://nam.edu/journey-construct-encompassing-conceptual-model-factors-affecting-clinician-well-resilience/.
3. Shanafelt TD, Hasan O, Dyrbye LN, et al. Changes in burnout and satisfaction with work-life balance in physicians and the general US working population between 2011 and 2014. Mayo Clin Proc. 2015;90(12):1600–13.
4. Dyrbye LNS, Sinsky TD, Cipriano CA, Bhatt PF, Ommay J, West A, Meyers CP. Burnout among health care professionals: a call to explore and address this underrecognized threat to safe, high-quality care. NAM perspectives; 2017. https://nam.edu/burnout-among-health-care-professionals-a-call-to-explore-and-address-this-underrecognized-threat-to-safe-high-quality-care/.
5. Salles A, Liebert CA, Greco RS. Promoting balance in the lives of resident physicians: a call to action. JAMA Surg. 2015;150(7):607–8.
6. Salles A, Liebert CA, Esquivel M, Greco RS, Henry R, Mueller C. Perceived value of a program to promote surgical resident Well-being. J Surg Educ. 2017;74(6):921–7.
7. Milam LA, Cohen GL, Mueller C, Salles A. The relationship between self-efficacy and Well-being among surgical residents. J Surg Educ. 2018;76(2):321–8.
8. Salles A, Cohen GL, Mueller CM. The relationship between grit and resident Well-being. Am J Surg. 2014;207(2):251–4.
9. Salles A, Lin D, Liebert C, et al. Grit as a predictor of risk of attrition in surgical residency. Am J Surg. 2017;213(2):288–91.
10. Salles A, Wright RC, Milam L, et al. Social belonging as a predictor of surgical resident Well-being and attrition. J Surg Educ. 2018;76(2):370–7.
11. Souba WW. Resilience-Back to the future. JAMA Surg. 2016;151(10):896–7.
12. Lebares CC, Hershberger AO, Guvva EV, et al. Feasibility of formal mindfulness-based stress-resilience training among surgery interns: a randomized clinical trial. JAMA Surg. 2018;153(10):e182734.
13. Farquhar J, Kamei R, Vidyarthi A. Strategies for enhancing medical student resilience: student and faculty member perspectives. Int J Med Educ. 2018;9:1–6.
14. Peters D, Horn C, Gishen F. Ensuring our future doctors are resilient. BMJ (Clinical Research Ed). 2018;362:k2877.
15. Bohman BD, Sinsky L, Linzer CA, Olson M, Babbott K, Murphy M, DeVries ML, Hamidi PP, Trockel MS. Physician Well-being: the reciprocity of practice efficiency, culture of wellness, and personal resilience. NEJM Catalyst; 2017. https://catalyst.nejm.org/physician-well-being-efficiency-wellness-resilience/.
16. University of Minnesota Medical School: Essential and Desired Qualities. https://www.med.umn.edu/admissions/how-apply/selection-criteria/essential-and-desired-qualities.
17. Shanafelt T, Trockel M, Ripp J, Murphy ML, Sandborg C, Bohman B. Building a program on Well-being: key design considerations to meet the unique needs of each organization. Acad Med. 2019;94(2):156–61.
18. Mehta N. Physician burnout: why it's not about resilience; 2018. https://www.medpagetoday.com/publichealthpolicy/generalprofessionalissues/72551.
19. Linzer M, Manwell LB, Williams ES, et al. Working conditions in primary care: physician reactions and care quality. Ann Inter Med. 2009;151(1):28–36.
20. Shanafelt TD, Dyrbye LN, Sinsky C, et al. Relationship between clerical burden and characteristics of the electronic environment with physician burnout and professional satisfaction. Mayo Clin Proc. 2016;91(7):836–48.
21. Talbot SD, W. Physicians aren't 'burning out.' They're suffering from moral injury. 2018. https://www.statnews.com/2018/07/26/physicians-not-burning-out-they-are-suffering-moral-injury/.

22. Shultz CG, Holmstrom HL. The use of medical scribes in health care settings: a systematic review and future directions. J Am Board Fam Med. 2015;28(3):371–81.
23. McCormick BJ, Deal A, Borawski KM, et al. Implementation of medical scribes in an academic urology practice: an analysis of productivity, revenue, and satisfaction. World J Urol. 2018;36(10):1691–7.
24. Gidwani R, Nguyen C, Kofoed A, et al. Impact of scribes on physician satisfaction, patient satisfaction, and charting efficiency: a randomized controlled trial. Ann Fam Med. 2017;15(5):427–33.

Part III
Individual Factors of Wellbeing

Chapter 5
Healthcare Role

Carl A. Johnson Jr and Britney L. Corey

5.1 Introduction

> I chose medicine–surgery–because it combined a quest for knowledge with a way to serve, to save lives, and to alleviate suffering.
> —C. Everett Koop, MD, FACS, Pediatric Surgeon and former U.S. Surgeon General

The vocation of surgery is one of incredible demands, with wonderful benefits and hefty costs. It is a weighty responsibility to be the individual who intervenes in a decisive way on patients with complex physiology, difficult co-morbidities, and varying degrees of social support. Surgeons have the unique role of performing operations daily that are often of such notable impact that they are life-defining moments for the patient.

Just as for all physician specialties, the decision to become a surgeon is usually made relatively early, prior to extensive exposure to the healthcare system. Some challenges are difficult to fully appreciate ahead of time, such as the emotional toll of difficult patient care decisions or what to do in cases with unclear diagnoses. The implications those situations may have on wellbeing is more readily apparent; however, dealing with all the factors surrounding and contributing to the care of a patient is also tremendously influential on the wellbeing of surgeons. Surgeons are susceptible to burnout and compassion fatigue [1, 2]. This chapter seeks to explore the positive and negative aspects of the healthcare role on surgeon wellbeing.

C. A. Johnson Jr
Department of Surgery, University of Alabama at Birmingham School of Medicine, Birmingham, AL, USA
e-mail: carljohnson@uabmc.edu

B. L. Corey (✉)
Department of Surgery, University of Alabama at Birmingham School of Medicine, Birmingham, AL, USA

Birmingham Veterans Affairs Medical Center, Birmingham, AL, USA
e-mail: blprince@uabmc.edu

© Springer Nature Switzerland AG 2020
E. Kim, B. Lindeman (eds.), *Wellbeing*, Success in Academic Surgery,
https://doi.org/10.1007/978-3-030-29470-0_5

5.2 Administrative Responsibilities

Surgeons choose the field of surgery because of their love of the operating room and the joy they find in providing definitive solutions to ill patients. But as new surgical interns quickly discover, there is a host of tasks and administrative responsibilities outside of the operating room that are required. These administrative tasks can range from documentation of operations, signing off on billing codes, and placing home health orders. Unfortunately, the staggering amount of time spent on medical documentation, paperwork, etc. can nearly equal the time spent on direct patient care [3] One prime example of both a source of frustration and opportunity for the physician community is the electronic medical record (EMR). The EMR has been a significant advancement for the medical community that was initially heralded as a mechanism to improve patient care. However there are many drawbacks - including that physicians are now responsible for computer order entry, electronic prescribing, medication reconciliation, and often billing [4, 5]. Data entry in the EMR has increased the clerical burden of physicians. Many physicians protest the lower-skilled work that clerks or scribes could do [5]. The amount of time spent on computerized tasks has been associated with higher levels of burnout [4]. There is great potential for continued advancements and innovation in technology so that the electronic medical record and other administrative tasks can be enhanced and/or reduced to decrease physician burnout. Engagement with EMR developers by interested surgeon and physician leaders is needed to continue enhancements that add to the value of the EMR for front-line clinicians.

In addition to the more daily administrative tasks of caring for patients that every medical provider faces, healthcare organizations need engaged surgeon leaders. Individual surgeons may find meaning in certain administrative responsibilities and tasks that allow them to uniquely advocate for their fellow surgeons and patients. Interested individuals may consider pursuing additional training or degrees with this focus, such as a Masters of Healthcare Administration. Providing opportunities for interested physicians to pursue additional training and leadership roles in these areas can benefit the entire department or healthcare organization, as engaged surgeons can address problems and provide solutions that can better the work environment for their fellow colleagues.

5.3 Alignment of Responsibility and Authority

The role of surgeon places the physician at the head of the care team, directing the treatment plan of the patient and the activities of the operating room, trauma bay, and ward, and using the judgement they have developed from years of training to make critical decisions. Within healthcare, there are many situations where physicians find themselves facing varying levels of responsibility and authority. For example, a surgeon may be criticized for not meeting productivity requirements. However, long operating room turnover times due to inadequate custodial staffing causes the surgeon to book less cases. The misalignment of responsibility and authority leads to job dissatisfaction and burnout. In contrast, when aligned ideally, it can provide a meaningful environment for physicians to thrive. A passionate surgical educator who is provided the resources and support to engage in a curriculum overhaul is likely to experience joy and satisfaction.

Burnout occurs "when there is a major mismatch between the nature of the job and the nature of the person who does the job" [6]. One major mismatch that causes burnout, as identified by Maslach and Leiter, is "lack of control" [6]. Similarly, loss of autonomy or lack of control over work leads to burnout [7]. The same research that identified that lack of control leads to burnout found that giving physicians control increases engagement [14]. This supports the conclusion that within the healthcare role, there is a need for alignment of responsibility and authority. Authority and responsibility can be misaligned at the institutional and national level by affiliations, rigid guidelines and policies [7]. One example of a rigid guideline with misaligned authority and responsibility is the decision made by a major academic center to set revenue-based goals on the percentage of patients who received the flu shot. Surgeons within that institution found themselves spending time counseling patients on the risks and benefits of receiving the flu shot; a task they were ill-prepared for and that fell outside of their area of expertise. Likewise, surgeons may become frustrated when they are asked to see complex patients within narrow windows of time. These factors worsen when reimbursement is tied to patient satisfaction scores, leading to a vicious cycle that physicians feel they cannot overcome. An antidote to the burnout this may cause is developing practice models that preserve physician work control. The ability to control the work environment can offset the stress imposed by high work demands [8].

Within this discussion of authority and responsibility, it is worth noting that the relationship physicians have with their supervisors and superiors is very important. Research by Shanafelt et al. found a link between the rate of burnout and leader rating, leadership scores and rates of satisfaction, with 11% of the variation in burnout and 47% of the variation in satisfaction explained by the leadership rating of the division/department leaders [9]. Likewise, other research has shown that the greatest disparities between unsatisfied and satisfied physicians were related to physician management, with the top factor being "trust-communication with chair/division head" [10]. This emphasizes the importance of developing leaders, specifically physician leaders, and the importance of considering leadership fit when making career decisions. It also suggests a solution to the problem of misaligned authority and responsibility – physician leadership should strive to ensure that physicians are held responsible for factors that they truly have the authority to control.

5.4 Clinical Responsibilities

When surgeons were surveyed in 2009, over 70% reported they would choose to become both a physician and surgeon again [11]. When American surgeons were surveyed in 2012 regarding their personal health habits and wellness practices, finding meaning in work was the highest ranked coping strategy, and was also associated with high overall quality of life scores [12]. Surgeons who spent more hours per week in the operating room had greater career satisfaction [11, 13]. As one can imagine, clinical responsibilities – when appropriately balanced – are a rich opportunity for surgeons to thrive and find a source of meaning.

When the work hours and practice characteristics of American surgeons were evaluated, the strongest correlation for burnout was hours worked. Surgeons working more than 80 h/week had a rate of 50%, while those working less than 60 h a week had a rate of 30.1% [20] A similar correlation was found when surgeons took two or more night calls a week. Ultimately, this impacted career satisfaction as a significant number of surgeons who worked longer hours and took more call reported that they would be less likely to choose a surgical career again [14]. Private practice surgeons are more at risk for burnout, while academic surgeons had better career satisfaction, and were less likely to be depressed or have suicidality [19]. Those with the best career satisfaction in academic surgery were full professors, while assistant professors had the least. The difference in burnout between academic and private practice surgeons are likely best explained by longer work hours and more days on call among private practice surgeons.

The high stakes environment of surgery and providing care during critical moments is a draw to the field, but it comes with a high rate of litigation and malpractice claims. The 2016 Benchmark Study performed by the American Medical Association showed that general surgery and obstetrics/gynecology are the two specialties most likely to be sued, with over 63% of general surgeons having a claim filed against them [15]. When members of the American College of Surgeons were surveyed in 2011 regarding the consequences of malpractice lawsuits, 24.6% of surgeons reported being involved in a malpractice suit in the 2 years prior [22]. Not surprisingly, experiencing a lawsuit was correlated with higher rates of burnout, depression, and suicidal ideation, as well as lower mean overall, physical, and mental quality of life scores, and less career satisfaction. Unfortunately, this may have a reciprocating effect on medical errors, as increased burnout is associated with increased medical errors [16].

Beyond the fear of litigation, surgeons live with stress as they worry about intraoperative adverse outcomes and post-operative complications in their patients [17, 18]. Studies have shown that intraoperative adverse events occur often and have a significant negative impact on surgeons' wellbeing. Surgeons struggle to share about these events due to the fear of litigation and lack of reporting systems, but report feelings of sadness, anxiety, and shame [17]. A continuous amount of stress is also present, primarily due to concern over the potential for complications in patients. Surgeons describe dealing with these emotional threats by distancing themselves from the patient and focusing on the technical act. This leads to emotional exhaustion, depersonalization, and a low sense of personal accomplishment – the hallmarks of burnout [12, 19]. Identifying methods and focusing research on ways to decrease intraoperative adverse events and post-operative complications are worthy goals; institutions and surgeon leadership should also consider offering additional emotional support and resources to surgeons who are dealing with these difficult situations.

Two potential solutions related to clinical responsibilities are worth noting. First, surgeons' incentives should not be directly tied to excessive workloads. Physicians primarily increase productivity by shortening time with patients, ordering more tests/procedures, or working long hours [7]. As increased work hours can lead to burnout, this method can easily backfire for the institution and lead to psychological harm for the physician. Institutions would be wise to consider this when developing compensation models. The second strategy is to ensure that physicians can spend at least 20% of their time on work that is meaningful to them. Studies have shown that physicians who spent approximately 1 day a week performing work that was meaningful were 50% less likely to experience burnout [20]. Surgeons placed great value on finding meaning in work, and achieving 20% of time spent on meaningful activities is a worthy goal for physician leadership to aspire to [12]. Indeed, the association between increased hours in the operating room and career satisfaction is likely related to this [13].

5.5 Learning and Career Stage

In 2014, US general surgery residents were surveyed to characterize rates of burnout [21]. The results were staggering: 69% of residents met the criteria for burnout; 44% of these residents had considered dropping out of residency, and the same percentage wished they had enrolled in an alternate residency. Female residents were more likely to be burned out, at a rate of 73%. Residents who were planning on a career in private practice were more susceptible to burnout. A study of a national sample of US physicians across specialties found that early career physicians had the lowest career satisfaction, greatest rates of work-home conflict, and greater depersonalization [22]. Middle career physicians (those with 10–20 years of practice) worked more hours, took more call, were less satisfied with their specialty and work-life balance, and had more emotional exhaustion and burnout. As one may expect, late career physicians had the best career satisfaction and lowest burnout.

One of the traps that residents and physicians can fall into is that of "delayed gratification". This is a superior cognitive skill that can be used as a coping strategy when work-life balance is unattainable. This strategy is typically used during residency and the early career stage, when individuals have little control over their schedules and time. Instead of making time for a personal life and other meaningful activities outside of work, they delay this for later once their careers are established. However, research suggests that this coping strategy can persist, transitioning from the wait to finish training to the wait for retirement [23, 24]. To combat this, surgeons and organizations need to prioritize discovering and nurturing activities at work and beyond that are meaningful, energizing, and are self-renewing [23, 24]. Dr. Mary Brandt, a pediatric surgeon with a passion for wellbeing, strongly recommends taking a "sabbath" each week to allow for this personal renewal, with a full or half-day dedicated to play, rest, and relaxation [25].

5.6   Patient Population

Academic surgeons often work at major referral centers that serve as safety-net hospitals. As a result, surgeons at these centers routinely care for a diverse group of patients, ranging from the well-informed and resource-rich to those with extremely limited resources and little health literacy. The percentage of patients with complex medical needs and diagnostic dilemmas is often high. Treating critically ill patients and guiding them to a full recovery can be rewarding, yet draining. The percentage of uninsured patients receiving care at an academic medical center can be substantial. The lack of medical insurance can place a financial strain on hospitals and increased numbers of uninsured patients may be negatively associated with physician satisfaction [26, 27]. Physicians can feel that quality of care is influenced by factors outside of their control, including having the time or resources necessary to address complex psychosocial problems [28]. By contrast, other patients have access to a virtually endless amount of medical information via the internet or other media and can present with a diagnosis and treatment plan already "in mind." This can increase the length of physician consultations as they have to explain when their care plans differ and counteract pressure to enact treatment plans they do not believe in. Increased numbers of such information-centric patients can decrease physician satisfaction [29, 30]. Academic surgeons typically have a large network of other surgeons around them to consult with, as well as access to other advanced specialties (i.e. interventional radiology) which can alleviate some of the pressures of treating these complex patients. Physician leadership should consider the complexity of patients being cared for and the specialized services being provided when decisions are made about clinic time slots, dedicated academic time, and resource allotment.

5.7   Specialty Related Issues

Wellbeing in the field of surgery encompasses all areas of the surgeon – beyond just avoiding burnout and attending to spiritual and emotional wellbeing. Surgery has some unique challenges as operating puts unusual stress on physical wellbeing. Exposure to hazards, musculoskeletal injuries and physical strain, as well as time constraints leave many surgeons ignoring their personal physical concerns.

Exposure to occupational hazards can occur in any clinical environment, but the opportunities are more frequent in the field of surgery [39]. Sharps injuries expose health care providers to pathogens such as Hepatitis B, Hepatitis C, and HIV. Exposure to fluoroscopy and surgical smoke are other occupational hazards that surgeons should actively attempt to limit their exposure to [25]. Physical strain from long hours of standing in awkward positions and with poor posture are not to be dismissed. This is particularly a problem in laparoscopic cases, although it also occurs during open surgery [31]. Musculoskeletal pain is reported by 50–85% of surgeons during and after performing surgery [25]. As more research brings these issues to light, it is important for academic surgeons to correct their techniques and to model this to trainees. It may also be in the best interest of health care entities to offer ergonomic training and evaluations to their physicians to decrease the rate of injuries and potentially prolong their practice. Robotic surgery may offer an ergonomic advantage to surgeons [32].

A surgical career can also impact other areas of health, with surgeons reporting poor rates of preventative health screenings [25]. Female surgeons also report more issues with infertility compared to the general population [33]. Evidence-based interventions and awareness of the physical health impacts of a surgical specialty is of utmost importance, and more research, support, and commitment to this is needed at the individual physician level and by health care organizations [23].

5.8 Student and Trainee Responsibilities

While training learners is a hallmark of academics, how these activities relate to burnout and career satisfaction in academic surgeons is not well understood. It is notable that involvement in education of trainees was considered a positive influence toward pursuing a career in academic surgery [34]. Likewise academic surgeons have less burnout and more career satisfaction, which may be related to the educational opportunities this career provides [13]. Surgeons who educate others can truly have a multiplying effect as the knowledge they impart impacts every patient cared for by their trainees.

Working with trainees requires substantial time and effort. Beyond instructing in the operating room and overseeing patient care activities, faculty members are expected to offer timely feedback, complete evaluations, participate in promotion committees and resident interviews, facilitate didactic sessions, and provide mentorship and career advising. In return, residents provide clinical care to their patients. Surgeons may also have student and trainee responsibilities outside of the traditional roles of resident and medical student. Academic surgeons typically engage in research that may involve an entire spectrum of trainees ranging from high school students to post-doctoral students. Mentoring and supporting these students and trainees may be very gratifying. One effective tool for fighting burnout is "job crafting," where individuals are encouraged to seek ways to participate in more activities that are personally meaningful to them [44]. Institutions and physician leaders that advocate for individuals to spend time doing meaningful work may be more likely to retain their physician talent and save the institution the costs of lost revenue and recruitment [25]. Academic surgeon leadership should seek ways to support these important roles by providing supporting personnel, advocating for funding, and facilitating connections and opportunities within the academic center.

5.9 Teaching and Research Responsibilities

Teaching the next generation of surgeons and surgeon scientists is a key attribute of today's academic surgeon and can be very rewarding [35–37]. Mentorship is crucial to surgical trainees and is considered to be an important factor in reducing surgical resident attrition [38, 39]. The persistent challenge faced by those who find educational activities meaningful is the relative lack of financial resources supporting it. The clinical care of patients leads to reimbursement, and research is often supported by grant funding. Recognizing, funding, and accounting for the educational service of faculty members is more difficult [7]. This impacts the salary support of educators, as well as the tenure and promotion process. Some have advocated for an educational value unit (EVU) system to be used to recognize and compensate individuals who provide educational services [40]. For the purpose of tenure and promotion, the Association for Surgical Education published recommendations on how to document, recognize, and reward teaching. The model is called "the educator's pyramid" and it provides a framework for departments to use to appropriately recognize and promote the surgeon educator [41].

It has been well documented that NIH funding has become more difficult to obtain in recent years, and this decrease has affected surgeons disproportionately [42, 43]. Difficulty in obtaining funding is a key reason fewer surgeons are pursuing basic science research. Increased clinical responsibilities is also a strong deterrent to performing research, as well as difficulty maintaining work-life balance. In a survey of academic surgeons, Keswani observed that 68% of surgical faculty believe it is unrealistic for a surgeon to be a successful basic researcher [44]. Despite these challenges, surgical research can be extremely rewarding. Many important contributions have come as a result of the efforts of surgeon-scientists including nine Nobel Prize winners [45]. The pressing need for more surgeon scientists has been outlined by many including a recent *Nature* editorial admonishing more surgeons to do basic science research [43, 45–47]. Academic centers can support surgeon scientists by providing protected research time, support personnel for grant applications, and collaborative research environments.

5.10 Conclusion

When one examines the healthcare role in surgeon wellbeing, it is easy to see a veritable minefield, as well as endless opportunities for joy, engagement, and meaning in work. The work of the surgeon is intense but deeply personal and meaningful. The experiences that are deeply draining can also be deeply meaningful. Surgeon wellbeing is influenced by individual factors, as well as healthcare organizations [7]. It is the responsibility of both the physician and the healthcare organization to ensure that each stay well. Maintaining the necessary balance requires creative solutions and committed surgeon leadership and advocacy.

References

1. Coetzee SK, Laschinger HKS. Toward a comprehensive, theoretical model of compassion fatigue: an integrative literature review. Nurs Health Sci. 2018;20(1):4–15. https://doi.org/10.1111/nhs.12387.
2. Wu D, Gross B, Rittenhouse K, Harnish C, Mooney C, Rogers FB. A preliminary analysis of compassion fatigue in a surgeon population: are female surgeons at heightened risk? Am Surg. 2017;83(11):1302–7.
3. Ammenwerth E, Spotl HP. The time needed for clinical documentation versus direct patient care. A work-sampling analysis of physicians' activities. Methods Inf Med. 2009;48(1):84–91.
4. Shanafelt TD, Dyrbye LN, Sinsky C, Hasan O, Satele D, Sloan J, West CP. Relationship between clerical burden and characteristics of the electronic environment with physician burnout and professional satisfaction. Mayo Clin Proc. 2016;91(7):836–48. https://doi.org/10.1016/j.mayocp.2016.05.007.
5. Friedberg MW, Chen PG, Van Busum KR, Aunon F, Pham C, Caloyeras J, Mattke S, Pitchforth E, Quigley DD, Brook RH, Crosson FJ, Tutty M. Factors affecting physician professional satisfaction and their implications for patient care, health systems, and health policy. Rand Health Q. 2014;3(4):1.
6. Rothenberger DA. Physician burnout and Well-being: a systematic review and framework for action. Dis Colon Rectum. 2017;60(6):567–76. https://doi.org/10.1097/DCR.0000000000000844.
7. Shanafelt TD, Noseworthy JH. Executive leadership and physician Well-being: Nine Organizational Strategies to Promote Engagement and Reduce Burnout. Mayo Clin Proc. 2017;92(1):129–46. https://doi.org/10.1016/j.mayocp.2016.10.004.
8. Linzer M, Levine R, Meltzer D, Poplau S, Warde C, West CP. 10 bold steps to prevent burnout in general internal medicine. J Gen Intern Med. 2014;29(1):18–20. https://doi.org/10.1007/s11606-013-2597-8.
9. Shanafelt TD, Gorringe G, Menaker R, Storz KA, Reeves D, Buskirk SJ, Sloan JA, Swensen SJ. Impact of organizational leadership on physician burnout and satisfaction. Mayo Clin Proc. 2015;90(4):432–40. https://doi.org/10.1016/j.mayocp.2015.01.012.
10. Demmy TL, Kivlahan C, Stone TT, Teague L, Sapienza P. Physicians' perceptions of institutional and leadership factors influencing their job satisfaction at one academic medical center. Acad Med. 2002;77(12 Pt 1):1235–40.
11. Shanafelt TD, Balch CM, Bechamps GJ, Russell T, Dyrbye L, Satele D, Collicott P, Novotny PJ, Sloan J, Freischlag JA. Burnout and career satisfaction among American surgeons. Ann Surg. 2009;250(3):463–71. https://doi.org/10.1097/SLA.0b013e3181ac4dfd.
12. Shanafelt TD, Oreskovich MR, Dyrbye LN, Satele DV, Hanks JB, Sloan JA, Balch CM. Avoiding burnout: the personal health habits and wellness practices of US surgeons. Ann Surg. 2012;255(4):625–33. https://doi.org/10.1097/SLA.0b013e31824b2fa0.
13. Balch CM, Shanafelt TD, Sloan JA, Satele DV, Freischlag JA. Distress and career satisfaction among 14 surgical specialties, comparing academic and private practice settings. Ann Surg. 2011;254(4):558–68. https://doi.org/10.1097/SLA.0b013e318230097e.
14. Balch CM, Shanafelt TD, Dyrbye L, Sloan JA, Russell TR, Bechamps GJ, Freischlag JA. Surgeon distress as calibrated by hours worked and nights on call. J Am Coll Surg. 2010;211(5):609–19. https://doi.org/10.1016/j.jamcollsurg.2010.06.393.
15. Guardado J. Policy Research Perspectives: Medical Liability Claim Frequency Among U.S. Physicians. 2017. https://www.ama-assn.org/sites/ama-assn.org/files/corp/media-browser/public/government/advocacy/policy-research-perspective-medical-liability-claim-frequency.pdf. Accessed 25 Feb 2019.
16. Shanafelt TD, Balch CM, Bechamps G, Russell T, Dyrbye L, Satele D, Collicott P, Novotny PJ, Sloan J, Freischlag J. Burnout and medical errors among American surgeons. Ann Surg. 2010;251(6):995–1000. https://doi.org/10.1097/SLA.0b013e3181bfdab3.

17. Han K, Bohnen JD, Peponis T, Martinez M, Nandan A, Yeh DD, Lee J, Demoya M, Velmahos G, Kaafarani HMA. The surgeon as the second victim? Results of the Boston intraoperative adverse events Surgeons' attitude (BISA) study. J Am Coll Surg. 2017;224(6):1048–56. https://doi.org/10.1016/j.jamcollsurg.2016.12.039.
18. Pinto A, Faiz O, Bicknell C, Vincent C. Acute traumatic stress among surgeons after major surgical complications. Am J Surg. 2014;208(4):642–7. https://doi.org/10.1016/j.amjsurg.2014.06.018.
19. Orri M, Farges O, Clavien PA, Barkun J, Revah-Levy A. Being a surgeon--the myth and the reality: a meta-synthesis of surgeons' perspectives about factors affecting their practice and Well-being. Ann Surg. 2014;260(5):721–8.; discussion 728-729. https://doi.org/10.1097/SLA.0000000000000962.
20. Shanafelt TD, West CP, Sloan JA, Novotny PJ, Poland GA, Menaker R, Rummans TA, Dyrbye LN. Career fit and burnout among academic faculty. Arch Intern Med. 2009;169(10):990–5. https://doi.org/10.1001/archinternmed.2009.70.
21. Elmore LC, Jeffe DB, Jin L, Awad MM, Turnbull IR. National Survey of burnout among US general surgery residents. J Am Coll Surg. 2016;223(3):440–51. https://doi.org/10.1016/j.jamcollsurg.2016.05.014.
22. Dyrbye LN, Varkey P, Boone SL, Satele DV, Sloan JA, Shanafelt TD. Physician satisfaction and burnout at different career stages. Mayo Clin Proc. 2013;88(12):1358–67. https://doi.org/10.1016/j.mayocp.2013.07.016.
23. Balch CM, Freischlag JA, Shanafelt TD. Stress and burnout among surgeons: understanding and managing the syndrome and avoiding the adverse consequences. Arch Surg. 2009;144(4):371–6. https://doi.org/10.1001/archsurg.2008.575.
24. Shanafelt T. A career in surgical oncology: finding meaning, balance, and personal satisfaction. Ann Surg Oncol. 2008;15(2):400–6. https://doi.org/10.1245/s10434-007-9725-9.
25. Brandt ML. Sustaining a career in surgery. Am J Surg. 2017;214(4):707–14. https://doi.org/10.1016/j.amjsurg.2017.06.022.
26. Pagan JA, Balasubramanian L, Pauly MV. Physicians' career satisfaction, quality of care and patients' trust: the role of community uninsurance. Health Econ Policy Law. 2007;2(Pt 4):347–62. https://doi.org/10.1017/S1744133107004239.
27. Coleman DL. The impact of the lack of health insurance: how should academic medical centers and medical schools respond? Acad Med. 2006;81(8):728–31.
28. Wetterneck TB, Linzer M, JE MM, Douglas J, Schwartz MD, Bigby J, Gerrity MS, Pathman DE, Karlson D, Rhodes E, Society of General Internal Medicine Career Satisfaction Study G. Worklife and satisfaction of general internists. Arch Intern Med. 2002;162(6):649–56.
29. Fang H, Rizzo JA. Information-oriented patients and physician career satisfaction: is there a link? Health Econ Policy Law. 2011;6(3):295–311. https://doi.org/10.1017/S1744133110000186.
30. Mechanic D. Physician discontent: challenges and opportunities. JAMA. 2003;290(7):941–6. https://doi.org/10.1001/jama.290.7.941.
31. Nguyen NT, Ho HS, Smith WD, Philipps C, Lewis C, De Vera RM, Berguer R. An ergonomic evaluation of surgeons' axial skeletal and upper extremity movements during laparoscopic and open surgery. Am J Surg. 2001;182(6):720–4.
32. Stylopoulos N, Rattner D. Robotics and ergonomics. Surg Clin North Am. 2003;83(6):1321–37. https://doi.org/10.1016/S0039-6109(03)00161-0.
33. Phillips EA, Nimeh T, Braga J, Lerner LB. Does a surgical career affect a woman's childbearing and fertility? A report on pregnancy and fertility trends among female surgeons. J Am Coll Surg. 2014;219(5):944–50. https://doi.org/10.1016/j.jamcollsurg.2014.07.936.
34. Goudreau BJ, Hassinger TE, Hedrick TL, Slingluff CL Jr, Schroen AT, Dengel LT. Academic or community practice? What is driving decision-making and career choices. Surgery. 2018;164(3):571–6. https://doi.org/10.1016/j.surg.2018.05.003.
35. Rosengart TK, Mason MC, LeMaire SA, Brandt ML, Coselli JS, Curley SA, Mattox KL, Mills JL, Sugarbaker DJ, Berger DA. The seven attributes of the academic surgeon: critical aspects of the archetype and contributions to the surgical community. Am J Surg. 2017;214(2):165–79. https://doi.org/10.1016/j.amjsurg.2017.02.003.

36. Rikkers L. The real job: recruit, mentor, and protect: comment on: "the modern surgery department chairman". JAMA Surg. 2013;148(6):515. https://doi.org/10.1001/jamasurg.2013.1233.
37. Kron IL. Surgical mentorship. J Thorac Cardiovasc Surg. 2011;142(3):489–92. https://doi.org/10.1016/j.jtcvs.2011.05.017.
38. Freischlag JA, Silva MM. Preventing general surgery residency attrition-it is all about the mentoring. JAMA Surg. 2017;152(3):272–3. https://doi.org/10.1001/jamasurg.2016.4096.
39. Wasserman MA. A strategy to reduce general surgery resident attrition: a Resident's perspective. JAMA Surg. 2016;151(3):215–6. https://doi.org/10.1001/jamasurg.2015.4607.
40. Stites S, Vansaghi L, Pingleton S, Cox G, Paolo A. Aligning compensation with education: design and implementation of the educational value unit (EVU) system in an academic internal medicine department. Acad Med. 2005;80(12):1100–6.
41. Sachdeva AK, Cohen R, Dayton MT, Hebert JC, Jamieson C, Neumayer LA, Sharp KW, Spence RK. A new model for recognizing and rewarding the educational accomplishments of surgery faculty. Acad Med. 1999;74(12):1278–87.
42. Narahari AK, Mehaffey JH, Hawkins RB, Charles EJ, Baderdinni PK, Chandrabhatla AS, Kocan JW, Jones RS, Upchurch GR Jr, Kron IL, Kern JA, Ailawadi G. Surgeon scientists are disproportionately affected by declining NIH funding rates. J Am Coll Surg. 2018;226(4):474–81. https://doi.org/10.1016/j.jamcollsurg.2017.12.047.
43. More surgeons must start doing basic science. Nature. 2017;544(7651):393–4. https://doi.org/10.1038/544393b.
44. Keswani SG, Moles CM, Morowitz M, Zeh H, Kuo JS, Levine MH, Cheng LS, Hackam DJ, Ahuja N, Goldstein AM, Basic Science Committee of the Society of University S. The future of basic science in academic surgery: identifying barriers to success for surgeon-scientists. Ann Surg. 2017;265(6):1053–9. https://doi.org/10.1097/SLA.0000000000002009.
45. Woldu SL, Raj GV. Surgery: the surgeon-scientist—a dying breed? Nat Rev Urol. 2016;13(12):698–9. https://doi.org/10.1038/nrurol.2016.236.
46. Henke PK, Mulholland MW. Response: Letter to Article by Keswani SG, et al. The Future of Basic Science in Academic Surgery: Identifying Barriers to Success for Surgeon Scientists. Ann Surg 2017:265:1053–1059. Ann Surg. 2018;268(6):e46–7. https://doi.org/10.1097/SLA.0000000000002492.
47. Kibbe MR, Velazquez OC. The extinction of the surgeon scientist. Ann Surg. 2017;265(6):1060–1. https://doi.org/10.1097/SLA.0000000000002192.

Chapter 6
Personal Factors

Margaret W. Arnold and Sandra R. Dibrito

6.1 Introduction

Cultivating wellbeing in the surgical workforce is an urgent need. In addition to systemic and environmental factors, several personal factors contribute to overall wellness. These can be individually examined to find intervenable points to elevate wellness and wellbeing in medicine. In this chapter, we will take a closer look at the personal factors identified by the National Academy of Medicine as related to wellness. Divided into intrinsic, extrinsic, and environmental personal factors, we aim to identify targets for future interventions to minimize burnout.

6.2 Intrinsic Personal Factors

6.2.1 Personality Traits

It is not a secret that surgeons are thought to be headstrong, argumentative, and perhaps even egotistical. These stereotypical personality traits suggest that surgeons are difficult to work with and inflexible. In a formal review of studies of personality traits of all medical specialties, one study reported that "surgeons were less agreeable and more antagonistic than other specialists." The authors of the review conclude that "surgeons, as a group, seem to be social, active, and dominant". This

M. W. Arnold (✉)
Department of Surgery, MedStar Health Baltimore, Baltimore, MD, USA
e-mail: marnol21@jhmi.edu

S. R. Dibrito
Department of Surgery, Johns Hopkins University School of Medicine, Baltimore, MD, USA
e-mail: dibrito@jhmi.edu

© Springer Nature Switzerland AG 2020
E. Kim, B. Lindeman (eds.), *Wellbeing*, Success in Academic Surgery,
https://doi.org/10.1007/978-3-030-29470-0_6

sounds relatively negative. However, these traits often drive the quick decision making that is necessary for success in minute-to-minute intraoperative care and allow for leadership in times of stress. The authors of the review state that surgeons are described as displaying characteristics of extroversion and "openness to experience". They postulate that "openness to experience", which they describe as imaginativeness, depth of feeling, curiosity, and need for variety, develops over the course of surgical training [1]. Solving surgical problems requires imagination and extemporaneous thinking, and it is not surprising that surgeons tend to appreciate variety in their day to day work.

What do these personality traits have to do with wellbeing? Recognition of the strengths within even the most negative sounding traits allows us to build on those traits to facilitate wellness. In order to care for ourselves as surgeons, we must make room for introspection about our own personality traits that facilitate patient care on the one hand but may hamper our interpersonal relationships on the other. Simple awareness of our personality traits, for the good and bad, help us approach people and problems in a more functional way.

With an increasing number of female surgeons, the comparison between male and female counterparts is inevitable, but the data can be used to target differential causes of burnout in these groups. In an international study of over 7000 physicians, females scored significantly higher in all components of empathy, although reported feeling less valued by patients, their colleagues, and their superiors as compared to male physicians. The authors of this suggest that increased empathic concern among female physicians may come with the higher cost of emotional exhaustion [2]. Similarly, a meta-analysis of 183 studies conducted by Purvanova and Muros found female physicians to be more emotionally exhausted than their male counterparts while having similar depersonalization and personal accomplishment scores [3].

If we appreciate that physicians have a tendency towards emotional exhaustion, the next step requires using these findings to help make meaningful change. As we aim towards wellness, pervasive feelings of emotional exhaustion should not be acceptable for ANY physician, regardless of gender. In naming personality traits of surgeons, in knowing where we struggle, we can better solve our burnout crisis on a large, systemic scale. But day to day, if we can appreciate ourselves as we are, headstrong and emotionally exhausted, we can work to build relationships and support systems to optimize our daily lives.

6.2.2 Flexibility and Ability to Respond to Change

In order to maintain mental well-being while simultaneously provide excellent patient care, it is imperative for physicians to find an appropriate emotional distance from which to provide empathic concern. As Decety et al. describe, "The ability to engage in self-other awareness and regulate one's emotions is pivotal to the adaptive experience of empathy in clinical practice" [2]. The clinical landscape is a fluid environment, the needs of patients changing daily and longitudinally, with the demands of each work day different from the last. The ability to adapt to these changes and remain empathic is at the forefront of preventing burnout.

Just as in athletics, flexibility prevents injury. Stretching to gain physical flexibility is akin to practicing accommodation of flux in the workplace with everyday decisions. If we are introspective enough to see that our limits and boundaries are being tested, if we are uncomfortable in a technically or interpersonally challenging situation, we can take the time to insist on flexibility and grow from that experience. In responding to change in a less rigid way, we can hone our flexibility as a skill and prevent injury in the form of emotional exhaustion, burnout, and lack of empathy.

There are ways that physicians can shape their day to feel more in-control and thus more satisfied. Discussing scheduling of operative cases, clinics, and academic pursuits at the departmental level can allow individual surgeons to have more control over their own personal practice. But even with the best intentions, OR day schedules can change to accommodate all sorts of emergencies. Patients cancel and others need emergency intervention. Being calm and flexible, recognizing the inevitability of these changes in a meditative way, can help surgeons feel less out-of-control in these circumstances and avoid negative emotions that come with lack of flexibility.

Freeborn et al. demonstrated that in an HMO model, "physicians who perceive greater control over their practice environment, who perceive that their work demands are reasonable, and who have more support from colleagues have higher levels of job satisfaction, commitment to their employer, and better psychological wellbeing" [4]. This suggests that as physicians, we should seek to participate in the organization of our practice and set the limits of what we allow our work to demand from us, actively addressing demands we find unreasonable. Just as we can individually be flexible, division heads and department leaders need to be flexible as they understand how to get the most out of their team members. Pushing every individual to the limit of their capability is the short-game of productivity and won't allow for a department to flourish over time.

6.2.3   Personal Values, Ethics, and Morals

The surgical world is demanding. It is a business where patients are seen and treated in a fee-for-service model, where volume is king, and resources are constrained by bureaucracy. On the other hand, it is a service based in compassion where the very personal relationship between surgeons and patients involves developing trust and mutual respect. As discussed by Wall et al.,

> Surgeons live and practice an intense form of applied ethics. They deliver bad news; guide patients and their families through complicated decisions; live a code of trust with colleagues, patients and trainees; and frequently address end-of-life issues. Moreover, surgeons must go to bed at night knowing that in the morning, they will spend hours with someone's life literally in their hands [5].

On a nearly daily basis, surgeons' personal values are challenged as they weigh the best options for patients and their families against what is available or considered reasonable by payors. We are acting on behalf of the patient, but cannot be blind to the needs of the medical system both nationally and locally. We need to be judicious with limited resources while simultaneously providing the best care we can, and navigating these conflicting interests can be a source of ethical dilemma and exhaustion.

Additionally, the power differential between surgeons and vulnerable patients is a set-up for ethical issues. We are compelled to describe disease processes and options to patients and families who have a limited understanding of medicine and guide them through perhaps some of the most difficult moments of their lives. This occurs with extreme frequency, many times daily. Only by focusing on the goals of patient autonomy and nonmaleficence can we stay true to our ethical compass and limit our tendency to come across as paternalistic.

It is suggested that the current burnout crisis among physicians is a symptom of the larger problem with the healthcare system. The pervasiveness of burnout suggests that it is a failure of the system, as opposed to individual failure due to inadequacy of resilience. The term "moral injury" has previously been applied to soldiers exposed to war, but has recently been suggested to apply to physicians suffering with the inability to provide high-quality care in our current healthcare system [6]. By forcing physicians to contemplate the financial obligations of medicine, our system has burdened physicians with a moral impasse, to be encountered on every patient visit.

There are no easy answers to ethical, moral, or values-based issues faced by surgeons in terms of maintaining personal wellbeing. While it is helpful to know that the entire system is suffering together, fighting the daily fight on behalf of patients, perhaps it is better to think about ways we as individuals can participate in systemic change to alleviate these burdens for future physicians.

6.3 Extrinsic Personal Factors

6.3.1 Relationships and Social Support

In a survey of nearly 8000 surgeons, 90% had a domestic partner. Almost half of those partners did not work outside of the home, 35% were working non-physicians, and 16% were physicians. Surgeons whose domestic partner was another physician were more likely to report depressive symptoms and low mental quality of life than those surgeons whose domestic partner stayed at home. Surgeons whose domestic partner stayed home reported feeling more satisfied with their career [7]. The stressors of life as a physician are magnified when both partners are physicians, and it requires extra effort to balance the needs of each person.

Maintaining social support outside of the workplace is key to remaining balanced. This could mean keeping tight connections with friends, immediate family members, or significant others. In a very demanding job, it is often difficult to keep up with and maintain these relationships. Especially during residency, relationships have been found to suffer [8]. Carving out dedicated time to spend with friends and family is worth the effort. It is easy to let work take over minutes or hours, because the tasks we are faced with can feel very pressing. But we must acknowledge that life in the hospital will continue without us, and that our friends and family cannot wait forever for attention.

6.3.2 Family Dynamics

A large body of research exists regarding the family dynamics of surgeons, particularly centering around female surgeons. Female surgeons tend to be younger, are less likely to be married, and less likely to have children than male surgeons. Among those who were married, 83% of female surgeons had a spouse who worked outside of the home, whereas only 48% of male surgeons' spouses worked. The spouses of 43% of female surgeons were physicians, and 27% were surgeons. Only 5% of male surgeons have a surgeon spouse [9]. One could only imagine balancing a household run by two surgeons – the constant demands of both surgical schedules opposing on almost a daily basis. In households of two physicians, only 63% of males and 45% of females reported high levels of marital satisfaction [10].

Freischlag et al. determined that 1 in 5 surgeons reported a conflict between their career and their spouse's career in the 3-week period preceding their survey. Among those reporting a conflict, it resolved in the favor of the female surgeon 59% of the time, compared to 87% of male surgeons [9]. There is an approximately 3% increase in having a work-home conflict with every additional hour worked as a surgeon per week [11]. It has also been demonstrated that although the number of hours worked per week by physicians does not correlate with marital or parental satisfaction, it does relate to the amount of "role conflict" in a household where both partners are physicians [10].

Adding children to the mix adds to the presence of work-home conflicts. Having children is independently associated with 1.65× higher odds of having work-home conflicts for surgeons [11]. Female surgeons were much less likely to rely on their spouse to care for a sick child or child out of school compared to male surgeons (25% vs. 70%, $p < 0.001$) [9]. This is not to say that having children is all negative. However, in medicine as we evaluate causes of burnout, we should be sensitive to the additional challenges that physicians face as they try to balance a demanding clinical workload with household responsibilities.

6.3.3 Work-Life Integration

In the last decade, the terminology work-life balance has given way to work-life integration, appreciating that there is no hard line of demarcation between "work" and "life". For many, work comes with rewards of feeling accomplished, helping people, completing tasks. Living life involves striving to excel at work. So, integrating the demands of work with the demands of family and those outside of work is more sensible than treating them like two opposing forces.

In many cases, unfortunately, success in the work environment and the home environment feel like competing forces. Of surgeons surveyed, 23% of those who have children reported that their commitment to child rearing slowed their career advancement. The difference was more stark when divided by gender, with 57% of female surgeons indicating that child rearing slowed career advancement, compared to 20% of males ($p < 0.001$) [12]. Of the 50% of surgeons who reported having a work-home conflict in the preceding 3 weeks, only 12% were resolved in favor of personal responsibilities rather than professional responsibilities [9].

There are only so many minutes in a day, and so it is important for the surgeon to have time to reflect on how they wish to spend those minutes. No matter how many minutes one dedicates to work or family time, it is possible to feel either fulfilled or unsatisfied. Only 36% of surgeons thought that the work schedule left enough time for personal time and family life [12]. For the remaining 64% - it must be asked whether or not the surgeon felt able to control their work circumstance in a way that would give them more joy. If they valued surgery or academic achievement more highly than having personal time, it may simply be that they wished there were more minutes in an hour. Part of wellness is reflecting on what the individual would like to prioritize, then acting on those desires. We cannot be everywhere at once and things have to be sacrificed. It is up to the individual to decide on how to divide their time. Most importantly, the leadership of the hospital is not aware at any given moment how their staff would choose to divide their time if given the choice. It is the responsibility of the individual to decide on their priorities and to communicate them upward. The administration, therefore, must also be receptive to this communication. If their priorities are not able to be satisfied in one job, it may be best to look elsewhere. If we can be honest with ourselves, making our own lives a priority, we can still practice medicine and surgery and be fulfilled. It just may be that we cannot be a "triple threat" of days gone by. But really, it is that we must find joy in the things we spend our time doing, whether it is work or "life".

6.3.4 Financial Stressors/Economic Vitality

The costs of medical training continue to increase. In a national survey of surgical residents, nearly 40% had >$200,000 in educational debt and 70% had a high debt-to-asset ratio. Meanwhile, only 6% of residents reported having any financial education during their residency. Nationally, 74–85% of residents report significant debt challenges [13]. Kolars et al. demonstrated that internal medicine residents with educational debt >$200,000 have 1.7 fold higher burnout scores than their peers [14]. These financial stressors, beginning in training, directly impact the wellness of physicians and contribute to burnout.

Unfortunately, surgical training is particularly lengthy, and interest adds up over time. Anxiety over increasing debt, about insecurity of the government's ability to follow through on loan forgiveness programs, and the daunting prospect of providing for a family while in training or finishing training adds an extraordinary amount of stress to trainees. And once trainees move on towards a higher salary, many are concerned that their salaries are less than equitable. In every specialty, female physicians have lower unadjusted salaries than male physicians, with an absolute difference of approximately $51,000. Following multivariable adjustment for rank, years in practice, specialty type, etc., the absolute difference was still $19,900 [15]. Even after gender pay equity efforts, one academic institution with only a 1.9% pay gap calculates a lifetime disparity in over $66,000. Continuing to advocate for pay parity would alleviate financial stress in households with female physicians.

6.4 Work Environment Personal Factors

6.4.1 Inclusion and Connectivity

We spend the majority of our waking weekday hours at work. Even in the fast-paced work environment of an academic hospital, it is not only possible but common to feel lonely. Loneliness increases the risk of cardiovascular disease, depression and anxiety and also decreases productivity and creativity. Feeling like part of the team at work, actively engaging with colleagues and patients, is important for the health of the physician and the hospital. A study by Cigna reported that only 15% of American employees feel engaged at work, and Forbes reports that this may be responsible for billions of dollars in lost productivity across the country each year.

Similarly, Gallup research has repeatedly shown a link between having a best friend at work and the amount of effort that employees expend in their job. Specifically, 63% of women who strongly agree they have a best friend at work also report being "engaged" in their work, compared to only 29% with no best friend at work. Those employees who do report having a best friend at work are less likely to be actively looking for job opportunities, are more likely to trust the integrity and ethics of their team members, rate their own and their organizations' performance more highly, and are less likely to report negative feelings such as worry, stress, and exhaustion [16, 17]. A study of nurses demonstrated a strong negative correlation between work-related social support and burnout [18].

It may seem difficult from the non-supervisory role to increase inclusion and connectivity in the workplace, however, there are ways to make the work place more inviting from every level. Even if it means sacrificing time for personal or family related tasks, attending work-related social events occasionally helps to build a sense of community and support among colleagues. These relationships will help stave off burnout in the future and can bring more joy to everyday life.

6.5   Conclusion

6.5.1   *Physical, Mental, and Spiritual Well-being*

Perhaps said best by Mark Nepo, "One of the mysteries of illness is that no one can be healed by anyone whose emptiness is greater than their own". The rate of suicide is 1.4× higher for male physicians and 2.3× higher for female physicians compared to the average population [19]. As healers, we must make time for our own wellbeing such that there is enough emotional energy to care for our patients. Professionalism in medicine includes empathy and humanism, and thus it is a professional imperative to stave off threats to these qualities that are inherent in our being [20].

It would be easy to say that surgeons and physicians should sleep more, exercise more, eat healthier, meditate, and find spiritual guidance to enable them to perform better and prevent burnout. Achieving all of these at once is well intentioned but nearly impossible. Small steps, like building in a specific time in the week for exercise, packing a lunch for work to avoid high-calorie cafeteria foods a couple of times a week, or going to bed 30 minutes earlier instead of watching one more episode of TV are more reachable goals. Sometimes, the pursuit of "wellness" is enough to cause burnout. Beating ourselves up for "failing" at maintaining our own health can make it worse.

6.5.2   *Sense of Meaning*

Cycling back to finding joy in everyday activities, we must allow ourselves the time to discover what makes us happy in our lives. We must feel some autonomy and control over our schedules and pursue what we love. If that means fewer OR days and more clinic time, maybe that is a good solution. If it is fewer days at work and more time with young children, it may be worth a pay cut. Maybe it means more operative cases in a more streamlined location, which may mean finding a different work setting. Finding the sense of meaning, the personal reward and accomplishment that comes with healing others, that drove us to pursue medicine in the first place is a good place to start preventing burnout. To burn out, we must once have been on fire. Keeping the fire going by seeking out a sense of meaning, and guarding our personal time, can prevent burnout. This reflection takes time and effort and can be painful. But as physicians, nothing leading up to our careers has been without time, effort, and occasional pain. We are capable of alleviating personal barriers to burnout if we are willing to ask ourselves what it would take to love our jobs and our lives simultaneously.

References

1. Borges NJ, Savickas ML. Personality and medical specialty choice: a literature review and integration. J Career Asses. 2002;10(3):362–80.
2. Gleichgerrcht E, Decety J. Empathy in clinical practice: how individual disposition, gender, and experience moderate empathic concern, Burnout, and emotional distress in physicians. PLoS One. 2013;8(4):e61526. https://doi.org/10.1371/journal.pone.0061526.
3. Purvanova R, Muros J. Gender differences in burnout: a meta-analysis. J Vocat Behav. 2010;77(2):168–85.
4. Freeborn DK. Satisfaction, commitment, and psychological Well-being among HMO physicians. West J Med. 2001;174(January):13–8.
5. Wall A, Angelos P, Brown D, Kodner I, Keune J. Ethics in surgery. Curr Probl Surg. 2013;50:99–134.
6. Talbot SG, Dean W. Physicians aren't 'burning out.' They're suffering from moral injury. Stat 2018:26–29.
7. Dyrbye LN, Shanafelt TD, Balch CM, Satele D, Freischlag J. Physicians married or partnered to physicians: a comparative study in the American College of Surgeons. J Am Coll Surg. 2010;211(5):663–71. https://doi.org/10.1016/j.jamcollsurg.2010.03.032.
8. Law M, Lam M, Wu D, Veinot P, Mylopoulos M. Changes in personal relationships during residency and their effects on resident wellness: a qualitative study. Acad Med. 2017;92(11):1601–6. https://doi.org/10.1097/ACM0000000000001711.
9. Dyrbye L, Shanafelt T, Balch C, Satele D, Sloan J, Freischlag J. Relationship between work-home conflicts and Burnout among American surgeons. Arch Surg. 2011;146(2):211–7.
10. Warde CM, Moonesinghe K, Allen W, Gelberg L. Marital and parental satisfaction of married physicians with children. J Gen Intern Med. 1999;14:157–65.
11. Dyrbye L, Freischlag JA, Kaups KL, Oreskovich M, Satele DV, Hanks JB, Sloan JA, Balch CM, Shanafelt TD. Work-home conflicts have a substantial impact on career decisions that affect the adequacy of the surgical workforce. Arch Surg. 2012;147(10):933–9. https://doi.org/10.1001/archsurg.2012.835.
12. Tait S, Balch C, Bechamps G, Russel T, Dyrbye L, Satele D, Collicott P, Novotny PJ, Sloan J, Burnout FJ. Career satisfaction among American surgeons. Ann Surg. 2009;250(3):463–71. https://doi.org/10.1097/SLA.0b013e3181ac4dfd.
13. Tevis SE, Rogers AP, Carchman EH, Foley EF, Harms B. Clinically competent and fiscally at risk: impact of debt and financial parameters on the surgical resident. J Am Coll Surg. 2018;227(2):163–171.e7. https://doi.org/10.1016/j.jamcollsurg.2018.05.002.
14. West CP, Shanafelt TD, Kolars JC. Quality of life, Burnout, educational debt, and medical knowledge among internal medicine residents. JAMA. 2011;306(9):952–60.
15. Jena A, Olenski A, Blumenthal D. Sex differences in physician salary in US public medical schools. JAMA Intern Med. 2016;176(9):1294–304. https://doi.org/10.1001/jamainternmed.2016.3284.
16. Mann A. Why we need best friends at work. GALLUP 2018:1–8. https://www.gallup.com/workplace/236213/why-need-best-friends-work.aspx?version=print.
17. Gallup. Women in America: Work and Life Well-Lived. 2016.
18. Eastburg MC, Williamson M, Gorsuch R, Ridley C. Social support, personality, and Burnout in nurses. J Appl Soc Psychol. 1994;24(13):1233–50.
19. Shanafelt T, Boone S, Tan L, Dyrbye L, Sotile W, Satele D, West C, Sloan J, Oreskovich M. Burnout and satisfaction with work-life balance among US physicians relative to the general US population. Arch Intern Med. 2012;172(18):1377–85. https://doi.org/10.1001/archinternmed.2012.3199.
20. West CP, Shanafelt TD. The influence of personal and environmental factors on professionalism in medical education. BMC Med Educ. 2007;7(29):1–9. https://doi.org/10.1186/1472-6920-7-29.

Chapter 7
Meaning/Purpose in Work

Paula Marincola Smith and Kyla P. Terhune

7.1 Background

Burnout can be characterized as loss of enthusiasm for work, depersonalization, or as having a sense that work is no longer meaningful. It is a pervasive problem amongst physicians and is estimated to affect nearly 40% of practicing surgeons in the United States [1–4]. The high prevalence for burnout is cause of concern, as the effects of burnout appear to impact the physician-patient relationship, the quality of care physicians provide, as well as rates of depression, substance abuse, and suicidality amongst physicians [5–7].

Factors that contribute to physician and surgeon burnout are complex. Several studies have suggested that lack of control over the practice environment, administrative obligations, workload, practice setting, lack of work-life-balance, medical errors, and risk of malpractice suits all may contribute to the development of burnout amongst physicians [4, 8]. Interestingly, despite many surgeons in the U.S. frequently working more than 60 hours per week, the number of hours worked does not appear to be associated with rates of burnout in surgeons [1, 3]. Each of these factors must be only part of the story though, as every individual physician's personality, coping strategy, resilience and support system may dramatically impact how the above stressors affect an individual provider. Those differences in how work-related stressors are processed likely accounts for the variation in burnout seen among physicians even when in similar professional circumstances [4, 9].

P. Marincola Smith
Department of Surgery, Vanderbilt University Medical Center, Nashville, TN, USA
e-mail: paula.m.smith@vumc.org

K. P. Terhune (✉)
Department of Surgery, Vanderbilt University Medical Center, Nashville, TN, USA

Office of Graduate Medical Education, Vanderbilt University Medical Center, Nashville, TN, USA
e-mail: kyla.terhune@vumc.org

© Springer Nature Switzerland AG 2020
E. Kim, B. Lindeman (eds.), *Wellbeing*, Success in Academic Surgery,
https://doi.org/10.1007/978-3-030-29470-0_7

Multiple studies have recently suggested that finding enhanced meaning in one's work may be an important factor in mitigating burnout for medical professionals [4, 10, 11]. In one anonymous survey of 7197 members of the American College of Surgeons (ACS), surgeons who noted "placing greater emphasis on finding meaning in work, focusing on what is important in life, maintaining a positive outlook, and embracing a philosophy that stresses work/life balance" were significantly less likely to be burned out than their colleagues who did not [11]. On a population level, it has been proposed that focusing on improving upon the experience of providing care by assisting healthcare providers to find joy and meaning in work is an essential element of The Quadruple Aim, a set of principles for healthcare reform in the U.S. and abroad [12].

In this chapter, we highlight elements of surgical practice that may positively contribute to a sense of meaning and purpose in our work. We then discuss the taxing aspects of a career in surgery that may detract from finding meaning in our jobs and in our personal lives, and we present an original, albeit simplistic model demonstrating that increasing factors (or the emphasis of factors) that add *positive meaning* to a surgeon's life while providing tools that mitigate stressors responsible for *negative meaning* may provide stabilization and protection from burnout during difficult times. We emphasize the importance of balancing positive and negative factors in order to create one's own *net meaning*. This *net meaning* could ultimately determine our ability to endure challenges and setbacks in our personal and professional lives. We recognize that this approach is very simplistic and the emphasis and importance of each factor for each individual may be different. However, we do believe that the basic concept of working to increase this gap between factors that promote positive and negative meaning in our jobs and in our lives has the potential to mitigate burnout for physicians and surgeons.

7.2 Empathy, Meaning, and Empathetic Distress

Neuroscience research demonstrates persuasively that human brains are hardwired to experience empathy, in particular when one observes intense negative emotions such as pain and suffering. This capacity for empathy offers both a susceptibility to share suffering as well as an instinct to respond with compassion [13–15]. This human instinct for empathic and compassionate response to human suffering is the very reason many medical professionals, including surgeons, chose their careers. Compassion can naturally allow a physician's challenging work to feel meaningful rather than taxing.

On the other hand, it is known that one's greatest strength is often one's greatest weakness. It is the physician's capacity for empathy and compassion that, when unchecked, can significantly contribute to stress and negative wellbeing. When a physician is confronted with human suffering and, for one reason or another, feels personally responsible for the suffering or is otherwise unable to ease the agony, this predisposition for empathy can lead to feelings of "empathetic distress". If experienced repeatedly and not balanced with opposing positive emotions or coping mechanisms, this empathetic distress can eventually lead to emotional exhaustion and burnout [13, 16–18].

Fig. 7.1 Model for a potential balance between factors that contribute to and detract from meaning in work. Difference is defined as "net meaning." Increasing magnitude and quantity of factors that contribute may effectively minimize those that detract

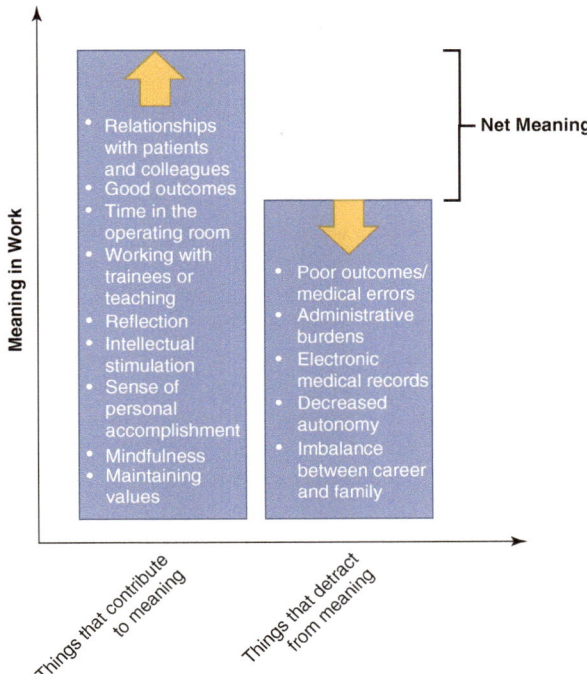

In the case of surgeons, such an experience may be even more pronounced than those experienced by other healthcare professionals. A surgeon may feel that a patient's suffering is the direct result of his or her personal actions in the operating room. Additionally, the opportunity for such encounters increases as one's patient and operative care increase. On the other hand, surgeons are also uniquely positioned to derive significant fulfillment from the immediate gratification of positive surgical outcomes. We propose, as demonstrated in Fig. 7.1, that it is the balance of these ever-opposing emotions—those that contribute to and those that detract from a sense of meaning—that create a *net meaning* that ultimately either protects physicians and surgeons from or predisposes them to burnout. If one can recognize the frequency, impact, or direct effect on oneself of various positive and negative factors, one has the potential to impact this net meaning.

7.3 Enhancers of Enjoyment and Meaning in Work

As suggested above, healthcare providers often choose their careers due to an innate desire to serve people, to relieve suffering and prolong quantity and quality of life. This role as a "healer" in all fields of medicine is at the essence of the profession.

The ability to utilize knowledge and expertise accumulated over many years of schooling and training uniquely positions physicians to intervene upon and change the trajectory of our fellow humans' lives for the better. This is perhaps why many physicians and healthcare providers are able to see their work as more than "just a job" or "just a paycheck".

Beyond the inherent satisfaction derived from positively impacting the lives of those around us, there are other essential elements that contribute to deriving enjoyment and meaning from our lives and our work. Mihaly Csikszentmihalyi wrote in *Flow: The Psychology of Optimal Experience* about the essential elements of human pleasure and enjoyment [19]. He distinguishes pleasure from enjoyment and notes that pleasure is "a feeling of contentment that one achieves whenever… expectations set by biological… or social conditioning have been met." Pleasure, while it improves quality of life, "does not produce psychological growth." Enjoyment, on the other hand, is characterized by "a sense of novelty or accomplishment" and occurs when a person has "gone beyond what he or she has been programmed to do and achieve[s] something unexpected." Csikszentmihalyi goes on to suggest that enjoyment has eight major components:

- Tasks with reasonable chance of completion
- Clear goals
- Immediate feedback
- Deep but effortless involvement that removes from awareness the frustrations and worries of everyday life
- Sense of control over our actions
- No concern for the self
- Alteration of the concept of time, hours can pass in minutes and minutes can look like hours

With these in mind, one can easily identify elements of medical practice that bring enjoyment through work. Such elements could include autonomy in patient care, opportunity to bring creativity into clinical or academic practice, and positively impacting the lives of our patients through good clinical outcomes. Due to the tangible and visible nature of surgery and the opportunity for direct and clear intervention, surgeons are particularly positioned to have "clear goals" in patient care and receive "immediate feedback" following their interventions. Time in the operating room for an attending surgeon also provides, in most cases, a "sense of control over our actions" as well as "alteration of the concept of time". These elements of medical and surgical practice contribute to the derivation of enjoyment from work, and ultimately can contribute to positive meaning in a surgeon's life.

Pushing the idea of mindfulness as directly contributing to quality of life even further, Csikszentmihalyi also introduced the concept of *Flow*. "Flow", known colloquially as "the zone", is a mental state in which a person performing an activity is fully immersed in a feeling of energized focus, full involvement, and enjoyment in the process of the activity [20]. This results in complete absorption in one's task, resulting in loss of one's sense of space and time [19]. In 2001, Nakamura and Csikszentmihalyi together identified six factors that together encompass a "flow" experience [19, 20]:

- Intense and focused concentration on what one is doing in the present moment
- Merging of action and awareness
- Loss of reflective self-consciousness (i.e. loss of awareness of oneself as a social actor)
- A sense that one can control one's actions; this is, a sense that one can in principle deal with the situation because one knows how to respond to whatever happens next
- Distortion of temporal experience (typically, a sense that time has passed faster than normal)
- Experience of the activity as intrinsically rewarding

Csikszentmihalyi proposes that when a person can organize his or her perception to experience "flow" as often as possible, quality of life starts to improve. During a "flow" state, he notes, one is in control of their psychic energy and everything done "adds order to consciousness". After a "flow" episode, one feels more "together", both "internally and with respect to other people and the world in general" [19].

Performing in the operating room is perhaps one of the most unambiguous examples of a "flow" state. While performing an operation, surgeons must proceed with complete focus. One must be aware of every detail from technicalities in the operative field to the physiologic state of the patient while simultaneously acting and moving in a deliberate and productive direction. One may lose a sense of self-consciousness and time. In most cases, there is a strong sense of complete control over the operation, and the experience of operating can be intrinsically rewarding. The operating room is one of the only places where one must disconnect from the outside world entirely, putting smartphones aside and ignoring constant streams of emails and text messages.

This regular experience of a "flow" state in the operating room may be an inherent piece of surgical practice that provides enjoyment, satisfaction, and meaning in a surgeon's career and life. While other elements of delivering patient care may be rewarding and contribute to a sense of meaning in their own ways, as suggested above, it is likely that this regular, almost meditative, experience of "flow" is particularly useful in improving a surgeon's quality of life. Csikszentmihalyi importantly notes that "the most important trait of people who find flow... is non self-conscious individualism... because of their intrinsic motivation, they are not easily disturbed by external events" [19]. It is perhaps this element of resilience achieved through regularly experiencing a "flow" state that provides an opportunity for surgeons to withstand the unavoidable stressors of medical practice.

Importantly, depending on the practice environment and hospital setting, some surgeons may also find gratification and meaning from work that is not directly related to patient care. For instance, teaching and/or research may be important elements of a surgeon's job that provide profound satisfaction. For those with leadership roles in both academic and private practice settings, mentorship or structural/practice development may be sources of gratification and meaning. In fact, Shanafelt and colleagues demonstrated that the extent to which academic physicians are able to focus on the aspect of their work that is most meaningful to them (research, education, patient care, or administration) has a strong inverse relationship to their risk of burnout [21]. Whatever the elements, it is important that surgeons gain insight into the elements of their careers that provide them with a sense of value and meaning, as intentionality and mindfulness surrounding these elements of practice may enhance their effectiveness as protective factors against the inevitable stressors of clinical practice (see Sect. 7.5).

7.4   Elements That Detract from Meaning in Work

While a career in surgery offers many opportunities to derive positive meaning and fulfilment, there are conversely many aspects of medical and surgical practice that either act as direct stressors or otherwise negatively impact a surgeon's overall sense of meaning. Several studies have examined common causes of burnout among physicians, and those frequently identified include lack of autonomy, difficulty balancing personal and professional life, excessive administrative tasks, insufficient protected time for academic endeavors, hostile work environments, and "gender/age-related issues" [1, 3, 8, 22–26]. How each of these factors impacts an individual surgeon is complex and is likely the result of many non-professional factors such as personality, health, personal circumstances, resilience, and support network (including marital status and children) [1].

In 2008, a survey was conducted by the ACS to examine the incidence of burnout among American surgeons and to evaluate the personal and professional characteristics associated with surgeon burnout. Of the 24,000 surgeons surveyed via email, 34% (n = 7905) returned surveys and were included in the final analysis [1, 3, 27]. Among other interesting findings, the results of this survey demonstrated that nearly 40% of surgeons met criteria for burnout, and the following factors were associated with burnout on multivariate logistic regression analysis: subspecialty choice (OR 1.2–1.6, all $p < 0.013$, with trauma, urology, otolaryngology, vascular surgery, and general surgery being associated with the highest odds of burnout), youngest child being ≤ 21 years old (OR 1.54, $p < 0.001$), compensation being entirely based on billing (OR 1.37, $p < 0.001$), spouse working as a healthcare professional (OR 1.23, $p = 0.004$), number of nights on call per week (OR 1.05, $p < 0.001$), and number of years in practice (OR 1.03, $p < 0.001$). On the other hand, having children (OR 0.82, $p = 0.006$) and spending more than half of one's time dedicated to non-patient care efforts (including research and administrative duties, OR 0.81, $p = 0.035$) were associated with reduced risk of developing burnout amongst the participating surgeons.

It is interesting to contemplate why some of these elements are risk factors for burnout. For instance, having children versus not having children appeared to be protective from developing burnout while having children ≤ 21 years old compared to having children >21 years old was a risk factor for burnout. There are many potential interpretations of this. It is known, though, that having young children is associated with various stressors (financial, childcare, sleepless nights, etc.) that may exacerbate job-related stressors such as long hours and hefty call schedules. These may fade as children age and are more independent, and adult children can then potentially contribute to strengthening support networks. Certainly, intrinsic qualities of the individual such as personality, coping strategies, and resilience, as well as external qualities impacting the work environment and home environment impact an individual's propensity for burnout.

In addition to the factors identified in the ACS survey described above, Balch and colleagues note that some essential elements for enduring medical education and training may directly propagate unhealthy and unbalanced habits amongst physicians and surgeons, even after the completion of training. For instance, many medical students, residents, and fellows, due to their long hours and lack of control over their call schedules and time, develop a coping strategy that justifies putting their personal lives on hold while fostering a mentality of delayed gratification (i.e. "things will get better when I'm done with this rotation/medical school/residency/fellowship") [1]. In many cases, this coping mechanism appears to carry forward through the end of training and into the lives of practicing physicians and surgeons. Rather than cultivating personal relationships and extra-professional interests once training is complete, many practicing physicians find themselves perpetually delaying these tasks to the future—until after they establish themselves in practice, until their grant is funded, until they are promoted to associate professor, etc. [1]. This habit of perpetually ignoring one's personal life for the sake of career development and advancement may contribute to an everlasting imbalance between personal and professional lives, dramatically impacting wellbeing and sense of meaning.

Other factors that can have potentially devastating effects include medical errors or experiencing bad patient outcomes. Medical errors (defined as a "commission or omission with potentially negative consequences for the patient that would have been judged wrong by skilled and knowledgeable peers at the time it occurred, independent of whether there were any negative consequences") are distinct from complications ("acknowledged risks of medical care or surgical procedures"). While the majority of medical errors cause little or no harm to patients, certainly they have the potential to lead to considerable morbidity or even mortality [27]. Medical errors, especially when associated with a poor outcome for the patient, can have a significant emotional impact on physicians that can persist for years after the error occurred [27]. As a result, physicians are sometimes referred to as the "second victim" of medical errors [28, 29].

While physicians and medical institutions put great attention and resources towards avoiding medical errors, most surgeons will be involved with a medical error at some point in their careers. Whether the error is the direct result of a technical mistake in the operating room, the result of miscommunication between treatment teams, documentation or technological oversights, or misinterpretation of diagnostic studies, each of these scenarios could lead to the devastating recognition that one has made a mistake with potentially fatal consequences. While the patient is the first and obvious victim of a medical error, physicians are also wounded by the same error [28].

Demanding operative and call schedules lead to imbalance between personal and professional lives. Policy changes and evolving medico-legal landscapes may lead to decreased surgeon autonomy in certain practice environments. The adaptation of new technologies and electronic medical records may result in disproportionate time spent on administrative tasks and documentation. Medical errors or unanticipated complications may occur. All of these stressors have the potential to detract from one's sense of meaning in work. If, in the same setting, one isn't deriving enough meaning from other elements of their career or actively working to mitigate these stressors through counseling or otherwise, there is risk of losing an overall sense of meaning in our work.

7.5   Net Meaning

Here we introduce the concept of *net meaning* (Fig. 7.1). Net meaning is the idea that every individual surgeon experiences things that contribute to meaning in work while simultaneously enduring other experiences that detract from meaning in work. What elements (and the degree to which those elements) contribute to a sense of meaning in work vary from physician to physician. Many of the most meaningful elements center on the concept of the individual provider being a healer, developing expertise in their field, being a teacher of colleagues or future providers, or making important scientific discoveries [4]. Specific examples that can contribute positively include strong relationships with patients, time in the operating room (experiencing "flow"), good outcomes, grateful patients, time spent on extra-clinical activities that one finds valuable (teaching, research), intellectual stimulation, support and recognition from colleagues. Elements that can detract from net meaning include poor outcomes, medical errors, administrative burdens, decreased autonomy, threat of medico-legal vulnerability, and imbalance between career and family.

We propose that it is possible for individual surgeons and surgical practices to deliberately focus on expanding the former while minimizing the latter. With the renewed interest nationally on the prioritization of physician wellbeing as well as the recognition that physician burnout has the potential to impact financial and business aspects of medical care [30], it seems possible and even advisable that surgical practices and medical centers begin taking notice of these elements that impact a physician's ability to derive meaning from their work.

Shanafelt and Noseworthy nicely summarize some of the ways that individual providers, work units, health care organizations, and the nation as a whole can work to enhance meaning in work for physicians [30]. On the individual level, self-awareness of the most personally meaningful aspects of work as well as making a point of recognizing and acknowledging positive events at work are ways that individual physicians and surgeons can enhance and expand the protective effect of factors that contribute to meaning in work. Additionally, when possible, advocating for shaping one's career to match one's personal interest (balance of clinical and non-clinical time, type of cases, etc.) has the capacity to significantly impact a physician's ability to derive meaning from work. On the "work unit" level, matching work to the talents and interests of the individual physician and identifying opportunities for physician involvement in education, research, or leadership is critical.

From the health care organizational level, creating an organizational culture and practice environment that values physician wellbeing as well as providing opportunities for professional development have the potential to improve physician engagement. On the national/policy level, research and educational grant funding opportunities, new regulations that result in additional time spent on clerical work, and evolving supervisory roles for physicians over midlevel providers have the potential to tip the balance of factors that detract from or enhance an individual physician's ability to derive meaning from work.

Several studies have demonstrated the efficacy of enhancing a physician's sense of meaning in work as a tool to increase physician satisfaction and reduce burnout [4]. The majority of these studies have examined interventions that focus on the individual providers rather than interventions that target organizations or policy. In a few studies, emphasis was placed on fostering self-awareness amongst physicians to assist them in identifying elements of their work that they most value and to connect with elements of their jobs that they find most meaningful [31, 32]. These studies utilized several interventions to enhance physician awareness and reflection, including writing brief narratives about personal experiences in their practice as well as asking the physicians to discuss their experiences in small groups. The goal of these types of interventions, known as "mindfulness training", is to increase awareness, intention, and self-reflection in an effort to decrease work-related distress. In a prospective trial conducted by Krasner and colleagues, 70 primary care physicians underwent mindfulness training and were examined by survey in a before-and-after study design. This intervention demonstrated increased levels of mindfulness, decreased levels of burnout, improved overall mood, and increased levels of conscientiousness and emotional stability following mindfulness training, and these changes were maintained for up to 15 months following the intervention [33]. This study, along with those previously mentioned, suggests that mindfulness training and encouraging physicians to be deliberate about identifying elements that contribute to positive meaning can improve physician wellbeing and be protective from burnout. Unfortunately, there have been many fewer studies aimed at addressing institutional factors that can contribute to physician distress, although this certainly also has the potential to be an efficacious strategy [34].

Based on the above, we would suggest that focusing attention on the following aspects of one's life and career may help increase either the quality or quantity of factors that contribute to meaning while decreasing or mitigating the impact of the features that detract from meaning.

- **Practice mindfulness and self-awareness.** Intentional reflection, narrative medicine or journaling, meditation, or even professional help in the form of trained counselors are all potential approaches. Employing these activities may blunt the negative effects of the detractors, allowing one to spend more time and energy focusing on aspects that contribute to meaning.
- **Be intentional about noting when things are going well.** In your workspace, display reminder of good patient outcomes (thank you notes, gifts) and items that remind you of your support network (photos, items). Turn to these in difficult times.

- **Strengthen support networks**. Don't fall into the trap of delaying the investment that friends and family require—be in it for the long-haul. Seek quality when quantity is not possible.
- **Find an umbrella of mentors who can provide perspective and share experience**. Don't rely on one individual to provide all aspects of mentorship. Seek to have a diverse portfolio of mentors, all for different reasons, decreasing the risk of potential feelings of disappointment or abandonment and increasing exposure to others' strategies and approaches in enhancing career satisfaction.
- **Establish and increase career elements that provide the highest value**. Look for positions, situations, and potential pivots that help accentuate these elements. One may need to execute realistic financial planning in order to achieve this.
- **Seek strong leadership and work environments**. The leadership of the department, group, or hospital establishes the culture and can significantly impact the degree of support in the workplace, autonomy, and job expectations for individuals.

Whatever the approach, it is clear that equipping physicians and surgeons with the ability to enhance factors that contribute to meaning in work and limit or diminish effects of factors that detract from meaning in work has the potential to greatly increase provider net meaning and, accordingly, increased overall job satisfaction and decreased burnout. It is impossible to eliminate the stressors that are inherent in the life of a surgeon. However, by recognizing and expanding the elements of one's career that contribute to positive meaning, we believe that surgeons can find protection from the inevitable stressors. It is this balance of positive and negative factors and one's reactions to them that will ultimately determine an individual provider's net meaning. If a positive balance it maintained, it could be protective from burnout. It is the authors' hope that future institutionally- and systems-focused research can lead to validated interventions that can be implemented to tip the scales in favor of positive net meaning in the lives of our hardworking surgeons.

References

1. Balch CM, Shanafelt T. Combating stress and burnout in surgical practice: a review. Adv Surg. 2010;44(1):29–47.
2. DeCaporale-Ryan L, Sakran JV, Grant SB, Alseidi A, Rosenberg T, Goldberg RF, et al. The undiagnosed pandemic: burnout and depression within the surgical community. Curr Probl Surg. 2017;54(9):453–502.
3. Shanafelt TD, Balch CM, Bechamps GJ, Russell T, Dyrbye L, Satele D, et al. Burnout and career satisfaction among American surgeons. Trans Meet Am Surg Assoc. 2009;127:107–15.
4. Shanafelt TD. Enhancing meaning in work. JAMA. 2009;302(12):1338–40.
5. West CP, Huschka MM, Novotny PJ, Sloan JA, Kolars JC, Habermann TM, et al. Association of perceived medical errors with resident distress and empathy. JAMA. 2006;296(9):1071–8.
6. Grol R, Mokkink H, Smits A, Van Eijk J, Beek M, Mesker P, et al. Work satisfaction of general practitioners and the quality of patient care. Fam Pract. 1985;2(3):128–35.
7. Dyrbye LN, Thomas MR, Massie S, Power DV, Eacker A, Harper W, et al. Burnout and suicidal ideation among U.S. medical students. Ann Intern Med. 2008;149:334–41.

8. Shanafelt TD, Sloan JA, Habermann TM. The well-being of physicians. Am J Med. 2003;114(6):513–9.
9. Linzer M, Visser M, Oort FJ, Smets E, McMurray JE, de Haes H. Predicting and preventing physician burnout: results from the United States and the Netherlands. Assoc Prof Med. 2001;111:170–5.
10. Tei S, Becker C, Sugihara G, Kawada R, Fujino J, Sozu T, et al. Sense of meaning in work and risk of burnout among medical professionals. Psychiatry Clin Neurosci. 2014;69(2):123–4.
11. Shanafelt TD, Oreskovich MR, Dyrbye LN, Satele DV, Hanks JB, Sloan JA, et al. Avoiding burnout. Ann Surg. 2012;255(4):625–33.
12. Sikka R, Morath JM, Leape L. The Quadruple Aim: care, health, cost and meaning in work. BMJ Qual Saf. 2015;24(10):608–10.
13. Ekman E, Halpern J. Professional distress and meaning in health care: why professional empathy can help. Soc Work Health Care. 2015;54(7):633–50.
14. Preston SD, de Waal FB. Empathy: its ultimate and proximate bases. Behav Brain Sci. 2002;25(1):1–71.
15. Ickes W. Empathic accuracy. J Pers. 1993;61(4):587–610.
16. Hatfield E, Rapson RL. Emotional contagion and the communication of emotion. Prog Commun Sci. 2006;14:73–89.
17. Hein G, Singer T. I feel how you feel but not always: the empathic brain and its modulation. Curr Opin Neurobiol. 2008;18(2):153–8.
18. Singer T, Klimecki OM. Empathy and compassion. Curr Biol. 2014;24(18):R875–8.
19. Csikszentmihalyi M. Flow—the psychology of optimal experience. New York: Harper Collins Publishers; 2008. 336 p.
20. Nakamura J, Csikszentmihalyi M. The concept of flow. In: Snyder CR, Lopez SJ, editors. Handbook of positive psychology; 2001. p. 89–93.
21. Shanfelt TD, West CP, Sloan JA, Novotny PJ, Poland GA, Menaker R, et al. Career fit and burnout among academic faculty. Arch Intern Med. 2009;169(10):990–5.
22. Balch CM, Freischlag JA, Shanafelt TD. Stress and burnout among surgeons. Arch Surg. 2009;144(4):371–6.
23. Shanafelt T, Chung H, White H, Lyckholm LJ. Shaping your career to maximize personal satisfaction in the practice of oncology. JCO. 2006;24(24):4020–6.
24. Shanafelt TD, Novotny P, Johnson ME, Zhao X, Steensma DP, Lacy MQ, et al. The well-being and personal wellness promotion strategies of medical oncologists in the North Central Cancer Treatment Group. Oncology. 2005;68(1):23–32.
25. Spickard A, Gabbe SG, Christensen JF. Mid-career burnout in generalist and specialist physicians. JAMA. 2002;288(12):1447–50.
26. Meier DE, Back AL, Morrison RS. The inner life of physicians and care of the seriously ill. JAMA. 2001;286(23):3007–14.
27. Shanafelt TD, Balch CM, Bechamps G, Russell T, Dyrbye L, Satele D, et al. Burnout and medical errors among American surgeons. Ann Surg. 2010;251(6):995–1000.
28. Wu AW. Medical error: the second victim. BMJ. 2000;320:726–7.
29. Wu AW, Folkman S, SJ M, Lo B. Do house officers learn from their mistakes? JAMA. 1991;265(16):2089–94.
30. Shanafelt TD, Noseworthy JH. Executive Leadership and Physician Well-being: nine organizational strategies to promote engagement and reduce burnout. Mayo Clin Proc. 2017;92(1):129–46.
31. Rabow MW. Doctoring to heal. West J Med. 2001;174:66–9.
32. Epstein RM. Mindful practice. JAMA. 1999;282(9):833–9.
33. Krasner MS, Epstein RM, Beckman H, AL S, Chapman B, Mooney CJ, et al. Association of an educational program in mindful communication with burnout, empathy, and attitudes among primary care physicians. JAMA. 2009;302(12):1284–93.
34. Dunn PM, Arnetz BB, Christensen JF, Homer L. Meeting the imperative to improve physician well-being: assessment of an innovative program. J Gen Intern Med. 2007;22(11):1544–52.

Chapter 8
Skills and Abilities

Lauren M. Theiss and Daniel I. Chu

8.1 Introduction

Rates of burnout among US physicians continue to climb at an alarming rate. In a 2014 survey, 53% of surgeons met the criteria for burnout [1] and studies have demonstrated up to 69% burnout rates in general surgery residents [2]. It is well known that physician burnout detracts from both physician wellbeing and patient care [3]. Recognizing the importance of physician wellbeing, the National Academy of Medicine launched The Action Collaborative on Clinician Well-Being and Resilience in January 2017. In order to identify the factors that contribute to clinician wellbeing, experts developed a conceptual model of wellness that examines both external factors, such as organizational and regulatory factors, and individual factors that directly impact physician wellbeing, and ultimately, patient care [4]. It is therefore imperative that our profession seek to understand those factors that contribute to physician wellbeing, including the individual skills and abilities that may protect physicians from burnout. These skills and abilities, many of which are identifiable, teachable and actionable, represent powerful tools to promote physician wellbeing (Table 8.1).

8.2 Clinical Competency

What role does clinical competency play in physician wellbeing? It is certainly reasonable to assume that physicians who perceive their clinical skills to be lacking or who have limited clinical confidence may suffer from more stress, an unfavorable work environment, and experience more burnout. Limited data exists, however, to

L. M. Theiss · D. I. Chu (✉)
Department of Surgery, University of Alabama at Birmingham, Birmingham, AL, USA
e-mail: laurentheiss@uabmc.edu; dchu@uabmc.edu

© Springer Nature Switzerland AG 2020
E. Kim, B. Lindeman (eds.), *Wellbeing*, Success in Academic Surgery,
https://doi.org/10.1007/978-3-030-29470-0_8

Table 8.1 Important skills and abilities that impact physical wellbeing

Skill/ability	Impact on wellbeing	Facilitators	Barriers	How to acquire
Clinical competency	+	Clinical confidence Positive emotions	Medical errors Malpractice Negative emotions	Optimal work and learning environment, medical education
Mentorship	+	Considered meaningful activity Emphasis on mentorship	Poor mentor/mentee relationship Poor mentorship skills	Mentorship programs, mentor education
Leadership	+	Autonomy Quality of supervising leadership	Poor communication and group skills	Leadership initiatives and courses
Efficiency, mastering new technologies	+	Institutional resources Organizational skills Adaptive	Clerical burden EMR Redundant processes	Examine institutional factors, maximize productivity
Resilience and grit	+	Hard work Adaptation Perseverance Interest	Stress Focus only on talent	Resilience training, Duckworth's grit tenants
Emotional intelligence	+	Empathy Social skills	Depersonalization Immaturity Work environment	EI coaching, age, experience

suggest that clinical competency directly contributes to wellbeing. Interestingly, the converse relationship between clinical *skills* and wellbeing has been well documented. Studies have shown that poor physician wellbeing is correlated with poor skills as reflected through medical errors and malpractice [5]. Additionally, physician burnout has been found to be associated with involvement in a recent malpractice suit and higher reported medical error in US surgeons [6, 7]. While clinical competency has not been directly linked to burnout, McConnell et al. have linked negative and positive emotions to both the acquisition of skills and clinical decision-making. Based on their review, the authors theorize that physicians with negative moods are more likely to commit medical errors due to prematurely terminated, and incomplete, workup and diagnosis [8]. Together, these early studies suggest that wellbeing and physician competency are likely co-dependent. Efforts to improve one cannot be done without including the other.

8.3 Mentorship

Mentorship is both an invaluable skill and a resource in augmenting physician wellbeing. Mentorship provides an important organizational tie that engages physician-mentors and makes these individuals feel more aligned with their institution(s). Providing mentorship to younger physicians, residents, and medical students is beneficial in preventing burnout, particularly if providing mentorship is a meaningful activity for that physician. Studies have shown that physicians who spend at least 20% of their work time on meaningful tasks to be less prone to burnout [9, 10]. Mentorship also enhances mentee wellbeing by providing a relationship and resource for guidance and encouragement. In a study of otolaryngology residents, institution of a formal mentorship program decreased levels of resident stress and improved scores on a burnout inventory, suggesting that mentorship programs serve to augment mentee wellbeing [11]. While there is little data on the efficacy of programs that teach mentorship skills to mentors themselves, mentorship programs represent a potential opportunity to enhance both mentor and mentee wellbeing.

8.4 Management, Delegation, Leadership, Communication, and Teamwork Skills

The ability to lead, communicate, and work with a team is essential in the health professions. Surgeons with poor communication and group skills are unlikely to function well on a team, and therefore are more likely to be unsuccessful and feel isolated in their work environment. Studies show that physicians crave the ability to lead, and both perceived and actual autonomy is an important contributor to wellbeing [9, 12]. Conversely, the quality and style of leadership of those who oversee physicians is important in preventing physician burnout. In a survey of over 3896 physicians, Shanafelt et al. found that decreased physician burnout was associated with high-quality leadership from their supervisors [13].

Several groups have reported improved leadership scores and self-assessed leadership ability with the institution of formal leadership programs [14]. Few studies, however, have linked leadership programs to improved patient outcomes or patient satisfaction [15, 16]. Nonetheless, these leadership programs ranged from formal classes and seminars to more intensive local or national physician leadership courses. Although further studies are needed to link leadership skills to decreased physician burnout, the dissemination of leadership skills is a worthy endeavor and may enhance both physician leadership and wellbeing.

8.5   Optimizing Workflow, Organizational Skills, Mastering New Technologies

Disorganized workflow and clerical burden contribute to worsening physician wellbeing. Recent studies indicate that physicians spend an astonishing amount of time on paperwork and the electronic medical record (EMR). One study of physicians across four specialties found that physicians spent on average 49.2% of their time on the EMR or desk work and only 27% of their time in direct contact with patients [17]. In a cohort of family medicine physicians, Arndt et al. observed that physicians spent on average 6 h of their 11 h day just on the EMR, with an average of 1.4 h of time spent after hours [18]. Inefficiency and paperwork mean more time spent away from what physicians perceive to be meaningful work, and studies have shown that these factors are associated with burnout [19, 20]. Inefficiency is often driven by inefficient institutional resources, such as poor integration of care and support staff, but it is also intimately tied to personal skills such as experience, prioritization, organizational skills, and the ability to say "no" [20, 21].

Additionally, the daunting task of mastering new technology such as the EMR can contribute to fatigue, burnout, and poor wellbeing, especially in a work environment that is increasingly digitized. Shanafelt et al. found that out of 5389 physicians who used EMRs, 57% met the criteria for burnout, while only 45% of physicians without EMRs were burned out. Physicians who used EMRs were also less likely to be satisfied with the amount of time spent on clerical work [22].

Physicians with organizational skills and the ability to quickly adapt will inherently spend less time navigating their institution's regulations and office duties. These physicians can therefore spend more time on meaningful work or optimizing work-life balance, both of which lead to improved physician wellbeing. By examining factors that contribute to redundant processes and inefficiency on a local level, institutions and their leaders can maximize physician efficiency and institute meaningful change [20]. These changes could ultimately decrease physician burnout, increase wellbeing and positively impact patient care. Physician wellbeing therefore can be also targeted through the acquisition, provision and maintenance of organizational skills at the individual and institutional-level.

8.6   Resilience and Grit

Resilience and grit equip individuals with the ability to combat adversity and achieve success. Although often used synonymously, resilience and grit are separate concepts. Herrman et al. define resilience as "positive adaptation… despite adversity," taking care to point out that resilience is both a "personal trait" and a "dynamic process" [23]. Resilience allows individuals to recover quickly and grow in response to stress. On the other hand, grit is an adjective used to describe individuals who are hard working and perseverant. Angela Duckworth explored this concept in her book *Grit,* defining grit as "the sustained application of effort towards a long term goal"

[24]. In the battle between effort and talent, Duckworth states that sheer effort is twice as important as natural talent in those who ultimately achieve success. Individuals who are "gritty" and recognize hard work and perseverance as critical skills are more likely to be successful than those who solely focus on talent. Perhaps unsurprisingly, several studies have demonstrated that surgical residents with more grit have less burnout, greater wellbeing, and are less likely to contemplate leaving surgical residency [25–27]. In a survey of 73 general surgery residents, Salles et al. found that residents with less grit as assessed with Duckworth's Short Grit Scale were more likely to have contemplated leaving residency [25]. This group also demonstrated that across 141 residents in surgical subspecialties, residents with more grit had lower rates of burnout [26].

Can grit and resilience be taught? The answer is likely "yes," but more research is needed. Several studies demonstrate the benefit of resilience training in improving physician communication, job satisfaction, and wellbeing, although there is no concrete curriculum or consensus on best training approach [19, 28]. Additionally, Duckworth argues that grit is a learnable trait and can be strengthened by focusing on four tenants: developing a fascination, seeking daily improvement, remembering greater purpose, and harboring a growth mindset. The point is made that physicians who integrate these principles into their careers will be well-equipped to battle adversity. And by teaching grit and resilience, we can positively impact physician wellbeing.

8.7   Coping Skills, Empathy, and Emotional Intelligence

Emotional intelligence (EI) is the awareness and ability to control one's own emotions and interact empathetically with others. Daniel Goleman further popularized the term in his 1995 book, describing five essential elements of emotional intelligence: emotional self-awareness, self-regulation, motivation, empathy, and social skills (Table 8.2) [29]. Arora et al. described EI as a "psychological construct" that encompasses many different social skills. The authors also keenly point out that EI could be considered either a personality trait or an ability, and this definition directly

Table 8.2 Key domains of emotional intelligence

Element of EI	Definition	This element allows one to:
Self-awareness	Aware of own thoughts and behaviors and their impact on others	Recognize and admit to strengths, weaknesses Ask for help when needed
Self-regulation	Ability to control behavior and impulses	Redirect disruptive behavior Remain calm in stressful situations
Motivation	Passion to work for a greater purpose	Stay focused and driven Overcome failure
Empathy	Understanding others emotions	Remain sensitive to others Have good bedside manner
Social skills	Ability to form and manage relationships with others, build rapport	Form strong connections with others Build teams

impacts attempts to measure and even teach EI [30]. Emotional intelligence has been well studied in many industries, but is relatively new to the medical field [31, 32]. EI is becoming increasingly recognized as a vital tool to help physicians cope with a high-stress work environment, and may be even more important for surgeons, who are often subject to unique pressures and expectations. EI has been correlated with wellbeing, higher job satisfaction, and lower rates of burnout in physicians [33–37]. In a 2011 study of internists and 2872 outpatients, physician burnout was correlated with lower patient satisfaction [34]. In general surgery residents, Hollis et al. found that higher levels of emotional intelligence were associated with higher job satisfaction [35]. This group also found that surgery residents with lower EI, particularly in the facet of self-control, were more likely to experience burnout, especially as related to personal accomplishment [37]. In addition to these associations, other studies have linked EI with improved patient trust, communication, and teamwork skills [30].

How can we teach emotional intelligence? Johnson et al. suggest that EI can be taught in an interdisciplinary setting embedded in existing work structures rather than a structured classroom environment. In this way, skills learned can be easily translated and applied [38]. Goleman described a business executive who improved emotional intelligence over several months through intensive self-reflection, videotapes of work interaction, and on-the-job coaching [39]. While the time and resources available to this business executive may not be available to most practicing physicians and residents, EI-specific principles could be adopted into existing surgical coaching and mentorship programs. Emotional intelligence can be taught and the skills it offers are invaluable ways to positively impact physician wellbeing and daily interactions in the surgical workplace.

8.8   Conclusion

Many individual skills and abilities are directly tied to physician wellbeing and burnout. Organizational efficiency, resilience, and emotional intelligence are three key examples that shape the way that physicians perceive and interact with their patients, colleagues, and the healthcare system. By identifying, teaching, and implementing these crucial skills, we can equip physicians to remain healthy, engaged, and grounded with the ultimate goal of improving physician wellbeing.

References

1. Shanafelt TD, et al. Changes in burnout and satisfaction with work-life balance in physicians and the general US working population between 2011 and 2014. Mayo Clin Proc. 2015;90(12):1600–13.
2. Elmore LC, et al. National survey of burnout among US General Surgery Residents. J Am Coll Surg. 2016;223(3):440–51.

3. Dimou FM, Eckelbarger D, Riall TS. Surgeon burnout: a systematic review. J Am Coll Surg. 2016;222(6):1230–9.
4. Brigham T, et al. A journey to construct an all-encompassing conceptual model of factors affecting clinician well-being and resilience, vol. 8. Washington, DC: National Academy of Medicine; 2018.
5. Tawfik DS, et al. Physician Burnout, Well-being, and Work Unit Safety Grades in Relationship to Reported Medical Errors. Mayo Clin Proc. 2018;93(11):1571–80.
6. Balch CM, et al. Personal consequences of malpractice lawsuits on American surgeons. J Am Coll Surg. 2011;213(5):657–67.
7. Shanafelt TD, et al. Burnout and medical errors among American surgeons. Ann Surg. 2010;251(6):995–1000.
8. McConnell MM, Eva KW. The role of emotion in the learning and transfer of clinical skills and knowledge. Acad Med. 2012;87(10):1316–22.
9. Rothenberger DA. Physician burnout and well-being: a systematic review and framework for action. Dis Colon Rectum. 2017;60(6):567–76.
10. Shanafelt TD, et al. Career fit and burnout among academic faculty. Arch Intern Med. 2009;169(10):990–5.
11. Zhang H, et al. Formal mentorship in a surgical residency training program: a prospective interventional study. J Otolaryngol Head Neck Surg. 2017;46(1):13.
12. Ariely D, Lanier WL. Disturbing trends in physician burnout and satisfaction with work-life balance: dealing with malady among the nation's healers. Mayo Clin Proc. 2015;90:1593–6.
13. Shanafelt TD, et al. Impact of organizational leadership on physician burnout and satisfaction. Mayo Clin Proc. 2015;90(4):432–40.
14. Frich JC, et al. Leadership development programs for physicians: a systematic review. J Gen Intern Med. 2015;30(5):656–74.
15. Green PL, Plsek PE. Coaching and leadership for the diffusion of innovation in health care: a different type of multi-organization improvement collaborative. Jt Comm J Qual Improv. 2002;28(2):55–71.
16. Korschun HW, et al. Realizing the vision of leadership development in an academic health center: the Woodruff Leadership Academy. Acad Med. 2007;82(3):264–71.
17. Sinsky C, et al. Allocation of physician time in ambulatory practice: a time and motion study in 4 specialties. Ann Intern Med. 2016;165(11):753–60.
18. Arndt BG, et al. Tethered to the EHR: primary care physician workload assessment using EHR event log data and time-motion observations. Ann Fam Med. 2017;15(5):419–26.
19. West CP, Dyrbye LN, Shanafelt TD. Physician burnout: contributors, consequences and solutions. J Intern Med. 2018;283(6):516–29.
20. Shanafelt TD, Noseworthy JH. Executive leadership and physician well-being: nine organizational strategies to promote engagement and reduce burnout. Mayo Clin Proc. 2017;92:129–46.
21. Shanafelt TD, et al. Longitudinal study evaluating the association between physician burnout and changes in professional work effort. Mayo Clin Proc. 2016;91(4):422–31.
22. Shanafelt TD, et al. Relationship between clerical burden and characteristics of the electronic environment with physician burnout and professional satisfaction. Mayo Clin Proc. 2016;91(7):836–48.
23. Herrman H, et al. What is resilience? Can J Psychiatr. 2011;56(5):258–65.
24. Duckworth A. Grit: the power of passion and perseverance. New York: Scribner; 2016.
25. Salles A, et al. Grit as a predictor of risk of attrition in surgical residency. Am J Surg. 2017;213(2):288–91.
26. Salles A, Cohen GL, Mueller CM. The relationship between grit and resident well-being. Am J Surg. 2014;207(2):251–4.
27. Burkhart RA, et al. Grit: a marker of residents at risk for attrition? Surgery. 2014;155(6):1014–22.
28. West CP, et al. Interventions to prevent and reduce physician burnout: a systematic review and meta-analysis. Lancet. 2016;388(10057):2272–81.

29. Goleman D. Emotional intelligence: why it can matter more than IQ. New York: Bantam Books, Inc.; 1995.
30. Arora S, et al. Emotional intelligence in medicine: a systematic review through the context of the ACGME competencies. Med Educ. 2010;44(8):749–64.
31. McKinley SK, Phitayakorn R. Emotional intelligence and simulation. Surg Clin North Am. 2015;95(4):855–67.
32. Thomas S, Tram S, O'Hara LA. Relation of employee and manger emotional intelligence to job satisfaction and performance. J Vocat Behav. 2006;67:461–73.
33. Satterfield J, Swenson S, Rabow M. Emotional intelligence in internal medicine residents: educational implications for clinical performance and burnout. Ann Behav Sci Med Educ. 2009;14(2):65–8.
34. Weng HC, et al. Associations between emotional intelligence and doctor burnout, job satisfaction and patient satisfaction. Med Educ. 2011;45(8):835–42.
35. Hollis RH, et al. Emotional intelligence in surgery is associated with resident job satisfaction. J Surg Res. 2017;209:178–83.
36. Lindeman B, Petrusa E, McKinley S, et al. Association of burnout with emotional intelligence and personality in surgical residents: can we predict who is most at risk? J Surg Educ. 2017;74(6):e22–30.
37. Cofer KD, et al. Burnout is associated with emotional intelligence but not traditional job performance measurements in surgical residents. J Surg Educ. 2018;75(5):1171–9.
38. Johnson DR. Emotional intelligence as a crucial component to medical education. Int J Med Educ. 2015;6:179–83.
39. Goleman D. What makes a leader? Harv Bus Rev. 1998;76(6):93–102.

Part IV
External Factors of Wellbeing

Chapter 9
Sociocultural Factors of Wellbeing

Jamie Knell and Erika L. Rangel

Multiple external factors contribute to clinician wellness, including societal expectations of the physician's role, the political and economic climate, and racial and gender discrimination manifesting as overt and unconscious bias. Stressors have been placed on clinicians through cultural changes in patient expectations, increased focus on safety and transparency, and the influence of media portrayal of clinicians. As we face workforce shortages, the effort to recruit and retain the most talented to the profession requires us to address the forces that negatively influence wellness, and to combat stigma that creates barriers to physicians seeking help.

9.1   Economic and Political Climate

Although a key tenant of the medical profession is a moral obligation to society, physicians have not traditionally engaged in political advocacy, with lower voting rates than the general population or other highly educated groups, such as lawyers [1, 2]. Over the past two decades, that paradigm has changed, with greater physician activism [3] and a shift in political orientation from predominantly Republican to predominantly Democrat [4]. Physician campaign contributions have increased by nearly tenfold. Clinicians are debating highly politicized topics such as women's wellness, abortion, vaccination, and gun violence, as seen in the #ThisIsMyLane movement.

J. Knell
Department of Surgery, Brigham and Women's Hospital, Boston, MA, USA
e-mail: jknell1@partners.org

E. L. Rangel (✉)
General and Gastrointestinal Surgery, Department of Surgery, Brigham and Women's
Hospital, Boston, MA, USA
e-mail: erangel@bwh.harvard.edu

© Springer Nature Switzerland AG 2020   85
E. Kim, B. Lindeman (eds.), *Wellbeing*, Success in Academic Surgery,
https://doi.org/10.1007/978-3-030-29470-0_9

With the passage of the Patient Protection and Affordable Care Act (ACA) in 2010, a series of significant changes to the practice of medicine have taken place. Increased coverage was offered largely through expansion of Medicaid eligibility and major changes to individual insurance markets. Both were funded through new taxes and cuts to Medicare provider rates and Medicare Advantage. With the ACA, a host of delivery system reforms were also enacted which were intended to improve quality and to curtail annual healthcare costs approaching \$3.5 trillion [5]. Certain proposed political changes, such as Medicare physician fee reductions, led to concern for reduction in physician compensation. Indeed, national surveys demonstrated decreases in physician salary by 7.1% from 1995 to 2003, despite growth in earnings of other healthcare workers [6]. With average medical school debt nearing \$200,000 [7] and lengthy training reducing overall career earnings, such salary cuts are concerning for many trainees and physicians. Other reforms include the development of the Center for Medicare and Medicaid Innovation within the Centers for Medicare and Medicaid (CMS), quality initiatives that reduce payment for hospital-acquired conditions and readmissions, bundled payment initiatives, and the creation of accountable care organizations (ACOs). Under an ACO, physician groups or hospitals are permitted to care for Medicare patients using a fee-for-service model, but must minimize cost while achieving quality benchmarks. Financial bonuses and penalties are tied to attainment of these metrics, which require complex tracking, accurate coding, and constant process improvement. Since being signed into law, the ACA has faced political opposition, legal challenges, and calls for repeal. While the long-term impact of the ACA for patients and providers remains unknown, the fluctuating political climate has left the future of healthcare coverage in question. Potential further centralization of medicine leads to questions regarding patient volume, rising regulatory burdens, and reimbursements. A recent physician survey found that the overall economic climate was one of the top three factors contributing to burnout [8].

Despite increasing complexity in insurance coverage and reimbursement plans, an understanding of the costs of healthcare delivery is expected from physicians, despite their lack of formal training. In the inpatient setting, physicians are often unaware of the expenses related to tests, medications, and devices they utilize. Although over 80% of patients wish to discuss out-of-pocket expenses for healthcare services, studies suggest most physicians are unable to answer these questions, undermining the physician-patient relationship [9]. As the gatekeepers of the healthcare system, physicians hold an important role in cost containment. In the future of ACOs, the stakes may continue to rise as reimbursement becomes tied to cost-efficient care [10].

Finally, care of uninsured patients causes financial challenges for many US hospitals and added stress to the physicians providing care. Although trauma is the second most costly medical condition in the United, States, one of every five trauma patients are uninsured [11]. The high proportion of uncompensated care provided to these patients leads to negative financial margins, potential financial insolvency, and closure of tertiary safety net hospitals [11]. Care of the uninsured and underinsured poses clinical challenges for physicians who must find "work-arounds" for patients who cannot afford diagnostic tests, specialty care, or basic treatments such as antibiotics. These may include referring patients to already overburdened safety net providers, forgoing indicated tests or therapies because of cost, or reducing out-of-pocket expenses with fee waivers or other adjustments in billing. Such concessions impact quality of care, jeopardize continuity, and add the liability risk of committing billing violations or offering nonstandard care. These challenges remain a problem despite the ACA, as coverage has not been extended to as many people as originally hoped [12], and many remain underinsured or face high copayments. The strain of being forced to compromise high standards of care for patients leads many physicians to avoid understaffed and underfunded institutions in favor of private nongovernmental organizations. This "brain drain" is similar to the phenomenon of talented physicians who leave underdeveloped countries to work in Western nations [11, 13]. Managing care for uninsured or underinsured patients was listed as one of the top four external stress factors for physicians [8].

9.2 Alignment of Societal Expectations and Clinician's Role

The last century has seen an exponential increase in medical knowledge, with the discovery of penicillin by Sir Alexander Fleming, the first successful organ transplant by Dr. Joseph E. Murray, and the development of most vaccines for common illnesses. The pace of acquisition of new medical knowledge is skyrocketing, with doubling time estimated to have dropped from 50 years in 1950 to 3.5 years in 2010. By 2020, the doubling time of such new knowledge is expected to be just 73 days [14]. It is no surprise that patients have developed high expectations of modern medicine. This may make it difficult for surgeons to set realistic treatment goals, as many diseases remain outside the realm of cure and treatments may involve substantial risks.

Studies suggest that many patients lack a deeper understanding of medical conditions, tests, and surgeries, often overestimating the benefit of interventions. They may harbor unrealistic expectations of treatment options and underestimate their inherent risks [15, 16]. For example, over 90% of patients surveyed in the UK overestimated the benefit of screening for breast and colon cancers [17]. Those with complex disease may not understand the morbidity of their conditions, such as patients with incurable lung cancer that often do not comprehend the palliative nature of chemoradiation and anticipate cure instead [18]. While some of these expectations may result from poor communication between physicians and patients, others may represent pre-existing beliefs about the power of medicine. Pressure to avoid direct conversations about outcomes may stem from a desire to satisfy the patient, as studies suggest patients perceive their physicians as better communicators when they convey a more optimistic prognosis [19]. Formal curricula to teach residents compassionate communication skills must be integrated into surgical training to reduce apprehension in the delivery of bad news and to help surgeons to establish realistic goals of care with their patients.

9.3 Media Portrayal

Throughout the decades, physicians have been portrayed in different ways on television. In the mid-1900s doctors were typically represented in a consistently positive and heroic fashion, such as in *Dr. Kildare* or *Ben Casey* [20, 21]. Studies in the 1960s and 1990s showed that watching television shows with positive depictions of physicians was generally associated with positive perceptions of doctors [22, 23]. By the late 1990s and the early 2000s, however, portrayals of physicians on TV began to change. Doctors were shown as less competent, having less ethical character, and less physically attractive [24]. For example, *House (2004)*, starred a rude, insensitive doctor with a drug addiction but the ability to solve seemingly unsolvable clinical puzzles. *Grey's Anatomy*, which premiered in 2005 and boasted almost 20 million viewers each week at its peak, focused on the relationships of the physicians it portrayed, often showing unprofessional behavior [25]. Studies that examined the content on medical television shows over time found a decrease in behavior that indicated rapport between physicians and patients, such as sitting while delivering medical news, while raising voices and inappropriate touching became more common [26]. The authors suggest that such portrayals of physicians in medical dramas may negatively influence patients' perceptions of physicians and reduce the efficacy of physician visits due to diminished trust.

The content of medical television dramas can also be questionable, leading to unrealistic patient expectations. For example, several studies have demonstrated that the rate of success of cardiopulmonary resuscitation (CPR) on television is significantly higher than the survival rate in real life [27, 28]. This may contribute to public overestimation of the success of resuscitative efforts [29, 30] with one study demonstrating no change in the decision to undergo CPR, even after education about the limited rates of survival to hospital discharge [31].

Media coverage of health information includes daytime medical talk shows and medical programs in news outlets. These programs have a significant impact on public health, with a survey performed by the National Health Council reporting that 75% of viewers pay a moderate to significant amount of attention to medical news, and that 58% of viewers changed their health habits as a result of media reports [32]. Popular syndicated daytime medical talk shows such as "The Dr. Oz Show" and "The Doctors" draw two to three million viewers per day [33]. The surge in healthcare information provided by the media led the American Medical Association to publish guidelines for "Ethical Physician Conduct in the Media" [34]. Despite an emphasis to uphold the tenets of the profession by presenting accurate information supported by science, a study in the British Medical Journal found that approximately half the recommendations made on daytime medical talk shows had either no evidence or were contradicted by the best available evidence. Potential risks were discussed for less than 10% of medical recommendations, and disclosure of potential conflicts of interest occurred less than 1% of the time [35]. Concerns about Dr. Oz's unfounded claims regarding dietary supplements ultimately led to a

Senate subcommittee hearing. His faculty position at Columbia University was subsequently called into question by physician colleagues due to his reported lack of integrity due to his promotional work [36].

9.4   Patient Behaviors and Expectations

The doctor-patient relationship is considered by many to be the bedrock of medical care but it has undergone significant changes in recent decades. For centuries this relationship was primarily paternalistic, with the physician making medical decisions on behalf of their patients [37, 38]. Physicians commonly made house calls or held "office hours" in their homes. Many had social relationships with their patients, living in the same neighborhoods and treating multiple members of the same family [39]. Today's physicians face increasing demands on their time, rising administrative costs, and pressures to provide increasingly cost-efficient care in the climate of ACOs. Physicians spend nearly twice the amount of time performing administrative tasks as they do seeing patients [40] and as much as half their workday documenting in the electronic health record. The pressure to transition to "Big Med", or systematic provision of services by larger integrated entities that control the majority of patient care, has resulted in physicians leaving smaller private practice models in favor of hospital employment or affiliation. Today, there are just half the number of physicians remaining in solo or small group private practice compared to 2000 [41]. The doctor-patient relationship is viewed by many as shifting towards medical consumerism, with shorter patient visits taking on the characteristics of a business transaction [38] and eroding both patient and physician satisfaction [42]. Efforts to systematically manage healthcare providers conflicts with the tenets of autonomy and hierarchy that physicians traditionally valued.

Technology has played a significant role in access to medical knowledge, access to care, and expectations for instant medical advice. Patients as consumers now seek information through nontraditional channels including self-management software, social media, and other informal networks. Although the quality and accuracy of such information is variable, surveys suggest that 60–80% of internet users obtain health information online, with over 160 million Google searches per day on healthcare related issues [43]. Patients expect convenient and instant access to their test results, to their medical notes [44], and to medical advice by messaging their physician online. Many practitioners express concern that this will increase the hours providers are expected to be available for care [45] and may lead to clinicians acting as curators of health information. Additionally, these communications are not typically covered by insurance reimbursement [45].

Surveys show an erosion in the overall level of trust between patients and the medical system in recent years [46, 47], with the proportion of Americans expressing confidence in the medical profession dropping from 73% in 1966 to only 34%

in 2012 [48]. The US ranks nearly last (24 of 29) among industrial countries in this regard. However, this may reflect poor confidence in medical leaders rather than distrust of individual physicians, with over half reporting they were still were satisfied with their own personal care. The reasons for deterioration in trust in the healthcare system are multifactorial and may relate to lack of a universal health care system, the complex US political process, and extensive media coverage which tends to make physician advocacy appear more adversarial than it appears in other countries. The controversial nature of medicine has been highlighted by highly politicized debates regarding universal healthcare coverage in the wake of the ACA and hotly debated bills to cut Medicaid and Medicare spending. In the US, the medical profession does not share management of the healthcare system with the government, and must therefore leverage influence of private medical organizations, which are divided among multiple specialty organizations that may not share similar viewpoints. The fragmented input from medical professionals reduces American public trust and the ability of physicians to influence policy decisions affecting patient care [48]. Physician organizations such as the AMA have been labeled self-serving and accused of placing profits before patients.

Media coverage may also contribute to public backlash against managed care by influencing public anxiety over key aspects of healthcare. For example, analysis of print and broadcast media in the US have found that the tone of coverage of healthcare has become more critical over time. Television programs focus on negative stories more than half the time and often emphasize controversies in patient care issues, using dramatic anecdotes and a "villains and victims" format to tell their stories instead of peer-reviewed research studies [49].

Erosion of public trust may have negative consequences for patient outcomes and healthcare costs. Numerous studies have shown that a positive relationship between physician and patient is associated with adherence to recommended treatments, greater utilization of preventative services [50–52], better outcomes in chronic disease, and higher levels of patient satisfaction [53]. The bond between physician and patient has historically been a special one and draws many into the medical profession. Loss of this trust can result in decreased fulfillment and a feeling of alienation among providers.

9.5   Culture of Safety and Transparency

In a field of constantly changing knowledge, sometimes ambiguous science, and physicians vulnerable to human error, medical errors are a reality in the care of patients. In 2000, a report from the Institute of Medicine (IOM), *To Err is Human, Building a Safer Health System*, described up to 98,000 hospital deaths per year from medical error [54]. Although this generated attention-grabbing headlines, the intended message was that improvements in patient safety require systemwide changes including prevention, recognition, and mitigation of harm from error. The IOM committee understood that placing blame on individuals for specific errors would create a culture of reticence in admission of adverse events or discussing "near misses". The National Center for Patient Safety within the Agency for Healthcare Research and Quality (AHRQ) was created based on this committee's recommendations to establish safety goals, track progress in meeting these goals, invest in research to learn more about preventing errors, and to share effective practices. The IOM committee also recommended mandatory national public reporting systems for medical errors, growth of voluntary and confidential reporting systems, provision of incentives for safe practices through insurers and regulators, and building a culture of safety within healthcare leadership.

Since the IOM report, many studies have demonstrated that effective communication with patients and families immediately after patient harm reduces medical liability, leads to organizational learning, and fosters improvements in patient safety mechanisms. In 2017, over 200 US healthcare institutions adopted open, non-defensive approaches to handling medical errors called communication and resolution programs (CRPs) [55]. These CRPs advocate for early reporting and analysis of the event, full explanations for families and patients, emotional support for healthcare professionals involved in the event, and apologies and compensation to patients when the hospital is at fault. With increased transparency and safety reporting, incident reports have increased and claims have decreased, with accompanying reductions in legal costs and settlement amounts [56]. In May 2016, the AHRQ introduced the CANDOR toolkit, a free resource to help hospitals adopt this approach [57].

Although this movement has built accountability and improvements in patient safety, less focus has been given to alleviating the emotional toll on physicians after making a medical error. Such mistakes can be devastating for physicians, who may struggle with their own fallibility, worry about loss of patient trust and litigation, and experience guilt, anxiety, embarrassment, depression, fear, decreased job satisfaction, and even thoughts of suicide [58, 59]. These reactions may be heightened for physicians who have difficulty disclosing the error to the patient and their family [59]. Surgeons, in particular, are challenged by these disclosures because it belies the culture of decisiveness and certainty they are expected to uphold. Surgeons have described the stress of feeling the need to portray qualities of strength despite powerful negative feelings after an adverse event [60]. Studies of residents involved in medical errors show similar concerns, with increased rates of burnout, depression, lower quality of life, decreased empathy, and perceptions of further errors in the subsequent months [61] Despite efforts by institutions to support physicians after patient harm occurs, a recent study suggests more progress is needed, with only 10% of physicians reporting adequate help for error-related stress [59].

As a result of public pressure to achieve greater patient safety, the Accreditation Council on Graduate Medical Education (ACGME) implemented duty-hour regulations for U.S. medical trainees in 2003. Despite these limitations on work hours and regulatory pressure to increase resident supervision, data demonstrating improvements in patient safety-related outcomes are equivocal [62]. However, many experts believe the combination of the 80-h work week, decreased autonomy, and increasing operative complexity have led to decreased confidence of graduating surgical residents over the past 10 years [63]. This topic has been discussed at length in editorials, at national meetings, and even in the lay press. The ongoing narrative may be a self-fulfilling prophecy as it further undermines the confidence of trainees [64]. When attending senior surgeons reminisce about the past and lament that today's training is inferior to the "good old days", residents may learn the technical aspects of the operation while believing they lack the judgement and skill of historic controls. Fostering self-doubt within surgical training is of great negative consequence, as the development of confidence is as critical as the acquisition of cognitive and technical competence. A surgeon lacking confidence despite having adequate skills results in uncertainty during crucial decision-making points in patient care. The future of surgical training requires educational experiences to focus on providing sufficient autonomy and operative experience while fostering professional role confidence. Senior surgeons must be aware that the way they relate to trainees has a strong impact on the surgeons they become. Collaborative efforts to enhance efficient and effective faculty teaching through objective assessment of teaching performance may produce sustainable improvements in the learning environment. Surveys of residents have linked autonomy and confidence with increased satisfaction with training [65] and greater work-related wellbeing [66].

9.6   Discrimination and Overt and Unconscious Bias

Over the past decades, innovative legislation and a focus on civil rights led to the development of programs to ensure opportunities for racial minorities and women in the workforce. Despite significant improvements in gender and racial inequalities, women and underrepresented minorities (URMs) in surgery still face disparities in recruitment, training, salary, academic advancement, and conduct from patients and other healthcare professionals, which can significantly contribute to burnout.

In the 1940s–1950s, only 5% of medical students were women. By 2017, female medical students outnumbered males. However, women remain underrepresented in surgery, making up just 18% of faculty and 40% of residents in the United States [67, 68]. In residency, nearly 90% of female trainees experience gender discrimination in interactions with faculty, other members of the healthcare team, and patients [69]. Studies show women residents may be given less autonomy in the operating room compared to their male colleagues at the same level of training [70]. Outside of the work environment, they are invited less frequently to socialize with their attendings, thereby limiting opportunities for professional development and reducing faculty approachability during times of stress [71]. Other common sources of gender discrimination include female nursing and clerical staff. The female surgeon may struggle to balance attainment of agency and leadership with the need to exhibit the communal or nurturing qualities that are considered positive in women. This is made more difficult in a healthcare environment dominated by female nurses and support staff, as women find other women in leadership positions to be less qualified and less desirable than a man with identical characteristics [72]. Such same-sex bias is prevalent in other male-dominated professions, where the assertive and agentic qualities that are seen as favorable in men are considered undesirable in women. This phenomenon perpetuates the cycle of prejudice by undermining a surgeon's sense of self-efficacy, her colleagues' and patients' respect, and her job satisfaction.

Surgical training is long, with completion at age 34 for those taking a traditional academic pathway with a one-year fellowship. These are common years for marriage and childbirth, though studies show female surgical residents face a different set of challenges in these life events. Most female surgeons delay childbearing until they have completed residency [73], although the majority report they would rather have had children earlier [74]. The delay in starting a family may be related to the difficulties of pregnancy during surgical training. A recent national survey of women surgeons who had at least one child during residency found 80% worked an unmodified schedule until birth [75], though the majority expressed concern about adverse health risks to themselves or their unborn child. Indeed, the rate of pregnancy complications, including preeclampsia and preterm labor, occur at higher frequency among residents who work long hours compared with matched controls [76, 77]. Although most women preferred a longer maternity leave, 78% received 6 weeks or less. Lactation support was problematic, with more than half describing inadequate lactation facilities, 85% reporting they were uncomfortable asking to scrub out of long cases to pump, and over half stopped nursing before they wanted to due to challenges balancing work duties with time to express milk. The perception of stigma was prevalent and fear of "appearing weak" and loss of reputation may preclude pregnant surgical residents from asking for accommodations [78]. This stigma may be perpetuated by unconscious bias within surgical education leadership, with almost half of surgical program directors reporting that the research years are the best time for a woman to have a baby, and nearly two-thirds reporting that having a child adversely affects a female trainee's work. These challenges and biases negatively influence career satisfaction for many, with 39% strongly considering leaving surgical residency and nearly 30% reporting they would discourage a female medical student from pursuing a surgical career due to the challenges of balancing the profession with motherhood [75, 79]. As the surgical workforce faces changing demographics and generational shifts in lifestyle priorities, surgical leaders must consider the needs of childbearing residents to recruit and retain the best candidates.

Following residency, women in surgery begin their careers with fewer academic resources, tend to be promoted less quickly, and earn significantly lower salaries than their male counterparts [80]. At the time of this publication, there were 22 female chairs of surgical departments, representing 12% of chairs nationally. Although this is an improvement from only two women leading surgical departments in 2001 [81], the "glass ceiling" that limits women from the highest, most prestigious positions in academic surgery is still a reality. This concept has been supplemented with the term "sticky floor", which refers to a phenomenon in academic medicine where fewer women are promoted or given institutional resources such as laboratory space at the start of their career. Although some have argued this disparity is related to the tendency for female surgeons to prioritize their family over their career or to work fewer hours, this theory has been refuted by studies demonstrating fewer promotions for women compared to men, even after adjusting for grant support, hours worked, publications, and tenure tracks. In academia, women may be more likely to assume roles referred to as "institutional housekeeping", including underpaid and unpaid tasks [82], clinician roles, and educator duties that do not lead to top leadership positions [80].

The pipeline theory, which endorses the idea that the number of women in leadership roles will increase with the influx of female medical students, is not supported by the data. Association of American Medical Colleges (AAMC) statistics suggest that women are not ascending to the ranks of full professors of surgery. In fact, there has been no change in the representation of women in academic surgery at higher faculty ranks over the past 15 years despite an increase in the absolute number of women entering academic surgery [83]. The paucity of women in leadership roles reduces the number of female mentors for residents and new faculty, further continuing the cycle. Such personal and professional mentorship is critical to prevent attrition in residents [84], to guide young female faculty away from taking on tasks that do not support leadership roles, and to increase their visibility at the regional and national level.

Women physicians on average earn 64 cents on the dollar compared to their male colleagues, with pay disparities as high as $83,000 among general surgeons after adjusting for volume, experience, geography, benefits, and practice type [85]. This gap may be even larger in academia, where women physicians were found to make 39% less than men despite controlling for age, rank, years since completing residency, specialty, clinical trial participation and publication count [86]. Women without children demonstrate similar pay gaps, suggesting that lower salaries for women physicians cannot be explained by intangible differences such as the need for scheduling flexibility for childcare [87]. Unsurprisingly, women in surgery are more likely to feel discriminated against than men [88] and to feel their gender limits their chance for promotion [83]. Limited access to professional advancement and support is associated with greater job strain, burnout, and lower work satisfaction [83, 89].

Women surgeons face unique challenges with respect to family responsibilities. Multiple large studies have shown that female surgeons spend more time childrearing [90], are more likely to experience a conflict between work and home duties, are more likely to believe that childrearing had slowed their career advancement, and are less likely to have a spouse who is a homemaker compared to their male counterparts. Those who experienced such work-home conflicts were less likely to feel they had enough time for their personal and family life and had significantly higher rates of burnout. Nearly 40% of women surgeons are partnered with another physician, half of whom are surgeons [73, 91]. Surgeons in these dual-physician partnerships are at higher risk of depressive symptoms and low mental quality of life [92], perhaps indicative of the complexity of work-life balance in these relationships.

Over the last decade, there is rising concern that faculty in our medical institutions lack adequate representation by URMs. African Americans represent 12.6% of the US population but only 7.8% of medical school graduates [93], 5% of surgical residents, and less than 3% of academic surgeons in the US [93, 94]. Minority physicians have historically cared for underserved populations more readily than their majority counterparts, may put URM patients at greater ease with their care, may increase participation by URM patients in clinical research studies, and provide valuable mentorship for future URM surgeons. Such benefits in patient care are seen in African American patients, who have improved outcomes when cared for by African American physicians [95]. Despite compelling evidence that minorities in the medical profession may improve racial inequities in health care, URMs are less likely to pursue academic careers in medicine [96]. The causes are likely multifactorial and include the low number of minority medical school graduates, the shortage of role models and mentors, poor preparation of URM residents for academic careers, and other factors such as institutional racism and educational debt. Similar to women surgeons, minority faculty are less likely to receive promotions, even after controlling for gender, degree, NIH funding, and tenure status. [97]. URMs are less likely to feel happy at work, less likely to feel comfortable asking attendings for help, and less likely to report being able to rely on their peers [93]. Although minority residents have reported overt discrimination such as racial or ethnic slurs [98], stories of implicit bias permeate even the lay press. In 2018, Dr. Fatima Stanford shared her experience with racial discrimination on a Delta Airlines flight when she attempted to aid a passenger in distress and was reportedly questioned repeatedly about her credentials by flight attendants [99]. Navigating such racial bias, particularly when it occurs at one's own institution, can have a deleterious effect on career satisfaction [100].

These disparities among female and minority surgeons are noted by medical students. Studies examining the influences on medical student career choice suggest women are discouraged from a surgical profession by perceptions of bias against women, lack of female role models, and lifestyle considerations [101, 102]. Twenty-five years ago, 96% of women students in described surgery as "unfavorable" to their gender, though no men claimed the same [103]. Despite gradual improvements in gender bias in our profession, another study done in the last decade still shows female students are less likely to be interested in surgery at the beginning of medical school, are more likely to lose interest during school, and are less likely to develop a new interest in surgery [102]. Studies also indicate that the lack of racial diversity among residents and faculty in a surgical training program may affect ranking by URMs [104], who may feel isolated or feel that the institution does not value minority participation. These negative perceptions contribute to our inability to capture the attention of a gifted pool of candidates, an increasing concern as the profession faces impending workforce shortages. To recruit and retain the most talented individuals to surgery, institutional leaders must recognize the importance of addressing barriers to academic advancement, provide transparency in salary and promotion, endorse leadership development for talented URMs and women, support mentorship for URM and women residents, and provide workplace family support.

9.7   Stigmatization of Mental Illness

Although the incidence of depression among physicians is similar to that in the general population [105], suicide is a disproportionately high cause of mortality for physicians relative to other professionals and the general population [106]. A study of members of the American College of Surgeons found that 1 in 16 reported suicidal ideation in the prior year, a number 1.5- to 3-fold greater than the general population [107]. Most of these surgeons reported symptoms of depression, though only 26% had sought psychiatric or psychologic help.

The culture of medicine has not historically been supportive of physician mental health, with punitive action often taken against the physician seeking help. This includes overt and subtle discrimination in medical licensing, hospital privileges, and professional advancement. Approximately 80% of state medical boards question the applicant about mental illness and over 30% of surveyed licensure board executive directors report that a diagnosis of mental illness is sufficient grounds for sanctioning a physician [108]. As a result, over half of physicians with self-reported mental health diagnoses worry about being placed on a restricted medical license [109] and 60% of surgeons with suicidal ideation report they did not seek care due to concerns that it would affect their licensure [107]. Apprehension regarding limitations in clinical practices, mandatory psychiatry evaluations, out-of-pocket expenses for required tests and evaluations, and public disclosure of personal health information create barriers to physicians seeking treatment [110]. In 2003, the American Foundation for Suicide Prevention published a consensus statement in the Journal of the American Medical Association to reduce obstacles to treating mental health disorders for physicians, suggesting that disclosures on licensure paperwork be limited to questions on impairment of professional abilities rather than mental health diagnoses, and that hospitals and malpractice insurers encourage physicians to seek help for suicidality and depression [111].

Only a third of physicians routinely seek health care, supporting the observation that the professional culture of the field discourages vulnerability and promotes self-reliance, perfectionism, and high-function. Although multiple studies have confirmed depression and burnout are major risk factors for suicide in physicians, many do not pursue treatment for fear of diminished reputation, loss of respect, and shame or embarrassment in seeking help for mental illness [105]. Physicians with mental health diagnoses often attempt management of their disease on their own, with those experiencing suicidal ideation more likely to prescribe their own antidepressants [109]. Concern for stigma is particularly prevalent within surgical subspecialties [109]. Fortunately, surgical residency programs have begun to develop wellness programs designed to reduce sources of stress [112] and recognize warning signs of depression and suicide [113]. Longitudinal studies of surgical trainees and practicing surgeons have shed greater understanding on the factors contributing to burnout. Building education and awareness are the first steps in prevention and treatment of an insidious disease in physicians and surgeons.

9.8 Conclusion

The climate of surgery is rapidly changing with numerous sociocultural pressures that affect wellness and contribute to burnout. Economic and political changes, alterations in societal expectations and reimbursement patterns, influence imposed by media, and unconscious bias toward minority groups have created a complex environment that challenges the traditional model of surgical practice. This new era of healthcare provides an exciting challenge to focus on constructive advocacy. In addition, recent evidence of the direct relationship between burnout, patient outcomes, physician wellness, and attrition have attracted national attention and laid a robust framework for improvements in our training environment, hospital practice, and mentorship models. To continue recruiting and retaining the most talented students to our profession, organizations and individual surgeons must share the responsibility of developing these programs for future surgeons.

References

1. Grande D, Asch DA, Armstrong K. Do doctors vote? J Gen Intern Med. 2007;22(5):585–9.
2. Gruen RL, Campbell EG, Blumenthal D. Public roles of US physicians: community participation, political involvement, and collective advocacy. JAMA. 2006;296(20):2467–75.
3. Huddle TS. Perspective: medical professionalism and medical education should not involve commitments to political advocacy. Acad Med. 2011;86(3):378–83.
4. Bonica A, Rosenthal H, Rothman DJ. The political polarization of physicians in the United States: an analysis of campaign contributions to federal elections, 1991 through 2012. JAMA Intern Med. 2014;174(8):1308–17.
5. CMS. National health expenditures 2017 highlights. 2017. https://www.cms.gov/research-statistics-data-and-systems/statistics-trends-and-reports/nationalhealthexpenddata/national-healthaccountshistorical.html. Accessed 2 Jan 2019.
6. Seabury SA, Jena AB, Chandra A. Trends in the earnings of health care professionals in the United States, 1987-2010. JAMA. 2012;308(20):2083–5.
7. Grischkan J, George BP, Chaiyachati K, Friedman AB, Dorsey ER, Asch DA. Distribution of medical education debt by specialty, 2010-2016. JAMA Intern Med. 2017;177(10):1532–5.
8. Rosenstein AH. Physician stress and burnout: prevalence, cause, and effect. AAOS Now. 2012:31.
9. Henrikson NB, Chang E, Ulrich K, King D, Anderson ML. Communication with physicians about health care costs: survey of an insured population. Perm J. 2017;21.
10. Song Z, Lee TH. The era of delivery system reform begins. JAMA. 2013;309(1):35–6.
11. Scott JW, Neiman PU, Najjar PA, Tsai TC, Scott KW, Shrime MG, et al. Potential impact of affordable care act-related insurance expansion on trauma care reimbursement. J Trauma Acute Care Surg. 2017;82(5):887–95.
12. Jaffe S. USA gears up for next round of enrollment under the ACA. Lancet. 2015;386(10004):1613–4.
13. Walden J. An overlooked cause of physician burnout. Fam Pract Manag. 2016;23(1):6–7.
14. Densen P. Challenges and opportunities facing medical education. Trans Am Clin Climatol Assoc. 2011;122:48–58.
15. Fagerlin A, Sepucha KR, Couper MP, Levin CA, Singer E, Zikmund-Fisher BJ. Patients' knowledge about 9 common health conditions: the DECISIONS survey. Med Decis Mak. 2010;30(5):35–52.

16. Hoffman BL, Shensa A, Wessel C, Hoffman R, Primack BA. Exposure to fictional medical television and health: a systematic review. Health Educ Res. 2017;32(2):107–23.
17. Hudson B, Zarifeh A, Young L, Wells JE. Patients' expectations of screening and preventive treatments. Ann Fam Med. 2012;10(6):495–502.
18. Chen AB, Cronin A, Weeks JC, Chrischilles EA, Malin J, Hayman JA, et al. Expectations about the effectiveness of radiation therapy among patients with incurable lung cancer. J Clin Oncol. 2013;31(21):2730–5.
19. Weeks JC, Catalano PJ, Cronin A, Finkelman MD, Mack JW, Keating NL, et al. Patients' expectations about effects of chemotherapy for advanced cancer. N Engl J Med. 2012;367(17):1616–25.
20. Chory-Assad RM, Tamborini R. Television exposure and the public's perceptions of physicians. J Broadcast Electron Media. 2010;47(2):197–215.
21. Jiwa M. Doctors and the media. Australas Med J. 2012;5(11):603–8. https://doi.org/10.4066/AMJ.2012.1562.
22. Blumenfeld W. Some correlates of TV medical Drama viewing. Psychol Rep. 1964;15(3):901–2.
23. Pfau M, Mullen LJ, Garrow K. The influence of television viewing on public perceptions of physicians. J Broadcast Electron Media. 1995;39(4):441–58.
24. Chory-Assad RM, Tamborini R. Television doctors: an analysis of physicians in fictional and non-fictional television programs. J Broadcast Electron Media. 2001;45(3):499–521.
25. Berger E. From Dr. Kildare to Grey's anatomy: TV physicians change real patient expectations. Ann Emerg Med. 2010;56(3):21–3.
26. Gross AF, Stern TW, Silverman BC, Stern TA. Portrayals of professionalism by the media: trends in etiquette and bedside manners as seen on television. Psychosomatics. 2012;53(5):452–5.
27. Diem SJ, Lantos JD, Tulsky JA. Cardiopulmonary resuscitation on television. Miracles and misinformation. N Engl J Med. 1996;334(24):1578–82.
28. Portanova J, Irvine K, Yi JY, Enguidanos S. It isn't like this on TV: revisiting CPR survival rates depicted on popular TV shows. Resuscitation. 2015;96:148–50.
29. Nava S, Santoro C, Grassi M, Hill N. The influence of the media on COPD patients' knowledge regarding cardiopulmonary resuscitation. Int J Chron Obstruct Pulmon Dis. 2008;3(2):295–300.
30. Van den Bulck JJ. The impact of television fiction on public expectations of survival following in hospital cardiopulmonary resuscitation by medical professionals. Eur J Emerg Med. 2002;9(4):325–9.
31. Schonwetter RS, Teasdale TA, Taffet G, Robinson BE, Luchi RJ. Educating the elderly: cardiopulmonary resuscitation decisions before and after intervention. J Am Geriatr Soc. 1991;39(4):372–7.
32. Johnson T. Shattuck lecture: medicine and the media. N Engl J Med. 1998;339(2):87–92.
33. Block AB. "Dr. Oz' and 'Ellen' see ratings growth, 'Kelly & Michael' topping 2011 in demo. The Hollywood Reporter. 2012. https://www.hollywoodreporter.com/news/dr-oz-ellen-see-ratings-387407. Accessed 12 Jan 2019.
34. AMA. Ethical physician conduct in the media. 2017. https://www.ama-assn.org/delivering-care/ethics/ethical-physician-conduct-media. Accessed 12 Jan 2019.
35. Korownyk C, Kolber MR, McCormack J, Lam V, Overbo K, Cotton C, et al. Televised medical talk shows—what they recommend and the evidence to support their recommendations: a prospective observational study. BMJ. 2014;349:g7346.
36. Dell SJ. What's wrong with Dr. Oz? Mo Med. 2015;112(5):332–3.
37. Choi CJ, Hwang SW, Kim HN. Changes in the degree of patient expectations for patient-centered care in a primary care setting. Korean J Fam Med. 2015;36(2):103–12.
38. Kaba R, Sooriakumaran P. The evolution of the doctor-patient relationship. Int J Surg. 2007;5(1):57–65.
39. Hafferty FW. What society and medicine want-for themselves and from each other. Virtual Mentor. 2007;9(4):305–9.

40. Sinsky C, Colligan L, Li L, Prgomet M, Reynolds S, Goeders L, et al. Allocation of physician time in ambulatory practice: a time and motion study in 4 specialties. Ann Intern Med. 2016;165(11):753–60.
41. Moses H, Matheson DH, Dorsey ER, George BP, Sadoff D, Yoshimura S. The anatomy of health care in the United States. JAMA. 2013;310(18):1947–63.
42. Dugdale DC, Epstein R, Pantilat SZ. Time and the patient-physician relationship. J Gen Intern Med. 1999;14(Suppl 1):S34–40.
43. Powell JA, Darvell M, Gray JAM. The doctor, the patient and the world-wide web: how the internet is changing healthcare. J R Soc Med. 2003;96(2):74–6.
44. Levingston SA. How is the doctor-patient relationship changing? It's going electronic. The Washington Post. 2015.
45. Katz SJ, Moyer CA. The emerging role of online communication between patients and their providers. J Gen Intern Med. 2004;19(9):978–83.
46. Calnan MW, Sanford E. Public trust in health care: the system or the doctor? Qual Saf Health Care. 2004;13(2):92–7.
47. Huang EC, Pu C, Chou YJ, Huang N. Public trust in physicians-health care commodification as a possible deteriorating factor: cross-sectional analysis of 23 countries. Inquiry. 2018;55:46958018759174.
48. Blendon RJ, Benson JM, Hero JO. Public trust in physicians—U.S. medicine in international perspective. N Engl J Med. 2014;371(17):1570–2.
49. Brodie M, Brady LA, Altman DE. Media coverage of managed care: is there a negative bias? Health Aff. 1998;17(1):9–25.
50. Bauer AM, Parker MM, Schillinger D, Katon W, Adler N, Adams AS, et al. Associations between antidepressant adherence and shared decision-making, patient-provider trust, and communication among adults with diabetes: diabetes study of northern California (DISTANCE). J Gen Intern Med. 2014;29(8):1139–47.
51. Musa D, Schulz R, Harris R, Silverman M, Thomas SB. Trust in the health care system and the use of preventive health services by older black and white adults. Am J Public Health. 2009;99(7):1293–9.
52. Schoenthaler A, Montague E, Baier Manwell L, Brown R, Schwartz MD, Linzer M. Patient-physician racial/ethnic concordance and blood pressure control: the role of trust and medication adherence. Ethn Health. 2014;19(5):565–78.
53. Birkhauer J, Gaab J, Kossowsky J, Hasler S, Krummenacher P, Werner C, et al. Trust in the health care professional and health outcome: a meta-analysis. PLoS One. 2017;12(2):e0170988.
54. IOM. To err is human: building a safer health system. Washington, DC: National Academy Press; 2000.
55. Brin DW. The best response to medical errors? Transparency. AAMC News. 2018.
56. Kachalia A, Kaufman SR, Boothman R, Anderson S, Welch K, Saint S, et al. Liability claims and costs before and after implementation of a medical error disclosure program. Ann Intern Med. 2010;153(4):213–21.
57. AHRQ. Communication and Optimal Resolution (CANDOR) Toolkit. 2018. https://www.ahrq.gov/professionals/quality-patient-safety/patient-safety-resources/resources/candor/introduction.html. Accessed 23 Jan 2019.
58. Han K, Bohnen JD, Peponis T, Martinez M, Nandan A, Yeh DD, et al. The surgeon as the second victim? Results of the Boston Intraoperative Adverse Events Surgeons' Attitude (BISA) study. J Am Coll Surg. 2017;224(6):1048–56.
59. Waterman AD, Garbutt J, Hazel E, Dunagan WC, Levinson W, Fraser VJ, et al. The emotional impact of medical errors on practicing physicians in the United States and Canada. Jt Comm J Qual Patient Saf. 2007;33(8):467–76.
60. Luu S, Leung SO, Moulton CA. When bad things happen to good surgeons: reactions to adverse events. Surg Clin North Am. 2012;92(1):153–61.
61. West CP, Huschka MM, Novotny PJ, Sloan JA, Kolars JC, Habermann TM, et al. Association of perceived medical errors with resident distress and empathy: a prospective longitudinal study. JAMA. 2006;296(9):1071–8.

62. Shelton J, Kummerow K, Phillips S, Arbogast PG, Griffin M, Holzman MD, et al. Patient safety in the era of the 80-hour workweek. J Surg Educ. 2014;71(4):551–9.
63. Elfenbein DM. Confidence crisis among general surgery residents: a systematic review and qualitative discourse analysis. JAMA Surg. 2016;151(12):1166–75.
64. Kellogg KC, Breen E, Ferzoco SJ, Zinner MJ, Ashley SW. Resistance to change in surgical residency: an ethnographic study of work hours reform. J Am Coll Surg. 2006;202(4):630–6.
65. Bucholz EM, Sue GR, Yeo H, Roman SA, Bell RH Jr, Sosa JA. Our trainees' confidence: results from a national survey of 4136 US general surgery residents. Arch Surg (Chicago, Ill : 1960). 2011;146(8):907–14.
66. Lases SS, Slootweg IA, Pierik E, Heineman E, Lombarts M. Efforts, rewards and professional autonomy determine residents' experienced well-being. Adv Health Sci Educ Theory Pract. 2018;23(5):977–93.
67. AAMC. Association of Medical Colleges. Distribution of women MD faculty by department and rank. 2014. https://www.aamc.org/download/411788/data/2014_table4a.pdf. Accessed 13 Apr 2017.
68. ACGME. ACGME residents and fellows by sex and specialty. 2015. https://www.aamc.org/data/workforce/reports/458766/2-2-charthtml. Accessed 4 Feb 2019.
69. Bruce AN, Battista A, Plankey MW, Johnson LB, Marshall MB. Perceptions of gender-based discrimination during surgical training and practice. Med Educ Online. 2015;20:2592–3.
70. Meyerson SL, Sternbach JM, Zwischenberger JB, Bender EM. The effect of gender on resident autonomy in the operating room. J Surg Educ. 2017;74(6):e111–e8. https://doi.org/10.1016/j.jsurg.2017.06.014.
71. Sullivan MC, Bucholz EM, Yeo H, Roman SA, Bell RH, Sosa JA. "Join the club": effect of resident and attending social interactions on overall satisfaction among 4390 general surgery residents. Arch Surg. 2012;147(5):408–14.
72. Buchanan F, Warning R, Tett R. Trouble at the top: women who don't want to work for a female boss. J Bus Divers. 2012;12(1):33–46.
73. Troppmann KM, Palis BE, Goodnight JE Jr, Ho HS, Troppmann C. Women surgeons in the new millennium. Arch Surg. 2009;144(7):635–42.
74. Hamilton AR, Tyson MD, Braga JA, Lerner LB. Childbearing and pregnancy characteristics of female orthopaedic surgeons. J Bone Joint Surg Am. 2012;94(11):e77, 1-9.
75. Rangel EL, Smink DS, Castillo-Angeles M, Kwakye G, Changala M, Haider AH, et al. Pregnancy and motherhood during surgical training. JAMA Surg. 2018c;153(7):644–52.
76. Gabbe SG, Morgan MA, Power ML, Schulkin J, Williams SB. Duty hours and pregnancy outcome among residents in obstetrics and gynecology. Obstet Gynecol. 2003;102(5):948–51.
77. Klebanoff MA, Shiono PH, Rhoads GG. Outcomes of pregnancy in a national sample of resident physicians. N Engl J Med. 1990;323(15):1040–5.
78. Rangel EL, Castillo-Angeles M, Changala M, Haider AH, Doherty GM, Smink DS. Perspectives of pregnancy and motherhood among general surgery residents: a qualitative analysis. Am J Surg. 2018a;216(4):754–9.
79. Rangel EL, Lyu H, Haider AH, Castillo-Angeles M, Doherty GM, Smink DS. Factors associated with residency and career dissatisfaction in childbearing surgical residents. JAMA Surg. 2018b;153(11):1004–11.
80. Zhuge Y, Kaufman J, Simeone DM, Chen H, Velazquez OC. Is there still a glass ceiling for women in academic surgery? Ann Surg. 2011;253(4):637–43.
81. Bickel J, Wara D, Atkinson BF, Cohen LS, Dunn M, Hostler S, et al. Increasing women's leadership in academic medicine: report of the AAMC Project Implementation Committee. Acad Med. 2002;77(10):1043–61.
82. Greenberg CC. Association for Academic Surgery presidential address: sticky floors and glass ceilings. J Surg Res. 2017;219:ix–xviii.
83. Sexton KW, Hocking KM, Wise E, Osgood MJ, Cheung-Flynn J, Komalavilas P, et al. Women in academic surgery: the pipeline is busted. J Surg Educ. 2012;69(1):84–90.

84. Bongiovanni T, Yeo H, Sosa JA, Yoo PS, Long T, Rosenthal M, et al. Attrition from surgical residency training: perspectives from those who left. Am J Surg. 2015;210(4):648–54.
85. Medscape. Medscape general surgeon compensation report. 2016. https://www.medscape.com/sites/public/physician-comp/2016. Accessed 4 Feb 2019.
86. Jena AB, Olenski AR, Blumenthal DM. Sex differences in physician salary in US Public Medical Schools. JAMA Intern Med. 2016;176(9):1294–304.
87. Jagsi R, Griffith KA, Stewart A, Sambuco D, DeCastro R, Ubel PA. Gender differences in the salaries of physician researchers. JAMA. 2012;307(22):2410–7.
88. Wright AL, Schwindt LA, Bassford TL, Reyna VF, Shisslak CM, St Germain PA, et al. Gender differences in academic advancement: patterns, causes, and potential solutions in one US College of medicine. Acad Med. 2003;78(5):500–8.
89. Cochran A, Hauschild T, Elder WB, Neumayer LA, Brasel KJ, Crandall ML. Perceived gender-based barriers to careers in academic surgery. Am J Surg. 2013;206(2):263–8.
90. Mayer KL, Ho HS, Goodnight JE Jr. Childbearing and child care in surgery. Arch Surg. 2001;136(6):649–55.
91. Dyrbye LN, Shanafelt TD, Balch CM, Satele D, Sloan J, Freischlag J. Relationship between work-home conflicts and burnout among American surgeons: a comparison by sex. Arch Surg (Chicago, Ill : 1960). 2011;146(2):211–7. https://doi.org/10.1001/archsurg.2010.310.
92. Dyrbye LN, Shanafelt TD, Balch CM, Satele D, Freischlag J. Physicians married or partnered to physicians: a comparative study in the American College of Surgeons. J Am Coll Surg. 2010;211(5):663–71.
93. Wong RL, Sullivan MC, Yeo HL, Roman SA, Bell RH Jr, Sosa JA. Race and surgical residency: results from a national survey of 4339 US general surgery residents. Ann Surg. 2013;257(4):782–7.
94. Williams M. The diverse surgeons initiative and increasing underrepresented minorities in academic surgery. J Am Coll Surg. 2011;212(5):914–5.
95. Saha S, Komaromy M, Koepsell TD, Bindman AB. Patient-physician racial concordance and the perceived quality and use of Health care. Arch Intern Med. 1999;159(9):997–1004.
96. Nivet MA. Minorities in academic medicine: review of the literature. J Vasc Surg. 2010;51(4 Suppl):53S–8S.
97. Madsen TE, Linden JA, Rounds K, Hsieh YH, Lopez BL, Boatright D, et al. Current status of gender and racial/ethnic disparities among academic emergency medicine physicians. Acad Emerg Med. 2017;24(10):1182–92.
98. Baldwin DC Jr, Daugherty SR, Rowley BD. Racial and ethnic discrimination during residency: results of a national survey. Acad Med. 1994;69(10 Suppl):S19–21.
99. Camero K, Anderson T. MGH voices support for doctor who says she was racially profiled on flight to Boston. The Boston Globe. 2018.
100. Peterson NB, Friedman RH, Ash AS, Franco S, Carr PL. Faculty self-reported experience with racial and ethnic discrimination in academic medicine. J Gen Intern Med. 2004;19(3):259–65.
101. Sanfey HA, Saalwachter-Schulman AR, Nyhof-Young JM, Eidelson B, Mann BD. Influences on medical student career choice: gender or generation? Arch Surg. 2006;141(11):1086–94.
102. Snyder RA, Bills JL, Phillips SE, Tarpley MJ, Tarpley JL. Specific interventions to increase women's interest in surgery. J Am Coll Surg. 2008;207(6):942–7.
103. Lillemoe KD, Ahrendt GM, Yeo CJ, Herlong HF, Cameron JL. Surgery—still an "old boys' club"? Surgery. 1994;116(2):255–9.
104. Ku MC, Li YE, Prober C, Valantine H, Girod SC. Decisions, decisions: how program diversity influences residency program choice. J Am Coll Surg. 2011;213(2):294–305. https://doi.org/10.1016/j.jamcollsurg.2011.04.026.
105. Schwenk TL, Davis L, Wimsatt LA. Depression, stigma, and suicidal ideation in medical students. JAMA. 2010;304(11):1181–90.
106. Broquet KE, Rockey PH. Teaching residents and program directors about physician impairment. Acad Psychiatry. 2004;28(3):221–5.

107. Shanafelt TD, Balch CM, Dyrbye L, Bechamps G, Russell T, Satele D, et al. Special report: suicidal ideation among American surgeons. Arch Surg. 2011;146(1):54–62.
108. Hendin H, Reynolds C, Fox D, Altchuler SI, Rodgers P, Rothstein L, et al. Licensing and physician mental health: problems and possibilities. J Med Licensure a Disc. 2007;93(2):6–11.
109. Gold KJ, Andrew LB, Goldman EB, Schwenk TL. "I would never want to have a mental health diagnosis on my record": a survey of female physicians on mental health diagnosis, treatment, and reporting. Gen Hosp Psychiatry. 2016;43:51–7.
110. Dyrbye LN, West CP, Sinsky CA, Goeders LE, Satele DV, Shanafelt TD. Medical licensure questions and physician reluctance to seek care for mental health conditions. Mayo Clin Proc. 2017;92(10):1486–93.
111. Center C, Davis M, Detre T, Ford DE, Hansbrough W, Hendin H, et al. Confronting depression and suicide in physicians: a consensus statement. JAMA. 2003;289(23):3161–6.
112. Salles A, Liebert CA, Esquivel M, Greco RS, Henry R, Mueller C. Perceived value of a program to promote surgical resident well-being. J Surg Educ. 2017;74(6):921–7.
113. Hochberg MS, Berman RS, Kalet AL, Zabar SR, Gillespie C, Pachter HL. The stress of residency: recognizing the signs of depression and suicide in you and your fellow residents. Am J Surg. 2013;205(2):141–6.

Chapter 10
Regulatory, Business, and Payer Environment

Janelle F. Rekman and Adnan Alseidi

10.1 Introduction

Spending on healthcare in North America is out of control, and there has never been a more important time for surgeons to understand how legislative and regulatory actions affect their patient care and fiscal decisions. However, the complexity of systems influencing the 'business of surgery', and the speed at which they change, can be very intimidating for the average surgical provider. In addition, this topic has the potential to make junior surgeons perceive that the healthcare industry is losing its focus on patients, turning them from clinical care providers into business professionals [1]. It is imperative, however, that surgeons are involved in regulatory changes to prevent development of policies that hinder their ability to care for patients and contribute to rampant professional burnout [2]. Burnout, or "the consequences of severe or prolonged stress and anxiety experienced by people working in the healing profession" [3], is a much greater problem among surgeons than among the general population (53% vs. 28%) [4] and continues to increase in North America.

The goal of this chapter is to outline, at a high level, the current evidence describing how the regulatory, business, and payer aspects of a surgeon's practice contribute to their overall wellness (see Fig. 10.1). Additionally, ways in which the reader can get involved with advocacy action and ongoing conciliatory efforts will be highlighted.

J. F. Rekman
HPB and General Surgery, Virginia Mason Medical Center, Seattle, WA, USA
e-mail: janelle.rekman@virginiamason.org

A. Alseidi (✉)
HPB and Endocrine Surgery, Virginia Mason Medical Center, Seattle, WA, USA
e-mail: adnan.alseidi@virginiamason.org

© Springer Nature Switzerland AG 2020

E. Kim, B. Lindeman (eds.), *Wellbeing*, Success in Academic Surgery,
https://doi.org/10.1007/978-3-030-29470-0_10

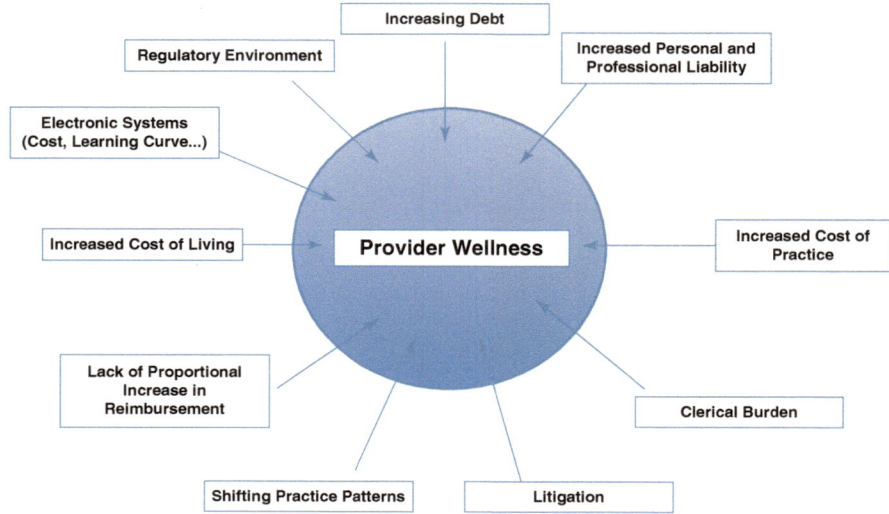

Fig. 10.1 Factors affecting provider wellness related only to the regulatory, business, and payer environment

10.2 Regulatory and Business Factors Affecting Surgeon Wellness

10.2.1 Regulatory Environment

North American surgeons have the daunting task of complying with a growing number of federal regulations affecting their day-to-day practice, and subsequently their overall wellness. The focus of many recent regulations has been to increase patient safety and define standards of care, but unfortunately studies show that provider workload has increased as a direct result [5]. The American Hospital Association (AHA) [6] published a comprehensive review of federal laws and regulations affecting providers and found that health systems and hospitals must comply with 629 discrete regulatory requirements as of 2017. To give an idea of the work hours necessary for compliance with these regulations, the average-sized hospital dedicates 59 full-time equivalents (FTEs) to these efforts (over one-quarter of which are nurses and doctors). For the average surgeon, the scope of regulatory burden is wide, including domains of: quality reporting, value-based payment models, meaningful use of electronic health records, hospital conditions of participation (CoPs), fraud and abuse, privacy and security (HIPAA), billing, and coverage verification requirements. The greatest proportion of provider resources are dedicated to CoP and billing/coverage verification processes, such as insurance pre-authorization. These two domains also represent 63% of the total average annual cost of regulatory compliance [6]. For providers, increased regulation means a larger burden of phone calls, increased paperwork, and more negotiating with payers, resulting in fewer hours to spend with family, exercise, or spend building relationships with their patients and/or colleagues.

Regulations surrounding reimbursement and billing of Medicare are complex, have recently changed, and continue to undergo massive overhaul. In 2015 Congress repealed the sustainable growth rate (SGR) formula that was used to calculate Medicare reimbursement and passed the Medicare Access and CHIP (Children's Health Insurance Program) Reauthorization Act (MACRA). SGR has now been replaced with the Quality Payment Program (QPP) that physicians can participate in through either the MIPS (Merit-based Incentive Payment System) or Alternative Payment Model (APM). MIPS has four components including an adjustment to the Physician Quality Reporting System (PQRS) and the Advancing Care Information (ACI) act which builds on the Electronic Health Record (EHR) incentive program also known as Meaningful Use [7]. If not familiar with these terms and acronyms, it is quite easy to understand the confusion and angst that can surround beginning a surgical practice or changing locations. In fact, as noted later in this chapter, surgeons are beginning to choose employment options over solo practice in part to allow someone else (namely a hospital employer) to manage these regulatory burdens.

The American Medical Association (AMA) joined over 100 other medical societies to warn the Centers for Medicare and Medicaid Services (CMS) that MACRA stands to increase regulatory burden and along with it, surgeon burnout [8, 9]. It is very frustrating for surgical providers to use valuable time fulfilling new regulatory reporting requirements, which can feel duplicative and inefficient in the face of already decreasing patient contact time. This can easily result in decreased surgeon work satisfaction and increased burnout.

In an effort to change policies impeding surgeons' ability to provide timely and high-quality surgical care, the American College of Surgeons (ACS) has launched the *Stop Overregulating My OR (SOMO)* initiative. The SOMO Initiative has gained Congressional traction on working to eliminate unnecessary requirements and regulatory obstacles. It especially focuses on issues such as MACRA/MIPS, physician reimbursement, electronic health records, and prior authorization. Individual surgeons can become involved in these activism efforts by getting involved in *Surgeons Voice*, the grass roots advocacy arm of the ACS.[1] The Health Policy Advocacy Committee (HPAC) and Surgeons PAC (Political Action Committee) are also open to surgeon-member participation. As Ross Goldberg stated during his ten Hot Topics in Health Reform lecture at the ACS General Assembly [10], "If you don't like something, the only way to change it is to participate. Things will be done to us [surgeons], rather than with us, if we don't advocate".

The ACS has seen a number of regulatory wins in 2018, with the help of surgeon involvement, as a result of negotiation for regulatory reform with the Department of Health and Human Services (HHS) and CMS. Goals of these negotiations were to

---

[1] See more information on *Surgeons Voice* here: www.facs.org/advocacy/surgeonsvoice.

highlight the burdens imposed by incoming legislation and identify mutually beneficial adjustments. A few highlights of changes proposed and accepted include:

1. Surgeons are only required to report six quality metrics rather than the nine previously required under the Physician Quality Reporting System (PQRS) program.
2. Surgeons are excluded from being required to participate in MIPS if they see less than 200 Medicare Part B patients or bill less than $90,000 for part B services annually
3. There is an increased focus on CMS data collection and review methodologies in order to accurately calculate physician reimbursement [11].

The AHA is also involved in the effort. In a series of letters to the President, Congress and CMS, the AHA made clear recommendations for immediate release of some of the regulatory burden on hospitals and providers, summing up their views with, "A reduction in administrative burden will enable providers to focus on patients, not paperwork, and reinvest resources in improving care, improving health and reducing costs" [6].

10.2.2 *Clerical Burden and Electronic Systems*

Increased regulatory burden naturally translates into a large volume of clerical work for providers. The Electronic Health Record (EHR) Incentive Program (also known as Meaningful Use) from CMS is a frequently-cited example of good intent gone bad. This program was designed to increase the ability of EHRs to easily collect outcome data, provide simpler access for patients to their own health information, and help physicians coordinate care [9]. With the rollout of this program, however, the design of EHR systems has prevented physicians from receiving adequate compensation when errors and communication gaps caused penalties [12]. Although EHR systems introduce many advantages and can increase patient safety (e.g. avoiding patient allergies, improving clarity of orders, etc.), there is potential for misuse of these systems, increasing the burden of clerical work. When electronic systems do not talk to each other, work is duplicated. In addition, regulations without proper vetting by clinicians can result in data points gathered that only satisfy regulatory purposes without clinical relevance (i.e., garbage in, garbage out). Physicians can begin to feel like data entry clerks, especially since some specific requirements of the policy require physicians to be the ones to attest to the majority of the outcome data rather than other medical staff.

To further complicate the issue, ancillary medical staff also feel the burden of increased clerical requirements. These increased responsibilities contribute to their already-full schedules, decrease work satisfaction, and contribute to an all-time high staff turnover rate. A surgeon counts on their staff for so many components of running an efficient and effective practice that their wellness can be directly affected from staff turnover because more effort will need to be invested into new staff training, 'mistake proofing', and carrying increased office work burden during adjustment periods.

Few studies have looked at the relationship between clerical burden and physician burnout, despite a widespread understanding that a shift is occurring. To enhance objective data in the area, a survey was distributed via the AMA Physician Masterfile in 2014. Results showed that only 20–35% of surgeons (General or Subspecialty) were 'Satisfied' or 'Very Satisfied' with the volume of clerical burden directly related to patient care [13]. Sadly, approximately the same number (75–80%) thought their Electronic Health Records (EHRs) were hindering, not helping these efforts. In addition to federal quality data reporting, providers must become familiar with other new software capabilities, including patient portals, electronic prescribing, and computerized physician order entry (CPOE) [14, 15]. All these systems, designed to improve patient care through decreased systematic errors, can instead easily lead to information overload, steep learning curves (especially for those already in practice), and potentially even early retirement [16, 17].

Other unanticipated effects of the electronic documentation surge besides increased workload have been noted. Electronic documentation has led to a relative depersonalization of medicine, as providers focus on computer screens rather than making eye contact with patients [18]. Overall increase in data entry and screen time for providers decreases the meaningful elements of the patient-physician interaction, such as non-goal-oriented conversation [19]. In addition, time constraints on physicians increase as costs to cover EHR systems are covered via the elimination of physician transcription services, which traditionally have accelerated the workflow of surgeons after a long OR or clinic day. Even if these systems are replaced by self-entry voice recognition software, the learning curve to master these systems is a slow ascent [20]. Physicians in large hospital systems ruled by corporate productivity are encouraged to streamline their team's productivity by documenting on an ongoing basis, rather than stacking a pile of paperwork to complete at the end of the day, however this can lead to a surgeon's work feeling subsequently interrupted and distracted [21].

Furthermore, the staggering cost of EHR systems has been a tremendous burden. A recent study showed the annual cost of an electronic medical record for a moderate-sized practice in 2015 was $32,500 per physician, a 40% increase since 2009 [22], not even accounting for the up-front costs of installation or training. Small groups or private practice surgeons most acutely feel these costs, with the average-sized hospital spending nearly $760,000 annually to meet administrative requirements of information technology (IT) systems and investing $411,000 annually for upgrades and consistent regulatory compliance to those same IT systems [6].

A continued exponential rise in clerical and administrative burden for surgeons with already full schedules has the potential to increase the rate of physician burnout rapidly. Our societies are aware of this, but are our patients and legislatures? At the risk of irony, another task facing surgeons moving forward is coming up with effective solutions for future generations. Rao et al. [23], after conducting an institution-wide survey of the effect of clerical and electronic burden on their physicians, suggest three broad strategies for reducing this burden:

1. Organizations that develop requirements for physicians must work together to reduce the overall load and skim the unimportant regulations.
2. The management of the flow of requirements must be improved.
3. Physicians need to be allowed to delegate tasks to appropriately trained non-physician providers (scribes, human assistance technology such as voice recognition software, etc.).

In the same study, they observed an increasing number of their providers choosing to take a salary penalty rather than complete and submit data for incentive programs like Meaningful Use and the Physician Quality Reporting System (PQRS), signaling a potential tipping point if a change is not made.

10.2.3   Financial Reimbursement

In a cross-sectional survey looking at the connection between surgeon career dissatisfaction and burnout, Jackson et al. [24] found that the three most prevalent variables were dissatisfaction with hospital culture, hospital support, and financial reimbursement. The latter comes up in study after study. Conversations about money can be challenging for new graduates who have always had a fixed trainee salary. In some cases, these conversations have become so complex that junior surgeons are tempted to just accept anything they are offered without considering their overall worth to an organization. The speed and extent of reimbursement evolution mandates individual graduates spend a lot of time learning even the basic elements of financial compensation, as these will affect their workload and practice. A brief description of this changing environment is included here.

The current system of payment for surgeons is based on Relative Value based Units (RVUs). This system was created in 1992 by William Hsaio's group at Harvard to standardize the Medicare reimbursement process through CMS, and it subsequently has been adopted by most payers. In pure form, the RVU system accounts for all resources used to provide a service and was intended to improve and stabilize the system, while at the same time allowing physicians to have ongoing involvement in its improvement.

RVUs are broken down into three components: work (pre-service, intra-service, post-service up to 90 days post-operative), practice expense (facility/hospital, non-facility/office), and professional liability. Theoretically an RVU value is assigned to a procedure according to the time, effort, skill, mental stress, and amortized training expense required to perform it. There is a geographic modifier to account for location of practice influencing costs, and a conversion factor (CF) that converts RVU values into a dollar amount. This conversion factor has been a contentious issue. The Medicare CF has remained consistently between $36 and $35 per RVU between 1997 and 2017, during which time the cost of goods increased by 78% [25]. This can cause a narrow margin for keeping up with business expenses. It is important to understand that RVUs are assigned to procedures based on a typical patient. Patients who become outliers based on unexpected bad complications, fall outside the ability of the reimbursement process to account for.

After applying a normalization process, organizations can use RVUs as a comparative tool for measuring inter-surgeon productivity [26] and make decisions regarding promotion and contract renewal [27]. This has interesting implications for surgeons practicing in academic environments in which the conflicting responsibilities of clinical practice, education, and research have differing rates of reimbursement (see Shifting Practice Patterns below).

Overall, contemporary healthcare reimbursement reform aims to simultaneously curb costs of the current system while increasing efficiency and quality of care. Bundled payments of a single lump sum to all healthcare providers involved in an episode of care (out to 90 days) represent one attempt to improve upon the past pure fee-for-service system. These bundled payments are based off reported quality outcomes. The Bundled Payments for Care Improvement initiative from CMS has three key goal areas for cost saving: acute care cost reduction, post-acute care utilization management, and readmission reduction [28].

Bundled payments are meant to account for the complex interdependent relationship between physicians, patients and hospitals (both hospital, patient, and surgeon factors need to come into the cost equation), using objective and fair outcome variables. For example, despite the increasing emphasis healthcare leaders have placed on surgeon wellness, patient satisfaction remains the focus of outcome data points for administrators [29]. Interestingly, there is more emphasis placed on improving patient satisfaction data, despite limited evidence to link improved patient satisfaction with overall improved patient health outcomes. There is, however, a strong link supporting a correlation between physician job satisfaction and improved patient care, as well as between physician job satisfaction and increased productivity and retention [30–32]. A survey of hospital Chief Financial Officers estimated that when a surgeon misses 2 weeks of work, the hospital loses more than $80,000 in revenue [33]. If a surgeon retires early or leaves the institution due to burnout, replacing them can cost upwards of $two million in lost revenue and recruiting fees [34]. This supports the argument that our physician reimbursement systems need to increase focus on alternate metrics such as physician satisfaction.

Paying attention to the unintended consequences of reimbursement plans can prove enlightening as well. For example, surgeons who receive bonuses based on work above an expected baseline may have the unintended consequence of decreasing wellness and attention to personal needs [31]. Call schedules made by institutions have also been shown to correlate with markedly increased risk of burnout when surgeons are on call more than two nights per week [35, 36]. It has been shown that individuals can take steps to decrease burnout, but changes at the institutional level (often relating to systems of reimbursement) can be the most effective method of decreasing physician burnout [37].

10.2.4 Litigation

An American Medical Association survey in 2007–2008 showed that 90% of surgeons aged 55 years and older had been sued sometime during their career [38].

Despite 90% of claims decided by a trial verdict being decided in favor of the surgeon [39], these cases take an average of 5 years to resolve and exact a protracted, high emotional toll [40]. Essentially, if you practice long enough as a surgeon, you will be sued.

A survey of 7197 fellows and associate fellows in the ACS investigated the relationship between litigation and surgeon burnout. When comparing surgeons who had experienced a malpractice suit in the previous 24 months (1764) with those who had not been sued (5400), higher rates of burnout (31.9% versus 25.2%, OR 1.39, $p < 0.0001$), depression (46.6% versus 36.9%, OR 1.49, $p < 0.0001$), and suicidal ideation (6.4% versus 4.0%, OR 1.64, $p < 0.0001$) were found amongst those recently involved in a lawsuit [41, 42]. In line with this is a study [35, 36] demonstrating that the greatest risk factors for suicidality among physicians are major medical error in the previous 3 months and being sued (along with recent divorce or break up and depression). Malpractice allegations can induce self-doubt, anger, and a type of post-traumatic stress disorder termed malpractice stress syndrome [43, 44]. Therefore, the surgeon can become a 'second victim' as a result of emotional trauma.

There is an oppressive relationship between burnout and litigation in surgery. Many lawsuits are due to surgeons simply having their name on the chart or systems errors. Despite this, research shows that once sued by one patient or family, care of a surgeon's other patients can suffer due to decreased memory, knowledge recall and attention to detail [45]. Lawsuits can taint future interactions with patients and decrease job satisfaction.

In addition, those physicians already suffering from burnout are associated with a decrease in quality and quantity of patient care as well as an increased risk of malpractice suits [46, 47]. For example, medical errors increase 5–11% with each point a surgeon scores higher on the Depersonalization Scale (validated measure of burnout) [48].

Thankfully there is some good news for physicians. A study linking malpractice claims in the National Practitioner Data Bank (NPDB) paid on behalf of physicians between 1992 and 2004 showed that the rate of malpractice claims declined substantially during that time [49]. There were wide variations in rates of decline between specialties, with general surgery at 35.5%, neurosurgery 43.5%, otolaryngology 50.3%, and plastic surgery 59.9%. The same was true in a study of the AMA's Physician Masterfile population between 1994 and 2013, which found a decrease in paid malpractice claims by a third over the last decade [50, 51].

In addition, the majority of malpractice insurers have held their rates steady or have reduced them since 2006. Medical liability insurance is often the single most expensive cost of doing business for physicians (average medical malpractice premium in the US ranges from $50,000 to $200,000) [52] and most physicians still feel these rates are unacceptably high, however volatility in the rates has decreased. In the early 2000s, doctors' medical malpractice premiums increased by at least 25% annually.

Flattening of the rates is generally attributed to changes in regulation on malpractice claims (referred to as tort reform). Caps on the amount of compensation a claimant can receive, regulations imposing barriers to bringing suits or reaching trial, and changes to the ways damages are paid are examples of recent proposals. These tort reforms are handled at the State level, and the response of state legislatures has been mixed, with some embracing changes and others blocking them [53].

Interestingly, despite overall revenue decreases for insurance companies, there is no sign of premium increases on the horizon due to competitive forces in the medical professional liability market. Consolidation of the health care industry has pushed many surgeons to seek employment by hospitals or larger surgeon groups rather than self-insuring. This reduces the demand for primary medical liability coverage and decreases individual premiums. Also, malpractice claim frequency is at a historic all-time low in 2018 as drug makers, instead of physicians, have become the primary targets.

There have been some recent efforts at the legislative level to look critically at the current medical malpractice climate and try to come up with less fault-based options of reconciliation for patients and physicians alike. The Obama administration funded grants for experimental projects looking to decrease the litigious nature of healthcare. The first pilot program is called communication-and-resolution. These programs aim to bring providers and institutions into open dialogue with patients to proactively seek resolution, including offering an apology, an explanation of what happened, and possible compensation if the standard of care was not met with the intention of promoting candor, defusing emotions, and preventing misunderstanding if an apology is not offered. Another legislative change being pursued is referred to as 'apology laws'. These laws protect statements of regret, apology, or fault made by healthcare practitioners from being used against them in court, encouraging surgeons to communicate candidly with patients. Descriptions of other grant-funded projects with great potential to improve surgeon wellness are summarized in Mello et al. [50].

It is important not to underestimate the damage done to surgeons by the way our society channels remediation for adverse outcomes. Given that most surgeons get sued, helping individual practitioners recognize the occurrence of a lawsuit does not correlate with their surgical competence is a good starting point [54]. Collegial mental health support before, during, and after legal negotiations can support a surgeon's wellbeing in the process.

10.2.5 Shifting Practice Patterns

A surgeon's practice setting and specialty also play a role in job satisfaction and subsequent rates of burnout. Recent key shifts in the practice patterns of North American surgeons will drastically change the conversation regarding their wellness and therefore deserve mention.

Private practice surgeon numbers in North America are decreasing. Surgeons are finding it more challenging and out of reach to run their own business in the current regulatory and risk environment. Recent surveys show a drastic decline between

2000 and 2016 from 63% to 35% of surgeons in private practice [55]. Multivariate analysis of a 2008 survey of ACS Fellows shows that private practice surgeons are more likely to be burned out than those in an academic setting (OR 1.17, 95% CI 1.02–1.34). Increased nights on call, lack of replacement support during conferences and holidays, and increased administrative duties can contribute [41, 42]. This difference between academic and community surgeons, however, most likely varies greatly by practice location and size of call group. As insurers increasingly transfer risk to providers, private practitioners have begun forming larger teams out of necessity. To be a private practice surgeon today is not impossible, but it requires both an entrepreneurial spirit and a great degree of business acumen.

For these reasons and more, there has been an explosive growth of hospital-employed surgeons [56] and medical groups owned by hospitals [57]. The Avalere Health and Physicians Advocacy Institute indicates that the percentage of hospital-employed physicians increased by 63% between 2012 and 2016 [58]. This number even excludes the many physicians employed by institutions such as medical schools and conglomerates such as Kaiser Permanente [59]. From the hospital perspective, surgeons greatly enhance a service line and provide a reliable referral base to other services. Therefore, the demand by institutions to actively recruit and incentivize surgeons is growing daily [55].

Employment by hospitals can be attractive to young surgeon graduates who have accumulated high debt loads and who find a guaranteed salary with benefits provides a sense of security in uncertain times. As legislative changes to surgeon reimbursement push towards the bundling of payments into team-based reimbursement (accountable care organizations), a hospital-physician integrated system is better positioned to benefit than a private practitioner [60]. Finally, the cost of electronic health systems and information technology systems, mandated by federal regulation (Meaningful Use), can be cost prohibitive for those in private practice and are contributing to surgeon employment increase.

When selecting a practice environment, surgeons must recognize the heavy overlay of law and regulation applying specifically to the financial relationship they are entering. The most important of these, the Federal Anti-Kickback Statute (AKS) must be followed. Ideally this law is meant to prevent hospitals from paying providers to induce referrals into their system and joins the "Stark" law, which makes it illegal for physicians to refer to any organization in which they have a financial interest. Following these regulations can become quite complex for surgeons who have a relationship with more than one institution and hiring legal advice when signing new contracts is generally warranted.

In addition to selecting which surgeon-hospital relationship to enter, new surgical graduates choose varying degrees of academic involvement. Academic surgeons are facing continued constraints in the pursuit of research productivity [61]. With a push towards procedure-generated income as the focus of hospitals, high income-generating surgeons can be disproportionately positively affected [62]. Combined with a decrease in National Institutes of Health (NIH) and other outside grant funding for research, it is not surprising that the majority of grant funding in the US is applied for, and received by, non-surgeons. In fact, recent studies have shown an estimated

19% decrease in NIH funding was allotted to surgical research between 2003 and 2013 [63]. As a result, an unfortunate 68% of surgeons surveyed in 2015 thought it was not feasible to be successful as both a surgeon and a basic scientist in the current environment [64]. These challenges, including contract negotiation and setting expectations for protected research time, are often placed on new graduates who lack knowledge and experience in these arenas. For a new graduate hoping to start an academic surgical practice, these constraints provide an intense source of stress.

Mentorship relationships are key when preparing for these negotiations and when making career decisions. Interestingly, these relationships have been shown to benefit not only the trainee but also the faculty by enhancing their career satisfaction [65]. Given that residency training occurs primarily in the academic environment, it is important for residents who are considering private or small group practices to have intentional opportunity for mentorship by surgeons working in those models too.

These mentorship relationships are the building blocks for starting healthy dialogue regarding the business elements of a surgical practice. Traditional hierarchical and non-transparent models of surgical success promote an environment of competition and self-promotion, rather than collaboration. Whether or not these values and leadership styles are intentional, they can result in new faculty feeling alienated or undervalued [66, 67]. It is therefore important to promote open discussion regarding fair payment models that also promote quality patient-centered care and limit clerical burden.

In response to changing patterns of practice, and to reduce the tension of navigating employment contracts, the ACS Division of Advocacy and Health Policy has created a resource manual for practicing surgeons considering hospital employment [68]. Topics such as whether the terms of employment are fair and equitable, how the surgeon will be compensated, and what steps to take if an individual decides to change practice setting are covered in this resource manual.

10.3 Conclusions

Understanding the complex interplay between well-meaning regulatory and legal systems and the overall health and wellness of surgical providers has never been more important. Rates of surgeon burnout and suicides have sky-rocketed [69] and, as evidenced above, some of this can be attributed to the "corporatization of medicine" through increased regulation, clerical burden, and the litigatory environment. Many surgeons unfortunately view burnout as a personal failure and it is important to shift this perception moving forward.

A recent national survey assessing the professional satisfaction and career planning of US physicians between Aug 2014 and Oct 2014 reported 19.8% of respondents thought it "likely" or "definite" that they would reduce their clinical work hours in the next 12 months [70]. The most commonly cited reason was "to spend more time with family".

Surgeons, hospital administrators, and regulators should work to develop policies to support a culture which recognizes the importance of supporting physician efforts at self-care, attaining fair reimbursement, and limiting time at the hospital, while simultaneously allowing sufficient meaningful time caring for patients.

References

1. Ghaly R, Knezevic N. What happened to "patient first" and "do not harm" medical principles? Surg Neurol Int. 2018;9:176.
2. Shanafelt T, Hasan O, Dyrbye LN, et al. Changes in burnout and satisfaction with work-life balance in physicians and the general US working population between 2011 and 2014. Mayo Clinic Proc. 2015;91(2):276.
3. Freudenberger H. Staff burn-out. J Soc Issues. 1974;30(1):159–65.
4. Pratti M, Schlottmann F, Sarr M. The problem of burnout among surgeons. JAMA Surg. 2018;153(5):403–4.
5. Lindstrom R. Regulatory burdens contribute to physician occupational burnout. In: Ocular surgery news, US Edition. 2016. https://www.healio.com/ophthalmology/regulatory-legislative/news/print/ocular-surgery-news/%7Bd29e74c1-0ee8-4d8b-9a70-2b943620c54b%7D/regulatory-burdens-contribute-to-physician-occupational-burnout. Accessed 25 Jan 2019.
6. American Hospital Association & Manatt: Regulatory overload: assessing the regulatory burden on health systems, hospitals, and post-acute care providers. Executive Summary. 2017 report. https://www.aha.org/regrelief. Accessed 25 Jan 2019.
7. Welsh D, Puls M, Paramo J, Andreone P. Are surgeons ready? In: 2016 ACS governors survey: MACRA. 2017. https://bulletin.facs.org/2017/06/2016-acs-governors-survey-macra-are-surgeons-ready/. Accessed 25 Jan 2019.
8. American Medical Association. Letter to Andrew Slavitt. In: Merit-Based Incentive Payment System (MIPS) and Alternative Payment Model (APM) incentive under the physician fee schedule, and criteria for physician-focused payment models; proposed rule (CMS-5517-P). 2016. https://www.ama-assn.org/sites/ama-assn.org/files/corp/media-browser/public/about-ama/pr-statements/ama-macra-comments-27june2016.pdf. Accessed 25 Jan 2019.
9. Luh J. MACRA regulatory burdens and the threat of physician burnout. Mayo Clinic Proc. 2016;91(11):1667–72.
10. American College of Surgery. Stop over-regulating my OR initiative. 2018. https://facs.org/advocacy/regulatory/somo. Accessed 25 Jan 2019.
11. ACS 'Stop Overregulating My OR' website. ACS Regulatory Relief Wins. 2018. https://www.facs.org/advocacy/regulatory/somo/wins. Accessed 15 Dec 2018.
12. Caudle J. Finding meaning in a flawed meaningful use program: pathways toward physician compliance. 2016. https://reachmd.com/programs/everyday-family-medicine/finding-meaning-flawed-meaningful-use-program-pathways-toward-physician-compliance/7740/. Accessed 25 Jan 2019.
13. Shanafelt T, Dyrbye L, Sinsky C, Hasan O, Satele D, Sloan J, West C. Relationship between clerical burden and characteristics of the electronic environment with physician burnout and professional satisfaction. Mayo Clin Proc. 2016;91(7):836–48.
14. Dyrbye L, West C, Burnss T, Shanafelt T. Providing primary care in the United States; the work no one sees. Arch Intern Med. 2012;172(18):1420–1.
15. Friedberg M, Chen P, Van Busum K, et al. Factors affecting physician professional satisfaction and their implications for patient care, health systems, and health policy. 2013. In: RAND Health and the American Medical Association Reports 2013. https://www.rand.org/pubs/research_reports/RR439.html. Accessed 15 Jan 2019.

16. Beasley J, Wetterneck T, Temte J, et al. Information chaos in primary care; implications for physician performance and patient safety. J Am Board Fam Med. 2011;24(6):745–51.
17. Holden RJ. Cognitive performance-altering effects of electronic medical records: an application of the human factors paradigm for patient safety. Cogn Technol Work. 2011;13(1):11–29.
18. Frankel R, Altschuler A, George S, et al. Effects of exam-room computing on clinician-patient communication; a longitudinal qualitative study. J Gen Intern Med. 2005;20(8):677–82.
19. Shanafelt T, Gradishar W, Kosty M, et al. Burnout and career satisfaction among U.S. oncologists. J Clin Oncol. 2014;32(7):678–86.
20. Babbott S, Manwell L, Brown R, et al. Electronic medical records and physician stress in primary care: results form the MEMO study. J Am Med Inform Assoc. 2014;21(e1):e100–6.
21. O'Malley A, Grossman J, Cohen G, Kemper N, Pham HH. Are electronic medical records helpful for care coordination? Experiences of physician practices. J Gen Intern Med. 2010;25(3):177–85.
22. Bazzoli F. Group IT expenses reach $32,500 per physician. In: Health data management. 2016. https://www.healthdatamanagement.com/news/group-practice-it-expenses-reach-32-500-per-physician. Accessed 15 Jan 2019.
23. Rao S, Kimball A, Lehrhoff S, Hidrue M, Colton D, Ferris T, Torchiana D. The impact of administrative burden on academic physicians: results of a hospital-wide physician survey. Acad Med. 2017;92:237–43.
24. Jackson T, Pearcy C, Khorgami Z, Agrawal V, Taubman K, Truitt M. The physician attrition crisis: a cross-sectional survey of the risk factors for reduced job satisfaction among US surgeons. World J Surg. 2018;42:1285–92.
25. Bureau of Labor Statistics Consumer Price Index. 2018. https://www.bls.gov/data/. Accessed 15 Jan 2019.
26. Bendix J. RVUs: a valuable tool for aiding practice management. Understanding the basics of the RVU can assist physicians and practice managers in a wide variety of finance and management-related tasks. Med Econ. 2014;91:48–91.
27. Kentros C, Barbato C. Using normalized RVU reporting to evaluate physician productivity. Healthc Financ Manage. 2013;67:98–105.
28. Greenwald A, Bassano A, Wiggins S, et al. Alternative reimbursement models: bundled payment and beyond: AOA critical issues. J Bone Joint Surg Am. 2016;98:e45.
29. Bentley-Kumar K, Jackson T, Holland D, et al. Trauma patient: I can't get no (patient) satisfaction? Am J Surg. 2016;212:1256–60.
30. Alshallah S. Job satisfaction and motivation: how do we inspire employee? Radiol Manag. 2004;26:47–51.
31. Brandt M. Sustaining a career in surgery. Am J Surg. 2017;214:707–14.
32. Regehr C, Glancy D, Pitts A, LeBLanc V. Interventions to reduce the consequences of stress in physicians: a review and meta-analysis. J Nerv Ment Dis. 2014;202:353–9.
33. Davis W, Feltcher S, Guillamondegui O. Musculoskeletal occupational injury among surgeons: effects for patients, providers, and institutions. J Surg Res. 2014;189:207–212 e6.
34. Marmon LM, Heiss K. Improving surgeon wellness: the second victim syndrome and quality of care. Semin Pediatr Surg. 2015;24:315–8.
35. Balch C, Shanafelt T. Combating stress and burnout in surgical practice: a review. Adv Surg. 2010;44:29–47.
36. Balch C, Shanafelt T, Dyrbye L, et al. Surgeon distress as calibrated by hours worked and nights on call. J Am Coll Surg. 2010;211:609–19.
37. Choong P. Burnout: a leadership challenge. ANZ J Surg. 2013;83:495–6.
38. Guardado J. Medical liability claim frequency among U.S. physicians. In: Policy research perspectives: American Medical Association Economic and Health Policy Research. 2017. https://www.ama-assn.org/sites/ama-assn.org/files/corp/media-browser/public/government/advocacy/policy-research-perspective-medical-liability-claim-frequency.pdf. Accessed 25 Jan 2019.
39. Guardado J. Professional liability insurance indemnity and expenses, claim adjudication, and policy limits, 2006-2015. In: American Medical Association economic and health policy

research. 2018. https://www.ama-assn.org/sites/ama-assn.org/files/corp/media-browser/public/government/advocacy/policy-research-perspective-liability-insurance-claim.pdf. Accessed 25 Jan 2019.
40. Studdert D, Mello M, Gawande A, et al. Claims, errors, and compensation payments in medical malpractice litigation. N Engl J Med. 2006;354:2024–33.
41. Balch C, Oreskovich M, Dyrbyre L, Colaiano J, Satele D, Sloan J, Shanafelt T. Personal consequences of malpractice lawsuits on American surgeons. J Am Coll Surg. 2011a;213:657–67.
42. Balch C, Shanafelt T, Sloan J, Satele D, Freischlag J. Distress and career satisfaction among 14 surgical specialties, comparing academic and private practice settings. Ann Surg. 2011b;254(4):558–68.
43. Jena A, Seabury S, Lakdawalla D, Shandra A. Malpractice risk according to physician specialty. N Engl J Med. 2011;365:629–36.
44. Reading EG. The malpractice stress syndrome. NEJM. 1986;83(5):289–90.
45. Wetzel C, Kneebone R, Woloshynowych M, Nestel D, Moorthy K, Kidd J, Darzi A. The effects of stress on surgical performance. Am J Surg. 2006;191:5–10.
46. Orri M, Farges O, Clavien P, Barkun J, Revah-Levy A. Being a surgeon—the myth and the reality: a meta-synthesis of surgeons' perspectives about factors affecting their practice and well-being. Ann Surg. 2014;260:721–8.
47. Oskrochi Y, Maruthappu M, Henriksson M, Davies A, Shalhoub J. Beyond the body: a systematic review of the nonphysical effects of a surgical career. Surgery. 2016;159:650–64.
48. Shanafelt T, Balch C, Bechamps G, et al. Burnout and medical errors among American surgeons. Ann Surg. 2010;251:995–1000.
49. Schaffer A, Jena A, Seabury S, Singh H, Chalasani V, Kachalia A. Rates and characteristics of paid malpractice claims among US physicians by specialty, 1992-2004. JAMA Intern Med. 2017;177(5):710–9.
50. Mello M, Studdert D, Kachalia A. The medical liability climate and prospects for reform. JAMA. 2014;312(20):2146–55.
51. Palik M, Black B, Hyman D. The receding tide of medical malpractice litigation, I: national trends. J Empir Leg Stud. 2013;10(4):612–38.
52. Advisory Board. Malpractice premiums haven't risen in a decade. Here's why. In: Today's daily briefing. 2018. https://www.advisory.com/daily-briefing/2018/11/13/malpractice-premiums. Accessed 15 Dec 2018.
53. Avraham R. An empirical study of the impact of tort reforms on medical malpractice settlement payments. J Leg Stud. 2007;36(S2):S183–229.
54. Sachs C. Malpractice claims: it's a crapshoot—time to stop the self-blame and ask different questions. Ann Emerg Med. 2018;71:165–7.
55. Charles A, Ortiz-Pugols S, Ricketts T, Fraher E, Neuwahl S, Cairns B, Sheldon G. The employed surgeon: a changing professional paradigm. JAMA Surg. 2013;148:323–8.
56. Kocher R, Sahni N. Hospitals' race to employ physicians—the logic behind a money-losing proposition. N Engl J Med. 2011;364(19):1790–3.
57. Neprash H, Chernew M, Hicks A, Gibson T, McWilliams M. Association of financial integration between physicians and hospitals with commercial health care prices. JAMA Intern Med. 2015;175(12):1932–9.
58. Physicians Advocacy Institute. Updates physician practice acquisition study: national and regional changes in physicians employment. 2018. http://www.physiciansadvocacyinstitute.org/Portals/0/assets/docs/2016-PAI-Physician-Employment-Study-Final.pdf. Accessed 20 Jan 2019.
59. Kim D, Duco B, Wolterman D, Stokes C, Brace R, Solomon R, et al. A review and survey of neurosurgeon-hospital relationships: evolution and options. Neurosurgery. 2017;80:S10–8.
60. Napolitano L. Surgeons as hospital employees; good, bad, or indifferent. JAMA Surg. 2013;148(4):329–30.
61. Goudreau B, Hassinger T, Hedrick T, Slingluff C, Screen A, Dengel L. Academic or community practice? What is driving decision-making and career choices? Surgery. 2018;164:571–6.

62. Resnick A, Corrigan D, Mullen J, Kaiser L. Surgeon contribution to hospital bottom line. Ann Surg. 2005;242:530–9.
63. Hu Y, Edwards B, Brooks K, Newhook T, Slingluff C. Recent trends in National Institutes of Health funding for surgery: 2003 to 2013. Am J Surg. 2015;209:1083–9.
64. Keswani S, Moles C, Morowitz M, et al. The future of basic science in academic surgery. Ann Surg. 2017;265:1053–9.
65. Horner D. Mentoring: positively influencing job satisfaction and retention of new hire nurse practitioners. Plast Surg Nurs. 2017;37:7–22.
66. Krupat E, Pololi L, Schnell E, Kern D. Changing the culture of academic medicine: the C-change learning action network and its impact at participating medical schools. Acad Med. 2013;88:1252–8.
67. Wai P, Dandar V, Radosevich D, Brubaker L, Kuo P. Engagement, workplace satisfaction, and retention of surgical specialists in academic medicine in the United States. J Am Coll Surg. 2014;219:31–44.
68. American College of Surgeons Division of Advocacy and Health Policy. Resources for the practicing surgeon: the employed surgeon. Volume 1. 2018. https://www.facs.org/publications/primers. Accessed 25 Jan 2019.
69. Shanafelt T, Boone S, Tan L, et al. Burnout and satisfaction with work-life balance among US physicians relative to the general US population. Arch Intern Med. 2012;172:1377–85.
70. Sinsky C, Dyrbye L, West C, Satele D, Tutty M, Shanafelt T. Professional satisfaction and the career plans for US physicians. Mayo Clinic Proc. 2017;92(11):1625–35.

Chapter 11
Organizational Factors

Michaela Gaffley and Amy Hildreth

11.1 Introduction

Healthcare organizations today currently face tremendous external challenges and must partner with a healthy physician workforce to accomplish their goals. Physician and surgeon wellness are of utmost importance, as wellness has a profound influence on a clinician's ability to continue to practice safe, effective care as well as to maintain engagement with his or her work. In varying studies, the prevalence of burnout among physicians and surgeons has been found to be between 35 and 50% [1]. Many clinician well-being models of the past focused on individual factors contributing to burnout; however, research demonstrates that external factors exert more influence on wellness [2]. In a newly developed conceptual model, the National Academy of Medicine Action Collaborative on Clinician Well-Being and Resilience described a number of external factors that affect well-being, including a group of organizational factors [3] (Table 11.1). Organizational factors to be discussed in this chapter include organizational mission and values; leadership, culture, and staff engagement; professional development opportunities; workload, performance, compensation, and value attributed to work elements; bureaucracy and scope of practice; level of support for all healthcare team members; data collection requirements; diversity and inclusion; and harassment and discrimination. For organizations to be successful in the mission of providing excellent care in an increasingly competitive environment, they must attend to each of these factors that influence well-being in a way that increases joy and engagement among all members of the healthcare team.

M. Gaffley · A. Hildreth (✉)
Wake Forest School of Medicine, Department of Surgery, Winston-Salem, NC, USA
e-mail: mgaffley@wakehealth.edu; ahildret@wakehealth.edu

© Springer Nature Switzerland AG 2020
E. Kim, B. Lindeman (eds.), *Wellbeing*, Success in Academic Surgery,
https://doi.org/10.1007/978-3-030-29470-0_11

Table 11.1 Organizational factors within conceptual model of factors affecting clinician well-being and resilience

1	Congruent organizational mission and values
2	Culture, leadership, and staff engagement
3	Professional development opportunities
4	Workload, performance, compensation, and value attributed to work elements
5	Data collection requirements
6	Diversity and inclusion
7	Level of support for all healthcare team members
8	Bureaucracy
9	Scope of practice

Adapted from https://nam.edu/journey-construct-encompassing-conceptual-model-factors-affecting-clinician-well-resilience/

11.2 Congruent Organizational Mission and Values

An organization's mission and values play a key role in influencing the well-being of the clinicians that work within [4]. Values connect clinicians to their work, and their contribution to a pursuit they find meaningful can be a strong incentive [5]. Health care professionals bring with them to work a set of values developed through their personal experiences, and organizations similarly have values that may be expressed through their written and unwritten policies and procedures. Clinician values may either be congruent or incongruent with the values of the organizations in which they practice. If there exists incongruence between individual and organizational values, if there is conflict between the mission statement and the practice in the organization, or if the organization espouses competing values, these situations may create distress [2]. Conflicting personal and organizational values have been found to correlate with all three dimensions of burnout [6]. An American Medical Association (AMA)-sponsored study by Friedberg and colleagues found that values alignment with respect to the provision of patient care was particularly important for professional satisfaction [7]. Additionally, certain groups are at risk for incongruence with organization values more than others; a recent survey demonstrated that women are less likely to feel their institution's values are in line with their own [8]. Organizations must balance missions of service and quality versus profit in a way that aligns with the personal missions of their employed physicians in order to avoid dissonance [9].

11.3 Leadership, Culture, and Staff Engagement

As approximately 75% of United States physicians [10] and 68% of surgeons [11] are currently employed by hospitals, academic medical centers, or practice groups, organizational leadership has become an important influence on clinician well-being and job satisfaction. Significant challenges to effective leadership include a complex regulatory environment, new technologies, and the need to provide high-value care within significant financial constraints [12].

The impact of supervisors and leaders within the organization has been shown to influence an individual physician's state of mind and, therefore, productivity. Shanafelt and colleagues studied leadership qualities of physician supervisors and their impact on the well-being and satisfaction of individual physicians using a Likert scale of evaluation. They surveyed almost 4000 physicians with a high response rate and found that the supervisor ratings in leadership dimensions, including interest in supervisee's opinions, feedback, and career development, strongly correlated with wellness scores of individual physicians. In fact, a 1-point increase in leadership score resulted in a 3.3% decrease in likelihood of burnout and a 9% increase in likelihood of satisfaction. Eleven percent of the variation in burnout at the work unit level could be attributed to the leadership rating of the division or department chairperson. They discussed that physicians are a highly selected group of motivated people who work through obstacles to achieve a high degree of competency. The leaders that are needed should "inform, engage, inspire, develop and recognize," as these actions were highly valued in their survey [10]. Additional leadership behaviors shown to decrease burnout rates include keeping staff informed, soliciting suggestions for improving the work environment, supporting leadership development, and recognizing good performance [13]. Certainly, the absence of burnout does not guarantee the presence of engagement, but the two are closely related [14].

To improve organizational leadership, physicians must also take ownership. In a large survey of medical practices, it was noted that there was a heightened sense of values alignment when those in leadership had significant clinical experience [7]. After potential leaders in the medical community are identified, they must further develop their leadership skills, as these are not often explicitly taught in undergraduate or graduate medical education curricula. Shanafelt and Noseworthy suggest that we promote effective leaders by careful selection and preparation as well as performance evaluation by those they supervise. Leaders should also be trained to identify the unique talents of individual physicians and help them spend time on the tasks they find most meaningful [9].

A skilled leader helps establish the culture of an organization, which plays a significant role in clinician engagement and wellness. In fact, one study examining dissatisfaction and attrition in academic medicine noted that negative perceptions of the culture at work, including feelings of unrelatedness and moral distress, were associated with leaving an academic position [15]. The effect of culture on the quality of healthcare was set forth in a conceptual model crafted by Williams and colleagues. They found that stress in the workplace affected the quality of patient care and that increased stress was significantly correlated with burnout. They utilized a self-reporting method and found a statistically significant correlation for medical errors and suboptimal care with burnout. Thus, a culture that fostered pervasive stress decreased the quality of the healthcare that was delivered. However, when the interests of leadership and physicians were aligned, less physician stress was perceived [16].

In recognition of the importance of physician leadership to address burnout and increase the joy in our profession, CEOs of ten large health care organizations convened a summit to discuss these topics in 2017 at the American Medical Association (AMA) headquarters. They concluded that physician well-being was a "critical factor" in the provision of health care and made several commitments to address well-being based on available data (Table 11.2). These commitments included the need to measure and include well-being as an indicator of performance, to address clerical burden, to develop skills of physician leaders and support collaborative teams. They also pledged to support advocacy efforts to find ways to decrease organizational, regulatory, and payer environment sources of physician burnout [17].

The interplay of leadership, culture, and ultimately staff engagement affects patient care and its quality. It is important for leaders to promote cohesiveness, openness, team growth, and to create a safe environment to discuss medical error [16]. It is easier to mitigate or prevent mistakes in a culture that fosters quality and low stress, thereby decreasing burnout. Given the significant impact of leadership on well-being, organizations must hold leaders accountable to high standards and remove those leaders who are not effective [18].

Table 11.2 Prominent healthcare CEO's commitments to action after meeting at AMA summit 2016

1	**Regularly measure the well-being[a] of our physician workforce at our institutions using one of several standardized, benchmarked instruments**
2	**Include measures of physician well-being** along with financial and other performance metrics in our **institutional performance dashboards**
3	**Evaluate and track** the institutional costs of physician turnover, early retirement, and reductions in clinical effort
4	Emphasize the importance of **leadership skill development** for physicians and managers leading physicians throughout our organization
5	Understand and **address the clerical burden** and inappropriate allocation of work to physicians that is contributing to professional burnout
6	Support **collaborative, team-based models of care** where physician expertise is maximally utilized for patient benefit
7	Encourage government/regulators to **address the increasing regulatory burden** that is driving inefficiency, redundancy, and waste in health care
8	National support to **align technology and policy** with advanced models of team-based care and to reduce the burden of the EHR on all users
9	National support for **compiling and sharing best practices** from institutions that have successfully begun to address burnout, profiling case studies of effective well-being programs, efficient and satisfying changes in task distribution, and outlining a set of principles for achieving the well-being of health professionals
10	Continue to **educate our fellow CEOs** as well as other stakeholders in the health care ecosystem about the importance of reducing burnout and improving the well-being of physicians as well as other health care professionals
11	Support and **use organizational research** at our centers to determine the most effective policies and interventions to improve professional well-being among our physicians and other health care professionals

Noteworthy et al. "Physician Burnout Is A Public Health Crisis: A Message To Our Fellow Health Care CEOs"
[a]**Bold** added for emphasis

11.4 Professional Development

Although often focused on the needs of individuals, professional development activities sponsored by an organization may impact physician wellness and engagement. Professional development may take a variety of forms, including workshops, fellowships, individual activities, and mentoring systems [19]. These may be useful in increasing physician wellness and engagement because, as Bligh states, "Faculty development programmes are outward signs of the inner faith that institutions have in their workforce" [20]. Professional development programs designed to increase engagement have been reported at the student, resident, and faculty level. Torbeck and Dunnington describe an increase in engagement through development of a program with multiple components including a variety of opportunities such as workshops, teaching observations, "vitality" interventions, leadership training, and independent study modules targeted to the needs of the individual faculty learner [19]. There are also early indications that coaching may be useful when deployed systematically by an organization. Coaching may help physicians re-establish joy in their work by increasing a sense of control over one's work circumstances. Additionally, physicians may be more willing to seek out coaching than they are to seek services from mental health providers. Preliminary data from several Boston hospitals suggest that an intervention using coaches with distressed physicians can increase engagement and lead to improvements in job satisfaction [21]. Although coaching focuses on the individual, the improved function of individuals within an organization and a focus on solutions can enhance team performance and well-being. There are only emerging data about this aspect of organizational culture; the impact of professional development activities on physician wellness is an area where further study should be directed.

11.5 Workload, Performance, Compensation, and Value Attributed to Work Elements

Burnout risk is correlated with workload and hours spent at work. In a large survey comparing physicians to population controls, physicians were found to work a median of 10 more hours per week than their non-physician peers. In fact, 40% worked more than 60 h per week, and only 60% felt their work hours left them with enough time for personal and family life [22]. When evaluating surgeons for burnout, there is a strong connection between hours worked and burnout, with the prevalence of burnout increasing to 50% in those surgeons working greater than 80 h per week. Burnout was also increased in those who took two or greater nights of call per week (44–46%), and depression rate was strongly correlated with both hours worked and nights of call per week [23]. In addition to hours worked, the perception of time pressure contributes to increased physician stress. Greater job satisfaction is correlated with control over the working and clinical environment, increased emphasis on quality of care, and increased support for work-life balance. Conversely, lower job satisfaction has been correlated with a greater focus on productivity.

The more physicians are compensated on individual productivity, the less satisfaction they glean from their work [4].

Systems that emphasize quality of care over volume and promote the use of flexibility may be more successful in improving physician wellness. Specifically, the use of salaried compensation structures, sabbaticals, and organizational assistance with meeting self-care needs are potential strategies for increasing wellness in the physician workplace [9].

11.6 Bureaucracy and Scope of Practice

Bureaucracy, while essential for an organization's survival, may contribute to the components of burnout. Decision-making is often far removed from those who care directly for patients. Additionally, bureaucracies are impersonal entities; whereas caring for patients is considered by most physicians to be highly personal [24]. Within these constraints, however, scope of practice variations can influence physician wellness. Shanafelt and colleagues (2009) undertook a survey at a large academic medical center in which physicians' work characteristics, career satisfaction, and demographics were recorded. Over 550 physicians were sampled, and 84% responded. Of those who responded, 34% met burnout criteria by the Maslach Burnout Inventory, and 68% reported that patient care was the most meaningful component of their work. Those physicians who spent less than 20% of their time on the activity they found most meaningful were at increased risk of suffering from burnout [25]. Lower amounts of time allotted to their most meaningful activity was the greatest predictor of burnout. Based on these data, as little as 1 day per week spent on personally meaningful activities at work could result in a lower turnover rate, lower costs, more patient and physician satisfaction and a better healthcare system.

11.7 Level of Support for All Healthcare Team Members

Teams function best when there is support for the well-being of all team members. It is important that organizational efforts be implemented broadly, as students, residents, nurses, pharmacists, and others are at risk for burnout and distress. Importantly, it may not be immediately obvious when another team member is struggling. A multi-institutional cross-sectional study of general surgery residents and faculty evaluated the perception of burnout and depression of general surgery residents. The results illustrate a disconnect between reality and perception: 12% of residents had suffered from suicidal ideation in the prior 2 weeks, 75% suffered from burnout and 39% met depression criteria. Yet the attending surgeons correctly assessed the prevalence of burnout (of their residents) only 23% of the time. Seventy-five percent of faculty underestimated the presence of depression among their residents despite the close working conditions and long hours spent together. A large majority of respondents in both groups identified the common barriers to seeking help: time, denial and stigma [26]. Physician burnout has been shown to lead to a decrease in the sense of being connected to one's patients, but it may also be associated with disconnection and inability to appropriately support the patient care team.

11.8 Data Collection Requirements

Data collection requirements for physicians have increased exponentially in recent years. This phenomenon is an important factor in physician wellness, as time spent on administrative tasks can contribute to distress if they are not perceived to directly improve patient care. Clerical burden is a significant predictor of burnout symptoms, and physicians may spend up to half of their time on data collection and documentation [27]. Clinical documentation requirements have changed because of increasingly detailed documentation required for reimbursement, the computerization of the medical record, and the Health Insurance Portability and Accountability Act (HIPAA) that led health systems to limit potentially useful communication tools that were seen as a threat to patient privacy [28]. As a result, clinicians spend increasing amounts of time on non-clinical activities and are pressured to save documentation for evening hours following work. Excess time spent on documentation can lead to a loss of autonomy and collegiality and interfere with the physician-patient relationship [7].

Although many of these concerns are outside of the sphere of influence of individual organizations, there are a number of organizational interventions that may be beneficial. For instance, organizations can ensure that inbox messages to physicians are clear and targeted. Medical assistants and other support personnel may improve clinician satisfaction by supporting documentation efforts. Scribes and other support mechanisms may also play a role in increasing physician quality of life by increasing efficiency and allowing for more direct physician-patient interaction [28]. Changes to data collection requirements must be addressed at the regulatory level, but individual institution support can play a valuable role.

11.9 Diversity, Inclusion, and Discrimination

Efforts to increase diversity in our medical workforce continue; unfortunately, the reality falls short of the ideal. African Americans comprise 13% of the U.S. population but only 7.5% of students entering medical school [18]. According to the Association of American Medical Colleges (AAMC), in 2015, 6% of medical school graduates and 3% of medical school faculty were African American. Five percent of medical school graduates and 2% of medical school faculty were Latino [29]. These and other underrepresented minority (URM) physicians may experience unconscious bias that can effect institutional climate, career opportunities, mentoring opportunities, and doctor-patient relationships [30]. In a study of both minority and nonminority students, nearly half reported symptoms of depression and burnout. Minority students noted that racial discrimination, feelings of isolation, and different cultural expectations had adversely affected their medical school experience [31]. A recent AAMC analysis of faculty burnout based on responses to the 2018 StandPoint Faculty Engagement Survey demonstrates that URM women report symptoms of burnout at a rate that is greater than either URM men or non-URM men or women [32].

Although women are more well-represented in the workforce than in prior years, they also experience a lack of inclusion in many settings. In general surgery, for instance, women are less likely to become board certified than men after entering residency [33]. Female surgery residents are more likely to be dissatisfied with their own well-being and health as well as the surgical environment around them [34]. Half of women consider dropping out of surgery residency at some point [35], and their attrition rates are significantly higher than those of male surgery residents [36]. Women in surgery are more likely to experience burnout, as reported by one study, with an odds ratio of 1.6 [37]. Women are also less likely to advance to become full professor or department chair and are less likely to earn grants from the National Institutes of Health [35]. Additionally, women surgeons earn less money, with a reported $44,000 pay gap [38]. A survey of pregnant residents published in JAMA Surgery found that 39% considered leaving surgery because of their experience becoming a mother while being a resident [39]. A factor cited by many was the need for mentorship and organizational support in parenthood in the form of daycare mirroring their work hours, lactation facilities, and lifting of the stigma. Women are additionally less likely to feel to feel a sense of belonging in the workplace and perceive lower gender equity in their institutions [8].

Exclusion in the workplace creates significant barriers to physician wellness; focused attention on diversity and inclusion has the potential to create more functional teams and improve the work environment significantly. One study in particular notes that a diversity culture, defined as an organizational climate that is open to and appreciates individual differences, improves outcomes [40]. A number of interventions may be useful in generating such a climate. These interventions may include improving institutional diversity by proactively seeking out learners and health care providers, developing and evaluating strategies to improve the diversity culture of the institution, and ensuring that institutional objectives are aligned with community benefit. Local stakeholders should be included in key decisions [41].

The AAMC's Diversity and Innovation Forum on Unconscious Bias developed recommended actions to reduce and mitigate the impact of unconscious bias in health care settings. Leaders are encouraged to make a commitment to identify and decrease bias in their institutions as well as to create an inclusive climate while acknowledging bias and its effects. Education through team training, the implicit association test (IAT), and further research can help individuals recognize bias. Additionally, committees involved in admissions, appointment, promotion, and tenure should be diverse in makeup and identify clear goals before beginning deliberations [30].

11.10 Harassment and Bullying

While most studies in medical settings have not directly linked harassment and burnout, connections have been demonstrated in other workplace settings. Increased burnout rates in women in medicine as compared to men may be related to higher rates of workplace harassment and discrimination for women. A 1995 survey of female faculty members from a variety of specialties found that 52% of women had experienced sexual harassment, while only 5% of the men surveyed had similar experiences [42]. A recent review and meta-analysis of the surgical literature on this topic found an estimate of discrimination and harassment at 22% and 31%, respectively [43].

Although harassment of women in medical workplaces is well documented, discrimination and harassment of other groups have not been studied widely. However, there is some evidence that lesbian, gay, bisexual, and transgender (LGBT) physicians face these threats to well-being regularly. A group of LGBT physicians were recently surveyed. Ten percent stated they were denied referrals from heterosexual colleagues, and 15% had been harassed by a colleague. Over 20% had been socially ostracized, and 34% had witnessed discriminatory care of an LGBT patient. It is clear that these experiences can negatively impact physician wellness, and we must urgently consider ways to create a safer environment for our LGBT and other at-risk physicians [44].

Additionally, bullying is not uncommon in the medical field and in surgery. Bullying is different than discrimination or harassment in that it does not necessarily target race, ethnicity, religion, sex, nationality, or disability and is not prohibited by state or federal laws. A recent survey of Australian surgeons reports that 47% of surgeons surveyed had been bullied and 68% had witnessed bullying behavior [45]. Survey respondents reported bullying from a variety of sources including faculty surgeons and even administration. Further study on this significant threat to physician well-being is warranted given these concerning statistics and the paucity of data in the United States surgical workplace.

Organizations may take measures to systematically decrease harassment and bullying. For example, authors from the Group on Women in Medicine and Science at the AAMC recommend a number of measures for organizations to take in order to implement a zero-tolerance policy for sexual harassment in the workplace. These measures include the implementation of mechanisms for reporting without fear, mandatory training, monitoring and sanctioning for those who commit harassment, no tolerance for "locker room talk", and the development of research programs to generate more data-guided solutions to the problem [46].

11.11 Conclusions

Health care organizations are currently at a critical juncture for physician wellbeing. Rates of burnout among clinicians have reached alarming levels. Many of the factors that either foster wellbeing and engagement or promote burnout are under the control of organizations. These organizations must closely attend to internal influences on physician well-being in order to build a strong work force and successfully navigate the challenges of providing care in today's complex healthcare environment.

References

1. Dimou FM, Eckelbarger D, Riall TS. Surgeon burnout: a systematic review. J Am Coll Surg. 2016;222:1230–9.
2. Maslach C, Schaufeli WB, Leiter MP. Job burnout. Annu Rev Psychol. 2001;52:397–422.
3. Brigham T, Barden C, Legreid Dopp A, Hengerer A, Kaplan J, Malone B, Martin C, Mchugh M, Margaret Nora L. A journey to construct an all-encompassing conceptual model of factors affecting clinician well-being and resilience. NAM Perspect. 2018. https://doi.org/10.31478/201801b.
4. Williams ES, Konrad TR, Linzer M, McMurray J, Pathman DE, Gerrity M, Schwartz MD, Scheckler WE, Douglas J. Physician, practice, and patient characteristics related to primary care physician physical and mental health: results from the Physician Worklife Study. Health Serv Res. 2002;37:121–43.
5. Leiter MP, Maslach C. Areas of Worklife: a structured approach to organizational predictors of job burnout. In: Research in occupational stress and well being, vol. 3. 2003. p. 91–134.
6. Leiter MP, Harvie P. Correspondence of supervisor and subordinate perspectives during major organizational change. J Occup Health Psychol. 1997;2:343–52.
7. Friedberg MW, Chen PG, Van Busum KR, et al. Factors affecting physician professional satisfaction and their implications for patient care, health systems, and health policy. Rand Health Q. 2014;3:1.
8. Pololi LH, Civian JT, Brennan RT, Dottolo AL, Krupat E. Experiencing the culture of academic medicine: gender matters, a national study. J Gen Intern Med. 2013;28:201–7.
9. Shanafelt TD, Noseworthy JH. Executive leadership and physician well-being: nine organizational strategies to promote engagement and reduce burnout. Mayo Clin Proc. 2017;92:129–46.
10. Shanafelt TD, Gorringe G, Menaker R, Storz KA, Reeves D, Buskirk SJ, Sloan JA, Swensen SJ. Impact of organizational leadership on physician burnout and satisfaction. Mayo Clin Proc. 2015;90:432–40.
11. Charles AG, Ortiz-Pujols S, Ricketts T, Fraher E, Neuwahl S, Cairns B, Sheldon GF. The employed surgeon. JAMA Surg. 2013;148:323–8.
12. Stoller JK. Developing physician-leaders: a call to action. J Gen Intern Med. 2009;24:876–8.
13. Kruskal JB, Shanafelt T, Eby P, Meltzer CC, Rawson J, Essex LN, Canon C, West D, Bender C. A road map to Foster wellness and engagement in our workplace—a report of the 2018 summer intersociety meeting. J Am Coll Radiol. 2018;16:869–77. https://doi.org/10.1016/J.JACR.2018.10.025.
14. Taris TW, Ybema JF, van Beek I. Burnout and engagement: identical twins or just close relatives? Burn Res. 2017;5:3–11.
15. Pololi LH, Krupat E, Civian JT, Ash AS, Brennan RT. Why are a quarter of faculty considering leaving academic medicine? A study of their perceptions of institutional culture and intentions to leave at 26 representative U.S. medical schools. Acad Med. 2012;87:859–69.
16. Williams ES, Manwell LB, Konrad TR, Linzer M. The relationship of organizational culture, stress, satisfaction, and burnout with physician-reported error and suboptimal patient care: results from the MEMO study. Health Care Manag Rev. 2007;32:203–12.
17. Noseworthy J, Madara J, Cosgrove D, et al. Physician burnout is a public health crisis: a message to our fellow health care CEOs. Health Aff Blog. 2017. https://doi.org/10.1377/hblog20170328.059397.

18. National Academy of Medicine Organizational Factors—Clinician Well-Being Knowledge Hub. https://nam.edu/clinicianwellbeing/causes/organizational-factors/. Accessed 1 Feb 2019.
19. Torbeck L, Dunnington G. Designing a comprehensive professional development program in a surgery department: process, measures, and lessons learned. J Surg Educ. 2018;76:727–37. https://doi.org/10.1016/j.jsurg.2018.09.008.
20. Bligh J. Faculty development. Med Educ. 2005;39:120–1.
21. Adelman SA, Liebschutz JM. Health care provider coaching to enhance well-being, teamwork, and the system. In: NEJM Catal. 2017. https://catalyst.nejm.org/health-care-provider-coaching-wellness-teamwork/. Accessed 15 Feb 2019.
22. Shanafelt TD, Boone S, Tan L, Dyrbye LN, Sotile W, Satele D, West CP, Sloan J, Oreskovich MR. Burnout and satisfaction with work-life balance among US physicians relative to the general US population. Arch Intern Med. 2012;172:1377–85.
23. Balch CM, Shanafelt TD, Dyrbye L, Sloan JA, Russell TR, Bechamps GJ, Freischlag JA. Surgeon distress as calibrated by hours worked and nights on call. J Am Coll Surg. 2010;211:609–19.
24. Gunderman RB, Lynch JW. How bureaucracy can Foster burnout. J Am Coll Radiol. 2018;15:1803–5.
25. Shanafelt TD, West CP, Sloan JA, Novotny PJ, Poland GA, Menaker R, Rummans TA, Dyrbye LN. Career fit and burnout among academic faculty. Arch Intern Med. 2009;169:990–5.
26. Williford ML, Scarlet S, Meyers MO, et al. Multiple-institution comparison of resident and faculty perceptions of burnout and depression during surgical training. JAMA Surg. 2018;153:705–11.
27. Shanafelt TD, Dyrbye LN, Sinsky C, Hasan O, Satele D, Sloan J, West CP. Relationship between clerical burden and characteristics of the electronic environment with physician burnout and professional satisfaction. Mayo Clin Proc. 2016;91:836–48.
28. Ommaya AK, Cipriano PF, Hoyt DB, Horvath KA, Tang P, Paz HL, DeFrancesco MS, Hingle ST, Butler S, Sinsky CA. Care-centered clinical documentation in the digital environment: solutions to alleviate burnout. NAM Perspect. 2018. https://doi.org/10.31478/201801c.
29. Association of American Medical Colleges. Diversity in medical education: facts & figures 2016. 2016. http://www.aamcdiversityfactsandfigures2016.org/report-section/section-1/. Accessed 14 Feb 2019.
30. Association of American Medical Colleges; The Kirwan Institute for the Study of Race and Ethnicity. In: Proceedings of the diversity and inclusion innovation forum: unconscious bias in academic medicine. 2017.
31. Dyrbye LN, Thomas MR, Eacker A, Harper W, Massie FS, Power DV, Huschka M, Novotny PJ, Sloan JA, Shanafelt TD. Race, ethnicity, and medical student well-being in the United States. Arch Intern Med. 2007;167:2103–9.
32. Association of American Medical Colleges. Burnout among U.S. Medical School faculty. Anal Br. 2019. https://doi.org/10.1067/j.cpsurg.2011.12.001.
33. Andriole DA, Jeffe DB. Certification by the American Board of Surgery among US Medical School Graduates. J Am Coll Surg. 2012;214:806–15.
34. Ban KA, Chung JW, Matulewicz RS, Kelz RR, Shea JA, Dahlke AR, Quinn CM, Yang AD, Bilimoria KY. Gender-based differences in surgical residents' perceptions of patient safety, continuity of care, and well-being: an analysis from the flexibility in duty hour requirements for surgical trainees (FIRST) trial. J Am Coll Surg. 2017;224:126–136.e2.
35. Greenberg CC. Association for Academic Surgery presidential address: sticky floors and glass ceilings. J Surg Res. 2017;219:ix–xviii.
36. Yeo HL, Abelson JS, Mao J, Lewis F, Michelassi F, Bell R, Sedrakyan A, Sosa JA. Who makes it to the end? Ann Surg. 2017;266:499–507.
37. Elmore LC, Jeffe DB, Jin L, Awad MM, Turnbull IR. National Survey of burnout among US general surgery residents. J Am Coll Surg. 2016;223:440–51.
38. Jagsi R, Griffith KA, Stewart A, Sambuco D, DeCastro R, Ubel PA. Gender differences in salary in a recent cohort of early-career physician-researchers. Acad Med. 2013;88:1689–99.

39. Rangel EL, Smink DS, Castillo-Angeles M, Kwakye G, Changala M, Haider AH, Doherty GM. Pregnancy and motherhood during surgical training. JAMA Surg. 2018;153:644–52.
40. Hofhuis J, van der Rijt PGA, Vlug M. Diversity climate enhances work outcomes through trust and openness in workgroup communication. Springerplus. 2016;5:714. https://doi.org/10.1186/s40064-016-2499-4.
41. The Committee on Institutional and Policy-Level Strategies for Increasing Diversity of the U.S. Healthcare Workforce. In the nation's compelling interest: ensuring diversity in the health care workforce. Washington, DC: National Academies Press; 2004.
42. Carr PL, Ash AS, Friedman RH, Szalacha L, Barnett RC, Palepu A, Moskowitz MM. Faculty perceptions of gender discrimination and sexual harassment in academic medicine. Ann Intern Med. 2000;132:889–96.
43. Huang Y, Chua TC, Saw RPM, Young CJ. Discrimination, bullying and harassment in surgery: a systematic review and meta-analysis. World J Surg. 2018;42:3867–73.
44. Eliason MJ, Dibble SL, Robertson PA. Lesbian, gay, bisexual, and transgender (LGBT) physicians' experiences in the workplace. J Homosex. 2011;58:1355–71.
45. Ling M, Young CJ, Shepherd HL, Mak C, Saw RPM. Workplace bullying in surgery. World J Surg. 2016;40:2560–6.
46. Bates CK, Jagsi R, Gordon LK, et al. It is time for zero tolerance for sexual harassment in academic medicine. Acad Med. 2018;93:163–5.

Chapter 12
Learning and Practice Environment

Rebecca F. Brown, Mahesh S. Sharma, and Melina R. Kibbe

12.1 Introduction

Data from a recent physician workforce survey indicates an impending and critical shortage of surgical specialists [1]. Although the reasons for this shortage are multifactorial, physician attrition, which is impacted by reduced job satisfaction and burnout, may account for one aspect of this shortage. According to the agency for Healthcare Research and Quality, burnout is defined as "a long-term stress reaction marked by emotional exhaustion, depersonalization, and a lack of sense of personal accomplishment" [2]. Workplace dissatisfaction has negative downstream consequences such as increased job turnover, rising healthcare costs, reduced patient satisfaction, and diminished patient safety [3]. Given the significant amount of time physicians and trainees dedicate to clinical medicine, it is not surprising that the learning and practice environment has been identified in the National Academy of Medicine (NAM) Conceptual Model for Clinician Wellbeing and Resilience [4] as an important factor that impacts clinician wellness. In the NAM Model, the learning and practice environment is further subdivided into smaller domains including:

- Autonomy
- Collaborative vs. competitive environment
- Curriculum
- Health IT operability and usability/Electronic Health records

R. F. Brown · M. S. Sharma
Department of Surgery, University of North Carolina at Chapel Hill, Chapel Hill, NC, USA
e-mail: Mahesh_Sharma@med.unc.edu

M. R. Kibbe (✉)
Department of Surgery, University of North Carolina at Chapel Hill, Chapel Hill, NC, USA

Department of Biomedical Engineering, University of North Carolina at Chapel Hill, Chapel Hill, NC, USA
e-mail: melina_kibbe@med.unc.edu

© Springer Nature Switzerland AG 2020
E. Kim, B. Lindeman (eds.), *Wellbeing*, Success in Academic Surgery,
https://doi.org/10.1007/978-3-030-29470-0_12

- Learning and practice setting
- Mentorship
- Physical learning and practice conditions
- Professional relationships
- Student affairs policies
- Student-centered and patient-centered focus
- Teams structures and functionality
- Workplace safety and violence

Identifying factors within each domain of the learning and practice environment that affect clinician wellbeing and working towards optimization of this climate is paramount in the overall pursuit of clinician resilience. Each of these domains will be examined individually below and suggestions offered, when possible, to maximize clinician resilience.

12.2 Autonomy

Autonomy, which is simply defined in the Cambridge English Dictionary as "the ability to make your own decisions without being controlled by anyone else", is a quality long valued by physicians as they facilitate the work up and treatment of their patients [5]. However, increasing regulations, documentation requirements, and performance expectations imposed on clinicians by insurance companies, government agencies, and hospital administration have led to limitations in physicians' clinical decision making (e.g., which tests to order, which treatments to administer, etc.) and even how much time a physician is able to spend with patients [6]. This loss of control experienced by physicians has been identified in numerous studies as a major contributor to stress and burnout [6–8].

In the face of our evolving practice environment, how can physicians combat the loss of autonomy in the healthcare system and the burnout associated with it? Empowering clinicians to proactively participate in the improvement of the healthcare systems in which they work has been proposed as a mechanism through which physicians can reclaim autonomy while also providing invaluable guidance to their respective health care systems [6, 9, 10]. Additionally, incorporating business principles into student, resident, and early faculty education will allow providers to understand the health care system, its financial foundations, and numerous payment systems. Furthermore, such curricula will teach physicians effective leadership and conflict management skills which are critical for administrative success [11].

While ever-changing regulations will always be a factor, the loss of physician autonomy does not have to accompany them. Empowering physicians to become more involved in high-level decision making processes, both on a local and national level, and providing them with the education and experience to appropriately advise healthcare systems is a viable strategy that has been shown to not only foster clinician resilience, but also contribute to improvements in the overall delivery of health care [9].

12.3   Collaborative vs Competitive Environment

Competition in the workplace has been used by many corporations to inspire motivation and increase productivity within the workforce by comparing employee performance and incentivizing production and efficiency. While this strategy can lead to increased output from individual workers, the nature of a competitive work environment has also been shown to promote undue stress and lack of collegiality [12]. Historically, the pyramidal structure of early surgical residencies created a competitive environment in which a surplus number of trainees were pitted against each other for a limited number of coveted house staff positions. The training period was long, arduous, and, at times, indefinite. Trainees who were not selected to advance often returned to their communities with limited expertise, yet continued to perform surgeries without restriction [13]. Surgical educators recognized the need for broad standardization of surgical training and certification in the 1930s and 1940s, which eventually led to the transition of surgical residencies from the competitive pyramidal structure to the more modern rectangular structure. This paradigm shift in surgical education proved that a collaborative environment could produce well trained surgeons without the inefficiencies and toxic culture created by the pyramidal system [13]. As health care has continued to evolve, successful collaboration within service lines and amongst different specialties throughout the hospital is paramount to providing quality health services. While there may be a place for friendly competition amongst teams with regards to non-patient care issues, such as quality improvement projects, research, or even in-training examination scores, the cultivation of a cooperative workplace within a health care system is vital in creating a holistic patient care environment centered around provider wellbeing.

12.4   Curriculum

As physician burnout has been appropriately recognized as an important issue in healthcare that affects not only clinicians but also influences the quality of care provided to patients, the call for the adoption of a wellness curriculum to combat burnout and promote wellbeing and resilience has surfaced. While traits conferring resilience are intrinsic to some clinicians' personalities, research suggests that learned behaviors, such as mindfulness and reflective practice, along with social support and healthy sleep, can also contribute to clinician wellbeing [14]. Based on this, numerous conceptual models for resilience have been developed for medical students and trainees, with the goal that early incorporation of wellness strategies will convey physical and emotional hardiness throughout an individual's career [14, 15]. Likewise, numerous interventions thought to contribute to clinician wellbeing, including mindfulness training, cognitive behavioral therapy, and even yoga and nutrition courses, have been offered to medical students, residents, and faculty alike, with positive results on measures of clinician wellbeing [14]. The variability of these unique but successful interventions demonstrates that there is no single cookie-cutter curriculum to combat the ongoing burnout suffered by clinicians of all ages. However, incorporating programs that support and instill wellness into curricula can help clinicians gain skills to foster resilience throughout their careers.

12.5 Health It Operability and Usability/Electronic Medical Record (EMR)

As a part of the American Recovery and Reinvestment Act, all public and private healthcare providers were required to adopt and incentivized to demonstrate "meaningful use" of electronic medical records (EMR) by January 1, 2014 [16]. The resultant clerical burden expected of physicians has quickly become a top contributor to clinician burnout. Research suggests that every one hour spent with patients translates to 1–2 hours of additional after visit documentation and other care coordination, with much of this unreimbursed "work after work" being completed in between other activities at night, on weekends, and during time off [17]. Furthermore, the elimination of transcription services and replacement with physician self-entry, either by typing or voice recognition software, has further increased the amount of time clinicians spend on documentation [18]. In addition to increasing the documentation requirements for clinicians, the use of EMRs has also altered the patient-physician interaction and many say detracts from more meaningful aspects of medical practice [18]. Of note, these studies do not take into account the continuous need to update logins and passwords, navigate complex and difficult to troubleshoot networking and printing systems within the hospital, learn how new software updates impact daily work flow patterns, and manage other software and hardware malfunctions that can add further frustration and time to a clinician's daily workload.

While many studies have confirmed the association of EMR use and burnout, interventions to employ the EMR more effectively and help decrease the charting demands placed on clinicians are only now beginning to surface. Improving usability of the EMR and matching functionality with clinician needs are long-term goals, which require not only revamping of the EMR platform, but also involve workflow reassessment and evolution of medical practice to match progress made possible with continual technological advances. The use of artificial intelligence for task automation in the future is also promising, but has yet to be incorporated into current EMR systems. While these long term solutions should remain high on the priority list as EMRs evolve, a few more immediate solutions to "tame the EMR" have been suggested [19].

Redistribution of data entry tasks to patients and non-physician team members can help offload a large portion of data entry from the physician [19]. Populating the EMR with data from templated questionnaires completed by patients or employing assistants for order entry and documentation support are promising approaches. The latter can be accomplished through the use of scribes, who document physician-patient encounters in real time under clinician supervision, or through an advanced care team model, in which clinically trained individuals assist with all facets of the patient visit—clinical documentation, order entry, healthcare maintenance, health coaching, and care coordination [18]. The ambulatory process excellence, or APEX model, developed at the University of Colorado, employs medical assistants, under the supervision of a provider, to gather data, reconcile medications, set an agenda for patient visits and subsequently document the visit. The medical assistant can also assist with patient education as well as health coaching [17]. While this program requires additional workforce in clinics as well as rigorous training and protocol development, after its introduction, APEX remained cost neutral due to increased productivity and efficiency in clinics, while also demonstrating improved compliance with healthcare maintenance and, most importantly, a 40% decrease in physician burnout scores [17]. Another immediate solution suggested in other studies recommends scheduling longer office visits to match the additional time for documentation or designating "EMR catch-up time" during patient care sessions [20]. Lastly, ongoing evaluation of a clinician's EMR use and observation of workflow patterns can identify additional areas for targeted training to improve an individual's efficiency in use of the EMR [19].

Recognizing EMR use as a major contributor to physician burnout is an important first step, and ongoing improvements in the usability of the EMR, workflow processes, and clinician efficiency as well as redistribution of tasks have been suggested as both long term and immediate solutions to help alleviate clerical burden on physicians and, ultimately, combat clinician burnout.

12.6 Learning and Practice Setting

The learning and practice setting refers to the environment in which staff physicians as well as trainees work. This milieu is influenced by factors including institutional culture, physical environment, setting (private versus academic practice), employment model (hospital employee versus practice owner versus locum tenens), patient mix (private insurance versus Medicare/Medicaid), and geographic location. National surveys have demonstrated that surgeons employed in private practices report lower job satisfaction and higher rates of burnout than surgeons working in an academic setting [21, 22]. The underlying etiology that contributes to these findings is not well defined, but may be related to differential support systems, reimbursement strategies, level of intellectual curiosity and stimulation, or collegiality within practices. However, with the changing tide of the private practice environment, as many independent practices are now being purchased by large healthcare organizations, the effects on burnout amongst private practitioners remains to be determined. Additional research to evaluate how wellness changes based on practice setting, as well as to further delineate reasons for this discrepancy amongst settings are still needed.

With respect to resident doctors, the learning environment resembles the practice setting, but also includes elements from three broad domains: the content of the program, the interpersonal aspects of and atmosphere of the program, and the structure and organization of the program [23]. Improving the climate of learning can be achieved by healthcare systems paying particular attention to elements within these three domains with a focus on the appropriate integration of work and training, and tailoring education to the learning needs of the individual trainee. A better learning environment has been associated with fewer symptoms of burnout and a better quality of life for trainees [24, 25].

12.7 Mentorship

The history of surgical training is rooted in mentorship. Just as Mentor helped to guide Telemachus on his journey in search of his father, Odysseus, in Homer's epic poem *The Odyssey*, surgical trainees receive instruction and navigation from learned mentors who assist in counseling them during their surgical journeys. Dating back to the mid sixteenth century, when teenagers sought guidance and education under the direct tutelage of a master surgeon for 5–7 years before entering practice, the apprenticeship model had been the principle method of training and remained the standard for over three centuries [26]. While our training methods have evolved over time, the importance of mentorship in medicine remains a vital part of clinician growth. Mentors in medicine not only provide clinical education and training, but also help mentees navigate difficult situations throughout their professional development and play a vital role in successful training programs, while also contributing to resident retention, and continued career advancement [27]. Not surprisingly, these relationships have also been shown to be a source of resilience for clinicians at all stages in their career [14, 28, 29].

As the field of surgery has matured, our discipline has become much more deliberate in the identification and practice of good mentorship. Numerous studies have systematically identified qualities of exceptional mentors, which include acting as a professional role model, remaining involved and available to trainees, and being a compassionate critic. Coupling these qualities with investment from the mentee has been shown to help garner successful, long-term mentor-mentee relationships. While informal mentorship, that which has historically occurred in the operating room, on surgical wards, and during planned and unplanned interactions with educators, is a mainstay in surgery, the incorporation of formal mentorship programs into residency training and early attending-hood to create a renewable environment in which trainees can thrive has been shown to decrease resident burnout [29, 30]. Integral to the success of such programs are designation of protected time for mentoring, deliberate mentor-mentee pairing, identification and ongoing training of successful mentors, continued investment from the mentee, and tracking and evaluation of mentorship activities [29]. While day-to-day teaching and informal mentorship should continue, formalization of mentorship programs can help programs deliberately foster the mentor-mentee relationships that not only influence career progression, but can also contribute to clinician resilience.

12.8 Physical Learning and Practice Conditions

In his book, *Frames of Mind: The Theory of Multiple Intelligences*, Gardner introduces the concept of kinesthetic intelligence, or using the body to create or do something [31]. As technical acumen in surgery is predicated on physical learning and practice, it is imperative that trainees as well as practicing surgeons are engaged in this process continuously. While time spent in residency and fellowship often involves ongoing coaching and assessment of achievement for both intellectual and technical milestones, deliberate practice, which is defined by Ericsson as applying effort to skills that one cannot do well or at all, is not distinctly required in postgraduate training [32]. The concept of deliberate practice over an extended period of time (10,000 hours), which he noted is required to achieve expert performance, often supersedes formal training when surgeons begin their journeys as independent practitioners. Regrettably, the continuation of oversight or coaching during early and ongoing faculty development is often informal at best. However, research suggests that focusing on these imperfect skills under the continued tutelage of a coach can allow a learner to increase the overall reach and range of skills—a factor very important in a surgical career [32]. One major challenge that arises during surgical training lies in the fact that many of the elusive skills are often related to relatively uncommon presentations or emergent situations, where the opportunity for an unskilled learner to practice would present too great of a risk to the patient. Simulation and virtual reality have emerged as high-fidelity alternatives in the performance of rare procedures necessary during dire situations. These can allow for deliberate practice to occur without causing undo patient harm [32]. Ongoing coaching and deliberate practice that leads to increasing expertise also encourages clinicians to gain independent skills and set future development goals. Ultimately, this mastery allows for autonomy of practice, which has a major positive impact on surgeon wellbeing.

12.9 Professional Relationships

As our healthcare system continually shifts toward an environment rich in collaboration, the professional and dynamic relationships between physicians and other healthcare workers have begun to shift as well. Gone are the days that throwing instruments in the operating room occurs without retribution. While this was never truly acceptable behavior, the focus on emotional intelligence as a vital competency for effective leadership amongst physicians has emerged. Emotional intelligence, as introduced by Salovey and Mayer in the 1990s, is commonly described as "the ability to monitor one's own and others' emotions, to discriminate among them, and to use this action to guide one's thinking and actions" and is considered an intrinsic characteristic that is distinct from one's personality in that it can be learned and altered [33]. Studies have demonstrated that higher emotional intelligence in physicians is linked to increased job satisfaction, and, not surprisingly, has also been shown to be protective against physician burnout [33–35]. While healthcare-specific emotional intelligence differs slightly from the initial model described, the overarching theme of the need to provide physicians with insight on their personal emotional intelligence scores remains strong. Early incorporation of emotional intelligence curricula in a clinician's medical training, as well as ongoing and deliberate evaluation of emotional intelligence, has been shown to not only improve clinician leadership and interactive skills, but also portends a protective benefit in burnout, likely related to increased coping mechanisms for stress management and improved emotional regulation [33, 35].

12.10   Student Affairs Policies

A quick Google search querying the availability of medical student affairs policies as they relate to wellness returned a staggering 21.6 million results, indicating that wellness has also risen as a priority in undergraduate medical education. Linked medical school websites offer support and a commitment to medical student wellness, and list various local healthcare, mental health, and healthy living resources available to physicians in training. In addition to these resources, policies have been created outlining appropriate treatment of medical students and mandating an environment conducive to learning with freedom from discrimination and harassment. Integral to the existence of this safe work and learning environment is the availability of an anonymous reporting mechanism with a commitment to investigation of reports with inherent protection from retribution. The ready availability and easy accessibility of student affairs policies related to wellness and appropriate treatment of medical students exhibits the commitment of undergraduate medical education to clinician resilience from the onset of medical training.

12.11   Student-Centered and Patient-Centered Focus

While the hospital is a hallowed teaching ground where surgeons and other physicians learn, hone, and perfect their craft, the obligation to maintain patient safety throughout their treatment and hospital course is also of the utmost importance. The ability of the teacher, regardless of level of training, to balance student-centered education with patient-centered care presents a difficult challenge and requires awareness of the instructor to create a welcoming environment that allows learners to participate to the extent of their ability while monitoring and ensuring the patient continues to receive appropriate care. Ensuring that all members of the health care team participating in the care of the patient, including nurses, aides, students, residents, etc. have been introduced and understand and respect each other's roles is an important first step in creating such an environment.

12.12 Team Structures and Functionality

With the ongoing evolution of our healthcare system, the formation and development of healthcare teams, which are defined as two or more healthcare providers working together with patients and caregivers to accomplish shared goals, has become a central component of high quality patient care [36]. Successful execution of a team-based approach has been shown to improve patient outcomes in various healthcare settings and increase compliance with performance measures. Additionally, a positive team culture and climate has been correlated with clinician job satisfaction, wellness, and resilience [17, 18, 36, 37]. Clinicians remain central to the patient care team, sharing expert medical knowledge and often acting as the natural leader of clinical, management, and quality improvement teams throughout their healthcare system. However, many physicians lack familiarity and training in team-based approaches and leadership [38, 39]. In a two-part manuscript series on high performance teams for physician leaders, Schwartz et al. describe a model of team performance specific to healthcare that defines a framework for a team model and provides an introduction to the *common language* critical to team function [38, 39]. The model is divided into four major conceptual domains: (1) structure, (2) context, (3) process, and (4) productivity (see Table 12.1 below). Central to this model is the role of the physician leader.

12.13 Major Domains of Teamwork

Additional research on high performance teams that have been successful in healthcare have elucidated a number of similar principles that have also been shown to impact clinician wellbeing. These include establishing shared goals, identifying clear expectations for team members' functions to optimize efficiency, developing mutual trust amongst team members to enhance idea development, encouraging effective bidirectional communication within the team, and continuously assessing team structure and function through measurable processes and outcomes [36]. Clinician awareness of the major domains of teamwork (Table 12.1) as well as the principles of a successful high performance team can help inform leadership abilities of clinicians, which, in turn, leads to a positive team culture and climate, that ultimately garners clinician wellness and mitigates burnout.

12.14 Workplace Safety and Violence

Numerous high profile and disturbing cases of workplace violence have occurred within health care systems and have received substantial media attention in the recent past; sadly, workplace violence perpetrated against medical providers is, unfortunately, a daily occurrence [40]. The different types of workplace violence are outlined in Table 12.2 below.

Table 12.1 Major domains of teamwork with descriptive highlights from text [38, 39]

Domain		Highlights
Structure—team composition	**Team**—Members, role, and hierarchy	Stages of team development include *forming* (initial team introduction), *storming* (early, short term power struggles within team), *norming* (each team member develops own identity within group), and *performing* (clearly defined culture necessary for goal accomplishment)
	Organization—Compatibility and support for teams	Allocation of support and resources for team(s) in specific disciplines to provide patient-centered care, organizational structures like service lines, or the development of multidisciplinary clinics and centers of excellence
Context—environment in which the team performs	**Team**—Emotional or operational climate for members	Socioemotional atmosphere of the team. Leadership can help foster team cohesiveness
	Organization—Operational climate for teams	Climate created by organization to support teamwork and individual team members. Organizational policies and structures that lead to employee satisfaction foster more engagement and dedication to team structure and function
Process—manner in which the team functions	**Interdependence**—Defining member roles and team strategy	Allows for effective use of team resources by allocating tasks to the highest performer of the task. In the medical arena, experienced guidance must be available constantly to balance education and efficiency
	Growth and development—Aligning personal and team goals	Individuals in the team learn and prosper, which in turn benefits the individual, team and organization
Productivity—strategies used by teams to produce desired outcomes	**Measures and metrics**—Assessing team performance	Objective measurement of results. Platform for development of healthcare team
	Plan of action—A blueprint for team success	Integrated combination of the team's primary purpose (short- and long-term goals) and extension to institution's mission that includes strategies and timelines for execution

Table 12.2 Types of workplace violence

Type	Description	Example
I	Violence by outside criminals	A health care worker is robbed at gun point on the way to their car at the end of their workday
II	Violence by service recipients	An intoxicated patient punches a member of the health care team
III	Violence by current or former coworkers	A heated argument arises between two residents about the care of a patient
IV	Violence by close personal contacts	The spouse of an employee assaults the employee at their place of work

While healthcare workers are subject to all types of workplace violence, data suggest that assaults directed at healthcare workers by patients make up the majority of type II assaults that occur in U.S. workplaces annually [40]. Healthcare workers are nearly four times as likely to require time away from work as result of workplace violence, and it has been cited as a major contributor to burnout for all healthcare workers [40, 41]. In the realm of physicians, residents have been identified as particularly at-risk for experiencing workplace violence, with 20–40% of residents reporting assaults and 67–79% describing verbal abuse or threats from patients or family members in recent surveys [42].

Ensuring safety in the workplace is a vital component of clinician wellbeing. While it is impossible for healthcare facilities to control the individual behavior of all patrons and employees, it is imperative that "universal precautions for violence" be used across systems to not only control an acute crisis, but also to manage long term effects on employees while working to prevent future workplace violence. Recognition of the benefit of a violence-free workplace and a commitment to supporting this goal with both financial and administrative resources is vital in reducing workplace violence in healthcare systems [42]. Enacting a zero-tolerance policy for all violence, including verbal assault, is an important first step, and should be supported by the introduction of a reliable, complainant-protective reporting system that requires investigation of all reported incidents as well as tracking and identification of patients with known history of violence. Having an acute incident response team comprised of trained security personnel to de-escalate and control acute violent outbursts that is readily available and easily accessible is also mandatory to ensuring a safe workplace environment. Clinicians should receive training on measures that can be used to prevent violence, as well as to de-escalate aggression and minimize resultant injury when violence does occur. Workplaces should regularly be checked for the presence of potential hazards or weapons, and corrective measures employed and audited to ensure effectiveness in workplace violence reduction. Lastly, ensuring counseling services are available to clinicians who are victims of workplace violence can help manage long-term effects. While these suggestions will have to be tailored at each institution, adopting the attitude that workplace violence is not "part of the job" for clinicians, and optimizing reporting systems and work environment while training physicians in violence prevention and de-escalation are pivotal to the creation of a safe workplace and clinician resilience.

12.15 Conclusion

Burnout amongst physicians is a state of mental and physical exhaustion that affects not only clinician job satisfaction and career longevity, but also can negatively impact the quality of care physicians provide to patients. While burnout is a complex entity with numerous internal and external influences, the environment in which clinicians learn, train, and work is a major contributor. Each aspect of the learning and practice environment, as discussed above, is integrally related to each other and as such has the propensity to influence clinician wellness individually and collectively. Addressing each domain of the learning and practice environment in a proactive fashion while keeping resilience at the forefront of the strategic armamentarium to enhance provider wellbeing is paramount. Although there is no "magic pill" for the epidemic of burnout that clinicians, and especially surgeons, are currently facing, drawing from wellbeing practices of other high-risk occupations combined with systematically addressing each domain within the learning and practice environment in healthcare, will assist clinicians to achieve career satisfaction, work-life balance, and individual wellbeing. The translation of this effort will most definitely lead to sustained improvements in patient care while also having a positive impact on healthcare organizations and more importantly, society at large.

References

1. Inc. IM. The complexities of physician supply and demand. Washington, DC: Association of American Medical Colleges; 2017.
2. Physician Burnout Rockville: Agency for Healthcare Research and Quality; 2017. https://www.ahrq.gov/professionals/clinicians-providers/ahrq-works/burnout/index.html.
3. Jackson TN, Pearcy CP, Khorgami Z, Agrawal V, Taubman KE, Truitt MS. The physician attrition crisis: a cross-sectional survey of the risk factors for reduced job satisfaction among US surgeons. World J Surg. 2018;42(5):1285–92.
4. Brigham T, Barden C, Legreid Dopp A, Heneger A, Kaplan J, Malone B, et al. A Journey to Construct an All-Encompassing Conceptual Model of Factors Affecting Clinician Well-Being and Resilience. Washington, DC: National Academy of Medicine; 2018. Available at: https://nam.edu/journey-constructencompassing-conceptual-model-factors-affecting-clinician-well-resilience/.
5. Dictionary C. Cambridge University Publisher; 2018. https://dictionary.cambridge.org/us/dictionary/english/autonomy.
6. Southwick FS, Southwick SM. The loss of a sense of control as a major contributor to physician burnout: a neuropsychiatric pathway to prevention and recovery. JAMA Psychiatry. 2018;75(7):665–6.
7. Blechter B, Jiang N, Cleland C, Berry C, Ogedegbe O, Shelley D. Correlates of burnout in small independent primary care practices in an urban setting. J Am Board Fam Med. 2018;31(4):529–36.
8. Lee RT, Seo B, Hladkyj S, Lovell BL, Schwartzmann L. Correlates of physician burnout across regions and specialties: a meta-analysis. Hum Resour Health. 2013;11:48.
9. Swensen S, Kabcenell A, Shanafelt T. Physician-organization collaboration reduces physician burnout and promotes engagement: the Mayo Clinic experience. J Healthc Manag. 2016;61(2):105–27.
10. Shanafelt TD, Noseworthy JH. Executive leadership and physician well-being: nine organizational strategies to promote engagement and reduce burnout. Mayo Clin Proc. 2017;92(1):129–46.
11. Khan TW. Improving wellness by improving autonomy through physician leadership development. Acad Med. 2017;92(7):895.
12. Ramsay D. Is competition in the workplace good or bad? Adventure Associates; 2015. www.adventureassoc.com/is-competition-in-the-workplace-god-or-bad/.
13. Grillo HC. Edward D. Churchill and the "rectangular" surgical residency. Surgery. 2004;136(5):947–52.

14. Winkel AF, Honart AW, Robinson A, Jones AA, Squires A. Thriving in scrubs: a qualitative study of resident resilience. Reprod Health. 2018;15(1):53.
15. Dunn LB, Iglewicz A, Moutier C. A conceptual model of medical student well-being: promoting resilience and preventing burnout. Acad Psychiatry. 2008;32(1):44–53.
16. American Recovery and Reinvestment Act of 2009: P.L. 111-5, as signed by the President on February 17, 2009: law, explanation and analysis. Chicago: CCH; 2009. 678 p.
17. Wright AA, Katz IT. Beyond burnout—redesigning care to restore meaning and sanity for physicians. N Engl J Med. 2018;378(4):309–11.
18. Shanafelt TD, Dyrbye LN, Sinsky C, Hasan O, Satele D, Sloan J, et al. Relationship between clerical burden and characteristics of the electronic environment with physician burnout and professional satisfaction. Mayo Clin Proc. 2016;91(7):836–48.
19. DiAngi YT, Longhurst CA, Payne TH. Taming the EHR (Electronic Health Record)—there is hope. J Fam Med. 2016;3(6):1072.
20. Babbott S, Manwell LB, Brown R, Montague E, Williams E, Schwartz M, et al. Electronic medical records and physician stress in primary care: results from the MEMO Study. J Am Med Inform Assoc. 2014;21(e1):e100–6.
21. Balch CM, Shanafelt TD, Sloan JA, Satele DV, Freischlag JA. Distress and career satisfaction among 14 surgical specialties, comparing academic and private practice settings. Ann Surg. 2011;254(4):558–68.
22. Dyrbye LN, Varkey P, Boone SL, Satele DV, Sloan JA, Shanafelt TD. Physician satisfaction and burnout at different career stages. Mayo Clin Proc. 2013;88(12):1358–67.
23. Schonrock-Adema J, Visscher M, Raat AN, Brand PL. Development and validation of the scan of postgraduate educational environment domains (SPEED): a brief instrument to assess the educational environment in postgraduate medical education. PLoS One. 2015;10(9):e0137872.
24. Dyrbye LN, Thomas MR, Harper W, Massie FS Jr, Power DV, Eacker A, et al. The learning environment and medical student burnout: a multicentre study. Med Educ. 2009;43(3):274–82.
25. van Vendeloo SN, Prins DJ, Verheyen C, Prins JT, van den Heijkant F, van der Heijden F, et al. The learning environment and resident burnout: a national study. Perspect Med Educ. 2018;7(2):120–5.
26. Polavarapu HV, Kulaylat AN, Sun S, Hamed OH. 100 years of surgical education: the past, present, and future. Bull Am Coll Surg. 2013;98(7):22–7.
27. Mian A. True mentorship in medicine. Can Fam Physician. 2011;57(2):252.
28. Yeung M, Nuth J, Stiell IG. Mentoring in emergency medicine: the art and the evidence. CJEM. 2010;12(2):143–9.
29. Wasserman MA. A strategy to reduce general surgery resident attrition: a resident's perspective. JAMA Surg. 2016;151(3):215–6.
30. Zhang H, Isaac A, Wright ED, Alrajhi Y, Seikaly H. Formal mentorship in a surgical residency training program: a prospective interventional study. J Otolaryngol Head Neck Surg. 2017;46(1):13.
31. Gardner H. Frames of mind: the theory of multiple intelligences. New York: Basic Books; 2011. lii, 467 p.
32. Ericsson KA, Prietula MJ, Cokely ET. The making of an expert. Harv Bus Rev. 2007;85(7–8):114–21, 93.
33. Lindeman B, Petrusa E, McKinley S, Hashimoto DA, Gee D, Smink DS, et al. Association of burnout with emotional intelligence and personality in surgical residents: can we predict who is most at risk? J Surg Educ. 2017;74(6):e22–30.
34. Weng HC, Hung CM, Liu YT, Cheng YJ, Yen CY, Chang CC, et al. Associations between emotional intelligence and doctor burnout, job satisfaction and patient satisfaction. Med Educ. 2011;45(8):835–42.
35. Lin DT, Liebert CA, Tran J, Lau JN, Salles A. Emotional intelligence as a predictor of resident well-being. J Am Coll Surg. 2016;223(2):352–8.

36. Smith CD, Balatbat C, Corbridge S, Dopp AL, Fried J, Harter R, et al. Implementing optimal team-based care to reduce clinician burnout. NAM Perspectives. Discussion Paper. Washington, DC: National Academy of Medicine; 2018. Available from: https://nam.edu/implementing-optimal-team-based-care-toreduce-clinician-burnout.
37. Welp A, Manser T. Integrating teamwork, clinician occupational well-being and patient safety—development of a conceptual framework based on a systematic review. BMC Health Serv Res. 2016;16:281.
38. Jain AK, Thompson JM, Chaudry J, McKenzie S, Schwartz RW. High-performance teams for current and future physician leaders: an introduction. J Surg Educ. 2008;65(2):145–50.
39. Majmudar A, Jain AK, Chaudry J, Schwartz RW. High-performance teams and the physician leader: an overview. J Surg Educ. 2010;67(4):205–9.
40. Phillips JP. Workplace violence against health care workers in the United States. N Engl J Med. 2016;375(7):e14.
41. Zafar W, Khan UR, Siddiqui SA, Jamali S, Razzak JA. Workplace violence and self-reported psychological health: coping with post-traumatic stress, mental distress, and burnout among physicians working in the emergency departments compared to other specialties in Pakistan. J Emerg Med. 2016;50(1):167–77.e1.
42. Wax JR, Pinette MG, Cartin A. Workplace violence in health care-It's not "part of the job". Obstet Gynecol Surv. 2016;71(7):427–34.

Part V
Improving Wellbeing

Chapter 13
Addressing Individual Factors

Robyn Richmond and Sharmila Dissanaike

In this chapter, we present a few practical suggestions for improving personal well-being, which can be included within a busy career in a less-than-perfect healthcare system. Rather than create yet another checklist of things to-do, we encourage the reader to identify one or two areas where attention may currently be lacking in their lives, and consider making only one change at a time. While these are individual factors, humans remain innately social animals; pairing with one or more friends to undertake a new wellness initiative has been shown to increase long-term success and is encouraged where feasible.

13.1 Healthcare Role

As a surgeon, her profession often defines her. She has trained for years to gain the knowledge, skills and expertise to get to where she is. When she is faced with a poor patient outcome or her days are filled with tasks unrelated to the care of her patients, it is easy to understand how burnout can set in.

A medical error is a commission or omission that a knowledgeable peer would have deemed wrong, with potential negative consequences for the patient [1]. Medical errors include medication errors, patient misidentification and errors or delays in diagnosis [2]. Medical errors by surgeons can be substantial and lead to significant consequences [2]. This is to be distinguished from a surgical complication, defined as any deviation from the normal postoperative course [3]. Although medical errors do not always lead to a complication, they still weigh heavily in the mind of the surgeon. Similarly, surgical complications can adversely affect a surgeon's mental wellbeing, even if they are not a result of a medical error.

R. Richmond (✉) · S. Dissanaike
Department of Surgery, Texas Tech University Health Sciences Center, Lubbock, TX, USA
e-mail: Robyn.Richmond@ttuhsc.edu; Sharmila.Dissanaike@ttuhsc.edu

© Springer Nature Switzerland AG 2020
E. Kim, B. Lindeman (eds.), *Wellbeing*, Success in Academic Surgery,
https://doi.org/10.1007/978-3-030-29470-0_13

A survey sent out on behalf of the American College of Surgeons found that reporting an error within the previous 3 months had a large, statistically significant association with symptoms of burnout and depression [2]. While causality cannot be determined from a survey, other studies have confirmed the impact of medical errors on the emotional wellbeing of physicians, showing that the detrimental effects may even last for years [4, 5]. Physicians have been referred to as the "second victim" of medical errors, a term first coined in the British Medical Journal by Wu [6]. A study evaluating the psychological repercussions in health care professionals in an intensive care setting, found that many reported feelings of shame, guilt, anxiety, loss of confidence and anger [7]. The relationship between medical errors and poor psychological states is likely bidirectional, as previous studies have shown that burnout and depression may undermine the quality of care physicians provide [8, 9] developing into a vicious cycle.

As vigilant as individual surgeons and systems are, medical errors and complications will still occur. When a surgeon causes a medical error or has a complication, verbalization is an important tool to help him cope [7]. Discussing the event with colleagues and mentors who are familiar with this territory allows the surgeon to share his experience, recognize that he is not unique in his predicament, and reinforces the motivation to learn and develop [10]. Morbidity and mortality reviews and root cause analysis discussions are a part of this approach, and allow the surgeon to discuss the case in a protected environment with peers and develop strategies for prevention in the future [7]. Within a supportive environment this process can be both cathartic and educational; without it, it may feel punitive and further worsen the situation for the individual. Having a culture of safety, which is an organizational factor, with supportive leadership, good communication and strong cooperation is therefore key to these forums being successful [11].

While these forums may help the surgeon discuss the medical aspects of the case in question, venues that allow her to process the inevitable emotional response are also important. Discussing the emotional impact of a complication with friends and family is both appropriate and helpful, and serves as an important means to prevent compartmentalization of our lives, however, discussion with colleagues is invaluable [12–14]. The natural history of recovery after an adverse patient event, as described by S. D. Scott and colleagues, includes restoring personal integrity as the third stage, which includes seeking support from colleagues [12]. A colleague can relate more closely with the experience and understand the personal impact such an event has on the surgeon [12]. Disclosure to a colleague and acceptance of criticism has been shown to reduce the negative effects of adverse events [14]. More formalized organizational meetings designed for this purpose, such as Schwartz Center Rounds or Balint groups, can be helpful tools to discuss the emotional impact of a case [15]. During these longitudinal programs the emotional aspect of patient care is discussed, instead of clinical particulars [15]. Literature suggests that participants receive multiple benefits including improved self-awareness, resilience, job satisfaction and empowerment [15].

Critical incident stress debriefing is an incident-specific session or sessions with the medical team directly involved in an event [16]. Following a critical incident, such as a cardiac arrest or other high-acuity patient scenario, the team members directly involved meet shortly after the conclusion of the event. The medical particulars of the scenario are discussed and opportunities for improvement are considered. These sessions involve peer support, feedback, mentoring and problem solving [16]. Debriefings provide an opportunity for the surgeon to share his emotional responses with the medical team involved, and help with the emergence of coping strategies [17, 18]. In a study of recent medical student graduates, debriefing sessions did not decrease rates of burnout, but were perceived as beneficial by participants [16]. Over 60% of physicians stated that they would recommend them to other physicians and 89% reported emotional and social support from the sessions [16].

After an error or complication, disclosure to a patient or their family, although difficult, has been shown to reduce physician distress [5]. Retaining good patient relationships following an error increases the likelihood of a good emotional outcome for the physician [19, 20]. Better coping is observed if a bad outcome is accepted and disclosed [21]. Training that assists surgeons in disclosure is beneficial to help us perform this difficult yet necessary step [7]. Whether formal or informal, verbalization following an error or complication with attention given to the emotional toil with colleagues, friends, family and patients is key to the wellbeing of the surgeon.

Less dramatic than medical complications and errors, yet vitally important due to the daily impact on our lives, is the structure of a surgeon's daily workload. A surgeon who is unhappy with the degree of administrative responsibilities, the amount of teaching (too little or too much) or research demands will ultimately have difficulty finding satisfaction in his job. While not every one of these aspects may be open to change, they are all open to negotiation—a fact that may not always be apparent, especially to a surgeon early in his career. While negotiation skills are not routinely taught in medical school or surgical training, there are plenty of resources available to help develop this important life skill. If the factors resulting in daily job dissatisfaction are not able to be changed, then a decision to change jobs should be considered. A job that causes more distress than joy on a daily basis will not be sustainable over the long term; therefore, it is important that the surgeon clearly assesses which components are the most impactful and important part of his overall job satisfaction and proceeds accordingly.

13.2 Personal Factors

There are many personal factors that contribute to a surgeon's wellbeing. A surgeon must pay attention to his own self-care, including his own medical health, nutritious eating, regular exercise and good sleep hygiene to help avoid symptoms of burnout.

While maintaining good medical health seems to be obvious for healthcare workers, studies have shown that physicians often neglect their own medical needs [22, 23]. In a study evaluating family medicine trainees, 92% self-prescribed their own medications and 49% felt that they neglected their own health [22]. This is may be due to the fact that 30% of them had not seen a physician within 5 years and 65% of them felt unable to take time off if ill [22].

Unfortunately, the chances of having poor health increase with age. A large cohort study suggests that 50% of US surgeons will experience a major health issue by age 50 years, and that their career may be influenced by personal health issues [24]. While there is no clear evidence that routine physicals reduce morbidity or mortality [25], in a survey of members of the American College of Surgeons, surgeons who reported seeing their primary care provider within the previous 12 months were more likely to be up to date with all age- and sex-appropriate health care screening guidelines [23]. Furthermore, surgeons who followed national screening guidelines for their own health reported higher quality of life scores and decreased rates of burnout [23].

Healthy eating sounds easy, but is often difficult for a busy surgeon to fit into her life. While nutrition is not a cure for burnout, fueling the body with balanced foods boosts energy levels, and prevents medical problems that develop as a complication of obesity. A study of residents found that post-graduate year 3 residents were more likely to be overweight than post-graduate year 1 residents, suggesting an adverse impact of lifestyle and workload on their ability to maintain a healthy weight [26]. Additionally, another study involving residents showed a statistically significant increase in weight gain throughout training [27]. There are no shortage of meal plans and advice, dieticians, meal delivery services, healthy snack options and other resources available to help prevent a busy surgeon's lifestyle from compromising healthy eating habits, and we recommend this expenditure of time and resources as a long-term investment in ourselves.

Regular exercise can easily become another chore or item on a crowded "To Do" list for an already over-scheduled surgeon. The Centers for Disease Control (CDC) recommend that adults participate in a minimum of 150 min of aerobic activity per week and muscle strengthening exercises twice per week [28]. In addition to promoting cardiovascular health, boosting energy levels and helping with maintenance of a healthy weight, regular exercise is associated with lower rates of burnout [23]. An American College of Surgeons survey found that surgeons who adhered to the recommended exercise guideline outlined by the CDC had higher quality of life scores and lower rates of burnout [23].

Inadequate sleep is also associated with higher rates of burnout and depression in physicians [29–31]. A study of medical students reported higher rates of burnout and depression in those who did not get adequate sleep or exercise [30]. Another study of interns showed after logistic regression analysis that chronic sleep deprivation had the highest association with becoming depressed [31]. While individuals may have slightly different sleep requirements, evidence shows that the majority of healthy adults require an average of 7–9 h of sleep each night [32]. Getting enough sleep can be especially difficult for a surgeon, given the unique clinical demands of covering night call. When her clinical duties allow, practicing good sleep hygiene is important to get quality sleep. This includes reducing or eliminating afternoon caffeine intake, noise and visual adjustments in her sleeping environment, limiting screen-time just before bed, regular exercise and avoidance of excessive alcohol consumption. When emergencies or on-call duties disrupt a night or several nights of sleep, it is important to recognize the sleep debt that accumulates. Sleep debt must be "repaid" in order to avoid chronic fatigue, so adjusting a post-call schedule to accommodate a nap or relaxation is important [33].

13.3 Skills and Abilities

There is some evidence that a high level of emotional intelligence (EI) is inversely correlated with burnout among healthcare professionals [34]. Unfortunately, it is near-impossible to discern if this is a cause and effect relationship, and if so, in which direction. Nonetheless, it seems likely that the traits of EI—the capacity to be aware of, control, and express one's emotions, and to handle interpersonal relationships judiciously and empathetically—may help surgeons cope better with the many stressors that accumulate over time, and result in burnout. To this end, developing the skills associated with EI, which are related to resiliency and the capacity to maintain wellbeing in the face of adversity, may serve as a component of developing individual wellness. As mentioned previously, these should never be considered as a panacea in isolation, but rather developed in conjunction with systemic and organizational changes aimed at improving the work environment.

There is debate as to how much of EI is innate or fixed after early childhood development, versus how much potential we have to consciously develop these skills as an adult; regardless, the importance of EI to success in many fields of human endeavor, has led to the teaching of these skills becoming a major industry in and of itself. A detailed discussion of how to develop EI is outside the scope of this chapter. However, in brief, EI is commonly described using five components: self-awareness, self-regulation, motivation, empathy and social skills [35].

Many high achievers, surgeons included, spent their formative years acquiring the intellectual and technical skills necessary to succeed in their highly demanding profession. They are already highly motivated, since it is impossible to get to this stage of our career without intrinsic motivation. However, they may not have taken the time and invested in the very different type of effort necessary to develop self-awareness, emotional self-regulation and social skills such as active listening and effective communication. Therefore, these aspects of EI are often the focus of adult education in professionals such as surgeons.

While there are many books and online resources available to those seeking to develop these skills by themselves, it is likely more effective to pursue this training in a formal setting, with a coach who can provide an external perspective. Usually this involves personal interviews and an initial 360 evaluation to establish a baseline, identification of the most critical areas for improvement, a structured program to develop skills in these areas and a final evaluation of the success of these measures. Unfortunately, this type of intervention is usually very labor intensive and thus costly, so may not be feasible for everyone. However, for those being recruited to a new position, especially one with any leadership or administrative responsibilities, or who have identified a particular area that is hindering their success at an existing workplace, it is reasonable to negotiate employer support for the time and resources necessary to participate in this type of program. Surgeons are a valuable and relatively scarce human resource; therefore, an investment that retains a surgeon in the workforce or helps ensure their success in a new job will be cost-effective for the employer in the long run. Given the widespread use of coaching, 360 evaluations and EI training in the business world, it should not be considered a sign of failure or weakness to request this type of support, even in the healthcare professions.

For those seeking to increase their self-awareness and emotional regulation at their own pace, incorporating a mindfulness-based meditation practice into daily life can be beneficial. Even short durations of low-intensity meditation practice have been shown to improve concentration, blood pressure, sleep and multiple other facets of wellbeing [36]. The methodology can be as simple as learning to focus on the sensation of one's breath, which is a foundational mindfulness technique taught in nearly all traditions. Over time, the practitioner learns to use this skill not just in formal meditation practice but as an anchor in daily life, especially useful in stressful situations. Progressively, awareness of the breath is expanded to a heightened awareness of thoughts, emotions and feelings—aspects of our lives that often have great impact but lurk unnoticed in the subconscious, often only being given serious consideration after unwise actions have been committed. Heightened awareness leads naturally to an increased capacity for self-regulation—the first two components of emotional intelligence. Together, self-awareness and self-regulation help us lead easier lives regardless of the external circumstance, by reducing the unnecessary anxiety and distress that we often unconsciously add to the inevitable stresses and conflicts of modern life. Over time, this can develop into a heightened and durable sense of wellbeing.

As with EI, there are now many published resources that provide instructions to the beginner; a brief list of suggested reading is at the end of this chapter. However, for those who wish to develop these skills at a higher level, it is usually necessary to have access to a teacher in person, who can provide guidance as the practice develops.

13.4 Conclusion

As surgeons, we all trained for many years to focus on our patient's wellbeing, with implicit or explicit instruction that it should be placed above our own. It may therefore seem indulgent, even frivolous, to discuss personal wellbeing among surgeons, who are a highly privileged group in our society. However, the skills required for a surgeon to function at peak performance require a baseline level of health and personal wellbeing; furthermore, the ethos of valuing all lives equally requires that we take care of ourselves as we would our patients. We have presented several strategies for improving surgeon wellbeing; it is our hope that the reader will choose to adopt at least one or two of these, as an important investment in yourself that will pay dividends for many years.

References

1. Wu AW, Folkman S, McPhee SJ, Lo B. Do house officers learn from their mistakes? JAMA. 1991;265(16):2089–94.
2. Shanafelt TD, Balch CM, Bechamps G, Russell T, Dyrbye L, Satele D, et al. Burnout and medical errors among American surgeons. Ann Surg. 2010;251(6):995–1000.
3. Dindo D, Demartines N, Clavien P. Classification of surgical complications: a new proposal with evaluation in a cohort of 6336 patients and results of a survey. Ann Surg. 2004;240(2):205–13.
4. Christensen JF, Levinson W, Dunn PM. The heart of darkness: the impact of perceived mistakes on physicians. J Gen Intern Med. 1992;7(4):424–31.
5. Waterman AD, Garbutt J, Hazel E, Dunagan WC, Levinson W, Fraser VJ, et al. The emotional impact of medical errors on practicing physicians in the United States and Canada. Jt Comm J Qual Patient Saf. 2007;33(8):467–76.
6. Wu AW. Medical error: the second victim. The doctor who makes the mistake needs help too. BMJ. 2000;320(7237):726–7.
7. Laurent A, Aubert L, Chahraoui K, Bioy A, Mariage A, Quenot JP, et al. Error in intensive care: psychological repercussions and defense mechanisms among health professionals. Crit Care Med. 2014;42(11):2370–8.
8. West CP, Huschka MM, Novotny PJ, Sloan JA, Kolars JC, Habermann TM, et al. Association of perceived medical errors with resident distress and empathy: a prospective longitudinal study. JAMA. 2006;296(9):1071–8.
9. Fahrenkopf AM, Sectish TC, Barger LK, Sharek PJ, Lewin D, Chiang VW, et al. Rates of medication errors among depressed and burnt out residents: prospective cohort study. BMJ. 2008;336(7642):488–91.
10. Engel KG, Rosenthal M, Sutcliffe KM. Residents' responses to medical error: coping, learning, and change. Acad Med. 2006;81(1):86–93.
11. Garrouste-Orgeas M, Philippart F, Bruel C, Max A, Lau N, Misset B. Overview of medical errors and adverse events. Ann Intensive Care. 2012;2(1):2.
12. Scott SD, Hirschinger LE, Cox KR, McCoig M, Brandt J, Hall LW. The natural history of recovery for the healthcare provider "second victim" after adverse patient events. Qual Saf Health Care. 2009;18(5):325–30.
13. Sirriyeh R, Lawton R, Gardner P, Armitage G. Coping with medical errors: a systematic review of papers to assess the effects of involvement in medical errors on healthcare professionals' psychological well-being. Qual Saf Health Care. 2010;19(6):e43.
14. Aasland OG, Forde R. Impact of feeling responsible for adverse events on doctors' personal and professional lives: the importance of being open to criticism from colleagues. Qual Saf Health Care. 2005;14(1):13–7.
15. Taylor C, Xyrichis A, Leamy MC, Reynolds E, Maben J. Can Schwartz Center Rounds support healthcare staff with emotional challenges at work, and how do they compare with other interventions aimed at providing similar support? A systematic review and scoping reviews. BMJ Open. 2018;8(10):e024254.
16. Gunasingam N, Burns K, Edwards J, Dinh M, Walton M. Reducing stress and burnout in junior doctors: the impact of debriefing sessions. Postgrad Med J. 2015;91(1074):182–7.
17. Mitchell AM, Sakraida TJ, Kameg K. Critical incident stress debriefing: implications for best practice. Disaster Manag Response. 2003;1(2):46–51.

18. Staender SE, Manser T. Taking care of patients, relatives and staff after critical incidents and accidents. Eur J Anaesthesiol. 2012;29(7):303–6.
19. Fisseni G, Pentzek M, Abholz HH. Responding to serious medical error in general practice—consequences for the GPs involved: analysis of 75 cases from Germany. Fam Pract. 2008;25(1):9–13.
20. Kroll L, Singleton A, Collier J, Rees Jones I. Learning not to take it seriously: junior doctors' accounts of error. Med Educ. 2008;42(10):982–90.
21. Crigger NJ, Meek VL. Toward a theory of self-reconciliation following mistakes in nursing practice. J Nurs Scholarsh. 2007;39(2):177–83.
22. Uallachain GN. Attitudes towards self-health care: a survey of GP trainees. Ir Med J. 2007;100(6):489–91.
23. Shanafelt TD, Oreskovich MR, Dyrbye LN, Satele DV, Hanks JB, Sloan JA, et al. Avoiding burnout: the personal health habits and wellness practices of US surgeons. Ann Surg. 2012;255(4):625–33.
24. Harms BA, Heise CP, Gould JC, Starling JR. A 25-year single institution analysis of health, practice, and fate of general surgeons. Ann Surg. 2005;242(4):520–6.
25. Krogsboll LT, Jorgensen KJ, Gronhoj Larsen C, Gotzsche PC. General health checks in adults for reducing morbidity and mortality from disease: cochrane systematic review and meta-analysis. BMJ. 2012;345:e7191.
26. Leventer-Roberts M, Zonfrillo MR, Yu S, Dziura JD, Spiro DM. Overweight physicians during residency: a cross-sectional and longitudinal study. J Grad Med Educ. 2013;5(3):405–11.
27. Battles SM, Williams CJ, Duldner JE. Body composition change during the intern year of emergency medicine residency. Ann Emerg Med. 2004;44(4):S76–7.
28. Centers for Disease Control and Prevention. Physical activity for everyone [Internet]. Updated 2018 Nov 12; cited 2018 Dec 10. www.cdc.gov/physicalactivity/everyone/guidelines/adults. html#aerobic.
29. Soderstrom M, Jeding K, Ekstedt M, Perski A, Akerstedt T. Insufficient sleep predicts clinical burnout. J Occup Health Psychol. 2012;17(2):175–83.
30. Wolf MR, Rosenstock JB. Inadequate sleep and exercise associated with burnout and depression among medical students. Acad Psychiatry. 2017;41(2):174–9.
31. Rosen IM, Gimotty PA, Shea JA, Bellini LM. Evolution of sleep quantity, sleep deprivation, mood disturbances, empathy, and burnout among interns. Acad Med. 2006;81(1):82–5.
32. Hirshkowitz M, Whiton K, Albert SM, Alessi C, Bruni O, DonCarlos L, et al. National Sleep Foundation's sleep time duration recommendations: methodology and results summary. Sleep Health. 2015;1(1):40–3.
33. Dickinson DL, Wolkow AP, Rajaratnam SM, Drummond SP. Personal sleep debt and daytime sleepiness mediate the relationship between sleep and mental health outcomes in young adults. Depress Anxiety. 2018;35(8):775–83.
34. Vlachou EM, Damigos D, Lyrakos G, Chanopoulos K, Kosmidis G, Karavis M. The relationship between burnout syndrome and emotional intelligence in healthcare professionals. Health Sci J. 2016;10:52.
35. Goleman D. Emotional intelligence: why it can matter more than IQ. Bantam Books; 1996.
36. National Center for Complementary and Integrative Health. 8 things to know about meditation for health [Internet]. Bethesda: National Institutes of Health. [Updated 2018 Jan 30; Cited 2019 Jan 10]. https://nccih.nih.gov/health/tips/meditation.

Suggested Reading

Emotional Intelligence

Bradberry T, Greaves J. Emotional Intelligence 2.0. San Diego: Talentsmart; 2009.

Chapman D, Dethmer J, Klemp K. The 15 Commitments of Conscious Leadership: A new paradigm for sustainable success. Kaley Warner Klemp Conscious Leadership Group; 2015. ISBN: 970990976905.
Eurich T. Insight: Why we're not as Self-Aware as we think, and how seeing ourselves clearly helps us succeed at work and life. Crown Business; 2017. ISBN: 9780451496812.

Mindfulness

Gunaratna BH. Mindfulness in plain English. Boston: Wisdom Publications; 2014.
Tan C-M. Search inside yourself. Harper Collins; 2013.
Zinn JK, Hahn TN. Wherever you go, there you are: Mindfulness meditation in daily life. New York: Hyperion; 1994.

Chapter 14
Addressing External Factors

Hilary Sanfey

14.1 Introduction

Burnout is characterized by emotional exhaustion (EE), depersonalization (DP), and a diminished sense of personal accomplishment (PA) [1]. It is the emotional manifestation of a profound mismatch between high expectations for one's future and the reality of daily life. At its most extreme it can lead to substance use, depression, and suicide [2–7]. Furthermore, burnout can lead to a deterioration in professionalism, patient care, a higher incidence of medical errors, reduced patient satisfaction and an increase in staff turnover [8]. Compassion fatigue is a reduced capacity for empathy occurring in individuals whose work requires an intense involvement with people and is one symptom of burnout. While other domains of burnout may improve in more supportive environments, compassion fatigue will persist if one continues to work with the same demanding, emotionally draining patient population.

The percentage of surgeons with one or more manifestations of burnout has been increasing along with an equivalent decrease in the proportion who report high job satisfaction [6, 9, 10]. Risk factors include having young children, purely incentive-based pay, having a spouse who works as a healthcare professional, increasing nights on call, years in practice, and number of hours worked per week [11, 12]. In addition, the rapidly changing health care environment has profoundly affected clinician wellbeing [13–16]. The situation is further exacerbated by a surgeon's reluctance to seek assistance for themselves or others even in the presence of impairment [17–19].

H. Sanfey (✉)
Department of Surgery, SIU School of Medicine, Springfield, IL, USA
e-mail: hsanfey@siumed.edu

© Springer Nature Switzerland AG 2020
E. Kim, B. Lindeman (eds.), *Wellbeing*, Success in Academic Surgery,
https://doi.org/10.1007/978-3-030-29470-0_14

14.2   Conceptual Model

Wellbeing is a function of the relationship between demands and resources [20]. While there are rewards associated with clinical demands, clinicians can become demoralized if an organizational environment is insufficiently resourced to sustain their efforts to provide good care. Brigham et al. [20] developed a conceptual model for wellbeing that can be applied to a range of disciplines, settings, and career stages and takes into account socio-cultural, regulatory and organizational factors as well as the learning environment [20] (Fig. 14.1). This model illustrates the relationship between the clinician and patient and the individual and external factors that contribute to burnout or wellbeing [20]. This chapter will address the external factors that impact physician wellbeing using this model as a conceptual framework. While individual characteristics certainly contribute to burnout, the evidence suggests that system attributes such as workload, autonomy, control over practice, and quality of the work environment play a more significant role [15, 21].

14.3   Socio-cultural Factors

This category includes societal and patient expectations as well as discrimination or bias based on characteristics of personal identity (Table 14.1, Fig. 14.1). Surgery is a challenging profession due to the length of training, the physical demands of com-

FACTORS AFFECTING CLINICIAN WELL-BEING AND RESILIENCE

This conceptual model depicts the factors associated with clinician well-being and resilience; applies these factors across all health care professions, specialties, settings, and career stages; and emphasizes the link between clinician well-being and outcomes for clinicians, patients, and the health system. The model should be used to understand well-being, rather than as a diagnostic or assessment tool. In electronic form, the external and individual factors of the conceptual model are hyperlinked to corresponding landing pages on the Clinician Well-Being Knowledge Hub. The Clinician Well-Being Knowledge Hub provides additional information and resources. The conceptual model will be revised as the field develops and more information becomes available.

Copyright 2018 National Academy of Sciences

NATIONAL ACADEMY OF MEDICINE
Learn more at *nam.edu/ClinicianWellBeing*

Fig. 14.1 Factors affecting clinician well-being and resilience. (Reprinted from [20])

EXTERNAL FACTORS

SOCIETY & CULTURE

- Alignment of societal expectations and clinician's role
- Culture of safety and transparency
- Discrimination and overt and unconscious bias
- Media portrayal
- Patient behaviors and expectations
- Political and economic climates
- Social determinants of health
- Stigmatization of mental illness

RULES & REGULATIONS

- Accreditation, high-stakes assessments, and publicized quality ratings
- Documentation and reporting requirements
- HR policies and compensation issues
- Initial licensure and certification
- Insurance company policies
- Litigation risk
- Maintenance of licensure and certification
- National and state policies and practices
- Reimbursement structure
- Shifting systems of care and administrative requirements

ORGANIZATIONAL FACTORS

- Bureaucracy
- Congruent organizational mission and values
- Culture, leadership, and staff engagement
- Data collection requirements
- Diversity and Inclusion
- Harassment and discrimination
- Level of support for all healthcare team members
- Power dynamics
- Professional development opportunities
- Scope of practice
- Workload, performance, compensation, and value attributed to work elements

LEARNING/PRACTICE ENVIRONMENT

- Autonomy
- Collaborative vs. competitive environment
- Curriculum
- Health IT interoperability and usability/Electronic health records
- Learning and practice setting
- Mentorship program
- Physical learning and practice conditions
- Professional relationships
- Student affairs policies
- Student-centered and patient-centered focus
- Team structures and functionality
- Workplace safety and violence

HEALTH CARE RESPONSIBILITIES

- Administrative responsibilities
- Alignment of responsibility and authority
- Clinical responsibilities
- Learning/career stage
- Patient population
- Specialty related issues
- Student/trainee responsibilities
- Teaching and research responsibilities

INDIVIDUAL FACTORS

PERSONAL FACTORS

- Access to a personal mentor
- Inclusion and connectivity
- Family dynamics
- Financial stressors/economic vitality
- Flexibility and ability to respond to change
- Level of engagement/connection to meaning and purpose in work
- Personality traits
- Personal values, ethics and morals
- Physical, mental, and spiritual well-being
- Relationships and social support
- Sense of meaning
- Work-life integration

SKILLS & ABILITIES

- Clinical Competency level/experience
- Communication skills
- Coping skills
- Delegation
- Empathy
- Management and leadership
- Mastering new technologies or proficient use of technology
- Optimizing work flow
- Organizational skills
- Resilience skills/practices
- Teamwork skills

Fig. 14.1 continued

plex operative procedures and the emotional toll associated with unexpected, often highly visible, complications. Despite believing we are more resilient than our non-surgical colleagues, surgeons are more at risk for depression, broken relationships, substance dependence, and possibly suicide, all of which impact women differently [2, 3, 12]. Furthermore, there is a cultural expectation that suffering should take place in silence. The most common coping strategies are keeping stress to oneself, concentrating on what to do next, and going on as if nothing happened [22]. These responses positively correlate with feeling emotionally exhausted.

In most studies, women have been found to have a slightly increased risk of burnout compared with men possibly due to greater work-home conflict [6, 9, 10, 12]. In addition, patients expect a longer and more empathetic interaction with female physicians compared with male physicians. Female doctors have more female patients than male doctors, and more patients with psychosocial complexity. Patients also tolerate uncertainty less well from a female compared with a male physician. Mechanisms to address this include brief increments in visit time, training in patient expectations during medical school, and adjusting for patient gender in compensation plans [23–26].

Physicians frequently neglect their own health and tend not to seek help even when they know it is needed [27, 28]. Furthermore, surgeons' subjective assessment of their wellbeing relative to colleagues is unreliable [29]. In one report, a majority of surgeons (89.2%) believed that their wellbeing was at or above average, including 70.5% with scores in the bottom 30% relative to national norms. After receiving

Table 14.1 External factors contributing to burnout based on the conceptual model developed by Brigham et al.

Socio-cultural factors	Regulatory business and payer environment
• Alignment of societal expectations and clinicians role • Culture of Safety and Transparency • Discrimination and overt and unconscious bias • Media portrayal • Patient behaviors and expectations • Political and economic climates • Social determinants of health • Stigmatization of mental illness	• Accreditation, high stakes assessments, and publicized quality ratings • Documentation and reporting requirements • HR policies and compensation issues • Initial Licensure and compensation issues • Litigation risk • Maintenance of licensure and certification • National and state policies and practices • Reimbursement structure • Shifting systems of care and administrative requirements
Organizational factors	Learning practice environment
• Bureaucracy • Congruent organizational mission and values • Culture, leadership and staff engagement • Data collection requirements • Diversity and inclusion • Level of support for all healthcare team members • Professional development opportunities • Scope of practice • Workload, performance, compensation and value attributed to work elements	• Autonomy • Collaborative vs. competitive environment • Curriculum • Health IT interoperability, and usability/ Electronic Health Records • Learning and practice setting • Mentorship • Physical practice and learning conditions • Professional relationships • Student Affairs policies • Student-centered and patient-centered focus • Team structure and functionality • Workplace safety and violence

objective, individualized feedback, 46.6% of surgeons indicated that they intended to make specific changes as a result. Furthermore, suicidal ideation among surgeons over 45 years old is one and a half to three times higher than among the general population [5] and only 26% of surgeons describing suicidal ideation sought help. This trend of sacrificing self-care begins during medical school and residency and continues throughout a career. Fifty percent of residents report putting their life on hold until completion of residency and 37% oncologists report "Looking forward to retirement" as a "wellness promotion strategy" [19, 30]. Heavy workload, per se, is not a predictor of burnout, as surgeons are accustomed to difficult work and long hours. Studies on the impact of duty hours on burnout have been conflicting [31–33] and the intensity of the workday and its interference with the resident's home life appear to play a more influential role than the amount of sleep the resident has had. However, chronic sleep deprivation is a common risk factor for burnout [34].

Individuals with burnout can be less attentive to patient care resulting in a higher rate of adverse events and errors. Furthermore, burnout may result from the aftermath of an adverse event particularly if litigation is involved, thus perpetuating the vicious cycle of burnout [35, 36]. In the immediate aftermath of error, clinicians frequently feel isolated and receive unsupportive, judgmental reactions from peers and superiors [37, 38]. Environments that promote a culture of infallibility create high standards and expectations that one may fail to meet, resulting in clinicians blaming one another, avoiding disclosure, and failing to learn from negative experiences [37, 38]. Commonly cited concerns about seeking help after an adverse event include lack of confidentiality and a fear that seeking help would affect their medical license or professional privileges. Concerns about one's personal reputation can result in a range of negative emotions that last for weeks or even years following an adverse event [39]. Even though the culture of surgery is slowly changing, Mortality and Morbidity conferences may still unintentionally shame those involved in a medical error [40]. A culture shift is necessary to create space for more open discussion amongst colleagues to process negative events [41]. Including surgeon career satisfaction and measures of personal wellbeing in institutional metrics for success would help to ensure that warning signs of burnout are recognized early and treatment is initiated. Studies have demonstrated that in the case of physicians with substance abuse, the results of treatment are generally better than that of the general public and the majority of physicians who undergo treatment recover and return to practice [42].

Traditional views of diligent, hardworking, "self-sacrificing" physicians must change to allow work-life integration [43]. However, individual physicians have a professional responsibility to take care of themselves, to proactively identify personal and professional priorities, and take deliberate steps to integrate their personal and professional lives. Building community at work and connections with colleagues has been shown to reduce burnout and should be pursued [44, 45]. The recently announced National Academy of Medicine Action Collaborative on Clinician Well-Being and Resilience is one example of the unified approach necessary to address this issue that will require cooperation at every level of the health care system [45].

14.4   Regulatory Business and Payer Environment

This category includes matters pertaining to accreditation, documentation, certification and risk of litigation (Table 14.1, Fig. 14.1). The top causes of burnout include *too many bureaucratic tasks, increasing computerization of practice, maintenance of certification requirements* and *the Affordable Care Act*, indicating that the main causes are related to regulation rather than direct patient care [46]. Additional factors include a loss of control over work and erosion of meaning in work [15, 27, 44]. The "devaluing" of physician expertise is further perpetuated by the prevalent use of the term "providers" to collectively describe physicians and all other care providers [47]. This link between burnout and a reduction in the amount of time physicians devote to providing clinical care to patients is both a marker of dysfunction in the health care delivery system and a factor contributing to dysfunction [27].

The acronyms that physicians need to understand have exploded and failure to correctly meet care standards results in significant payment penalties. These financial pressures and the increased complexity of reimbursement pathways add to physician job dissatisfaction and are the principal reasons physicians are leaving their medical practices, equating to an annual loss of over 1000 physicians [8, 48]. The direct costs of turnover do not take into account the disruptive impact on patients, other team members, and the organization's culture and reputation. The loss of any team member increases the risk of burnout among all other members over the next 12 months [49]. In addition to turnover, hospitals face increased financial risk associated with medical errors and malpractice, as well as the short- and long-term disability of physicians suffering from mental health problems [48]. It is not surprising, therefore, that wellness of physicians is increasingly proposed as a quality indicator in health care delivery [27].

The burden of documentation required to meet billing requirements for each clinic visit, quality reporting, and justification for each test ordered is unsustainable [50]. Recommendations to address this are outlined in Table 14.2. Other strategies include covering predictable life events with clinician float pools or adding a *time in the bank* model [51]. Such coverage may be cost effective by raising morale and reducing burnout-related turnover. The high work hours for physicians relative to other professions should be acknowledged with efforts made to improve flexibility and enhance work-life integration. One health care system revamped their scorecards to provide enlightening patient and physician stories while overhauling and reducing the number of metrics reported to streamline the data, presenting it in a more user-friendly, easy-to-read format [52].

One model that attempts to address the impact of adverse events on the patient and the clinician is The Michigan Model [53]. Realizing that deny-and-defend was costly, taxing on resources, and a barrier to patient safety, the University of

Table 14.2 Recommendations for improving the clerical load

• Reduce and streamline required documentation
• Clarify tasks, forms, and documentation elements that may be completed by appropriately trained non-physicians
• Eliminate requirements by insurers that physicians perform and document unnecessary elements of care to justify billing codes that do not contribute to good medical care
• Develop a more efficient preapproval process for tests, medications, and procedures
• Integrate maintenance of certification requirements with standard continuing medical education requirements
• Replace questions by State licensing boards regarding diagnosis or treatment for mental health conditions with questions regarding current impairment
• Build in "desktop" time to the clinic schedule
• Hire scribes to ease the burden of data entry, the use of templates
• Require harmonization and standardization between EMR systems to ensure compatibility, facilitate smooth transfer of information and reduce duplication of work
• Educate payors, administrators, and those who have the legislative and regulatory authority to provide the necessary perspective and insight to help guide lawmakers involved with these decisions

Adapted from Shanafelt et al. The Way Forward

Michigan Health System transitioned to an *open disclosure and offer* model built on three principles: (I) Patients should be compensated quickly and equitably if they received unreasonable medical care; (II) If the care delivered was reasonable or did not negatively affect the clinical outcome, caregivers and the institution should be given full support; (III) The institution should learn from adverse patient safety events to reduce patient injuries, and thereby legal claims. Boothman et al. [53] stress the importance of honesty in determining whether or not a patient received unreasonable care and emphasize that defending true errors is a waste of resources, inhibits health care improvement initiatives, and undermines the development of an institution's culture of safety [53]. With this program, the rate of claims resulting in a lawsuit decreased per year and there was a shorter time to resolution and a decrease in costs [54]. This model has been modified by others [55, 56]. A program at the Brigham and Women's Hospital operates on the principles that humans are fallible and will inevitably make mistakes, therefore the individual and institutional responsibility is to learn from these and to work towards preventing a recurrence in the future [56]. Learning from a medical error and working toward future safety improvements correlates positively with growth and resilience [41]. This learning cannot occur in a shame and blame environment. In order for an institution to support physicians and other healthcare team members to deliver high quality care, the organization needs to be a learning organization and promote a culture of psychological safety where individuals are not afraid to ask questions or raise concerns.

14.5   Organizational Factors

This category includes organizational culture, diversity and inclusion and support for healthcare workers (Table 14.1, Fig. 14.1). It is now evident that organizational leadership can have a profound impact on physician satisfaction and wellbeing [44]. Recent meta-analyses regarding the overall effectiveness of burnout interventions support the argument that burnout is rooted in the organizational coherence of the health care system [16, 57, 58]. Organization-directed interventions were associated with higher treatment effects compared with physician-directed interventions [56]. Interventions targeting experienced physicians and delivered in primary care showed evidence of greater effectiveness compared with interventions targeting less experienced physicians and delivered in secondary care, but these group differences were nonsignificant. Interventions that combined several elements such as structural changes, fostering communication between members of the health care team, and cultivating a sense of teamwork and job control tended to be the most effective in reducing burnout [43, 57, 59, 60].

Shanafelt et al. identified a number of organizational and individual strategies to address the drivers of burnout [44, 50]. These are summarized in Table 14.3. Implementation of many of these strategies resulted in the burnout rate of their physicians decreasing by 7%, despite an 11% rise in the rate of burnout in physicians

Table 14.3 Organizational strategies to reduce burnout and promote physician engagement

• Acknowledge and assess the problem
• Harness the power of leadership
• Develop and implement targeted work unit interventions
• Cultivate community at work
• Use rewards and incentives wisely
• Align values and strengthen culture
• Promote flexibility and work-life integration
• Provide resources to promote resilience and self-care
• Facilitate and fund organizational science

Adapted from [44]

nationally [44]. This reduction was achieved despite having to implement a variety of other changes to improve efficiency, decrease costs, and increase productivity during the same interval. The Action Collaborative on Clinician Well-Being and Resilience was launched in January 2017 [45]. This is a network of more than 60 organizations with the goals of raising the visibility of clinician anxiety, burnout, depression, stress, and suicide, improving baseline understanding of challenges to clinician wellbeing and advancing evidence-based, multidisciplinary solutions to improve patient care by caring for the caregiver [45]. An Accreditation Committee on Graduate Medical Education (ACGME) initiated physician wellbeing symposium was held in 2015 with more than 100 invited members from multiple stakeholders [61]. The participants made a number of recommendations including the need for education and building awareness on burnout, promoting research and collaboration across the continuum to promote cultural change. A task force has been charged with continuing to oversee ACGME efforts to address what many now perceive to be a crisis of burnout within the health care work-force.

The Center for Professional Health, at Vanderbilt University is an example of an institutional program that aims to support and mentor individuals by identifying their unique goals and motivations and developing plans to achieve these [62]. This program is based on creating professional health and wellness portfolios which combine information on stress, burnout, impairment, resiliency, etc. with self-reflection and workbook activities. Completing these portfolios allow participants to develop self-awareness and build personal goals toward a successful future. Another example is a Stanford program developed to promote resident wellbeing across several domains including physical, psychological and professional wellbeing [63]. The authors found that while resident satisfaction improved there was no demonstrated impact in psychological wellbeing or burnout scores after implementation. The most valued component of the program was the well-stocked refrigerator. Another Stanford program initiative is the "Time in the Bank" program [51]. This allows doctors to "bank" the time they spend doing the often-unappreciated work of mentoring, serving on committees, covering colleagues' shifts on short notice or deploying in emergencies, and earn credits to use as payment for various work or home-related services including meals, housecleaning, babysitting, elder care, handyman services, dry cleaning pickup, and more all aimed to ease work-life conflicts. This pilot program led to big increases in job satisfaction, work-life balance and collegiality, in addition to a greater number of research grants applied for and a higher approval rate compared with the Stanford faculty not in the pilot [51]. Furthermore, banking credits reduced the guilt associated with asking others for help and encouraged faculty to share responsibility to reduce workload when needed.

West et al. conducted a randomized controlled trial to evaluate whether a facilitated small-group curriculum was an effective way to use employer-provided protected time [64]. Volunteers in both arms of the study received 1 h of protected time every other week. Those in the control arm could use this hour in any manner they chose. Participants in the facilitated small-group intervention who attended sessions aimed at achieving balance and wellbeing experienced significant improvements in empowerment, and engagement in work beyond that seen in the physicians receiving only protected time. In addition, rates of depersonalization decreased markedly in the intervention arm of the study compared with the control arm; both results were sustained for 12 months following the study. These findings suggest that although receiving unstructured protected time offered some benefits by itself, the advantages of the small-group curriculum were greater. West et al. concluded that it is cost effective to provide time each week for clinicians to do what they are most passionate about [64]. Introducing flexible work schedules will reduce stress around work-life conflicts. The gender differences in burnout identified among US physicians are not seen in the Netherlands, where 75% of women physicians work part-time. Part-time options allow institutions to use a more flexible career life cycle approach to meet the needs of an increasingly diverse workforce and prevent burnout [65].

In summary, institutional changes to promote wellbeing include ensuring adequate staffing, accommodating part-time work, developing stress-reduction programs, enhancing support for health professionals, and ensuring a reasonable workload throughout the day. In addition, dimensions of wellbeing should be routinely assessed as institutional performance metrics along with more standard institutional measures.

14.6 Learning Practice Environment

This category includes professional relationships and educational and training factors (Table 14.1, Fig. 14.1). Burnout exists across the spectrum of medical education and is a significant predictor of poor performance among residents [66], attending surgeons [10] and of impaired academic performance in medical students [4]. Stressors may change during each year of medical school and suicidal ideation increases as medical trainees progress through the system [4, 5, 67, 68]. Over 50% of medical students experience burnout, with as many as 10% reporting suicidal ideation [4]. Stressors include academic pressure, financial concerns, sleep deprivation, life events, and student abuse [4]. Dyrbye et al. recommend that medical schools should consider offering a variety of intervention options so that students can select activities in which they want to engage [69]. Many medical schools have implemented successful stress reduction programs to decrease burnout [70–73].

It is now known that many interns enter training already manifesting signs and symptoms of depression that developed during medical school [74]. Overall, 50% of residents suffer from burnout with a range that varies from 27 to 75% across specialties [75, 76] and increases from the beginning to the end of the intern year [34]. The type of burnout may vary by specialty with surgical fields experiencing more EE, primary care fields experiencing more DP, and non-primary care/non-surgical fields experiencing feelings of less PA [76]. A national survey found that 69% of General Surgery residents met the criterion for burnout on at least one sub-scale. Among residents with moderate to severe depression, suicidal ideation can be as high as 53% [7]. Time demands, lack of control over time management, work organization, clerical workload, and interpersonal relationships contribute to burn-out in residency. Of added concern is that almost one third of residents who self-identified as being depressed received prescription medications from another provider without a formal evaluation (half of these, from fellow residents) and some self-prescribed prescription antidepressants [77]. Interventions focused on enhancing teamwork, mentoring, and leadership skills might be particularly suitable for young physicians and for physicians dealing with intense work and patients with complex care needs [49, 78], and a structured mentoring program was associated with lower burnout on each subscale [79].

Barriers to seeking help among students and residents include concerns of losing respect from faculty and peers, lack of recognition of symptoms, time constraints, and concerns over negative licensing action [80]. Residents fear being perceived as not having the "right stuff" for surgery [19]. Furthermore, 10% of surgeons in practice and 50% of residents would ignore behaviors that visibly impact clinical performance and 32% of surgeons in practice would ignore behaviors that adversely impact a surgeon's personal life or wellbeing and potentially their clinical judgment [18, 19]. It is important to learn to recognize the signs and symptoms of burnout, depression, and substance abuse and take appropriate steps. Private practice setting is associated with increased rate of burnout and depression, and lower career satisfaction than academic practice [9]. Having a dedicated non-patient care time allotment in an academic, administrative, educational or research capacity was associated with lower risk of burnout [10]. Furthermore faculty who spent more time on an activity that was most meaningful to them (clinical, academic, research) were found to have a lower incidence of burnout [81].

Emotional reactions to adverse events can be devastating, potentially leading to depression, anxiety, burnout, and even suicide. At such times, physicians prefer to receive support from physician colleagues [41, 82]. Based on this, Shapiro et al. developed a peer support program that was one of the first of its kind to rely on clinician colleagues rather than mental health professionals to provide support to clinicians involved in medical errors [83]. This program is designed to reach out directly to clinicians through a number of channels including risk management, clinician colleagues and offer peer support. Outreach is offered to all clinicians involved in a stressful event, so that the clinician in question is not singled out as having trouble coping. The support involves respectful listening, and helps the peer draw on sources of resilience. In these situations, peer advisors also need to recognize the limits of confidentiality as a listener. For example, if a colleague is a danger to himself or others then the information must be shared with the appropriate authority. Finally, respectful treatment of colleagues is correlated with workplace satisfaction and a decreased likelihood of burnout. Therefore, several institutions have instituted mandatory professionalism training sessions and/or remediation programs [55, 84].

14.7 Summary

Physicians today have to manage a rapidly expanding medical knowledge base, more onerous maintenance of certification requirements, increased clerical work and patient portals, new regulatory requirements, and face an unprecedented level of scrutiny. Both individual-focused and organizational-level solutions are required to address physician burnout. Individual-directed interventions typically involve mindfulness techniques to enhance job competence and improve communication skills and personal coping strategies. However, physicians expected to deal with burnout individually might blame themselves for being less resilient. Thus, individual-directed interventions are more effective when supported by organizational approaches [44]. Organization-directed interventions can involve simple changes in scheduling and reductions in the intensity of workload or more ambitious changes to the operation of practices and health care organizations. These usually involve improved teamwork, changes in work evaluation, and in supervision to reduce job demands and enhance job control, and increasing the level of participation in decision-making [57]. Health care institutions should recognize the potential effect of physician wellbeing on the long-term viability of their organization, and dimensions of wellbeing should be routinely assessed as institutional performance metrics. Physicians based in different health care settings or at different stages of their career might face unique challenges and have different needs [57]. In addition, young physicians are at higher risk for burnout compared with experienced physicians. Therefore, it is particularly important to focus efforts on junior faculty and surgeons less than 10 years out of training. Future research into organizational interventions to reduce physician burnout should address the optimal approaches to development and implementation of burnout reduction strategies, along with assessment of the feasibility and costs associated with these interventions [58]. Meaningful progress will require collaborative efforts by national bodies, health care organizations, leaders, and individual physicians, as each is responsible for factors that contribute to the problem and must own their part of the solution [50].

References

1. Maslach C, Schaufeli W, Lieter M. Job burnout. Annu Rev Psychol. 2001;52(1):397–422.
2. Balch CM, Freischlag JA, Shanafelt TD. Stress and burnout among surgeons: understanding and managing the syndrome and avoiding the adverse consequences. Arch Surg. 2009;144(4):371–6.
3. Bittner JGT, Khan Z, Babu M, et al. Stress, burnout, and maladaptive coping: strategies for surgeon well-being. Bull Am Coll Surg. 2011;96(8):17–22.
4. Dyrbye LN, Thomas MR, Shanafelt TD. Systematic review of depression, anxiety, and other indicators of psychological distress among U.S. and Canadian medical students. Acad Med. 2006;81(4):354–73.
5. Shanafelt TD, Balch CM, Dyrbye LN, et al. Special report: suicidal ideation among American surgeons. Arch Surg. 2011;146(1):54–62.
6. Shanafelt TD, Hasan O, Dyrbye LN, et al. Changes in burnout and satisfaction with work-life balance in physicians and the general US working population between 2011 and 2014. Mayo Clin Proc. 2015;90:1600–13.
7. Van der Heijden F, Dillingh G, Bakker A, et al. Suicidal thoughts among medical residents with burnout. Arch Suicide Res. 2008;12(4):344–6.
8. Shanafelt TD, Dyrbye LN, West CP, et al. Potential impact of burnout on the US physician workforce. Mayo Clin Proc. 2016;91(11):1667–8.
9. Balch CM, Shanafelt TD, Sloan JA, et al. Distress and career satisfaction among 14 surgical specialties, comparing academic and private practice settings. Ann Surg. 2011;254(4):558–68.
10. Shanafelt TD, Balch CM, Bechamps G, et al. Burnout and career satisfaction among American surgeons. Ann Surg. 2009;250(3):463–71.
11. Dyrbye LN, Shanafelt TD, Balch CM, et al. Physicians married or partnered to physicians: a comparative study in the American College of Surgeons. J Am Coll Surg. 2010;211(5):663–71.
12. Dyrbye LN, Shanafelt TD, Balch C, et al. Relationship between work-home conflicts and burnout among American surgeons: a comparison by sex. Arch Surg. 2011;146(2):211–7.
13. Dyrbye LN, Shanafelt TD, Sinsky CA, et al. Burnout among health care professionals: a call to explore and address this under recognized threat to safe, high-quality care. NAM Perspectives. Discussion Paper, 2017 National Academy of Medicine, Washington, DC. Washington, DC: National Academy of Medicine. https://nam.edu/Burnout-Among-Health-Care-Professionals. Accessed 1.12.19.
14. Shanafelt TD, Mungo M, Schmitgen J, et al. Longitudinal study evaluating the association between physician burnout and changes in professional work effort. Mayo Clin Proc. 2016;91(4):422–31.
15. Shanafelt TD, Dyrbye LN, Sinsky C, et al. Relationship between clerical burden and characteristics of the electronic environment with physician burnout and professional satisfaction. Mayo Clin Proc. 2016;91(7):836–48.
16. West CP, Dyrbye LN, Shanafelt T. Physician burnout, contributors, consequences and solutions. J Intern Med. 2018;283:516–29.
17. DesRoches CM, Rao SR, Fromson JA, et al. Physicians' perceptions, preparedness for reporting, and experiences related to impaired and incompetent colleagues. JAMA. 2010;304(2):187–93.
18. Sanfey H, Fromson J, Mellinger J, et al. Surgeons in difficulty: an exploration of differences in assistance-seeking behaviors between male and female surgeons. J Am Coll Surg. 2015;221(2):621–7.
19. Sanfey H, Fromson J, Mellinger J, et al. Residents in distress: an exploration of assistance-seeking and reporting behaviors. AJS. 2015;210(4):678–84.
20. Brigham T, Barden C, Legreid Dopp A, et al. A journey to construct an all-encompassing conceptual model of factors affecting clinician well-being and resilience. NAM Perspectives. Discussion Paper. Washington, DC: National Academy of Medicine; 2018. https://nam.edu/journey-constructencompassing-conceptual-model-factors-affectingclinician-well-resilience. Accessed 1.14.19.

21. Rassolian M, Peterson LE, Fang B, et al. Workplace factors associated with burnout of family physicians. JAMA Intern Med. 2017;177(17):1036–7.
22. Lemaire JB, Wallace JE. Not all coping strategies are created equal: a mixed methods study exploring physicians' self-reported coping strategies. BMC Health Serv Res. 2010;10(1):208.
23. Cousin G, Mast MS, Jaunin-Stalder N. When physician-expressed uncertainty leads to patient dissatisfaction: a gender study. Med Educ. 2013;47:923–31.
24. Linzer M, Harwood E. Gendered expectations: do they contribute to high burnout among female physicians? J Gen Intern Med. 2018;33(6):963–5.
25. Mast MS, Hall JA, Roter DL. Disentangling physician sex and physician communication style: their effects on patient satisfaction in a virtual medical visit. Patient Educ Couns. 2007;68:16–22.
26. Mast MS, Hall JA, Cronauer CK, et al. Perceived dominance in physicians: are female physicians under scrutiny? Patient Educ Couns. 2011;83:174–9.
27. Wallace JE, Lemaire JB, Ghali WA. Physician wellness: a missing quality indicator. Lancet. 2009;374(9702):1714–21.
28. Medscape National Physician Burnout & Depression Report 2018. https://www.medscape.com/slideshow/2018-lifestyle-burnout-depression-6009235#3. Accessed 1.12.19.
29. Shanafelt T, Kaups KL, Nelson H, et al. An interactive, individualized intervention to promote behavioral change to increase personal wellbeing in US surgeons. Ann Surg. 2014;259(1):82–8.
30. Shanafelt TD, Chung H, White H, et al. Shaping your career to maximize personal satisfaction in the practice of oncology. J Clin Oncol. 2006;24(24):4020–6.
31. Gelfand DV, Podnos YD, Carmichael J, et al. Effect of the 80-hour workweek on resident burnout. Arch Surg. 2004;139(9):933–40.
32. Goitein L, Shanafelt TD, Wipf JE, et al. The effects of work-hour limitations on resident wellbeing, patient care, and education in an internal medicine residency program. Arch Intern Med. 2005;165(22):2601–6.
33. Hutter MM, Kellogg KC, Ferguson CM, et al. The impact of the 80-hour resident workweek on surgical residents and attending surgeons. Ann Surg. 2006;243:864–75.
34. Rosen IM, Gimotty PA, Shea JA, et al. Evolution of sleep quantity, sleep deprivation, mood disturbances, empathy, and burnout among interns. Acad Med. 2006;81(1):82–5.
35. Shanafelt TD, Balch CM, Bechamps G, et al. Burnout and medical errors among American surgeons. Ann Surg. 2010;251(6):995–1000.
36. West CP, Huschka MM, Novotny PJ, et al. Association of perceived medical errors with resident distress and empathy: a prospective longitudinal study. JAMA. 2006;296:1071–8.
37. Luu S, Patel P, St-Martin L, et al. Waking up the next morning: surgeons emotional reactions to adverse events. Med Educ. 2012;46:1179–88.
38. DeCaporale-Ryan L, Sakran J, Grant SB, et al. The undiagnosed pandemic: burnout and depression within the surgical community. Curr Probl Surg. 2017;54(9):453–502.
39. Marmon LM, Heiss K. Improving surgeon wellness: the second victim syndrome and quality of care. In: Seminars in pediatric surgery. Elsevier; 2015.
40. Sakran JV, Kaafarani H, Mouawad NJ, et al. When things go wrong. Bull Am Coll Surg. 2011;96(8):13–6.
41. Plews-Ogan M, May N, Owens J, et al. Wisdom in medicine: what helps physicians after a medical error? Acad Med. 2016;91(2):233–41.
42. Carinci AJ, Christo PJ. Physician impairment: is recovery feasible. Pain Physician. 2009;12(3):487–91.
43. Linzer M, Levine R, Meltzer D, et al. 10 bold steps to prevent burnout in general internal medicine. J Gen Intern Med. 2013;29(1):18–20.
44. Shanafelt TD, Noseworthy JH. Executive leadership and physician well-being: nine organizational strategies to promote engagement and reduce burnout. Mayo Clin Proc. 2017;92(1):129–46. https://doi.org/10.1016/j.mayocp.2016.10.004. www.mayoclinicproceedings.org.
45. National Academy of Medicine. Action collaborative on clinician well-being and resilience. https://nam.edu/event/clinician-resilience-and-well-being/. Accessed 1.14.19.

46. Peckham C. Medscape survey lifestyle report 2016: Bias and burnout. 2016. http://www.medscape.com/features/slideshow/lifestyle/2016/general-surgery-page=1. Accessed 1.3.19.
47. Goroll AH. Eliminating the term primary care "provider": consequences of language for the future of primary care. JAMA. 2016;315(17):1833–4.
48. Shanafelt TD, Goh J, Sinsky C. The business case for investing in physician well-being. JAMA Intern Med. 2017;177(12):1826–32.
49. Helfrich CD, Simonetti JA, Clinton WL, et al. The association of team-specific workload and staffing with odds of burnout among VA primary care team members. J Gen Intern Med. 2017;32(7):760–6.
50. Shanafelt T, Dyrbye LN, West CP. Addressing physician burnout; the way forward. JAMA. 2017;317(9):901–2.
51. Stanford Time in the Bank Program. http://wellmd.stanford.edu/content/dam/sm/wellmd/documents/Time-banking-system.pdf. Accessed 1.10.19.
52. Martin L. Good news: how to extinguish physician burnout. Advisory Board. https://www.advisory.com/research/physician-executive-council/prescription-for-change/2016/07/3-hospitals-on-burnout. Accessed 1.12.19.
53. Boothman RC, Imhoff SJ, Campbell DA Jr. Nurturing a culture of patient safety and achieving lower malpractice risk through disclosure: lessons learned and future directions. Front Health Serv Manag. 2012;28:13–28.
54. Kachalia A, Kaufman SR, Boothman R, et al. Liability claims and costs before and after implementation of a medical error disclosure program. Ann Intern Med. 2010;153:213–21.
55. CANDOR Quality AfHRa. Communication and Optimal Resolution (CANDOR) Toolkit. 2016. https://www.ahrq.gov/professionals/quality-patient-safety/patient-safety-resources/resources/candor/index.html. Accessed 1.14.19.
56. Shapiro J, Whittemore A, Tsen LC. Instituting a culture of professionalism: the establishment of a center for professionalism and peer support. Jt Comm J Qual Patient Saf. 2014;40(4):168–77.
57. Panagioti M, Panagopoulou E, Bower P, et al. Controlled interventions to reduce burnout in physicians a systematic review and meta-analysis. JAMA Intern Med. 2017;177(2):195–205.
58. West CP, Dyrbye LN, Erwin PJ, et al. Interventions to prevent and reduce physician burnout: a systematic review and meta-analysis. Lancet. 2016;388(10057):2272–81.
59. Linzer M, Poplau S, Grossman E, et al. A cluster randomized trial of interventions to improve work conditions and clinician burnout in primary care: results from the Healthy Work Place (HWP) study. J Gen Intern Med. 2015;30(8):1105–11.
60. Swensen S, Kabcenell A, Shanafelt T. Physician-organization collaboration reduces physician burnout and promotes engagement: the Mayo Clinic experience. J Health Manag. 2016;61(2):105–27.
61. ACGME Symposium on Resident Well-being. http://www.acgme.org/What-We-Do/Initiatives/Physician-Well-Being/ACGME-Symposium-on-Physician-Well-Being. Accessed 1.14.19.
62. Center for Professional Health, Vanderbilt University Medical Center. https://ww2.mc.vanderbilt.edu/cph/. Accessed 1.13.19.
63. Salles A, Nandagopal K, Walton G. Belonging: a simple, brief intervention decreases burnout. J Am Coll Surg. 2013;217:S116.
64. West CP, Dyrbye LN, Rabatin JT, et al. Intervention to promote physician well-being, job satisfaction, and professionalism: a randomized clinical trial. JAMA Intern Med. 2014;174(4):527–33.
65. Linzer M, Visser MR, Oort FJ, et al. Society of General Internal Medicine (SGIM) Career Satisfaction Study Group. Predicting and preventing physician burnout: results from the United States and the Netherlands. Am J Med. 2001;111(2):170–5.
66. Shanafelt TD, Bradley KA, Wipf JE, et al. Burnout and self-reported patient care in an internal medicine residency program. Ann Intern Med. 2002;136(5):358–67.
67. Dyrbye LN, Thomas MR, Massie FS, et al. Burnout and suicidal ideation among U.S. medical students. Ann Intern Med. 2008;149(5):334–41.

68. Dyrbye LN, West CP, Satele D, et al. Burnout among U.S. medical students, residents, and early career physicians relative to the general U.S. population. Acad Med. 2014;89(3):443–51.
69. Dyrbye LN, Shanafelt TD, Werner L, et al. The impact of a required longitudinal stress management and resilience training course for first-year medical students. J Gen Intern Med. 2017;32(12):1309–14.
70. De Vibe M, Solhaug I, Tyssen R, et al. Mindfulness training for stress management: a randomised controlled study of medical and psychology students. BMC Med Educ. 2013;13:107.
71. Ishak W, Nikravesh R, Lederer S, et al. Burnout in medical students: a systematic review. Clin Teach. 2013;10(4):242–5.
72. Slavin SJ, Chibnall JT. Finding the why, changing the how: improving the mental health of medical students, residents, and physicians. Acad Med. 2016;91(9):1194–6.
73. Warnecke E, Quinn S, Ogden K, et al. A randomised controlled trial of the effects of mindfulness practice on medical student stress levels. Med Educ. 2011;45(4):381–8.
74. Dyrbye LN, Moutier C, Durning SJ, et al. The problems program directors inherit: medical student distress at the time of graduation. Med Teach. 2011;33(9):756–8.
75. Mata DA, Ramos MA, Bansai N, et al. Prevalence of depression and depressive symptoms among resident physicians: a systematic review and meta-analysis. JAMA. 2015;314(22):2373–83.
76. Martini S, Arfken CL, Churchill A, et al. Burnout comparison among residents in different medical specialties. Acad Psychiatry. 2004;28(3):240–2.
77. Stoesser K, Cobb NM. Self-treatment and informal treatment for depression among resident physicians. Fam Med. 2013;46(10):797–801.
78. Hakanen JJ, Schaufeli WB. Do burnout and work engagement predict depressive symptoms and life satisfaction? A three-wave seven-year prospective study. J Affect Disord. 2012;141(2–3):415–24.
79. Elmore LC, Jeffe DB, Jin L, et al. National Survey of Burnout among US General Surgery Residents. J Am Coll Surg. 2016;223(3):440–51.
80. Dyrbye LN, Eacker A, Durning SJ, et al. The impact of stigma and personal experiences on the help-seeking behaviors of medical students with burnout. Acad Med. 2015;90(7):961–9.
81. Shanafelt TD. Enhancing meaning in work: a prescription for preventing physician burnout and promoting patient-centered care. JAMA. 2009;302(12):1338–40.
82. Hu Y-Y, Fix ML, Hevelone MD, et al. Physicians' needs in coping with emotional stressors: the case for peer support. Arch Surg. 2012;147(3):212–7.
83. Shapiro J, Galowitz P. Peer support for clinicians: a programmatic approach. Acad Med. 2016;91(9):1200–4.
84. Hickson GB, Pichert JW, Webb LE, et al. A complementary approach to promoting professionalism: identifying, measuring, and addressing unprofessional behaviors. Acad Med. 2007;82(11):1040–8.

Chapter 15
Wellbeing Considerations for Medical Students

Brittany N. Hasty and James N. Lau

15.1 Introduction

Medical school matriculation signifies the start of medical students' formal training towards becoming a doctor and the realization of their dream of caring for patients. This exciting transition also brings a multitude of challenges. The first day denotes the beginning of an arduous journey without an instruction booklet. This transition into higher education has previously been identified as one of the most stressful periods for learners [1]. Each year of medical school brings considerable challenges in the students' environmental, social, cognitive, and psychological realms that are all simultaneously ubiquitous and unique to each student.

As medical students embark on their journey, typically 1–2 years are spent in classroom-based education. This student-centered phase of medical education is similar to college or graduate school, but the curriculum is far more intense, and the bell curve is tighter. Concurrently, students are often thrust into early clinical exposure all while the pressure to study for the USMLE Step 1 is moving earlier into the first year. Furthermore, students are encouraged to adopt extracurricular professional activities in order to increase their competitiveness for residency. All of this adds unanticipated stress and anxiety in medical students. The knowledge and understanding of this by those who teach and mentor medical students must lead to a support system, curricular structure, and learning environment that make student wellbeing a top priority.

B. N. Hasty
Loyola University Chicago School of Medicine, Maywood, IL, USA
e-mail: brittany.hasty@lumc.edu

J. N. Lau (✉)
Stanford School of Medicine, Stanford, CA, USA
e-mail: jnlau@stanford.edu

15.2 The Impact of Student Demographics on Wellbeing

In 2004, the AAMC defined underrepresented populations in medicine as those "racial and ethnic populations that are underrepresented in the medical profession relative to their numbers in the general population" [2]. Despite an ongoing commitment to increasing underrepresented students in medical school, enrollment remains disproportionately low. As of 2018, students who self-identify as White still make up nearly 65% of graduating students while the percentages of Black (5.8%), American Indian and Alaska Native (0.7%), and Native Hawaiian and other Pacific Islanders (0.2%) populations has essentially remained the same or slightly decreased [3]. In the same year, 3.3% of students reported being denied opportunities based on race or ethnicity and another 8.7% reported being subjected to racially or ethnically offensive comments [3]. These behaviors lend themselves to creating a hostile learning environment for underrepresented students, which has been related to a lower performance and a higher likelihood to fail the USMLE Step 1 [4].

There is another subgroup of medical students that are at high risk of suffering psychological distress and if left unaddressed may also result in professional and academic hardship. According to the AAMC GQ, for the past 3 years, the number of students who identify as gay, lesbian, bisexual, and gender nonconforming are increasing [3]. For example, in one survey among first-year sexual minority students, those who identified as non-heterosexual, as compared to heterosexual, were 1.5 times as likely to suffer from depressive symptoms, 1.6 times as likely to suffer from anxiety, and 1.8 times more likely to report low self-rated health. Additionally, they were significantly more likely to report harassment and isolation. In another study, students who self-identified as LGBT were 8.2 times as likely to experience heterosexism and 6.6 times as likely to experience anti-LGBT discrimination [5].

We must be diligent to ensure our efforts to improve the learning environment take into account all medical students, and these subgroups of students in particular. If we fail to target our wellbeing interventions to improve overall mental health for our medical students, especially for minority students, we risk undermining our goals of workplace diversity and inclusion. By growing the ranks of underrepresented physicians we will drastically improve our capability as a profession to provide culturally competent care to our patients.

15.3 The Impact of Step 1 on Wellbeing

The National Board of Medical Examiners (NBME) originally developed the United States Medical Licensing Exam (USMLE) Step 1 exam in the 1960s as a pass/fail pre-clinical licensing exam, however, its current structure as we know it came to be in the 1990s. Typically taken by students between their preclinical and clinical years, the exam is a broad assessment of whether medical students can apply important concepts of the basic sciences to the practice of medicine with special emphasis on principles and mechanisms underlying health, disease, and modes of therapy. For state licensure, the exam is pass/fail, however, residency programs often utilize the scaled score as a surrogate for clinical aptitude, and thus resident selection, despite no direct correlation to clinical competence [6]. As a result, the USMLE Step 1 exam has become a high-stakes exam for all medical students, but especially for those wishing to pursue competitive specialties.

Students push themselves to their limit in studying for this exam, often sacrificing their psychological and physical wellbeing and, as such, many unintended consequences can be found in the residency application and selection processes, workforce disparities, and overall student wellbeing. For one, the cost of the exam is $630 and in addition, many students rely on expensive commercial resources to prepare for this examination thus placing an additional financial burden on students [7, 8]. With over 50% of medical students who graduated in 2018 having more than $150,000 dollars in educational debt, this all adds up [3]. Second, due to the added pressure of Step 1 preparation, many students opt to disengage with their institution's curricula in favor of intensive test preparation [8]. As a result, students work to memorize high-yield facts and associations, often at the expense of learning how to develop a differential diagnosis and hone their clinical decision making. On top of this, underrepresented minorities and those with less parental income on average have lower Step 1 scores, which can limit their number of residency interview offers [9]. At one institution, students were provided with 18-months of access to a commercial question bank for Step 1 preparation at no cost to the students. They found that students' utilization of the question bank was significantly associated with their performance on Step 1, and this was even more profound for students with lower Medical College Admission Test (MCAT) scores [10]. At another institution, in the months leading up to their Step 1 exam, students were provided with more intensive emotional and educational support [11].

Despite calls by students, advisors, and medical school leaders to deemphasize Step 1 by removing the numeric score, this will likely not take place due to increasing number of residency applicants for a finite number of positions and increasing pressures on programs to systematically select applicants to interview [8]. This costly endeavor requires a screening mechanism and with many medical schools having migrated their course grading systems to pass/fail, the surrogate assessment of medical knowledge remains Step 1. Mindful of the stresses and anxieties surrounding this exam, most medical schools have made changes to the preclinical years to accommodate. Resilience training in various forms have been created and integrated into medical school curricula, however little change in measurable quality of life has resulted [12]. Others have implemented additional avenues to address this 'Step 1 climate' with concrete changes in the pre-clerkship years [11]. These include: (1) all courses to be pass/fail, (2) shortening the pre-clerkship course content and time to allow more time to study for Step 1, and (3) shorten the course hours per day and days per week. While unique to each individual medical school, the preclinical learning environment and "Step 1 climate," are significant stressors to students. As a result, the pre-clerkship curriculum should be diligently assessed via a thorough program evaluation and with all key stakeholders, including students, taking part in creating solutions to be implemented.

15.4 The Impact of Clinical Rotations on Wellbeing

As medical students transition from the classroom to the bedside, from a student-centered to a patient-centered learning environment, their roles rapidly evolve. Additionally, as students embark on their clerkship journey, the protective effect of belonging to a medical student cohort diminishes [13–16]. By immersing themselves in patient care, clinical rotations are the cornerstone of a medical student's education. The knowledge they spend countless hours acquiring in their preclinical years is brought to the bedside in order to integrate their basic science knowledge, clinical knowledge, professionalism, communication and teamwork skills. While this transition is essential to becoming a physician, the clinical learning environment will inevitably contain many unexpected and urgent patient situations, long shifts, working weekends and holidays, and taking call, all setting the stage for stress, anxiety, and sometimes mistreatment. The increasingly complex patients, systems in which we practice, and teams in medicine have made becoming a physician in the 1.5 to 2 years of the clerkship program daunting. Advanced practice providers, students from other schools at the same clerkship sites, and observers make the clinical learning environment crowded and often unnecessarily competitive. Life for students is still happening and how family and friends fit into the lives of highly intellectual and hardworking focused students learning the ropes of being a caring competent physician often goes neglected. Unfortunately, students come face-to-face with a culture of medicine in which mistreatment is a common occurrence and even culturally acceptable facet of clinical training.

15.4.1 Mistreatment and Wellbeing

Medical student mistreatment has been shown to have deleterious effects such as increased rates of burnout, symptoms of post-traumatic stress, depressive symptoms, drinking for escape, and decreased confidence in clinical skills. As of 2018, 98% of medical students were aware of the mistreatment policies at their relative institutions; however, mistreatment remains underreported [3]. The most common reason for non-reporting was student perception that the incident was not important enough to report (57.4%), they did not think anything would be done about it (38.3%), or they fear reprisal (27.2%) [3]. As a result of the increasing prevalence of mistreatment, there have been a number of programs implemented aimed to both increase reporting and reduce mistreatment [17]. Unfortunately, many programs limit their definition of mistreatment to explicit actions (i.e. verbal and physical abuse, sexual harassment, etc.) like those put forth by the AAMC and the Liaison Committee on Medical Education (LCME); and as such these definitions fail to capture behaviors that fall outside these official definitions (i.e. neglect, failure to teach, etc.). Also, it has been found that the definition of mistreatment utilized by students varies by student role and student career choice, suggesting that the perception of mistreatment is far more nuanced and unlikely to be fully captured by institutional or organizational definitions [18–20].

15.4.2 Defining Mistreatment

The first step to ensuring medical student well-being on clerkships is to understand how students define mistreatment within the clinical learning environment. A study looking to define what mistreatment meant to students collected individual student definitions from over 200 students [18]. They describe a conceptual framework for understanding medical student mistreatment based on the student's role within the clinical learning environment. Students' definitions of mistreatment centered around their three main roles on the medical team: individual, student-learner, and team member. The overarching themes regarding student definitions include: (1) *Obstruction of Learning* (student-learner role), (2) *Exploitation of Vulnerability* (individual role) and (3) *Exclusion from Medical Team* (team member role) (Fig. 15.1) [18]. Furthermore, a fourth theme, (4) *Contextual Amplifiers of Mistreatment*, emerged from student definitions, suggesting that there are factors that amplify or dampen the mistreatment behavior (Fig. 15.2) [18]. Faculty and institutions that wish to mitigate the effects of mistreatment on medical student well-being should ensure that these student-identified roles are acknowledged and validated.

Role	Student	Member of Medical Team	Individual
Goals	To learn • Educational opportunity • Participation in patient care	To be treated as member of the team • Social inclusion • Inclusion as member of patient care team	To be treated fairly and with respect • Appropriate interpersonal interactions
Mistreatment specific to role	Obstruction of learning	Exclusion from team	Exploitation of student vulnerability

Fig. 15.1 A conceptual framework describing the relationship between the three primary roles of the medical student within the clinical learning environment [18]

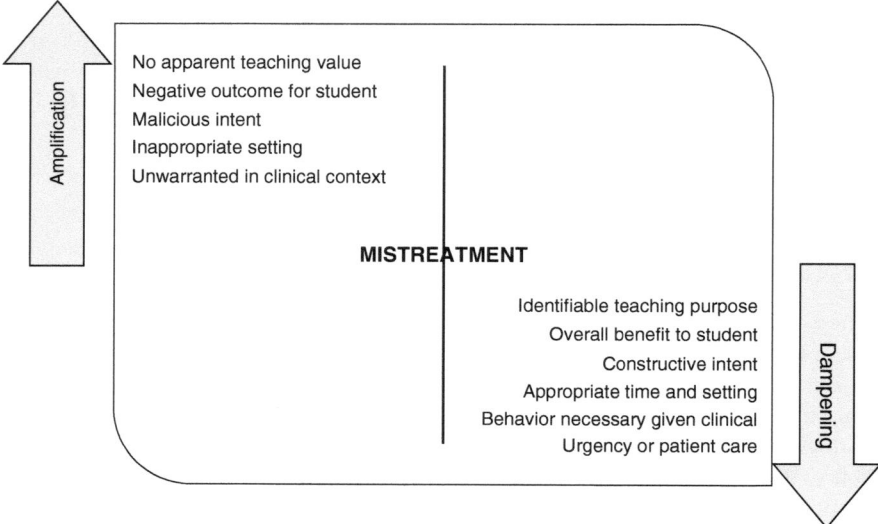

Fig. 15.2 A schematic to highlight the contextual modifiers of mistreatment based on student-generated definitions of mistreatment within the clinical learning environment [18]

15.4.3 Student-Centered Solutions

Not only should we focus on faculty and institutional interventions to improve medical student wellbeing, but we should encourage and empower medical students within the clinical learning environment. For certain clinical rotations, such as obstetrics and gynecology and surgery, the reported rates of student mistreatment are particularly high. In order to address this problem, a longitudinal mistreatment program was implemented on the surgery clerkship at a single institution [21]. This student-centric program had three core objectives: (1) To discuss preconceived expectations and concerns regarding the surgical culture; (2) To generate a student-driven definition of mistreatment; and (3) To inform students of available resources (informal and formal) to report and address mistreatment [21]. This program was well received by students as it provided them with an opportunity to define what mistreatment meant to them, a safe environment for them to discuss the learning environment, and staff to support and advocate for them [22]. As a result of this intervention, the surgery clerkship continues to see a decrease in the number of formal mistreatment reports 5 years after its implementation [21, 23].

A mistreatment program such as this has the potential to create long-term improvement in the clinical learning environment from the bottom up. Importantly, this student-centric program is facilitated by the Clerkship Director and Surgical Education Fellows—people who have the authority to make changes in the student's learning environment. As with any discussion regarding the clinical learning environment, it should stress the importance of setting bidirectional expectations between the student and faculty, address real-time conflict resolution, and create an environment of psychological safety. While this program reduced the number of mistreatment reports, it does not address the harm caused by mistreatment [23]. As a means to address this harm, restorative justice has been proposed as a possible solution. Restorative justice brings together the individuals involved in a mistreatment event in order to have a collaborative discussion [24]. The purpose is for the offender to accept responsibility, potentially find a way to repair the harm that was caused, and work to prevent future offenses [24].

Medical students learn and work in a wider context of our medical systems and clerkship leaders play a critical role in combating mistreatment. In order to address mistreatment, clerkship directors should: (1) Recognize that medical student mistreatment is pervasive and prevalent; (2) Accept a broader definition of mistreatment as defined by medical students; (3) Identify medical student advocates among faculty, residents, and fellows and; (4) Provide safe reporting methods for students without fear of reprisal. There must be action to address this increasingly ubiquitous and stressful environment that if unchecked can lead to broad and dangerous consequences for the students. We see this most seriously in the very high suicide and alcoholism rate for medical students [25].

Overall, a formal program in schools of medicine must be strengthened by initiatives in all the core clerkship departments. A culture change towards mindful teaching and reflection with mentorship espoused by the faculty, residents, and advanced practice providers must be fostered. Each core clerkship, sub-internship, and clinical elective must be formed around attention to the clinical learning environment. Utilizing all of these strategies, in whole or in part, may be meaningfully incorporated into the clinical learning environment as a means to address this important issue, and its implications for future generations of physicians. Ultimately, it is recognizing the student within the context of a constantly changing social, professional, and clinical environment that will allow us to design, implement, and evaluate a system that cares comprehensively for our future physicians and therefore ultimately our patients.

15.5 The Impact of Residency Applications on Wellbeing

Entry into the fourth year of medical school denotes the beginning of a powerful transition in the medical education journey. As students wind down their third year of medical school, they are simultaneously gearing up for applying to residency. The fourth year of medical school usually proceeds in three distinct phases. The first phase involves the student utilizing the Electronic Residency Application Service (ERAS) in order to generate a residency application and apply to programs. The second phase involves interview invites and interview acceptances. In this phase, students are obligated to travel to graduate medical education (GME) programs in order to interview. Finally, the third phase involves students and programs creating rank-ordered preference lists which then, through a computer algorithm, "matches" a student with a program. Since the 1950s, "the Match," or the National Resident Matching Program (NRMP) has dictated where medical students will spend their years in residency.

Today's match looks very different than the 1950s, as applicants far outnumber residency positions, the cost of applications and residency interviews have skyrocketed, we face an ongoing physician shortage, and for some specialties, the competition has grown fierce. For U.S. allopathic medical school graduates, those who successfully match into residency on average have higher Step 1 and Step 2 scores, higher mean number of research experiences, higher number of works of scholarship, and a higher number of contiguous ranks [26]. Since 2002 the average length of rank order lists have been increasing, yet the percentage of matched students is unchanged [26]. This means that students are applying, interviewing, and ranking more programs, but in 2018, 63.5% of U.S. seniors matched to their first or second ranked program [26].

The financial stresses of applying to residency are not to be taken lightly. Residency applicants are spending anywhere from $5000–10,000 in application fees and travel alone [27–29]. On top of the stress of residency applications, students must take and pass USMLE Step 2 prior to graduation. The Step 2 exam is made up of two parts, a Clinical Knowledge (CK) portion and the Clinical Skills (CS) portion. For both CK and CS, students spend nearly $2000 just for registration fees [7]. Additionally, the CS portion is held in select U.S. cities and thus many students have to incur additional travel and lodging fees in order to take the exam. Historically, Step 2 has not been as high-stakes of an exam as Step 1; however, programs are increasingly using the CK score not only as an application requirement but to rank applicants as well [30].

This combination of financial stress, another USMLE exam, and residency selection can make the final year of medical school one of the most stressful for students.

15.6 Student Support Instead of Remediation

Competency-based medical education (CBME) is currently being rolled out in undergraduate medical education. As a result, in 2014, the AAMC released 13 Core Entrustable Professional Activities (EPAs) for Entering Residency. The EPAs have been developed to guide medical schools to a fundamental set of observable skills thought to be necessary for entering interns and residents. Despite this move towards competencies, medical schools largely still have in place course exams and intermittent skills checks that fall far behind the intent of this paradigm [31]. Failure of these tests require remediation. Among the highly accomplished and select group that make up medical school students, this can cause anxiety in the 'failure to fail' environment [32].

Overall, the goal of medical schools is to train competent students who are prepared to enter residency, and this includes teaching students the clinical skills to care for patients. Most schools have a method in which to assess the clinical skills of students typically in their preclinical years prior to transitioning to clerkships and again prior to transitioning into residency. A summative assessment utilizing standardized patients and clinical case vignettes culminates the practice of medicine portion of the preclinical curriculum. The aim of this assessment is to discern those students who are ready for clerkship education from those who may need remediation prior to beginning clerkships. Many propose a thoughtful, individual, and comprehensive approach to student support instead of short bursts of remediation [31, 33].

Interestingly, frequent assessments have been suggested as a way to create wellness. Many participants cited individual faculty attention as a major strength of their remediation programmes. This observation is consistent with literature showing that remedial education has the greatest impact on the learner when it is individualized, highly interactive, and delivered in a meaningful context [34].

Coordinated student support contributes to medical student wellness since the intake is not through an acute remediation lens. The intake must take into account the student in the context of them as an individual, a member of a team, and as a student [18]. Counseling resources and cognitive testing may be considered in addressing wellbeing, clinical skills, professionalism, or a medical knowledge gap. In this way, the student can best be helped by tailoring their support program to their individual needs. Ideally, this would serve to improve their current state of wellness, but more importantly, reinvigorate enthusiasm and engagement in our profession that would contribute to their overarching success as a compassionate physician. Lastly, if engagement and fulfillment are lacking, then any intervention may first need to address if being a physician is the right career pathway for the struggling student. Allowing off-ramps at times of support may be able to redirect students to other fields, medical or unrelated, that would both contribute to humankind but also engage and fulfill the student [32].

15.7 Concluding Remarks

Positive psychological wellbeing is a critical aspect in becoming a physician and is an important predictor of medical student success, resilience, and personal fulfillment. A negative educational learning environment is a key source of anxiety, burnout, attrition, and frustration for medical students and directly threatens their wellbeing. Whether it be the challenges in the pre-clerkship realm with the looming USMLE Step 1 or the clerkship years with the communication mismatches that manifest in student mistreatment, changes in the educational environment are also where we can make the most impact. Structural changes likely best address the pre-clerkship simultaneous curricula of foundational science, clinical performance, and Step 1. Expectation setting, reflection, communication, and reframing may alleviate the transition to clinical clerkship training. Individualized, interactive, and evolving support throughout medical school is more effective at sustaining engagement than standard remediation of failed courses and high stakes competency assessments. This support could also assist in allowing off-ramps for mindful student life goal reassessment and possible realignment within the context of individual wellbeing [32]. Together we must all take into account and understand the experiences of our medical students within the context of them as an individual and as one who is deeply and intimately woven into our clinical learning environments. We must hesitate to make assumptions about what is best for them, and instead incorporate them as a key stakeholder in their wellbeing. Ultimately, throughout their tenure we must remain committed to treating medical students with respect and compassion in order to ensure our next generation of physicians can continuously find meaning in their work and thus deliver excellent care to our patients.

References

1. Zanardelli G, Sim W, Borges N, Roman B. Well-being in first year medical students. Acad Psychiatry. 2015;39:31–6.
2. Underrepresented in Medicine Definition—Initiatives—AAMC. https://www.aamc.org/initiatives/urm/. Accessed 31 Jan 2019.
3. Association of American Medical Colleges. Medical School Graduation Questionnaire 2018 All Schools Summary Report; 2018.
4. Wayne SJ, Fortner SA, Kitzes JA, Timm C, Kalishman S. Cause or effect? The relationship between student perception of the medical school learning environment and academic performance on USMLE step 1. Med Teach. 2013;35:376–80.
5. Nama N, MacPherson P, Sampson M, McMillan HJ. Medical students' perception of lesbian, gay, bisexual, and transgender (LGBT) discrimination in their learning environment and their self-reported comfort level for caring for LGBT patients: a survey study. Med Educ Online. 2017;22:1368850.
6. McGaghie WC, Cohen ER, Wayne DB. Are United States medical licensing exam step 1 and 2 scores valid measures for postgraduate medical residency selection decisions? Acad Med. 2011;86:48–52.
7. NBME USMLE Exam Fees | NBME. https://www.nbme.org/students/examfees.html. Accessed 30 Jan 2019.
8. Chen DR, Priest KC, Batten JN, Fragoso LE, Reinfield BI, Laitman BM. Student perspectives on the "step 1 climate" in preclinical medical education. Acad Med. 2018;94:302–4. https://doi.org/10.1097/ACM.0000000000002565.
9. Orom H, Semalulu T, Underwood W 3rd. The social and learning environments experienced by underrepresented minority medical students: a narrative review. Acad Med. 2013;88:1765–77.
10. Baños JH, Pepin ME, Van Wagoner N. Class-wide access to a commercial step 1 question bank during preclinical organ-based modules: a pilot project. Acad Med. 2018;93:486–90.
11. Slavin S. Reflections on a decade leading a medical student well-being initiative. Acad Med. 2019;94(6):771–4. https://doi.org/10.1097/ACM.0000000000002540.
12. Dyrbye LN, Shanafelt TD, Werner L, Sood A, Satele D, Wolanskyj AP. The impact of a required longitudinal stress management and resilience training course for first-year medical students. J Gen Intern Med. 2017;32:1309–14.
13. O'Brien B, Cooke M, Irby DM. Perceptions and attributions of third-year student struggles in clerkships: do students and clerkship directors agree? Acad Med. 2007;82:970–8.
14. Radcliffe C, Lester H. Perceived stress during undergraduate medical training: a qualitative study. Med Educ. 2003;37:32–8.
15. Mavor KI, McNeill KG, Anderson K, Kerr A, O'Reilly E, Platow MJ. Beyond prevalence to process: the role of self and identity in medical student well-being. Med Educ. 2014;48:351–60.
16. McNeill KG, Kerr A, Mavor KI. Identity and norms: the role of group membership in medical student wellbeing. Perspect Med Educ. 2014;3:101–12.

17. Mazer LM, Bereknyei Merrell S, Hasty BN, Stave C, Lau JN. Assessment of programs aimed to decrease or prevent mistreatment of medical trainees. JAMA Netw Open. 2018;1:e180870.
18. Brandford E, Hasty B, Bruce JS, Bereknyei Merrell S, Shipper ES, Lin DT, Lau JN. Underlying mechanisms of mistreatment in the surgical learning environment: a thematic analysis of medical student perceptions. Am J Surg. 2018;215:227–32.
19. Kemp MT, Smith M, Kizy S, Englesbe M, Reddy RM. Reported mistreatment during the surgery clerkship varies by student career choice. J Surg Educ. 2017;75:918–23. https://doi.org/10.1016/j.jsurg.2017.10.011.
20. Kulaylat AN, Qin D, Sun SX, Hollenbeak CS, Schubart JR, Aboud AJ, Flemming DJ, Dillon PW, Bollard ER, Han DC. Perceptions of mistreatment among trainees vary at different stages of clinical training. BMC Med Educ. 2017;17:14.
21. Mazer LM, Liebert CA, Bereknyei Merrell S, Lin D, Lau JN. Establishing a positive clinical learning environment in the surgery core clerkship: a video-based mistreatment curriculum. Washington, DC: MedEdPORTAL Publications; 2015.
22. Hasty BN, Miller SE, Berekynei Merrell S, Lin DT, Shipper ES, Lau JNB. Medical student perceptions of a mistreatment program in the surgery clerkship. Am J Surg. 2018;215(4):761–6.
23. Lau JN, Mazer LM, Liebert CA, Merrell SB, Lin DT, Harris I. A mixed-methods analysis of a novel mistreatment program for the surgery core clerkship. Acad Med. 2017;92:1028–34. https://doi.org/10.1097/ACM.0000000000001575.
24. Acosta D, Karp DR. Restorative justice as the Rx for mistreatment in academic medicine: applications to consider for learners, faculty, and staff. Acad Med. 2017;93:354–6. https://doi.org/10.1097/ACM.0000000000002037.
25. Jackson ER, Shanafelt TD, Hasan O, Satele DV, Dyrbye LN. Burnout and alcohol abuse/dependence among U.S. medical students. Acad Med. 2016;91:1251–6.
26. National Resident Matching Program. Results and data: 2018 Main Residency Match®. Washington, DC; 2018.
27. Camp CL, Sousa PL, Hanssen AD, Karam MD, Haidukewych GJ, Oakes DA, Turner NS. The cost of getting into orthopedic residency: analysis of applicant demographics, expenditures, and the value of away rotations. J Surg Educ. 2016;73:886–91.
28. Nikonow TN, Lyon TD, Jackman SV, Averch TD. Survey of applicant experience and cost in the urology match: opportunities for reform. J Urol. 2015;194:1063–7.
29. Agarwal N, Choi PA, Okonkwo DO, Barrow DL, Friedlander RM. Financial burden associated with the residency match in neurological surgery. J Neurosurg. 2017;126:184–90.
30. Green M, Jones P, Thomas JX Jr. Selection criteria for residency: results of a national program directors survey. Acad Med. 2009;84:362–7.
31. Ellaway RH, Chou CL, Kalet AL. Situating remediation: accommodating success and failure in medical education systems. Acad Med. 2018;93:391–8.
32. Bellini LM, Kalet A, Englander R. Providing compassionate off-ramps for medical students is a moral imperative. Acad Med. 2018;94:656–8. https://doi.org/10.1097/ACM.0000000000002568.
33. Hauer KE, Teherani A, Irby DM, Kerr KM, O'Sullivan PS. Approaches to medical student remediation after a comprehensive clinical skills examination. Med Educ. 2008;42:104–12.
34. Ishak W, Nikravesh R, Lederer S, Perry R, Ogunyemi D, Bernstein C. Burnout in medical students: a systematic review. Clin Teach. 2013;10:242–5.

Chapter 16
Wellbeing Consideration for Residents

Christina Cellini and Lauren Decaporale-Ryan

16.1 Introduction

Burnout in graduate medical education is a topic of recent and increasing interest. Several calls to action of late regarding resident wellbeing have been published highlighting the timeliness of this topic [1–3]. Percentages of burnout in medical students and residents are higher when compared to age-matched populations. A systematic review found a 29% rate of depression and/or depressive symptoms among resident physicians across studies, ranging from 21 to 43%, with similar or higher rates reported in other studies [4–7]. Attending surgeons appear to report similar rates of depression and burnout. In a study by the fellows of the American College of Surgeons (ACS), 40% of surgeons experienced burnout, 30% screened positive for depression and mental quality of life scores were below those reported for the population norm [8].

Burnout may change over the course of a training period/career and vary among specialties [7, 9, 10]. The implications of surgeon burnout include association with self-reported medical errors and patient safety concerns [11, 12]. As important as patient safety is, the impact of burnout to one's self deserves attention. A survey of ACGME residents conducted between 2000 and 2014 reported that after neoplastic malignancies, suicide was the second cause of death with suicide rates higher in early training [13]. Particularly in females, the risk of suicide is higher for doctors than in the general population [14]. The highlighting of resident suicides in the news and blogosphere as well as institutional experiences with resident suicide in programs around the country has led to increased scrutiny of resident training in terms of understanding burnout and preparation for a healthy life as a practicing surgeon.

C. Cellini (✉)
Department of Surgery, University of Rochester, Rochester, NY, USA
e-mail: christina_cellini@urmc.rochester.edu

L. Decaporale-Ryan
Departments of Psychiatry, Medicine and Surgery, University of Rochester, Rochester, NY, USA

© Springer Nature Switzerland AG 2020
E. Kim, B. Lindeman (eds.), *Wellbeing*, Success in Academic Surgery,
https://doi.org/10.1007/978-3-030-29470-0_16

16.2   Life of a Surgery Resident

The transition from medical school to residency is intense. No matter how difficult medical school is perceived to be by the student, it does not compare to the intense experience of residency. Medical school, to a great degree, offers a level of protection and control with built-in weeks for vacation, studying and choice in terms of clinical rotations and electives. Surgery residents now must transition from 4 years of anticipated schedules to 5 years of occupational stressors that include excessive workload, lack of control and poor balance between reward and effort [15]. Spouses and significant others of surgical residents may also be affected with similar rates of burnout and psychological distress [16].

The hidden curriculum of medicine refers to the set of influences that function at the level of organizational structure and culture. These may include understandings, cultures and rituals, taken-for-granted aspects, fundamental values, and "rules of the road" [17]. The notions of altruism, being the consummate workaholic, perfectionism, and obedience to authority are some of these cultural elements that discourage physicians from seeking self-care. While these broad areas of the hidden curriculum can be found across all medical specialties, the specific culture of surgery may harbor different or more intense feelings.

Some would say surgery has a distinct culture compared to other specialties. Surgery can be a polarizing rotation for medical students, eliciting a "love it or hate it" reaction [18]. In one study students rotating on a surgery clerkship perceived a clear surgery-specific hidden curriculum which, if unable to navigate, was found to exclude many from pursuing a surgical career [19]. Stereotypes of surgeons persist which include competitiveness, masculinity, requiring sacrifice, self-confidence, intimidation and having a poor work-life balance [20, 21]. Implications for surgical resident eduation may be a result of generational differences between the current medical student body and surgical faculty. The goals and expectations of today's graduating students differ from previous generations in many aspects of training. Absence of hierarchy, being less willing to sacrifice lifestyle and family time, and expectations of leisure time are such aspects to which younger generations of surgeons relate [22]. These generational differences may cause conflict when trainees need to seek help but feel like more senior faculty will not approve. The hidden curriculum of surgery puts this at odds with these expectations and may lead to or exacerbate the current issues with resident burnout.

16.3   Burnout and Wellness in Residency

It has been shown that compared to medical school, burnout rates rise once in residency. A 2014 large national study by Dyrbe et al. states that the peak time for distress in physicians in all specialty fields appears to be in residency/fellowship [7]. A systematic review by Pulcrano et al. found that across surgical specialties, surgery residents are at increased risk for burnout and tend to report a lower quality of life compared to attending surgeons [9]. Lebares et al. found that high levels of burnout, severe stress, and distress symptoms are experienced throughout general surgery training, with some improvement during lab years [23]. In this cross-sectional study, trainees with burnout and high stress were at increased risk for depression and suicidal ideation. Higher dispositional mindfulness was associated with lower risk of burnout, severe stress, and distress symptoms, supporting the potential of mindfulness training to promote resilience during surgery residency.

Other studies looking at surgery residents report similar concerns. In a survey study of PGY 2 residents, training in general surgery (in addition to urology, neurology and emergency medicine) was significantly associated with a higher relative risk (compared with internal medicine) of reporting symptoms of burnout [10]. Also in this study, career choice and specialty choice regret were reported by 19% and 17.1% of surgery residents respectively (RR 1.6 compared with internal medicine). In a similar study of surgery residents from two programs, burnout was found to have a direct relationship with both emotional intelligence and positive work experiences such as autonomy, social support, meaningful feedback, and opportunities for professional development, suggesting multiple potential areas for intervention [24]. In a study looking at six North Carolina surgery programs, prevalence of burnout in residents was 75% [25]. Forty percent were at risk for moderate-severe depression while 12% of residents reported suicidal ideation just prior to taking the survey. A concerning aspect was the finding that prevalence of burnout and depression was underestimated by both residents and attendings.

A cross-sectional national survey of surgery residents by Jackson et al. reported that bullying and overwhelming work responsibilities were reported as the most frequently existing stressors which accounted for high subsequent rates of post-traumatic stress disorder (PTSD) in surgical residents [26]. In this survey 22% of surgical residents responded screening positive for PTSD; 35% of residents were identified as at-risk for PTSD. Residents who screened positive for PTSD and at-risk for PTSD also were found to have an increased likelihood of screening high across all burnout components (emotional exhaustion, depersonalization, reduced personal accomplishment). This study's findings suggest a high degree of overlap between the risk of burnout and PTSD.

In a survey looking at utilization of duty hours, female surgery residents were found to work more hours and have less time off between shifts [27]. Unhappiness, depression and feelings of worthlessness were reported more often by female residents. On qualitative analysis, themes such as lack of female mentorship/leadership, challenges from hospital staff, patients and program culture emerged as contributors to these findings. As such, there may be value in approaching wellness interventions with gender in mind.

The ACGME has recognized trainee wellbeing as an important issue. In 2015, the ACGME Council of Review Committee Residents (CRCR), a 29-member multispecialty group of residents and fellows, conducted an appreciative inquiry exercise to define resident wellbeing. From these discussions, consensus themes in regards to improving the learning environment, addressing stress in residents, and providing systems to support wellbeing were identified [28]. More recently, the ACMGE released updated common program requirements that require every residency program to address physician wellbeing, burnout, self-care, and mental health issues [29]. Changes recommended by the ACGME and the CRCR include increasing awareness of the risk of depression during residency, creating confidential mechanisms through which to treat depression in trainees, developing formal peer/faculty mentoring programs, promoting a more supportive team-centered culture, and encouraging additional study of resident wellbeing with the aim of promoting better understanding and identifying best practices. The ACGME has established the Clinical Learning Environment Review Program (CLER) as a means to promote discussions and actions that will optimize the clinical learning environment [30]. The program provides feedback to ACGME-accredited institutions bi-annually in six areas—one of which is the wellbeing. Originally called "Duty Hours, Fatigue Management, and Mitigation", the focus of Wellbeing has evolved to address "work/life balance, fatigue, burnout, and support of those at risk of or demonstrating self-harm". This new area "recognizes the important role of clinical learning environments in designing and implementing systems that monitor and support the wellbeing of residents, fellows, faculty members, and other members of the clinical care team" [31]. A challenge to these expectations is that individual institutions have limited/varying resources and time within already packed educational schedules, leaving each program to develop and institute its own interpretation of these recommendations. Some institutions, including the University of Alabama at Birmingham and Johns Hopkins, have identified a need for institutional oversight of these issues by creating an Associate Designated Institutional Official focused on maintaining and enhancing the clinical learning environment.

16.4   What to Do from Here?

Burned out residents become burned out attendings which has implications for ongoing healthcare quality, access and cost, patient satisfaction, reduced productivity, increased job turnover, and earlier retirement [12, 32]. The business case for addressing burnout, therefore, should start in training. Numerous published studies have examined addressing burnout and improving physician wellness. Studies vary from personal interventions to organizational approaches, but many agree both are necessary for effective change [15, 33–35]. A study by Balch et al. identifies specific measures surgeons can take to decrease burnout and improve their personal and professional quality of life, such as placing greater emphasis on finding meaning in work, focusing on what is important in life, maintaining a positive outlook and embracing a philosophy of work/life balance [36]. Surgeons who reported taking these measures were significantly less likely to be burned out (all p < 0.0001). Goldman et al. propose a framework to combine organizational and individual factors to address the ACGME common program requirements [37]. However, they also acknowledge that competing financial strains and institutional and educational regulatory requirements challenge even the most dedicated of wellness champions in terms of the best way to implement the specific measures they suggest.

When thinking about addressing the issue of burnout in surgical trainees, many first tend to direct their attention to regulations regarding work hours. Work hour regulations were put into place to address patient safety issues, not resident burnout. Even so, conflicting results are found in studies looking at work hours and association with medical errors [38]. In a 2015 review the authors found that focusing on duty hours alone has not resulted in improvements in patient care or resident wellbeing [39]. In the Flexibility in Duty Hour Requirements for Surgical Trainees (FIRST) Trial which compared standard duty-hour policies with flexible, less-restrictive duty-hour policies for surgical residents, there was a trend favoring standard policies with respect to outcomes related to perceptions of personal time and resident satisfaction; however overall wellbeing did not differ significantly between study groups [40]. More recently in a study by Mendelsohn et al., activity trackers were used to measure sleep and activity in residents [41]. Of those studied, surgical residents worked the most hours per week and obtained fewer hours of sleep per day, however, there was no correlation between work hours and average daily sleep with burnout or wellbeing.

Perspectives of residents and program directors may differ when it comes to the topic of burnout and the priority of a wellness component to the educational curriculum within a training program. A survey in obstetrics and gynecology programs revealed discrepancies between the perspectives that residents and program directors (PDs) have on resident wellbeing and its priority within the training program [42]. While most PDs felt wellbeing programming was a priority, 10% of residents felt it should not be a priority. In a subsequent survey of obstetrics and gynecology residents, residents who responded that wellbeing was not a priority in their program were more likely to report wellbeing issues and burnout (p < 0.001) [43]. In internal medicine, residents reported that they would be more likely to seek help if their PDs inquired, recommended and/or facilitated help needed [44]. In ophthalmology a quarter of PDs reported resident issues with burnout and depression with 45% reporting the presence of a department wellness program [45]. Respondents without wellness programs reported a shortage of time (19/30; 63%) and lack of training and resources (19/30; 63%) as barriers to instituting these programs. From an ophthalmology resident perspective, 68% of residents reported that their program faced issues with resident burnout/depression, 45.6% reported that their residency programs placed moderate or major emphasis on resident wellbeing, and 26.7% reported that their department had a formal resident wellness program [46]. Finally, in a multispecialty survey of residents and PDs at a tertiary academic center, 69% of residents met criteria for burnout; however, 92% of PDs estimated burnout to be 49% or less [47]. Specifically, in general surgery and surgical subspecialties burnout was 89% and 82% respectively.

It is clear that there are high levels of resident burnout in surgery and that the majority of PDs and residents think addressing burnout is important. The importance of addressing burnout in residency also has more direct implications in terms of resident performance. Interestingly, in a study of general surgery chief residents and PDs reporting what should be included in a non-clinical curriculum, most topics were concordant except for management of burnout [48]. Almost 70% of PDs would include a lesson plan addressing the management of burnout compared with 30% of chief residents ($p < 0.0001$). While it is possible that many residents would find education on preventing burnout less important than other educational topics, there are many reasons why they should reconsider. For example, lower burnout scores are associated with better performance on the ABSITE, which for better or worse has implications for the fellowship match and board pass rates [49]. In addition, as with faculty, rates of burnout in general surgery residents are concerning in terms of the potential impact on quality of patient care. Major medical errors reported by surgeons are strongly related to a surgeon's degree of burnout and their mental QOL [11]. Higher degrees of burnout have been associated with negative patient care attitudes and behaviors, medication errors, and self-reported sub-optimal patient care by resident physicians [50, 51].

The burning question on everyone's mind is *how* resident burnout can best be addressed. Formal implementation of resident wellness curricula in the literature are few; however, many approaches to a structured program have been described in a variety of specialties [52–57]. The most comprehensive approaches to wellness curricula encompass both organizational and individual strategies to improving wellbeing. Few studies in the surgical literature describe structured wellness programs in general surgery training. At the University of Arizona, Riall et al. report their results with implementation of wellness program called The Energy Leadership Wellbeing and Resiliency Program [58]. This consisted of a year-long curriculum based on an executive coaching model called Energy Leadership [59]. This framework is based around self-awareness, mindfulness and emotional intelligence. Sessions throughout the year consisted of topics related to team building, communication, goal-setting, diet, ergonomics, mindfulness, among others. Healthy behavior was encouraged through challenges constructed to improve health and increase activity. Perceived stress scale, Maslach burnout inventory, Energy Leadership Index, Beck Depression inventory and the ACGME resident survey were used to assess residents on all these domains. Overall scores were improved compared from prior to implementation of the curriculum. Residents' reported level of satisfaction in leadership skills/communication skills, time management skills as well as other domains increased during the intervention, although was this not statistically significant. Positive perceptions of the program also increased from 80% to 96% on the annual ACGME resident survey.

At Stanford University, a resident wellness program called Balance in Life was initiated in 2011 [60]. The goal of the program was to improve resident wellness and work-life balance in the context of the stressful surgical training environment. This program addressed 4 components of resident wellbeing: physical, psychological, professional, and social. Program elements included a fully stocked refrigerator in the surgical workroom with a variety of healthy snacks to encourage healthy eating, regularly scheduled confidential group meetings with an experienced psychologist, mentorship and leadership training and organized social events. Residents were surveyed regarding utilization, barriers to use, and perceived value of the program components. Overall while there was no change in wellbeing or burnout after program implementation, residents' perception of the program was that it was feasible, highly valued, and positively viewed.

At the University of Rochester, a comprehensive resident wellness program was started in 2014. Like others, our program incorporates both organizational and individual components. Organizational aspects of the program include the explicit dedication of leadership to a culture of wellbeing in the department of surgery, appointment of a clinical psychologist as the associate program director for wellness, a structured resident wellness monthly curriculum, a yearly resident wellness retreat, and an annual 2-day leadership retreat and leadership training for rising chiefs. The yearly resident wellness retreat has been held since 2015 and residents are given the day free of clinical responsibilities and activities are held off-site. The day includes nationally recognized speakers on the topics of wellness and burnout, followed by several breakout sessions focused on topics of interest identified by residents (e.g., subjects connected to personal and/or professional development), a wellness fair with community resources (dental practices, behavioral health clinicians, meal delivery services) and free massages and pet therapy followed by an afternoon of resident-selected facilitated group activities (e.g., cooking class, art class, softball). One hundred percent of survey respondents indicated that the wellness day, especially the fair, should be hosted again, with 50% reporting direct moderate benefit to their wellbeing and 10% reporting extreme benefit. Departmental dedication to resident wellness includes protected time off for health maintenance appointments, including primary care, dental, ophthalmology, and behavioral health care. Residents are provided with contact information for on-site primary care physicians taking new patients and are given time off from clinical duties to attend these appointments. Allocation of funds was made for healthy snacks in the resident call room as well as social functions for residents and their families. Families are also "on-boarded" by participating in an orientation to residency life that includes information regarding the signs and symptoms of burnout and depression so that they have some of the tools to help support their loved ones during this highly stressful time, even from afar. Finally, the department identified space in proximity to the operating rooms to designate as lactation quarters. The associate program director for wellness is a clinical psychologist who is embedded in the department of surgery. Responsibilities of this person include: one-to-one communication, coaching, and leadership training; program development and strategic planning for annual wellness events; negotiation of contracts with local services for reduced fees (e.g., healthy meal delivery to residents); consultation for residents and faculty regarding improved team-based communication; support following a critical incident; consultation and referral for residents and faculty to community and University-based programming for behavioral health concerns; and consultation to the Clinical Competency Committee regarding the relationship between wellbeing/burnout and professionalism, communication, and technical skills. The one-to-one communication program is offered to support physicians in their delivery of care to patients in inpatient and outpatient settings, and the operating room. It is intended to improve patient and family satisfaction, as well as clinician satisfaction through emphasis on communication skills, professionalism, capacity to work on a team, time management and efficiency, and leadership skills. To address the individual components of wellness, a year-long wellness curriculum was developed, introduced and implemented by the author (Cellini) https://www.sciencedirect.com/science/article/pii/S1072751518318659?vi a%3Dihub. One hour sessions were held monthly during residents' protected education time to cover a variety of wellbeing-related topics including electronic medical record optimization, nutrition, ergonomics, sleep hygiene, mindfulness, finances, dealing with difficult people as well as processing sessions that included discussions centered around difficult clinical and personal scenarios. Residents were surveyed after each session and the Physician Well-being Index (PWBI) was administered on a quarterly basis [61]. Overall, our findings suggest that residents derived usefulness from the explored topics. Though preliminary, PWBI scores and qualitative feedback suggest that this curriculum is helping to change departmental culture and shows a trend towards improving resident wellbeing. We expect to publish our results in the upcoming year with the hope to create a sustainable curriculum that can be studied over time and expanded across other surgical specialties.

16.5 Conclusion

Residency training is a difficult and intense period in the lives of residents. The time is ripe to change the culture of the clinical learning environment to improving the health and wellbeing of our future physicians during their formative training years. The knowledge they gain and experiences they have during these years will shape their ability to handle the challenges to come. In doing so we hope they experience the practice of medicine as one where they can thrive and flourish, rather than merely survive.

References

1. Ripp JA, Privitera MR, West CP, Leiter R, Logio L, Shapiro J, et al. Well-being in graduate medical education: a call for action. Acad Med. 2017;92(7):914–7.
2. Salles A, Liebert CA, Greco RS. Promoting balance in the lives of resident physicians: a call to action. JAMA Surg. 2015;150(7):607–8.
3. Jennings ML, Slavin SJ. Resident wellness matters: optimizing resident education and wellness through the learning environment. Acad Med. 2015;90(9):1246–50.
4. Mata DA, Ramos MA, Bansal N, Khan R, Guille C, Di Angelantonio E, et al. Prevalence of depression and depressive symptoms among resident physicians: a systematic review and meta-analysis. JAMA. 2015;314(22):2373–83.
5. Lin DT, Liebert CA, Esquivel MM, Tran J, Lau JN, Greco RS, et al. Prevalence and predictors of depression among general surgery residents. Am J Surg. 2017;213(2):313–7.
6. Elmore LC, Jeffe DB, Jin L, Awad MM, Turnbull IR. National survey of burnout among US general surgery residents. J Am Coll Surg. 2016;223(3):440–51.
7. Dyrbye LN, West CP, Satele D, Boone S, Tan L, Sloan J, et al. Burnout among U.S. medical students, residents, and early career physicians relative to the general U.S. population. Acad Med. 2014;89(3):443–51.
8. Shanafelt TD, Balch CM, Bechamps GJ, Russell T, Dyrbye L, Satele D, et al. Burnout and career satisfaction among American surgeons. Ann Surg. 2009;250(3):463–71.

9. Pulcrano M, Evans SR, Sosin M. Quality of life and burnout rates across surgical specialties: a systematic review. JAMA Surg. 2016;151(10):970–8.
10. Dyrbye LN, Burke SE, Hardeman RR, Herrin J, Wittlin NM, Yeazel M, et al. Association of clinical specialty with symptoms of burnout and career choice regret among US resident physicians. JAMA. 2018;320(11):1114–30.
11. Shanafelt TD, Balch CM, Bechamps G, Russell T, Dyrbye L, Satele D, et al. Burnout and medical errors among American surgeons. Ann Surg. 2010;251(6):995–1000.
12. Dewa CS, Loong D, Bonato S, Trojanowski L, Rea M. The relationship between resident burnout and safety-related and acceptability-related quality of healthcare: a systematic literature review. BMC Med Educ. 2017;17(1):195.
13. Yaghmour NA, Brigham TP, Richter T, Miller RS, Philibert I, Baldwin DC Jr, et al. Causes of death of residents in ACGME-accredited programs 2000 through 2014: implications for the learning environment. Acad Med. 2017;92(7):976–83.
14. Schernhammer ES, Colditz GA. Suicide rates among physicians: a quantitative and gender assessment (meta-analysis). Am J Psychiatry. 2004;161(12):2295–302.
15. Maslach C, Leiter MP. The truth about burnout: how organizations cause personal stress and what to do about it. New York: Wiley; 2008.
16. Sargent MC, Sotile W, Sotile MO, Rubash H, Barrack RL. Quality of life during orthopaedic training and academic practice: part 2: spouses and significant others. J Bone Joint Surg Am. 2012;94(19):e145(1-6).
17. Koo K. Student narratives and the hidden curriculum in the surgery clerkship. J Surg Educ. 2013;70(1):1.
18. Cleland J, Johnston PW, French FH, Needham G. Associations between medical school and career preferences in year 1 medical students in Scotland. Med Educ. 2012;46(5):473–84.
19. Hill E, Bowman K, Stalmeijer R, Hart J. You've got to know the rules to play the game: how medical students negotiate the hidden curriculum of surgical careers. Med Educ. 2014;48(9):884–94.
20. Sanfey HA, Saalwachter-Schulman AR, Nyhof-Young JM, Eidelson B, Mann BD. Influences on medical student career choice: gender or generation? Arch Surg. 2006;141(11):1086–94; discussion 94
21. Hill EJR, Bowman KA, Stalmeijer RE, Solomon Y, Dornan T. Can I cut it? Medical students' perceptions of surgeons and surgical careers. Am J Surg. 2014;208(5):860–7.
22. J. W. Millennium Generation poses new implications for surgical resident education. Secondary Millennium Generation poses new implications for surgical resident education 2012. https://www.facs.org/education/division-of-education/publications/rise/articles/rap-archive/millennium-generation-poses-new-implications-for-surgical-resident-education.
23. Lebares CC, Guvva EV, Ascher NL, O'Sullivan PS, Harris HW, Epel ES. Burnout and stress among US surgery residents: psychological distress and resilience. J Am Coll Surg. 2018;226(1):80–90.
24. Lindeman B, Petrusa E, McKinley S, Hashimoto DA, Gee D, Smink DS, Mullen JT, Phitayakorn R. Association of burnout with emotional intelligence and personality in surgical residents: can we predict who is most at risk? J Surg Educ. 2017;74(6):e22–30.
25. Williford ML, Scarlet S, Meyers MO, Luckett DJ, Fine JP, Goettler CE, et al. Multiple-institution comparison of resident and faculty perceptions of burnout and depression during surgical training. JAMA Surg. 2018;153(8):705–11.
26. Jackson T, Provencio A, Bentley-Kumar K, Pearcy C, Cook T, McLean K, et al. PTSD and surgical residents: everybody hurts... Sometimes. Am J Surg. 2017;214(6):1118–24.
27. Dahlke AR, Johnson JK, Greenberg CC, Love R, Kreutzer L, Hewitt DB, et al. Gender differences in utilization of duty-hour regulations, aspects of burnout, and psychological Well-being among general surgery residents in the United States. Ann Surg. 2018;268(2):204–11.
28. Daskivich TJ, Jardine DA, Tseng J, Correa R, Stagg BC, Jacob KM, et al. Promotion of wellness and mental health awareness among physicians in training: perspective of a national, multispecialty panel of residents and fellows. J Grad Med Educ. 2015;7(1):143–7.
29. Accreditation Council for Graduate Medical Education 2017. 2019. https://www.acgme.org/Portals/0/PFAssets/ProgramRequirements/CPRs_2017-07-01.pdf.

30. Weiss KB, Bagian JP, Wagner R. CLER pathways to excellence: expectations for an optimal clinical learning environment (executive summary). J Grad Med Educ. 2014;6(3):610–1.
31. Education ACfGM. CLER pathways to excellence: expectations for an optimal clinical learning environment to achieve safe and high quality patient care, Version 1.1. https://www.acgme.org/Portals/0/PDFs/CLER/CLER_Pathways_V1.1_Digital_Final.pdf.
32. Bodenheimer T, Sinsky C. From triple to quadruple aim: care of the patient requires care of the provider. Ann Fam Med. 2014;12(6):573–6.
33. Wallace JE, Lemaire JB, Ghali WA. Physician wellness: a missing quality indicator. Lancet. 2009;374(9702):1714–21.
34. Shanafelt TD, Noseworthy JH. Executive leadership and physician well-being: nine organizational strategies to promote engagement and reduce burnout. Mayo Clin Proc. 2017;92(1):129–46.
35. Rothenberger DA. Physician burnout and Well-being: a systematic review and framework for action. Dis Colon Rectum. 2017;60(6):567–76.
36. Balch CM, Freischlag JA, Shanafelt TD. Stress and burnout among surgeons: understanding and managing the syndrome and avoiding the adverse consequences. Arch Surg. 2009;144(4):371–6.
37. Goldman ML, Bernstein CA, Konopasek L, Arbuckle M, Mayer LES. An intervention framework for institutions to meet new ACGME common program requirements for physician well-being. Acad Psychiatry. 2018;42(4):542–7.
38. Philibert I. What is known: examining the empirical literature in resident work hours using 30 influential articles. J Grad Med Educ. 2016;8(5):795–805.
39. Bolster L, Rourke L. The effect of restricting residents' duty hours on patient safety, resident well-being, and resident education: an updated systematic review. J Grad Med Educ. 2015;7(3):349–63.
40. Bilimoria KY, Chung JW, Hedges LV, Dahlke AR, Love R, Cohen ME, et al. National cluster-randomized trial of duty-hour flexibility in surgical training. N Engl J Med. 2016;374(8):713–27.
41. Mendelsohn D, Despot I, Gooderham PA, Singhal A, Redekop GJ, Toyota BD. Impact of work hours and sleep on well-being and burnout for physicians-in-training: the resident activity tracker evaluation study. Med Educ. 2019;53(3):306–15.
42. Winkel AF, Nguyen AT, Morgan HK, Valantsevich D, Woodland MB. Whose problem is it? The priority of physician wellness in residency training. J Surg Educ. 2017;74(3):378–83.
43. Morgan HK, Winkel AF, Nguyen AT, Carson S, Ogburn T, Woodland MB. Obstetrics and gynecology residents' perspectives on wellness: findings from a National Survey. Obstet Gynecol. 2019;133(3):552–7.
44. Kolarik RC, O'Neal RL, Ewing JA. Resident preferences for program director role in wellness management. J Gen Intern Med. 2018;33(5):705–9.
45. Tran EM, Scott IU, Clark MA, Greenberg PB. Resident wellness in US ophthalmic graduate medical education: the resident perspective. JAMA Ophthalmol. 2018;136(6):695–701.
46. Tran EM, Scott IU, Clark MA, Greenberg PB. Assessing and promoting the wellness of United States ophthalmology residents: a survey of program directors. J Surg Educ. 2018;75(1):95–103.
47. Holmes EG, Connolly A, Putnam KT, Penaskovic KM, Denniston CR, Clark LH, et al. Taking care of our own: a multispecialty study of resident and program director perspectives on contributors to burnout and potential interventions. Acad Psychiatry. 2017;41(2):159–66.
48. Sridhar P, Sanchez SE, DiPasco PJ, Novak L, Dechert T, Brahmbhatt TS. Educator and trainee perspectives on the need for a "real world" curriculum in general surgery. J Surg Res. 2019;233:268–75.
49. Smeds MR, Thrush CR, McDaniel FK, Gill R, Kimbrough MK, Shames BD, et al. Relationships between study habits, burnout, and general surgery resident performance on the American Board of Surgery In-Training Examination. J Surg Res. 2017;217:217–25.
50. Baer TE, Feraco AM, Tuysuzoglu Sagalowsky S, Williams D, Litman HJ, Vinci RJ. Pediatric resident burnout and attitudes toward patients. Pediatrics. 2017;139(3):e20162163.

51. de Oliveira GS Jr, Chang R, Fitzgerald PC, Almeida MD, Castro-Alves LS, Ahmad S, et al. The prevalence of burnout and depression and their association with adherence to safety and practice standards: a survey of United States anesthesiology trainees. Anesth Analg. 2013;117(1):182–93.
52. Spiotta AM, Fargen KM, Patel S, Larrew T, Turner RD. Impact of a residency-integrated wellness program on resident mental health, sleepiness, and quality of life. Neurosurgery. 2019;84(2):341–6.
53. Lebares CC, Hershberger AO, Guvva EV, Desai A, Mitchell J, Shen W, et al. Feasibility of formal mindfulness-based stress-resilience training among surgery interns: a randomized clinical trial. JAMA Surg. 2018;153(10):e182734.
54. Chakravarti A, Raazi M, O'Brien J, Balaton B. Anesthesiology Resident Wellness Program at the University of Saskatchewan: concept and development. Can J Anaesth. 2017;64(2):185–98.
55. Williamson K, Lank PM, Lovell EO. Development of an emergency medicine wellness curriculum. AEM Educ Training. 2018;2(1):20–5.
56. Arnold J, Tango J, Walker I, Waranch C, McKamie J, Poonja Z, et al. An evidence-based, longitudinal curriculum for resident physician wellness: the 2017 resident wellness consensus summit. West J Emerg Med. 2018;19(2):337–41.
57. Aggarwal R, Deutsch JK, Medina J, Kothari N. Resident wellness: an intervention to decrease burnout and increase resiliency and happiness. MedEdPORTAL. 2017;13:10651.
58. Riall TS, Teiman J, Chang M, Cole D, Leighn T, McClafferty H, et al. Maintaining the fire but avoiding burnout: implementation and evaluation of a resident well-being program. J Am Coll Surg. 2018;226(4):369–79.
59. Schneider BD. Energy leadership: transforming your workplace and your life from the Core. New York: Wiley; 2010.
60. Mueller CM, Buckle M, Post L. A facilitated-group approach to wellness in surgical residency. JAMA Surg. 2018;153(11):1043–4.
61. Dyrbye LN, Satele D, Sloan J, Shanafelt TD. Ability of the physician well-being index to identify residents in distress. J Grad Med Educ. 2014;6(1):78–84.

Chapter 17
Approaches to Study Wellbeing

Michael Kochis and Roy Phitayakorn

Because the concept of wellbeing encompasses so many different domains and disciplines, virtually any research method can be applied to its study. As such, this chapter is essentially an overview of the research methods relevant to the biomedical and social science fields in the broadest sense. There is no single best scheme to categorize research designs, but the classification presented here will consist of observational studies, correlational studies, and interventional studies (Fig. 17.1). The chapter concludes with a discussion how research can be used not just to study, but to also actively solve problems.

17.1   Observational Studies

17.1.1   A Note on Epistemology

Observational studies seek to describe the current state of affairs of the world. As simple as this objective may sound, it actually has significant philosophical underpinnings related to our very understanding of knowledge itself. While epistemological assumptions actually underpin all research questions, a discussion of them is particularly important here because the specific designs used to answer observational questions can arise from either of two different, but complimentary, schools of thought: a quantitative one, which incorporates numbers and statistics, and a

M. Kochis
Harvard Medical School, Boston, MA, USA
e-mail: michael_kochis@hms.harvard.edu; mkochis@mgh.harvard.edu

R. Phitayakorn (✉)
The Massachusetts General Hospital, Boston, MA, USA
e-mail: rphitayakorn@mgh.harvard.edu

© Springer Nature Switzerland AG 2020
E. Kim, B. Lindeman (eds.), *Wellbeing*, Success in Academic Surgery,
https://doi.org/10.1007/978-3-030-29470-0_17

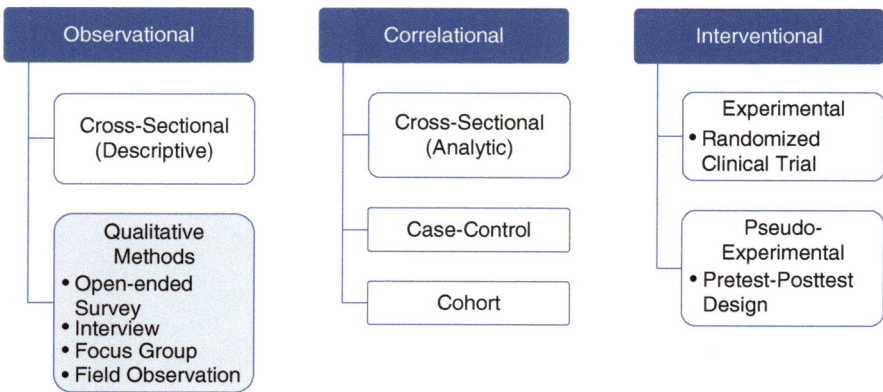

Fig. 17.1 Major research study categories with example methods. Observational studies seek to describe the world. Correlational studies assess for relationships between variables. Interventional studies involve the manipulation of an independent variable, and if they involve randomization, are the closest researchers can come to proving causation

Table 17.1 Comparison of quantitative and qualitative research

Quantitative research	Qualitative research
• Numerical statistics and relationships	• Personal experiences and opinions
• One objective and measurable reality	• Reality is socially constructed
• Deductively test hypotheses	• Inductively generate hypotheses
• Researcher is impartial	• Data gathering and analysis are subjective
• Predetermined design, often with controls	• Design is flexible and iterative
• Large sample sizes	• Perspectives of a few individuals
• Standardized across situations	• Highlights richness and nuance of context
• Generalizable on broad scale	• Limited generalizability
• Efficient data analysis	• Labor- and time-intensive
• Concise results are easily communicable	• Stories and quotations are compelling

Given the methodologies' advantages and disadvantages, they can be very complimentary when used together

qualitative one, which involves stories about personal experiences. Each methodology has its own respective advantages and disadvantages (Table 17.1). Correlational and interventional studies, as we will discuss later, are necessarily quantitative investigations.

Quantitative research has its origins in positivist thought, which maintains that truth is what can be determined by observations and measurements. While pure positivism's views about the world being governed by universal laws were fundamental in the development of the scientific method, a more tempered view called post-positivism arose in the mid-twentieth century and has since become the predominant mindset of the scientific community today. Post-positivism maintains that there is such a concept as objective "truth," and while it cannot always be definitively proven, it is still knowable to a reasonable extent. Objectivity manifests as a researcher acting in a detached manner and striving to let the data speak for themselves.

Under a post-positivist framework, truth can be approached via a hypothetico-deductive method that rules out alternative hypotheses using statistical tests [1]. Such quantitative approaches are fundamental to correlational and interventional studies, which seek to make claims about the existence of relationships between variables.

In all, quantitative research is suited to answer questions that can be answered with measurements and mathematical relationships. One major benefit of quantitative research is that it allows for great breadth of inquiry across a large number of cases. Furthermore, distilling the complexity of reality to a few key numbers—effect sizes and significance levels, for example—is useful for policy and decision-making.

In contrast to the objectivity of quantitative research, qualitative research emerges from a very different worldview. Qualitative research typically is framed from the theory of social constructivism, which argues that there is no single reality or truth, as "reality" is socially constructed. As such, reality needs to be interpreted and can only arise via an interaction between the researcher and the participant. The questions of qualitative research are open-ended and seek to understand what meaning people ascribe to certain experiences.

Unlike the hypothetico-deductive approach, in which data are used to test existing hypotheses, qualitative research uses an inductive approach in which the data are used to formulate theories about the world *de novo*. This approach is often called "grounded theory." Because these explorations are not constrained by pre-existing questions (e.g., response options on a multiple-choice survey), participants and the responses they give can help shape what the research questions become. These studies are often an iterative process, in which research questions are refined as new data are acquired.

Because qualitative data are usually situation-specific, investigators must be especially cautious in making generalizations beyond the population under study. However, such research can paint a more comprehensive and nuanced picture than quantitative investigations. Although qualitative results cannot be summarized in simple numbers, stories are powerful forces in highlighting issues and motivating others to change.

17.1.2 Cross-Sectional Studies

A quantitative observational approach has accounted for the majority of wellbeing research in recent years. This most commonly takes the form of surveys, which give a cross-sectional "snapshot" of the world at a given moment. Surveys are quick, inexpensive, simple to administer, and can acquire standardized responses from a wide range of respondents. One example of a cross-sectional observational study was conducted by Shanafelt et al. (2009), who emailed a survey to members of the American College of Surgeons [2]. Respondents answered questions derived from validated questionnaires on burnout and quality of life (see Chap. 19) and questions that offered five response options ranging from "definitely not" to "definitely yes" to describe how much they agreed with associated statements about their career satisfaction. Such numerical responses allowed descriptive summary statistics for the prevalence of certain outcomes: 40% of respondents met the researchers' criteria for burnout. Because that result does not involve a statistical test of correlation with another variable, it is considered a descriptive finding.

A benefit of surveys is that they allow for responses to be standardized across administrations, and results to be directly compared across different samples. Such investigations can thus be aggregated in a type of study called a meta-analysis. In fact, the previous study was one of 182 included in a meta-analysis conducted by Rotenstein and colleagues (2018) to determine the overall prevalence of burnout assessed by questionnaires [3]. Rather than finding a clear number, however, the authors' main conclusion was that there was substantial variability in individual studies' estimates of burnout amongst physicians, ranging from 0 to 87.1%, due to inconsistency in the definitions employed. This finding speaks to the limitations of quantitative research—it can only answer the specific question being asked, perhaps at the expense of meaningful interpretation. This, in turn, illustrates the major benefit of qualitative research.

17.1.3 Qualitative Methods

Common qualitative methods include open-ended surveys, interviews, or focus groups. Interviews can be conducted with varying levels of structure and need not strictly adhere to a script or set of questions—because such investigation is not constrained by a single hypothesis-driven research question, it can, and should, explore what the participant finds most important. Another type of qualitative research involves direct observations of people. Such "field research" is intended to document subjects' behaviors and interactions in the context of their natural environments and may or may not involve the researcher engaging and interacting with the subjects. In ethnographies, researchers incorporate themselves into different groups to better understand their dynamics through personally experiencing them. In naturalistic observation, the goal is to document things as they naturally occur, and the researcher remains inconspicuous so as to not alter the subjects' behaviors. The methods of interviews and observations may be packaged together into a case study, which is an in-depth exploration of a topic of interest (such as a project, policy, or program) and the parties involved [4].

Qualitative data analysis involves labeling the specific content of interview transcripts or field notes with codes that may represent bigger-picture ideas or trends. These codes used can be previously established (etic approach) or newly created from the data itself (emic approach). These codes then help organize the data into overarching themes. Given the amount of work required to gather and analyze qualitative data, the scope of qualitative studies is much narrower than that of quantitative work.

An important consideration about qualitative research is that data acquisition and analysis are subjective. Researchers must be aware of reflexivity, which involves reflecting on how their own presence or attitudes can impact their work. For interviews, this may manifest in how they phrase certain questions or how their own traits influence how subjects respond to them. In observations, their background experiences may impact how they notice and interpret certain actions.

A qualitative study on wellbeing conducted by Winkel et al. (2018) sought to "examine the experiences of obstetrics and gynecology residents to generate a theory of how residents learn to thrive" in their stressful work environment [5]. It took on a constructivist approach with grounded theory methodology, referring to the understanding that knowledge was created by the residents themselves and the study's conclusions would arise from the residents' responses, not some external standards initially conceptualized by the investigators. A purposive sampling approach targeted specific residents of interest: those suspected to "have an intense but not extreme experience of the phenomenon of resilience." Semi-structured interviews guided but did not dictate the discussions. Responses were transcribed, key content was coded with inductive labels, and a codebook was created. This codebook included 54 codes that the investigators then arranged into categories and revealed relationships between categories. The researchers reached thematic saturation, in which additional interviews did not produce substantively new data, after 18 interviews. In terms of the results, the manuscript presents the key categories, such as "Support System" and "Attention to Self," with illustrative quotations from participants. The findings often involve connections and tensions the residents perceive—experiences that could only surface through personal communication. The researchers demonstrate reflexivity in acknowledging how their background in narrative medicine might have influenced their findings: "ideas related to professional identity, empathy, and humanism might have emerged more prominently."

17.1.4   Mixed Methods Research

The fact that quantitative and qualitative research methods operate with different epistemological frameworks does not mean they are incompatible. In fact, each method's unique ability to answer specific types of questions means that the two can be especially potent when used together. Research projects that incorporate and integrate both quantitative and qualitative components are referred to as mixed-methods studies.

Mixed-methods studies can be described by the sequence of the two components in the research design. Convergent parallel design involves the simultaneous occurrence of quantitative data collection and analysis and qualitative data collection and analysis. The results are compared and related to yield the final interpretations. This is well suited to obtain multiple different perspectives about an issue and can help build comprehensive understanding.

Explanatory sequential design begins with quantitative data collection and analysis. It then seeks to explain those initial statistical findings in more depth with qualitative inquiry. Exploratory sequential design, on the other hand, begins with a qualitative study followed by a quantitative study. It is most appropriate for situations in which little is known about a topic, and it needs exploration before being explained. Performing a qualitative analysis first also helps researchers choose the most appropriate quantitative measurements to use later.

Clough et al. (2019) employed the explanatory sequential design in examining the barriers to treatment for stress and burnout-related difficulties experienced by doctors [6]. The investigation began with a survey in which Australian physicians completed the Perceived Barriers to Psychological Treatment (PBPT) scale, an instrument validated to examine the barriers preventing patients from seeking counseling for depression, rating how difficult each of 27 items would make it for them to seek care [7]. The 27 questions cluster around eight domains, including "negative evaluation of services" or "time constraints." The investigators ranked the domains' mean scores, and statistical tests assessed for differences in mean ratings between providers from rural and metropolitan environments. After that, the investigators conducted a total of 20 semi-structured interviews of doctors from both settings to identify their perceptions regarding the issue, as well as to develop strategies to promote help-seeking among doctors.

17.2 Correlational Studies

Correlational research involves quantitative studies that look for relationships between and among two or more variables. Although "correlation" also refers to a specific statistical analysis that can be used in correlational research, correlational research does not require any specific analysis. The main feature of correlational research is the design, in which multiple variables are measured. Variables of interest do not need to be continuous; correlations can exist between categories, as well.

In correlational studies, positive correlations mean that the variables increase or decrease in tandem, whereas negative correlations mean that one variable increases as the other decreases, or vice versa. No correlation implies that the variables are unrelated: knowing the change in one variable would not help predict a change in the other.

Like observational studies, correlational studies do not involve the manipulation of variables—only the documentation of what naturally occurs. As such, correlational research can be useful to study variables for which experimental testing is impractical or unethical. However, a correlation between two variables does not mean that the one variable was the cause for the other. Whereas it can be used to *predict* outcomes, it cannot explain them mechanistically.

17.2.1 Cross-Sectional Studies

These concepts are well illustrated by a study conducted by Shanafelt and colleagues (2010) assessing the relationship between surgeon burnout and medical errors [8]. A correlational design is appropriate because it is impossible to assign clinicians to different levels of burnout. Using additional data from the same survey of American College of Surgeons members mentioned before, this study looked at respondents' self-reported burnout scores and medical errors in the past 3 months. Higher levels of emotional exhaustion and depersonalization were each associated with higher likelihoods of reporting errors, in a dose-response manner. To be clear (and the authors note this), one cannot interpret from these data that burnout is what led to more error-making, or that error-making adversely affects physician mental health. The only thing that we can assert, with the support of statistical tests, is that there is a significant association between the two variables. This research can be described as cross-sectional correlational in that it takes a one-time snapshot of a population and shows the relationship between two variables.

There are two further correlational research designs common in epidemiology that can also be applied to the study of wellbeing: case-control, and cohort. Case-control studies differ from cross-sectional studies in that they provide information not about an entire population but rather only individuals with a specific characteristic. Cohort studies can shed light on an entire population but are often most useful in showing longitudinal effects.

17.2.2 Case-Control Studies

In a case-control study, the investigator finds "cases" that have some characteristic (or outcome) and then "controls" who do not. The controls are matched to the cases with regards to as many variables as possible in order to eliminate any confounding effects that may also influence the outcome. The investigator then retrospectively assesses exposures that each of the two groups experienced to see if there are differences in exposure rates between the two. The main outcome calculation for these studies is the odds ratio, which compares the odds of a case having some exposure to the odds of a control having the exposure. While these studies are helpful in revealing the relationship between risk factors and outcomes, can be performed quickly, and allow for the assessment of multiple factors at once, they are subject to recall bias and dependent on the quality of controls.

17.2.3 Cohort Studies

A cohort study follows a group of individuals prospectively, noting down exposures either initially or along the way. Eventually some members of the cohort develop the outcome of interest. The main outcome measure is "relative risk" (or rate ratio), which is calculated by comparing the risk of developing the outcome in an individual who did have an exposure to the risk of developing the outcome in an individual who did not have such an exposure. A major advantage of such a prospective study is that the criteria for exposure and outcome can be standardized. Cohort studies can also be retrospective, in which exposure and outcome have already been established and recorded at the time of the study.

Fahrenkopf and colleagues (2008) studied a cohort of pediatrics residents to assess the relationships between the depression and burnout, and medication errors [9]. The research team used validated instruments to assess residents for the exposures of depression and burnout and trained a team of nurses and physicians to collect outcome data on medical order errors in a standardized way prospectively over a month-long data collection period. The analysis found that depressed residents made more than six times as many errors as their non-depressed peers. Although the prospective results are compelling, this study is not suited to prove the claim that the errors occurred because the residents were depressed because both may be the result of some other confounding factor.

17.3 Interventional Studies

17.3.1 Experimental Studies

The last category of research designs, and the one best suited to answer questions about causality, examine the effect of an intervention. Interventional studies assess the impact of one or more experimental manipulations of an independent variable ("interventions") on a dependent variable. Because the manipulation of the independent variable occurs prior to the measurement of the dependent one, these experiments avoid the directionality issues that can appear in correlational studies (as illustrated in Shanafelt et al. [8]). A major distinguishing feature of experimental studies is random assignment of participants to the intervention or control groups. This promotes validity by reducing the effects of confounding factors besides the intervention between the two groups (as illustrated in Fahrenkopf et al. [9]).

These principles are well illustrated in the randomized controlled trial conducted by West et al. (2014), which set out to determine if a facilitated small-group curriculum would result in improvement in physician wellbeing [10]. Seventy-four practicing physicians in the Department of Medicine at the Mayo Clinic were randomized by a computer algorithm into two groups: 37 would receive 1 h of protected time every other week to participate in a curriculum involving facilitated small-group discussions, and 37 were allocated to a control group that received an equivalent amount of protected time but no formal curriculum. The manuscript presents a table common in trial manuscripts demonstrating that baseline demographic data between the intervention and control groups were equivalent. Surveys sent out at multiple time points during and after the intervention assessed such outcomes as job satisfaction, quality of life, and burnout, allowing statistical comparisons between the two groups. This study is unique in comparing data from the intervention and control arms with a non-trial cohort consisting of physicians who were eligible to participate but chose not to. The authors report that burnout rates decreased substantially in the trial intervention arm, decreased slightly in the trial control arm, and increased in the non-trial cohort.

17.3.2 Pseudo-Experimental Studies

Another type of interventional study is a pseudo-experimental study, which also involves the manipulation of an independent variable, but not the random assignment of groups. Potential differences between the groups in qualities besides their treatment status may threaten internal validity in such "non-equivalent group" designs. In the pretest-posttest design, a dependent variable is measured once before an intervention and then again after the intervention. Each participant serves as his or her own control. However, because there is no concurrent control group as the participants are undergoing the intervention, any change from before to after cannot be attributed to the intervention itself; there might have been some other effect besides the intervention that caused everyone to change. In the domain of wellbeing, it is worth considering the possibility of spontaneous remission, the phenomenon in which problems naturally improve over time regardless of an intervention. To be sure, an individual serving as his or her own control is not necessarily problematic: Randomized controlled trials can involve a crossover design in which subjects participate in both the intervention and control exposures at different times throughout the study. The problem with pretest-posttest studies is not having a control group during the same period of the study when others are receiving the intervention.

17.4 Research as Intervention

Whereas the primary objective of observational, correlational, and interventional studies is to generate knowledge about the world, research is not limited to simply understanding the status quo; it can also be a vehicle of impacting it. Within the context of wellbeing, research projects can be a way of addressing problems such as burnout and promoting improvements in the healthcare setting. Design-based research and (participatory) action research arose in the educational and social science fields, respectively, and have significant applications to the issues at hand. Although these approaches take on a stance that is less neutral or detached than traditional methods and are less focused on generalizability or reproducibility, the knowledge generated through them can be beneficial to other communities struggling with similar issues.

Design-based research is an iterative process involving testing interventions in the field, gathering information about their performance, updating them, and then trying again. Theory generation happens concurrently with refinement of the intervention. The actual work can involve a range of methods, and since it occurs in social environments, researchers are less interested in controlling variables than in understanding how complex interactions play out in real life. Action research is similarly focused on addressing issues that directly affect the studied population. Participatory action research blurs the line between "researcher" and "subject," including the participants in the design of the study so that they have a voice in expressing their lived experiences and particular needs. Since its constructivist epistemology emphasizes how knowledge is rooted in individuals' experiences, action research often involves qualitative approaches [11].

The ACGME used a form of action research called appreciative inquiry to "identify best current resources for promotion of wellness during training, what resources ideally should exist, and how the gap between the current reality and the ideal may be bridged" [12]. The investigators walked resident representatives on their Council of Review Committee Residents through a series of reflective steps discussing the "best of what is," then "what might be," "what can be," and finally "what should be." Using a qualitative approach, the residents' responses were analyzed for themes, which were then consensus-scored by two individuals outside the writing team. Example themes included "building systems to confidentially identify and treat depression in trainees" and "establishing a more formal system of peer and faculty mentoring".

17.5 Conclusion

Because the concept of wellbeing is so broad, almost any research method can be relevant to its study. There is no single optimal way to classify research, but a sound understanding of the benefits and limitations of different methods is critical in evaluating the potential merits of a study. Observational research simply seeks to describe the world as it is, not to measure relationships or assess the impact of an intervention or manipulation. Observational research can be accomplished via either quantitative or qualitative methods, depending on the type of question being asked. Quantitative observational approaches, like cross-sectional surveys, are quick, consistent, and therefore quite common, but are limited in what truths they can convey. Qualitative research like interviews, on the other hand, allows for deeper explorations of people's experiences and attitudes. Mixed methods studies integrate both quantitative and qualitative approaches.

The real benefit of quantitative research lies in its ability to perform statistical tests that can demonstrate mathematical relationships between variables. Correlational studies are those that reveal relationships between variables as they naturally occur. A variety of statistical methods can be applied to correlational studies, and the specific designs can be cross-sectional, case-control, and cohort. However, as compelling as such studies' statistical relationships may appear, they do not imply causation. The gold standard for that is experimental studies, which involve an independent variable being manipulated between two groups, with randomization, which eliminates the effect of confounding variables. Lastly, design-based and action research methodologies show how research can be a means of addressing problems. Involving those affected in the research process can be an effective way of determining practices most likely to succeed in the complexity of the real world.

References

1. Willig C. Introducing qualitative research in psychology. J Chem Inf Model. 2013;(9):1689–99.
2. Shanafelt TD, Balch CM, Bechamps GJ, Russell T, Dyrbye L, Satele D, et al. Burnout and Career Satisfaction Among American Surgeons. Ann Surg. 2009;250(3):463–70.
3. Rotenstein LS, Torre M, Ramos MA, Rosales RC, Guille C, Sen S, et al. Prevalence of burnout among physicians: a systematic review. JAMA [Internet]. 2018;320(11):1131–50. https://jamanetwork.com/journals/jama/fullarticle/2702871.
4. Starman AB. The case study as a type of qualitative research. J Contemp Educ Stud. 2013;1:28–43.
5. Winkel AF, Honart AW, Robinson A, Jones A, Squires A. Thriving in scrubs: understanding resilience in residents. Reprod Health. 2018;15:53.
6. Clough BA, March S, Leane S, Ireland MJ. What prevents doctors from seeking help for stress and burnout? A mixed-methods investigation among metropolitan and regional-based australian doctors. J Clin Psychol. 2019;75:418–32.
7. Mohr DC, Duffecy J, Baron KG, Lehman KA. Perceived barriers to psychological treatments and their relationship to depression. J Clin Psychol. 2010;66(4):394–409.
8. Shanafelt TD, Balch CM, Bechamps G, Russell T, Dyrbye L, Satele D, et al. Burnout and medical errors among American surgeons. Ann Surg. 2010;251(6):995–1000.
9. Fahrenkopf AM, Sectish TC, Barger LK, Sharek PJ, Lewin D, Chiang VW, et al. Rates of medication errors among depressed and burnt out residents: prospective cohort study. BMJ. 2008;336(7642):488–91.
10. West CP, Dyrbye LN, Rabatin JT, Call TG, Davidson JH, Multari A, et al. Intervention to promote physician well-being, job satisfaction, and professionalism a randomized clinical trial. JAMA Intern Med. 2014;174(4):527–33.
11. Jacobs S. The use of participatory action research within education-benefits to stakeholders. World J Educ. 2016;6(3):48–55.
12. Daskivich TJ, Jardine DA, Tseng J, Correa R, Stagg BC, Jacob KM, et al. Promotion of wellness and mental health awareness among physicians in training: perspective of a national, multispecialty panel of residents and fellows. J Grad Med Educ [Internet]. 2015;7(1):143–7. https://doi.org/10.4300/JGME-07-01-42.

Part VI
The Study of Wellbeing

Chapter 18
Tools of the Trade

Lindsey Gade and Heather L. Yeo

18.1 Introduction

Wellness is defined as "diverse and interconnected dimensions of physical, mental, and social wellbeing that… includes choices and activities aimed at achieving physical vitality, mental alacrity, social satisfaction, a sense of accomplishment, and personal fulfillment" [1]. The National Academy of Medicine's (NAM) model of wellbeing broadly categorizes the factors contributing to wellbeing into several factors that can be assessed and targeted for improvement [2]. These are categorized broadly as *individual factors*, including health care role, personal factors, and skills and abilities, and *external factors*, including sociocultural factors, regulatory/business/payer environment, organizational factors, and learning/practice environment. Figure 18.1 illustrates a simplified version of the NAM model of wellbeing adapted by our group.

Burnout is defined as a syndrome characterized by emotional exhaustion (EE), depersonalization (DP), and low sense of personal accomplishment (PA) produced by chronic occupational stress [3, 4]. An estimated 50% of surgeons suffer from burnout which has been associated with negative individual and external wellbeing factors [5]. Consequently, the American College of Surgeons (ACS) and the National Academy of Medicine (NAM) have issued a call to arms to help identify and remedy this epidemic. Despite two decades of research, there remains no consensual

L. Gade
Department of Surgery, New York-Presbyterian Hospital/Weill Cornell Medicine, New York, NY, USA
e-mail: lig9079@med.cornell.edu

H. L. Yeo (✉)
Department of Surgery, New York-Presbyterian Queens, Queens, NY, USA

Department of Healthcare Policy and Research, Weill Cornell Medicine, New York, NY, USA
e-mail: hey9002@med.cornell.edu

© Springer Nature Switzerland AG 2020
E. Kim, B. Lindeman (eds.), *Wellbeing*, Success in Academic Surgery,
https://doi.org/10.1007/978-3-030-29470-0_18

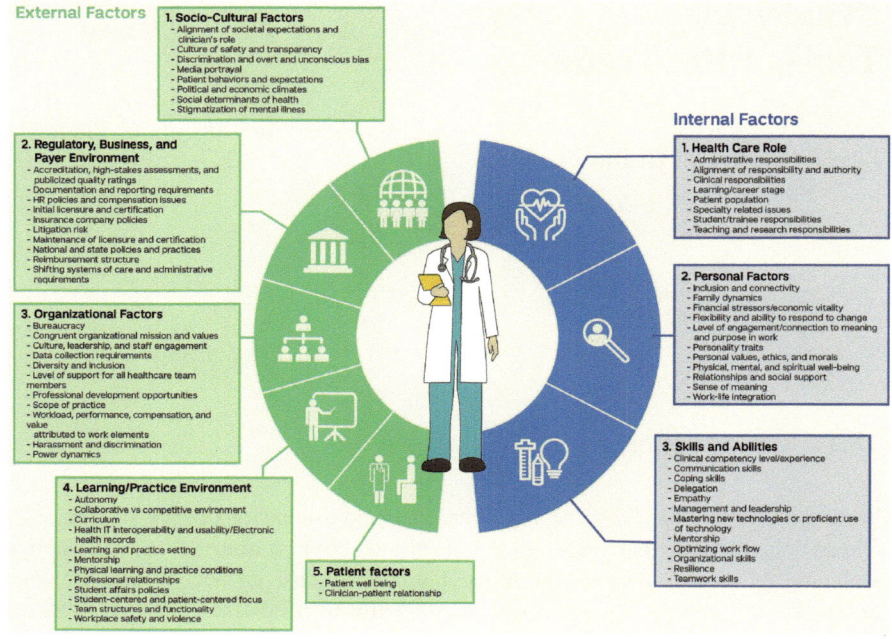

Fig. 18.1 Adaptation of the National Academy of Medicine's model of wellbeing depicting the external and individual factors contributing to wellbeing

diagnostic criteria, and evidence-driven interventions at the individual, organizational, and societal level are scarce. It is important for assessment and intervention purposes to understand the distinction between burnout and depression. Both are chronic processes that result in similar symptoms, but burnout distinctly refers to work related distress as opposed to the more global anhedonia described by depression [6–8]. Depression has been found to correlate with increased EE, but not with DP or PA [6–8]. Suicidal ideation, depression, job dissatisfaction, fatigue, and low mental quality of health have all been correlated with burnout, but they can be absent in the presence of burnout or present in the absence of burnout [9–11]. Accurate evaluation and diagnosis are necessary to direct intervention. Similarly, wellbeing is not just the absence of burnout or depression, but rather physical, mental, and social fulfillment.

Non-cognitive personality traits such as grit and resilience have been associated with improved wellbeing and performance [12–17]. Resilience is the ability to respond and adapt to stressful conditions in a positive way. Genetic, developmental, psychological, biological, and social factors contribute to the development and enhancement of resilience [18, 19]. Cognitive-behavioral, emotional regulation, and educational interventions have been effective in the development and enhancement of resilience which correlated with improved mental health and function [18, 20–23]. These interventions may be effective for surgeons and warrant further research. Grit is defined as perseverance and passion for long-term goals maintained over a prolonged period of time (years) regardless of failure, lack of progress, or adversity and can be thought of as a combination of perseverance and consistency [24, 25]. Psychologists initially characterizing grit argued that it could predict achievement almost as well as intelligence and believed it to be responsible for high levels of achievement, both academically and physically [25]. Unfortunately, grit is less well understood than resilience and more recent re-evaluation of these initial studies challenge the fundamental construct of grit. One such study suggests that grit is merely a repackaging of conscientiousness and demonstrates that conscientiousness is actually predictive of performance and achievement while grit has little to no predictive validity [26]. Another describes grit as the singular construct of "effortful persistence" that combines with the distinct entities of conscientiousness and intelligence to improve performance and produce achievement [27].

Below we will discuss screening tools for burnout and wellbeing in addition to grit and resilience valuations. They are meant to be used as initial assessments rather than comprehensive measurements.

18.2 Burnout Assessment Tools

18.2.1 Maslach Burnout Inventory (MBI)

Created by social psychologists in 1981, the MBI is the most widely used burnout assessment tool in the United States. After rigorous psychometric testing and validation in mental healthcare workers, Drs. Maslach and Jackson developed a 22-question survey divided into three core components with strong construct validity: emotional exhaustion (9 questions), depersonalization (5 questions), and low sense of personal accomplishment (8 questions) [4]. Responses for each component, or subscale, are measured via a 7 point Likert scale (never to daily) that correspond to the frequency of the attitude assessed. The sum total for each component corresponds to established low, average, or high burnout scores within that category [28]. Because these are continuous variables, there remains no accepted "yes/no" dichotomous definition of burnout which accounts for variability in the prevalence of burnout among health professionals [29]. While the MBI was originally created for individuals in health services, three versions have been developed including the MBI-HSS (Health Services Survey), MBI-GS (General Survey), and MBI-ES (Educator's Survey). The MBI-HSS most closely resembles the original survey developed by Maslach and Jackson and will be referred to as "MBI" in this chapter. The MBI has validity evidence among a wide variety of health professionals around the world and has adapted widespread use in the surgical community despite the lack of dedicated validation in United States attending surgeons [3, 28, 30–35]. The 22-item instrument is proprietary, requiring licensing agreements for use. Because of the practical limitations of a 22-item survey, items with the highest factor loading from the EE component, "I feel burned out for my work", and the DP component, "I have become more callous toward people since I took this job" were found not only to be appropriate surrogates for burnout when compared to the full MBI, but were also found to predict negative outcomes accurately and consistently [36, 37].

These studies were validated in surgeons and support the use of this abbreviated assessment in the future. Data from several studies using the MBI have demonstrated several risk factors that are associated with burnout (Table 18.1) and demonstrate negative outcomes associated with burnout (Table 18.2).

Table 18.1 Risk factors and protective factors associated with burnout/diminished wellbeing and the affected wellbeing domains

Risk factor	Wellness category	Citation	Population
Younger age	Individual—personal factors	Balch 2011 [38] Shanafelt 2009 [11] Campbell 2001 [39]	ACS members ACS members US surgical Attendings
Female gender	Individual—personal factors	Dyrbye 2011 [40] West 2011 [41]	ACS members ACS members
Children/number of children	Individual—personal factors	Campbell 2001 [39] Shanafelt 2009 [11] Balch 2011 [42]	US surgical Attendings ACS members ACS members
Spouse works in healthcare	Individual—personal factors	Balch 2011 [42]	ACS members
Subspecialty trauma cardiothoracic transplant urology	Individual—health care role	Balch 2010 [43] Shanafelt 2010 [44]	ACS members ACS members
Work home conflict	Individua—personal factors	Dyrbye 2011 [45] Dyrbye 2011 [40]	Internal medicine residents ACS members
Work hours	Individual—health care role External—organizational factors	Balch 2010 [43] Dyrbye 2011 [45] Balch 2011 [46] Dyrbye 2011 [40] Balch 2011 [42] Dewa 2014 [131]	ACS members ACS members ACS members ACS members ACS members Canadian physicians (multi-specialty including surgeons)
Nights on call	Individual—health care role External—organizational factors	Balch 2011 [42] Balch 2010 [43] Shanafelt 2009 [11]	ACS members ACS members
Practice setting—private practice	Individual—health care role External—organizational factors, learning/practice environment	Balch 2011 [47]	ACS members
>50% time dedicated to non-patient care	Individual—health care role External—organizational factors, learning/practice environment	Balch 2011 [46]	ACS members
Clerical burden	Individual—skills and abilities External—organizational factors, learning/practice environment	Shanafelt 2016 [48] West 2018 [49]	US physicians (multi-specialty including surgeons) US physicians (multi-specialty including surgeons)

Table 18.1 (continued)

Protective factor	Wellness category	Citation	Population
Time performing meaningful work	Individual—health care role, personal factors External—organizational factors, learning/practice environment	Shanafelt 2009 [11]	ACS members
Career fit	Individual—health care role, personal factors External—organizational factors, learning/practice environment	Shanafelt 2009 [11]	ACS members
Positive leadership qualities of immediate supervisor	External—organizational factors, learning/practice environment	Shanafelt 2015 [5]	US physicians (multi-specialty including surgeons)

Table 18.2 Negative outcomes associated with burnout/diminished wellbeing and the affected wellbeing domains

Outcome	Wellness category	Citation	Population
Medical error	Individual—skills and abilities, health care role	Shanafelt 2010 [44] West 2006 [50] West 2009 [51]	ACS members Internal medicine residents Internal medicine residents
Malpractice	Individual—skills and abilities, health care role External—regulatory, business, and payer environment	Balch 2011 [38]	ACS members
Suboptimal patient practices	Individual—skills and abilities, health care role	Williams 2007 [132] Klein 2010 [65] Shanafelt 2002 [133]	Primary care physicians German surgical Attendings Internal medicine residents
Physician turnover	External—organizational factors, learning/practice environment	Shanfelt 2011 [134]	ACS members
Early retirement	Individual—personal factors External—learning/practice environment	Campbell 2001 [39] Dewa 2014 [131]	Surgical residents/ attendings Canadian physicians (multi-specialty including surgeons)
Suboptimal professionalism	Individual—personal factors, skills and abilities, health care role External—learning/practice environment	Shanafelt 2016 [135] Tait 2016 [136]	US physicians US physicians
Alcohol abuse	Individual—personal factors	Oreskovich 2012 [137]	ACS members
Suicidal ideation	Individual—personal factors	Shanafelt 2011 [9]	ACS members
Motor vehicle accidents	Individual—personal factors	West 2009 [51]	Internal medicine residents

Take Home Points
- Gold standard of burnout worldwide
- Used as criterion variable to establish validity for Oldenburg Burnout Inventory (OBI), Copenhagen Burnout Inventory (CBI), and Physician Wellbeing Index (PWBI)
- Most extensive psychometric research of any burnout tool
- Does not address non-psychiatric effects of stress on wellbeing
- Long and complicated to use
- Is not specifically targeted to the stresses of being a surgeon

18.2.2   Oldenburg Burnout Inventory (OBI)

The OBI was constructed in Germany in the late 1990s by social psychologist Evangelia Demerouti and colleagues largely in response to the following criticisms of the MBI: inadequate assessment of burnout in populations not employed in health and human services, unidirectional language (EE and DP contain only negative statements, PA contains only positive statements), insufficient assessment of emotional exhaustion, and the belief that exhaustion and depersonalization without low personal achievement represent the core components of burnout [52, 53]. This 16-question survey contains only 2 core components, exhaustion (8 questions) and disengagement (8 questions), that stem from the Job Demands-Resource model of burnout, where high occupational demands and low occupational resources result in the above mentioned core components [53]. Each component contains an equal number of positive and negative statements (After work, I feel worn out vs after work, I feel fit for leisure activity) that are measured via a 4-point Likert scale (strongly agree to strongly disagree). Intended for use in all occupations, "exhaustion" encompasses physical and cognitive exhaustion in addition to emotional. Disengagement, as opposed to depersonalization, refers to negative attitudes toward work and distancing oneself from work [53]. The OBI has been validated in German nurses and "blue-collar workers", Dutch nurses, physicians, and "white-collar workers", and Americans employed in a variety of enterprises including education, healthcare, banking or financial services, government, manufacturing, retail, and telecommunications [52–55]. The American sample demonstrated acceptable internal consistency with each component maintaining Cronbach's $\alpha > 0.74$, a borderline acceptable 4 month test-retest reliability of 0.51 for exhaustion and 0.34 for disengagement, and convergent validity between the OBI and MBI-GS with $r = 0.6$ [54]. Outcomes associated with burnout as measured by the OBI include increased intent to leave, turnover, poor clinical performance, and absenteeism in Swedish nurses [56–58].

Take Home Points
- The OBI is a more general survey and can be used in any occupation.
- It is sensitive to physical and cognitive stress not detected by MBI which may be important considering the taxing nature of surgery.

- It lacks US literature linking performance on OBI to internal or external wellbeing outcomes.
- Limited generalizability to US surgeons as the literature is composed of small samples of non-surgeon healthcare professionals in international studies.

18.2.3 Copenhagen Burnout Inventory (CBI)

The CBI was constructed between 1997–2005 by Danish psychologists after the MBI was found to be insufficient to measure burnout in the Project on Burnout, Motivation, and Job Satisfaction (PUMA), a government funded project commissioned in response to increasing sick days and absenteeism in a union of ~2000 Danish human services workers. Criticisms of the MBI included disagreement with the fundamental components of MBI burnout (depersonalization is a coping mechanism, low personal accomplishment is a burnout consequence—neither should be included as part of the syndrome), inability to measure burnout in unemployed populations and in non-human services occupations, the "American" nature of some questions that generated negative reactions among many Dutch subjects, and the cost associated with the proprietary nature of the instrument. The authors of the CBI define burnout as severe physical and psychological exhaustion that develops within different spheres of life as personal burnout, or the degree of exhaustion experienced by the person, work-related burnout, or the degree to which exhaustion is perceived by the person to be related to work, and client-related burnout, or the degree of exhaustion that is perceived by the person to be related to work with clients [59]. The 19 question survey is divided into 3 components which reflect the domains of burnout: personal burnout (6 questions), work-related burnout (7 questions), and client-related burnout (6 questions). The survey contains negatively phrased questions (How often are you physically exhausted?) and responses are measured via 5-point Likert responses (always to never). Each component is scored individually. This compartmentalized definition of burnout allows the authors to measure burnout in unemployed populations as well as non-human service occupations. However, there are some major inherent flaws. Burnout is a work-specific phenomenon, so the utility of an instrument which measures burnout in an unemployed population should be addressed. Furthermore, life is the integration of personal and work-related responsibilities and it is unrealistic to measure them as distinct, compartmentalized entities. Unlike the MBI and OBI, the CBI has not been validated with factor analyses. Each domain had high internal reliability (Cronbach's $\alpha = 0.85–.87$) in the original sample of Dutch service workers (homecare services, psychiatric hospital staff, prison ward staff). Psychometric properties of the CBI have since been validated in a number of populations including Spanish healthcare workers, Iranian nurses, Chinese human service workers, Italian professors, and Japanese nurses [59–65]. Outcomes associated with high levels of burnout as measured by the CBI include decreased quality of care (German surgeons), academic motivation (Australian medical students), wellbeing (Canadian residents), work satisfaction (Canadian residents), social support (Taiwanese nurses, physicians, and administrators), and increased turnover (Iranian nurses), workplace incivility (US CRNAs), absenteeism (Dutch human service workers, Norwegian midwives), number of sick days, anti-depressant treatment, intent to quit, sleep problems, use of painkillers (Dutch human service workers), and administrative reorganization (Norwegian midwives) [65–72].

Take Home Points
- CBI is a general burnout survey that can be used in any occupation as well as in unemployed populations
- Components of CBI synthesized without factor analysis and support implausible work-life dichotomy
- The CBI lacks US validation
- The CBI has not been linked to other negative outcomes
- Limited generalizability to US surgeons as the literature is composed of small samples of non-surgeon healthcare professionals in international studies

18.3 Wellbeing Assessment Tools

18.3.1 Short Form-12 Health Survey (SF-12)

In the 1980s, the Short Form Health Survey-36 was developed by the RAND group in the United States during the Medical Outcomes Study, an NIH-funded study designed to assess variation in physician practice and patients' outcomes during the rise of HMOs and competing systems of care to produce reliable scales for the routine monitoring of patients' health and wellbeing [73–75]. It was intended to measure the general health of healthy individuals and those with chronic conditions, and to monitor clinical outcomes. The original survey consisted of 36 elements divided among 8 domains which was distilled using factor analysis into two summary measures, physical health and mental health [76, 77]. The survey was found to be psychometrically sound as a tool for health and wellbeing among healthy and chronically ill populations, and as a free instrument, gained widespread use in outcomes studies [73–75, 78]. The SF-12 was developed in 1996, out of limitations of the SF-36 due to its length and impractical application in large scale health measures and monitoring. This 12-element survey, derived from the SF-36 and tested in the US general population, contains 2 domains, physical health and mental health, which correlate well with the 2 summary measures of the SF-36 ($R^2 = 0.91$, $R^2 = 0.92$ respectively) [79]. Validity, reliability, and responsiveness were found to approximate that of the SF-36 in cross sectional studies assessing both physical and mental components and demonstrated the SF-12 to be a tool that was not only sensitive to change in mental and physical health status within a single individual, but a tool that was also able to discriminate between groups on the basis of age, diagnosis, and severity of mental or physical illness [79–82]. The survey has since been validated around the world and used as a tool to monitor clinical outcomes at both the individual and population level [79, 83–86].

Take Home Points
- The SF-12 is the gold standard for measurement of general health and wellbeing.
- It is used as a criterion variable to establish validity for PWBI.
- It incorporates both mental and physical health.
- It is quick and easy to use (<5 min).

18.3.2 Physician Wellbeing Index (PWBI)

The PWBI was initially conceptualized in 2010 by Dr. Dyrbye and colleagues at the Mayo Clinic as the Medical Student Wellbeing Index (MSWBI), a screening instrument intended to identify students in distress and monitor their wellbeing in the medical learning environment [87]. Created using literature review, correlational analysis with validated health assessments, and nominal group technique from medical students, deans, psychologists, and medical education experts from multiple institutions, the MSWBI included 7 items with dichotomous yes/no (1 point/0 points) responses to evaluate 5 domains of distress: burnout (emotional exhaustion, depersonalization), depression, fatigue, mental quality of life, and physical quality of life. The survey was validated by over 2000 medical students from numerous United States institutions and exhibited excellent content validity >0.90, acceptable internal reliability $\alpha = 0.68$, and ≥74% sensitivity and 63–100% specificity for identifying distress within each domain [87]. The WBI was then tested in physicians, residents, and a second cohort of medical students to assess its efficacy in detecting distress and associated negative outcomes [10, 88, 89]. In a sample of over 2500 medical students and 7500 physicians, a score of ≥4 was both sensitive and specific for low mental QOL, suicidal ideation (SI), and intent to quit [88, 90]. In the physician sample, a score of ≥4 was also associated with decreased career satisfaction, fatigue, and increased self-reported medical errors [91]. In a sample of 1700 residents, a score of ≥5 was sensitive and specific for low mental QOL and increased the likelihood of fatigue, suicidal ideation, and self-reported medical error [10]. With the support of the American College of Surgeons (ACS), the PWBI was then used in a surgery-specific intervention designed to assess surgeon wellbeing relative US physician norms, provide individualized feedback and education promoting health and self-care, and facilitate behavioral changes favoring wellbeing [90]. Findings demonstrated poor self-assessment of wellbeing in surgeons relative to other colleagues with ~70% of surgeons identifying themselves as having average or above average wellbeing, while their PWBI scores ranked in the bottom 30% of the population. This study is discussed in more detail below.

Take Home Points
- The PWBI is designed specifically for MDs and has been validated in surgeons.
- It is easy to use—accessible on the ACS website, <5 min, simple scoring + interpretation.

- It is weighted towards mental/emotional health but does include physical health.
- It is free on the ACS website.

18.3.3   Quality Work Competence (QWC)

Funded by the Swedish government as a quality improvement (QI) project at a regional hospital in 1994, the QWC project consisted of simultaneous QI studies addressing quality of care, work environment, and "internal service" with the aim of developing a series of instruments that would allow the hospital to quantify quality in each area and measure changes over time [92, 93]. The QWC instrument was initially composed of three surveys with 14 domains and over 90 elements, but was refined as an assessment of organizational and staff wellbeing with 10–14 components and >40 elements depending on the study [92–96]. The components include mental energy, work climate, work tempo, work-related exhaustion, performance feedback, participatory management, skills development, goal clarity, efficacy, leadership, employeeship, change focus, patient focus, and quality of care, and were measured via a 4-point Likert scale (strongly agree-strongly disagree) which is converted to a percentage. A "dynamic focus score" is calculated using different component weights based on the particular factor analysis within that study and the single number (0–100%) represents organizational and employee wellbeing [92–100]. The study was validated in Swedish hospital staff (nurses, physicians, managerial staff, non-managerial staff) and a small group of US primary care physicians and nurses. Outcomes associated with poor organizational and employee wellbeing include work performance, absenteeism, turnover, work performance, work productivity, and biological stress markers within hospital staff [92–100].

Take Home Points
- It is an assessment tool used to assess external wellbeing factors and is sensitive to institutional changes.
- It is a long survey with complex scoring.
- There are variable components from study to study—requires definitive factor analysis.
- Has been validated in a Swedish population but requires validation in US population.

18.4   Personality Assessments

18.4.1   Grit Scale (Grit-O)/Short Grit Scale (Grit-S)

In the early 2000s, social psychologists at the University of Michigan and University of Pennsylvania came to appreciate the importance of grit as a personality trait and its ubiquity in highly successful individuals from a variety of professions. This trait could not be adequately measured with existing scales, and in 2007, the Grit Scale was developed. This 12-item survey centered on 2 domains, consistency of interests and perseverance of effort, and contained both positively and negatively worded statements [25]. Responses were measured via a 5-point Likert scale (not at all like me to very much like me). Items for the survey were generated to "capture the attitudes and behaviors characteristic of high achieving individuals", were generic with regard to setting (i.e. work, school, military), and were applicable for both adolescents and adults [25]. Items were refined and factor analysis confirmed two domains with high internal consistency ($\alpha = 0.85$). The survey was then tested in several different populations including online adult volunteers, Ivy League undergraduates, West Point cadets, and National Spelling Bee contestants, and used a variety of tests including the Big Five Inventory (measure of conscientiousness, extraversion, neuroticism, agreeableness, and openness), the Brief Self-Control Scale (measure of self-control), and the Wechsler Intelligence Scale for Children-III to compare and contrast predictive validities. Increased grit was correlated with a number of positive outcomes including higher educational attainment and decreased number of career changes (adult volunteers), increased GPA (Ivy League undergraduates), increased summer training completion (West Point cadets), and improved performance and competition advancement (National Spelling Bee contestants). The Short Grit Scale, a more efficient version of the Grit Scale, consisted of 8 items from the original survey and preserved the 2 factor structure [24]. It was tested in the original populations and found not only to be psychometrically sound, but predicted outcomes better than the original [24]. Increased grit, as measured by the Short Grit Scale, was associated with improved psychological health and decreased burnout in a cohort of surgical residents [17].

This original concept of grit has come under attack in more current literature. A meta-analytic review analyzing 88 studies including over 66,000 subjects assessed the structure of grit, the relation of grit to performance, and the distinction of grit from conscientiousness [26]. The perseverance of effort domain strongly correlated with performance, but the consistency of effort domain did not correlate with performance and the combination of the two domains resulted in a significant loss of ability to predict performance. This suggests that the consistency of effort domain should not be a component of grit. Furthermore, the perseverance domain of the grit score and the overall grit score highly correlated with conscientiousness ($r = 0.89$ and $r = 0.84$ respectively). Taken together, this suggests that the value of the grit score in predicting performance stems from the perseverance domain and that this domain is basically a measure of conscientiousness. Another study evaluating the structure of grit also found a poor fit for the two factor model and instead defined grit as the singular construct of "effortful persistence" distinct from conscientiousness [27]. Effortful persistence was associated with "higher life course attainment" that could not be explained by IQ and conscientiousness. Further research is required to more accurately define grit and the components that distinguish and account for its unique effects.

Take Home Points
- Grit is a non-academic trait responsible for success.
- Initial studies of grit are promising, but subsequent work reveals major inconsistencies.
- Further research necessary to define grit, distinguish it from other constructs, and determine its role in improving performance and wellbeing.

18.4.2 Connor-Davidson Resilience Scale (CD-RISC)

The study of resilience over the last 30 years has rapidly increased as psychologists began to realize the importance of resilience in mental health and wellbeing in adults. Dissatisfied with current definitions and measures of resilience, Drs. Connor and Davidson set out to, "develop a valid and reliable measure to quantify resilience, to establish reference values for resilience in the general population and in clinical samples, and to assess the modifiability of resilience in response to pharmacologic treatment in a clinical population" [101]. Drawing on published work in resilience, a list of factors considered important in resilience were constructed. While it remains unclear how the authors selected the survey content from this list, the resultant survey contained 25 items from the following 5 domains: "notion of personal competence, high standards, and tenacity" (8 items), "trust in one's instincts, tolerance of negative affect, and strengthening effects of stress" (7 items), "positive acceptance of change and secure relationships" (5 items), "control" (3 items), and "spiritual influences" (2 items). Responses were measured via a 5-point Likert scale (not true at all to true nearly all of the time). The survey was evaluated in the general population (accessed via random-digit dial), primary care outpatients, psychiatric outpatients, subjects with Generalized Anxiety Disorder (GAD), and subjects with Post Traumatic Stress Disorder (PTSD). The survey demonstrated high internal consistency ($\alpha = 0.89$), high levels of agreement in test-retest reliability among PTSD patients with no clinical change, and appropriate convergence with validated tests among a combined sample of subjects from all groups. While the CD-RISC has been adapted internationally and rests upon psychometrically sound validation, UCSD psychologists sought to improve the quality of the survey by establishing a valid factor structure [102–110]. Using samples of undergraduates, the survey underwent exploratory factor analysis followed by confirmatory factor analysis which resulted in a 10-item survey (drawn from the original survey) with a single domain, persistence [110]. Scores on the 10-item survey correlated well with the initial CD-RISC ($r = 0.92$). In 2007, a 2 item CD-RISC (drawn from the original survey) was developed, containing the following two items: "I am able to adapt to change" and "I tend to bounce back after illness or hardship" [111]. These items correlated well with each of the other 23 items on the original CD-RISC and demonstrated good test-retest reliability, convergent validity, and divergent validity when tested in 6 different populations including subjects from the general population, family medicine outpatients, psychiatric outpatients, depressed patients, GAD patients, and PTSD patients. The positive effects of resilience in health professionals include decreased likelihood of depression [112], anxiety, stress [112–115], fatigue [112], burnout [116] and improved empowerment [117], academic performance [118], quality of life [112–114, 119], conflict management skills [117, 120], job satisfaction [115, 121], self-efficacy [115], purpose in life [121], patient and interpersonal relations [115], and positive perception of learning climate [112, 119]. It must be noted that only the interventional studies measured resilience with validated resilience surveys [113, 114, 122].

Take Home Points
- This is the current gold standard for measurement of resilience.
- It is not widely used despite gold standard status.
- Resilience correlates with improved mental health and wellbeing, so important to measure.
- Resilience is an actionable target for intervention, so important to measure.
- CD-RISC can be used individually and/or in research studies to measure and track resilience.

18.5 Burnout + Wellbeing Interventions

Because there are so many components of wellbeing, interventions to reduce burnout and promote wellbeing have been heterogenous, using varied assessments and targeting a wide array of outcomes. Applying the same conceptual framework of wellbeing to interventions, we will classify interventions as individual or external. Most interventions have focused on individual factors of wellness, but there are a handful of interventions targeting organizational improvement. Table 18.3 details interventions designed to improve individual and external wellbeing. Unfortunately, the majority of these studies are small, single-center interventions with poor generalizability and problematic methodology.

Shanafelt et al.'s electronic intervention supported by the ACS represents the strongest study to date, and is actively enrolling [90]. In an online three-step intervention, surgeons provided a self-assessment of their perceived wellbeing compared to other physicians, completed the PWBI assessment with immediate feedback that included their wellbeing relative to national norms, and provided education regarding common risk factors impacting wellbeing. Last, surgeons reported whether the information provided was useful and whether they planned to implement behavioral change based on the results.

This study is useful for the following reasons:
- Accessibility: the electronic format makes the intervention accessible to thousands of surgeons around the country so that its benefits are not limited to a narrow population
- Individualization: deficits identified are unique to each surgeon which allows tailored intervention specific to the needs of the individual rather than cookie-cutter group interventions

Table 18.3 Interventions to improve wellbeing in the medical community

Author	Wellness category	Intervention	Design	Measurement tool	Population	Outcomes
McCue et al. (1991) [123]	Individual— personal factors	Stress management education	Non-RCT (n = 64)	• MBI • ESSI stress systems instrument • Life experience survey	Medicine + pediatric residents	↓ Stress ↓ Emotional exhaustion
Ospina-Kammerer et al. (2003) [124]	Individual— personal factors	Respiratory one method (breathing relaxation technique)	RCT (n = 24)	• MBI	Family medicine residents	↓ Emotional exhaustion
Dunn et al. (2007) [96]	Individual— personal factors External—socio-cultural factors, organizational factors, learning/ practice environment	Organizational improvements targeting: • Control (physician influence over environment) • Order (environmental and staff improvements) • Meaning (increased emphasis on patient care over administration)	Prospective cohort (n = 32)	• MBI • QWC	PCPs	↓ Exhaustion ↑ Organizational health
Milstein et al. (2009) [125]	Individual— personal factors	Mindfulness education	Non-RCT (n = 15)	• MBI	Pediatric residents	No significant effect
Sood et al. (2011) [114]	Individual— personal factors	Single 90 min educational session in: • Stress management • Resiliency training • Structured relaxation	RCT (n = 32)	• Connor Davidson resilience scale • Perceived stress scale • Smith anxiety scale • Linear analog self-assessment scale	IM Attendings	↑ Resilience ↑ Overall QOL ↓ Perceived stress ↓ Anxiety
Weight et al. (2013) [126]	Individual— personal factors	Incentivized exercise program	Prospective cohort (n = 245)	• 2 item MBI • 1 item linear analog" overall QOL" • Physical activity assessment	Surgery, medicine, pediatrics, OB-GYN residents	↑ QOL ↑ Physical activity

Study	Category	Intervention	Study design	Measures	Population	Results
Moody et al. (2013) [127]	Individual—personal factors	Mindfulness course	RCT (n = 47)	• MBI • Perceived stress scale • Beck depression inventory • Qualitative—journal entries	Oncologists, nurses, social workers, psychologists, NPs, child life specialists	No significant effect on burnout, stress, or depression Journals: ↓ Stress ↑ Inner peace ↑ Compassion ↑ Self-awareness
West et al. (2014) [91]	Individual—personal factors	Biweekly educational/supportive meetings with facilitated discussions about mindfulness, reflection, and shared experience (protected time)	RCT (n = 74)	• Physician job satisfaction scale • Empowerment at work scale • 1 item linear analog "overall QOL" • SF-8 health survey • MBI • Perceived stress scale • Non-standardized Jefferson scale of physician empathy	IM Attendings	↑ Empowerment ↑ Engagement ↑ Self-efficacy ↓ Depersonalization ↓ Burnout No significant effect on stress, depression, overall QOL, job satisfaction
Shanafelt et al. (2014) [90]	Individual—personal factors	3 step electronic intervention: • Online self-assessment • Feedback + education about wellbeing and burnout • Assessment of intent to improve wellbeing in response	Prospective cohort (n = 1150)	• PWBI	Surgeons	↑ Self awareness Promotion of behavioral change

(continued)

Table 18.3 (continued)

Linzer et al. (2015) [128]	External—socio-cultural factors, organizational factors, learning/practice environment	Organizational improvements: • Monthly meetings to discuss work-related issues • Work-flow streamlining • Institution of a quality improvement measure	RCT (n = 135)	Non-standardized measures of: • Stress • Emotional exhaustion • Intent to leave • Satisfaction	PCPs	No significant effect on stress, intent to leave ↓ Emotional exhaustion ↑ Satisfaction
Ripp et al. (2016) [129]	Individual—personal factors	Bimonthly educational/supportive meetings with facilitated discussions about stress, balance, and job satisfaction (unprotected time)	RCT (n = 51)	MBI	IM interns	No significant effect on burnout
Riall et al. (2018) [130]	Individual—personal factors External—learning/practice environment, organizational factors	1 y of monthly "experiential and interactive" sessions addressing: • Energy leadership • Team building • Communication • Work-life integration • Goal setting • Empathy • Strategic diet and exercise • Posture for the surgeon/ergonomics • Stress reduction techniques • Mindfulness/meditation (protected time)	Prospective cohort (n = 49)	• MBI • Energy leadership index • Perceived stress scale • Beck depression inventory • Physician wellbeing index • ACGME resident survey	General surgery residents	↑ Energy leadership index scores ↓ Stress ↓ Emotional exhaustion ↑ Program evaluation scores on ACGME survey No significant effect on leadership skills, work relationships, communication skills, productivity, time management, personal freedom, and work-life balance

- Self-Awareness: providing an estimate of one's own wellbeing relative to others before seeing the results allows the surgeon to gauge the accuracy of his/her own self-assessment which is crucial to understanding oneself and implementing change
- Feasibility: the entire intervention is designed to take ~5 min making it practical for busy surgeons

Rooted in the transtheoretical model of health behavior change, this intervention allows one to identify deficits, provides tools to remedy the deficits, and encourages behavioral change. It currently resides on the American College of Surgery website and can be accessed at https://www.facs.org/member-services/surgeon-well-being.

18.6 Conclusion

Validated tools to measure and monitor wellbeing have been effective in identifying individuals at risk for and with diminished wellbeing. While there are a variety of tools to evaluate individual factors contributing to wellbeing, assessment tools evaluating external factors are in need. Surgeon-specific measures of burnout and wellbeing still do not exist due to the highly individualized nature of wellbeing, and group interventions have been limited in efficacy. Further research must be done to design adequate measures of external wellbeing, to develop and implement effective interventions at a population level, and to prospectively follow interventions to determine long-term outcomes and sustainability. In the immediate future, raising awareness, teaching surgeons to self-assess, providing easily accessible assessment tools, and creating a work environment that is supportive and receptive to change are all actions that can be implemented to enhance wellbeing now. Please see additional chapters in this text which provide further instruction and information on achieving and sustaining wellbeing.

References

1. Naci H, Ioannidis JPA. Evaluation of wellness determinants and interventions by citizen scientists. JAMA. 2015;314(2):121–2. https://doi.org/10.1001/jama.2015.6160.
2. Brigham T, Barden C, Legreid Dopp A, et al. A journey to construct an all-encompassing conceptual model of factors affecting clinician well-being and resilience. NAM Perspect. 2018;8. https://nam.edu/journey-constructencompassing-conceptual-model-factors-affectingclinician-well-resilience. https://doi.org/10.31478/201801b.
3. Maslach C, Jackson SE. The measurement of experienced burnout. J Occup Behav. 1981;2(2):99–113. https://doi.org/10.1002/job.4030020205.
4. Maslach C, Jackson SE, Leiter MP. Maslach burnout inventory manual. Palo Alto, CA: Consulting Psychologists Press; 1996.
5. Shanafelt TD, Hasan O, Dyrbye LN, et al. Changes in burnout and satisfaction with work-life balance in physicians and the general US working population between 2011 and 2014. Mayo Clin Proc. 2015;90(12):1600–13. https://doi.org/10.1016/j.mayocp.2015.08.023.

6. Bianchi R, Schonfeld IS, Laurent E. Burnout-depression overlap: a review. Clin Psychol Rev. 2015;36:28–41. https://doi.org/10.1016/j.cpr.2015.01.004.
7. Leiter MP, Durup J. The discriminant validity of burnout and depression: a confirmatory factor analytic study. Anxiety Stress Coping. 1994;7(4):357–73. https://doi.org/10.1080/10615809408249357.
8. Wurm W, Vogel K, Holl A, et al. Depression-burnout overlap in physicians. PLoS One. 2016;11(3):1–15. https://doi.org/10.1371/journal.pone.0149913.
9. Shanafelt TD, Balch CM, Dyrbye L, et al. Special report: suicidal ideation among American surgeons. Arch Surg. 2011;146(1):54–62. https://doi.org/10.1001/archsurg.2010.292.
10. Dyrbye LN, Satele D, Sloan J, Shanafelt TD. Ability of the physician well-being index to identify residents in distress. J Grad Med Educ. 2014;6(1):78–84. https://doi.org/10.4300/JGME-D-13-00117.1.
11. Shanafelt TD, Balch CM, Bechamps GJ, et al. Burnout and career satisfaction among american surgeons. Ann Surg. 2009;250(3):463–70. https://doi.org/10.1097/SLA.0b013e3181ac4dfd.
12. Steinhardt M, Dolbier C. Evaluation of a resilience intervention to enhance coping strategies and protective factors and decrease symptomatology. J Am Coll Health. 2008;56(4):445–53. https://doi.org/10.3200/JACH.56.44.445-454.
13. Medical Research Council. Lifelong health and well-being. 2010. http://www.mrc.ac.uk/Ourresearch/ResearchInitiatives/LLHW/index.htm#P61_3876.
14. Epstein RM, Krasner MS. Physician resilience: what it means, why it matters, and how to promote it. Acad Med. 2013;88(3):301–3. https://doi.org/10.1097/ACM.0b013e318280cff0.
15. Tugade MM, Fredrickson BL. Resilient individuals use positive emotions to bounce back from negative emotional experiences. J Pers Soc Psychol. 2004;86(2):320–33. https://doi.org/10.1037/0022-3514.86.2.320.
16. Waxman HC, Gray JP, Padron YN. Review of research on educational resilience. Santa Cruz, CA: Center for Research on Education, Diversity and Excellence, University of California; 2003.
17. Salles A, Cohen GL, Mueller CM. The relationship between grit and resident well-being. Am J Surg. 2014;207(2):251–4. https://doi.org/10.1016/j.amjsurg.2013.09.006.
18. Wu G, Feder A, Cohen H, et al. Understanding resilience. Front Behav Neurosci. 2013;7(February):1–15. https://doi.org/10.3389/fnbeh.2013.00010.
19. Southwick SM, Charney DS. The science of resilience: implications for the prevention and treatment of depression. Science (80). 2012;338(6103):79–82. https://doi.org/10.1126/science.1222942.
20. Howe A, Smajdor A, Sto A. The cross-cutting edge towards an understanding of resilience and its relevance to medical training. Med Educ. 2012;46:349–56. https://doi.org/10.1111/j.1365-2923.2011.04188.x.
21. Sood A, Sharma V, Schroeder DR, Gorman B. Stress management and resiliency training (SMART) program among Department of Radiology Faculty: a pilot randomized clinical trial. Explore (NY). 2014;10(6):358–63. https://doi.org/10.1016/j.explore.2014.08.002.
22. Maddi SR. Relevance of hardiness assessment and training to the military context. Mil Psychol. 2007;19(1):61–70.
23. Stoffel JM, Cain J. Review of grit and resilience literature within health professions education. Am J Pharm Educ. 2018;82(2):6150. https://doi.org/10.5688/ajpe6150.
24. Duckworth AL, Quinn PD. Development and validation of the short grit scale (grit-S). J Pers Assess. 2009;91(2):166–74. https://doi.org/10.1080/00223890802634290.
25. Duckworth AL, Peterson C, Matthews MD, Kelly DR. Grit: perseverance and passion for long-term goals. J Pers Soc Psychol. 2007;92(6):1087–101. https://doi.org/10.1037/0022-3514.92.6.1087.
26. Credé M, Tynan MC, Harms PD. Much ado about grit: a meta-analytic synthesis of the grit literature. J Pers Soc Psychol. 2017;113(3):492–511.
27. Abuhassàn A, Bates TC. Grit. J Individ Differ. 2015;36(4):205–14. https://doi.org/10.1027/1614-0001/a000175.

28. Jackson & Maslach. The Maslach burnout inventory manual, vol. 2. 2nd ed; 1986. p. 99–113. https://doi.org/10.1002/job.4030020205.
29. Dyrbye LN, West CP, Shanafelt TD. Defining burnout as a dichotomous variable. J Gen Intern Med. 2009;24(3):440. https://doi.org/10.1007/s11606-008-0876-6.
30. Hill JD, Smith RJH. Monitoring stress levels in postgraduate medical training. Laryngoscope. 2009;119(1):75–8. https://doi.org/10.1002/lary.20013.
31. Rafferty JP, Lemkau JP, Purdy RR, Rudisill JR. Validity of the Maslach burnout inventory for family practice physicians. J Clin Psychol. 1986;42(3):488–92. http://www.ncbi.nlm.nih.gov/pubmed/3711351.
32. Montiel-Company JM, Subirats-Roig C, Flores-Martí P, Bellot-Arcís C, Almerich-Silla JM. Validation of the Maslach burnout inventory-human services survey for estimating burnout in dental students. J Dent Educ. 2016;80(11):1368–75. http://www.ncbi.nlm.nih.gov/pubmed/27803209.
33. Pisanti R, Lombardo C, Lucidi F, Violani C, Lazzari D. Psychometric properties of the Maslach burnout inventory for human services among Italian nurses: a test of alternative models. J Adv Nurs. 2013;69(3):697–707. https://doi.org/10.1111/j.1365-2648.2012.06114.x.
34. Gil-Monte PR. Factorial validity of the Maslach burnout inventory (MBI-HSS) among Spanish professionals. Rev Saude Publica. 2005;39(1):1–8. S0034-89102005000100001.
35. Matejić B, Milenović M, Kisić Tepavčević D, Simić D, Pekmezović T, Worley JA. Psychometric properties of the Serbian version of the Maslach burnout inventory-human services survey: a validation study among anesthesiologists from Belgrade teaching hospitals. ScientificWorldJournal. 2015;2015:903597. https://doi.org/10.1155/2015/903597.
36. West CP, Dyrbye LN, Sloan JA, Shanafelt TD. Single item measures of emotional exhaustion and depersonalization are useful for assessing burnout in medical professionals. J Gen Intern Med. 2009;24(12):1318–21. https://doi.org/10.1007/s11606-009-1129-z.
37. West CP, Dyrbye LN, Satele DV, Sloan JA, Shanafelt TD. Concurrent validity of single-item measures of emotional exhaustion and depersonalization in burnout assessment. J Gen Intern Med. 2012;27(11):1445–52. https://doi.org/10.1007/s11606-012-2015-7.
38. Balch CM, Oreskovich MR, Dyrbye LN, et al. Personal consequences of malpractice lawsuits on American surgeons. J Am Coll Surg. 2011;213(5):657–67. https://doi.org/10.1016/j.jamcollsurg.2011.08.005.
39. Campbell DA, Sonnad SS, Eckhauser FE, Campbell KK, Greenfield LJ. Burnout among American surgeons. Surgery. 2001;130(4):696–705. https://doi.org/10.1067/msy.2001.116676.
40. Dyrbye LN, McMurray J, Linzer M, et al. Relationship between work-home conflicts and burnout among American surgeons. Arch Surg. 2011;146(2):211–7. https://doi.org/10.1001/archsurg.2010.310.
41. West CP, Shanafelt TD, Kolars JC. Quality of life, burnout, educational debt, and medical knowledge among internal medicine residents. JAMA. 2011;306(9):952–60. https://doi.org/10.1007/s11606-011-1730-9.
42. Balch CM, Shanafelt T. Combating stress and burnout in surgical practice: a review. Thorac Surg Clin. 2011;21(3):417–30. https://doi.org/10.1016/j.thorsurg.2011.05.004.
43. Balch CM, Shanafelt TD, Dyrbye L, et al. Surgeon distress as calibrated by hours worked and nights on call. J Am Coll Surg. 2010;211(5):609–19. https://doi.org/10.1016/j.jamcollsurg.2010.06.393.
44. Shanafelt TD, Balch CM, Bechamps G, et al. Burnout and medical errors among American surgeons. Ann Surg. 2010;251(6):995–1000. https://doi.org/10.1097/SLA.0b013e3181bfdab3.
45. Dyrbye LN. Work/home conflict and burnout among academic internal medicine physicians. Arch Intern Med. 2011;171(13):1207–9. https://doi.org/10.1001/archinternmed.2011.289.
46. Balch CM, Shanafelt TD, Sloan J, Satele DV, Kuerer HM. Burnout and career satisfaction among surgical oncologists compared with other surgical specialties. Ann Surg Oncol. 2011;18(1):16–25. https://doi.org/10.1245/s10434-010-1369-5.
47. Balch CM, Shanafelt TD, Sloan JA, Satele DV, Freischlag JA. Distress and career satisfaction among 14 surgical specialties, comparing academic and private practice settings. Ann Surg. 2011;254(4):558–68. https://doi.org/10.1097/SLA.0b013e318230097e.

48. Shanafelt TD, Dyrbye LN, Sinsky C, et al. Relationship between clerical burden and characteristics of the electronic environment with physician burnout and professional satisfaction. Mayo Clin Proc. 2016;91(7):836–48. https://doi.org/10.1016/j.mayocp.2016.05.007.
49. West CP, Dyrbye LN, Shanafelt TD. Physician burnout: contributors, consequences and solutions. J Intern Med. 2018;283(6):516–29. https://doi.org/10.1111/joim.12752.
50. West CP, Huschka MM, Novotny PJ, et al. Association of perceived medical errors: a prospective longitudinal study. JAMA. 2006;296(9):1071–8. https://doi.org/10.1001/jama.296.9.1071.
51. West CP. Association of resident fatigue and distress with perceived medical errors. JAMA. 2009;302(12):1294–300. https://doi.org/10.1001/jama.2009.1389.
52. Demerouti E, Bakker AB, Nachreiner F, Schaufeli WB. A model of burnout and life satisfaction amongst nurses. J Adv Nurs. 2000;32(2):454–64. https://doi.org/10.1046/j.1365-2648.2000.01496.x.
53. Demerouti E, Nachreiner F, Bakker AB, Schaufeli WB. The job demands-resources model of burnout. J Appl Psychol. 2001;86(3):499–512. https://doi.org/10.1037/0021-9010.86.3.499.
54. Halbesleben JRB, Demerouti E. The construct validity of an alternative measure of burnout: investigating the English translation of the Oldenburg burnout inventory. Work Stress. 2005;19(3):208–20. https://doi.org/10.1080/02678370500340728.
55. Bakker AB, Demerouti E. Towards a model of work engagement. Career Dev Int. 2008;13(3):209–23. https://doi.org/10.1108/13620430810870476.
56. Rudman A, Gustavsson JP. Burnout during nursing education predicts lower occupational preparedness and future clinical performance: a longitudinal study. Int J Nurs Stud. 2012;49(8):988–1001. https://doi.org/10.1016/j.ijnurstu.2012.03.010.
57. Rudman A, Gustavsson P, Hultell D. A prospective study of nurses' intentions to leave the profession during their first five years of practice in Sweden. Int J Nurs Stud. 2014;51(4):612–24. https://doi.org/10.1016/j.ijnurstu.2013.09.012.
58. Peterson U, Bergström G, Demerouti E, Gustavsson P, Åsberg M, Nygren Å. Burnout levels and self-rated health prospectively predict future long-term sickness absence: a study among female health professionals. J Occup Environ Med. 2011;53(7):788–93. https://doi.org/10.1097/JOM.0b013e318222b1dc.
59. Kristensen TS, Borritz M, Villadsen E, Christensen KB. The Copenhagen burnout inventory: a new tool for the assessment of burnout. Work Stress. 2005;19(3):192–207. https://doi.org/10.1080/02678370500297720.
60. Mahmoudi S, Atashzadeh-Shoorideh F, Rassouli M, Moslemi A, Pishgooie A, Azimi H. Translation and psychometric properties of the Copenhagen burnout inventory in Iranian nurses. Iran J Nurs Midwifery Res. 2017;22(2):117–22. https://doi.org/10.4103/1735-9066.205958.
61. Fong TCT, Ho RTH, Ng SM. Psychometric properties of the Copenhagen burnout inventory—Chinese version. J Psychol. 2014;148(3):255–66. https://doi.org/10.1080/00223980.2013.781498.
62. Sestili C, Scalingi S, Cianfanelli S, et al. Reliability and use of Copenhagen burnout inventory in Italian sample of university professors. Int J Environ Res Public Health. 2018;15(8):1708. https://doi.org/10.3390/ijerph15081708.
63. Molinero Ruiz E, Basart Gómez-Quintero H, Moncada Lluis S. Validation of the Copenhagen burnout inventory to assess professional burnout in Spain. Rev Esp Salud Publica. 2013;87(2):165–79. https://doi.org/10.4321/S1135-57272013000200006.
64. Shimizutani M, Odagiri Y, Ohya Y, et al. Relationship of nurse burnout with personality characteristics and coping behaviors. Ind Health. 2008;46(4):326–35. http://www.ncbi.nlm.nih.gov/pubmed/18716380
65. Klein J, Grosse Frie K, Blum K, von dem Knesebeck O. Burnout and perceived quality of care among German clinicians in surgery. International J Qual Health Care. 2010;22(6):525–30. https://doi.org/10.1093/intqhc/mzq056.
66. Kassam A, Horton J, Shoimer I, Patten S. Predictors of well-being in resident physicians: a descriptive and Psychometric study. J Grad Med Educ. 2015;7(1):70–4. https://doi.org/10.4300/JGME-D-14-00022.1.

67. Elmblad R, Kodjebacheva G, Lebeck L. Workplace incivility affecting CRNAs: a study of prevalence, severity, and consequences with proposed interventions. AANA J. 2014;82(6):437–45. http://www.ncbi.nlm.nih.gov/pubmed/25842642

68. Henriksen L, Lukasse M. Burnout among Norwegian midwives and the contribution of personal and work-related factors: a cross-sectional study. Sex Reprod Healthc. 2016;9:42–7. https://doi.org/10.1016/j.srhc.2016.08.001.

69. Borritz M. Burnout as a predictor of self-reported sickness absence among human service workers: prospective findings from three year follow up of the PUMA study. Occup Environ Med. 2006;63(2):98–106. https://doi.org/10.1136/oem.2004.019364.

70. Lyndon MP, Henning MA, Alyami H, et al. Burnout, quality of life, motivation, and academic achievement among medical students: a person-oriented approach. Perspect Med Educ. 2017;6(2):108–14. https://doi.org/10.1007/s40037-017-0340-6.

71. Chou L-P, Li C-Y, Hu SC. Job stress and burnout in hospital employees: comparisons of different medical professions in a regional hospital in Taiwan. BMJ Open. 2014;4(2):e004185. https://doi.org/10.1136/bmjopen-2013-004185.

72. Madsen IEH, Lange T, Borritz M, Rugulies R. Burnout as a risk factor for antidepressant treatment—a repeated measures time-to-event analysis of 2936 Danish human service workers. J Psychiatr Res. 2015;65:47–52. https://doi.org/10.1016/j.jpsychires.2015.04.004.

73. Jenkinson C, Wright L, Coulter A. Criterion validity and reliability of the SF-36 in a population sample. Qual Life Res. 1994;3(1):7–12. https://doi.org/10.1007/BF00647843.

74. McHorney CA, Johne W, Anastasiae R. The MOS 36-item short-form health survey (SF-36). Med Care. 1993;31(3):247–63. https://doi.org/10.1097/00005650-199303000-00006.

75. McHorney CA, Ware JE, Raczek AE. The MOS 36-item short-form health survey (SF-36): II. Psychometric and clinical tests of validity in measuring physical and mental health constructs. Med Care. 1993;31(3):247–63. http://www.ncbi.nlm.nih.gov/pubmed/8450681.

76. Harman H. Modern factor analysis. 3rd ed. Chicago: The University of Chicago Press; 1976.

77. SAS. SAS/STAT User's guide. 4th ed. Cary, NC: SAS; 1989.

78. Ware JE, Gandek B, Kosinski M, et al. The equivalence of SF-36 summary health scores estimated using standard and country-specific algorithms in 10 countries: results from the IQOLA Project International Quality of Life Assessment. J Clin Epidemiol. 1998;51(11):1167–70. https://doi.org/10.1016/S0895-4356(98)00108-5.

79. Ware J, Kosinski M, Keller SD. A 12-item short-form health survey: construction of scales and preliminary tests of reliability and validity. Med Care. 1996;34(3):220–33. http://www.ncbi.nlm.nih.gov/pubmed/8628042.

80. Jakobsson U. Using the 12-item short form health survey (SF-12) to measure quality of life among older people. Aging Clin Exp Res. 2007;19(6):457–64. http://www.ncbi.nlm.nih.gov/pubmed/18172367.

81. Gandhi SK, Salmon JW, Zhao SZ, Lambert BL, Gore PR, Conrad K. Psychometric evaluation of the 12-item short-form health survey (SF-12) in osteoarthritis and rheumatoid arthritis clinical trials. Clin Ther. 2001;23(7):1080–98. http://www.ncbi.nlm.nih.gov/pubmed/11519772.

82. Pettit T, Livingston G, Manela M, Kitchen G, Katona C, Bowling A. Validation and normative data of health status measures in older people: the Islington study. Int J Geriatr Psychiatry. 2001;16(11):1061–70. https://doi.org/10.1002/gps.479.

83. Burdine JN, Felix MR, Abel AL, Wiltraut CJ, Musselman YJ. The SF-12 as a population health measure: an exploratory examination of potential for application. Health Serv Res. 2000;35(4):885–904. http://www.ncbi.nlm.nih.gov/pubmed/11055454%0A; http://www.pubmedcentral.nih.gov/articlerender.fcgi?artid=PMC1089158.

84. Younsi M. Health-related quality-of-life measures: evidence from Tunisian population using the SF-12 health survey. Value Health Reg Issues. 2015;7:54–66. https://doi.org/10.1016/j.vhri.2015.07.004.

85. Gandek B, Ware JE, Aaronson NK, et al. Cross-validation of item selection and scoring for the SF-12 health survey in nine countries: results from the IQOLA project. International quality of life assessment. J Clin Epidemiol. 1998;51(11):1171–8. https://doi.org/10.1002/glia.440150307.

86. Lam CLK, Tse EYY, Gandek B. Is the standard SF-12 health survey valid and equivalent for a Chinese population? Qual Life Res. 2005;14(2):539–47. http://www.ncbi.nlm.nih.gov/pubmed/15892443.

87. Dyrbye LN, Szydlo DW, Downing SM, Sloan JA, Shanafelt TD. Development and preliminary psychometric properties of a well-being index for medical students. BMC Med Educ. 2010;10:8. https://doi.org/10.1186/1472-6920-10-8.

88. Dyrbye LN, Schwartz A, Downing SM, Szydlo DW, Sloan JA, Shanafelt TD. Efficacy of a brief screening tool to identify medical students in distress. Acad Med. 2011;86(7):907–14. https://doi.org/10.1097/ACM.0b013e31821da615.

89. Dyrbye LN, Satele D, Shanafelt T. Ability of a 9-item well-being index to identify distress and stratify quality of life in US Workers. J Occup Environ Med. 2016;58(8):810–7. https://doi.org/10.1097/JOM.0000000000000798.

90. Shanafelt TD, Kaups KL, Nelson H, et al. An interactive individualized intervention to promote behavioral change to increase personal well-being in US surgeons. Ann Surg. 2014;259(1):82–8. https://doi.org/10.1097/SLA.0b013e3182a58fa4.

91. West CP, Dyrbye LN, Rabatin JT, et al. Intervention to promote physicianwell-being, job satisfaction, and professionalism a randomized clinical trial. JAMA Intern Med. 2014;174(4):527–33. https://doi.org/10.1001/jamainternmed.2013.14387.

92. Arnetz JE, Arnetz BB. The development and application of a patient satisfaction measurement system for hospital-wide quality improvement. International J Qual Health Care. 1996;8(6):555–66. https://doi.org/10.1093/intqhc/8.6.555.

93. Arnetz BB. Physicians' view of their work environment and organisation. Psychother Psychosom. 1997;66(3):155–62. https://doi.org/10.1159/000289127.

94. Thomsen S, Dallender J, Soares J, Nolan P, Arnetz B. Predictors of a healthy workplace for Swedish and English psychiatrists. Br J Psychiatry. 1998;173(JULY):80–4. http://ovidsp.ovid.com/ovidweb.cgi?T=JS&PAGE=reference&D=emed4&NEWS=N&AN=1998228031.

95. Arnetz BB. Staff perception of the impact of health care transformation on quality of care. International J Qual Health Care. 1999;11(4):345–51. https://doi.org/10.1093/intqhc/11.4.345.

96. Dunn PM, Arnetz BB, Christensen JF, Homer L. Meeting the imperative to improve physician well-being: assessment of an innovative program. J Gen Intern Med. 2007;22(11):1544–52. https://doi.org/10.1007/s11606-007-0363-5.

97. Arnetz JE, Arnetz BB. The development and application of a patient satisfaction measurement system for hospital-wide quality improvement. International J Qual Health Care. 2011;8(6):555–66. https://doi.org/10.1093/intqhc/8.6.555.

98. Arnetz BB. Psychosocial challenges facing physicians of today. Soc Sci Med. 2001;52(2):203–13. https://doi.org/10.1016/S0277-9536(00)00220-3.

99. Anderzén I, Arnetz BB. The impact of a prospective survey-based workplace intervention program on employee health, biologic stress markers, and organizational productivity. J Occup Environ Med. 2005;47(7):671–82. https://doi.org/10.1097/01.jom.0000167259.03247.1e.

100. Gardulf A, Orton ML, Eriksson LE, Undén M, Arnetz B, Kajermo KN, Nordström G. Factors of importance for work satisfaction among nurses in a university hospital in Sweden. Scand J Caring Sci. 2008;22(2):151–60. https://doi.org/10.1111/j.1471-6712.2007.00504.x.

101. Connor KM, Davidson JRT. Development of a new resilience scale: the Connor-Davidson resilience scale (CD-RISC). Depress Anxiety. 2003;18(2):76–82. https://doi.org/10.1002/da.10113.

102. Xie Y, Peng L, Zuo X, Li M. The Psychometric evaluation of the Connor-Davidson resilience scale using a Chinese military sample. PLoS One. 2016;11(2):e0148843. https://doi.org/10.1371/journal.pone.0148843.

103. Blanco V, Guisande MA, Sanchez MT, Otero P, Vazquez FL. Spanish validation of the 10-item Connor-Davidson resilience scale (CD-RISC 10) with non-professional caregivers. Aging Ment Health. 2017;23:1–6. https://doi.org/10.1080/13607863.2017.1399340.

104. Guihard G, Deumier L, Alliot-Licht B, Bouton-Kelly L, Michaut C, Quilliot F. Psychometric validation of the French version of the Connor-Davidson resilience scale. Encéphale. 2018;44(1):40–5. https://doi.org/10.1016/j.encep.2017.06.002.

105. Wu L, Tan Y, Liu Y. Factor structure and psychometric evaluation of the Connor-Davidson resilience scale in a new employee population of China. BMC Psychiatry. 2017;17(1):49. https://doi.org/10.1186/s12888-017-1219-0.
106. Gulbrandsen C. Measuring older women's resilience: evaluating the suitability of the Connor-Davidson resilience scale and the resilience scale. J Women Aging. 2016;28(3):225–37. https://doi.org/10.1080/08952841.2014.951200.
107. Jorgensen IE, Seedat S. Factor structure of the Connor-Davidson resilience scale in south African adolescents. Int J Adolesc Med Health. 2008;20(1):23–32.
108. Jung Y-E, Min J-A, Shin AY, et al. The Korean version of the Connor-Davidson resilience scale: an extended validation. Stress Health. 2012;28(4):319–26. https://doi.org/10.1002/smi.1436.
109. Karaırmak Ö. Establishing the psychometric qualities of the Connor–Davidson resilience scale (CD-RISC) using exploratory and confirmatory factor analysis in a trauma survivor sample. Psychiatry Res. 2010;179(3):350–6. https://doi.org/10.1016/j.psychres.2009.09.012.
110. Campbell-sills L, Stein MB. Psychometric Analysis and Refinement of the Connor – Davidson Resilience Scale (CD-RISC): Validation of a 10-Item Measure of Resilience. J Trauma Stress. 2007;20(6):1019–28. https://doi.org/10.1002/jts.
111. Vaishnavi S, Connor K, Davidson JRT. An abbreviated version of the Connor-Davidson Resilience Scale (CD-RISC), the CD-RISC2 : Psychometric properties and applications in psychopharmacological trials. Psychiatry Res. 2007;152:293–7. https://doi.org/10.1016/j.psychres.2007.01.006.
112. Dyrbye LN, Power DV, Massie FS, et al. Factors associated with resilience to and recovery from burnout: a prospective, multi-institutional study of US medical students. Med Educ. 2010;44(10):1016–26. https://doi.org/10.1111/j.1365-2923.2010.03754.x.
113. Sood A, Sharma V, Schroeder DR, Gorman B. Stress management and resiliency training (SMART) program among Department of Radiology faculty: a pilot randomized clinical trial. Explore (NY). 2014;10(6):358–63. https://doi.org/10.1016/j.explore.2014.08.002.
114. Sood A, Prasad K, Schroeder D, Varkey P. Stress management and resilience training among Department of Medicine faculty: a pilot randomized clinical trial. J Gen Intern Med. 2011;26(8):858–61. https://doi.org/10.1007/s11606-011-1640-x.
115. Mache S, Bernburg M, Baresi L, Groneberg DA. Evaluation of self-care skills training and solution-focused counselling for health professionals in psychiatric medicine: a pilot study. Int J Psychiatry Clin Pract. 2016;20(4):239–44. https://doi.org/10.1080/13651501.2016.1207085.
116. Magtibay DL, Chesak SS, Coughlin K, Sood A. Decreasing stress and burnout in nurses: efficacy of blended learning with stress management and resilience training program. J Nurs Adm. 2017;47(7–8):391–5. https://doi.org/10.1097/NNA.0000000000000501.
117. Pines EW, Rauschhuber ML, Cook JD, et al. Enhancing resilience, empowerment, and conflict management among baccalaureate students: outcomes of a pilot study. Nurse Educ. 2014;39(2):85–90. https://doi.org/10.1097/NNE.0000000000000023.
118. Beauvais AM, Stewart JG, DeNisco S, Beauvais JE. Factors related to academic success among nursing students: a descriptive correlational research study. Nurse Educ Today. 2014;34(6):918–23. https://doi.org/10.1016/j.nedt.2013.12.005.
119. Tempski P, Santos IS, Mayer FB, et al. Relationship among medical student resilience, educational environment and quality of life. PLoS One. 2015;10(6):e0131535. https://doi.org/10.1371/journal.pone.0131535.
120. Pines EW, Rauschhuber ML, Norgan GH, et al. Stress resiliency, psychological empowerment and conflict management styles among baccalaureate nursing students. J Adv Nurs. 2012;68(7):1482–93. https://doi.org/10.1111/j.1365-2648.2011.05875.x.
121. Waite PJ, Richardson GE. Determining the efficacy of resiliency training in the work site. J Allied Health. 2004;33(3):178–83.
122. Magtibay DL, Chesak SS, Coughlin K, Sood A. Decreasing stress and burnout in nurses. JONA J Nurs Adm. 2017;47(7/8):391–5. https://doi.org/10.1097/NNA.0000000000000501.
123. McCue JD. A stress management workshop improves residents' coping skills. Arch Intern Med. 1991;151(11):2273–7. https://doi.org/10.1001/archinte.1991.00400110117023.

124. Ospina-Kammerer V, Figley C. An evaluation of the respiratory one method (ROM) in reducing emotional exhaustion among family physician residents. Int J Emerg Ment Health. 2003;5(1):29–32.
125. Milstein JM, Raingruber BJ, Bennett SH, Kon AA, Winn CA, Paterniti DA. Burnout assessment in house officers: evaluation of an intervention to reduce stress. Med Teach. 2009;31(4):338–41. https://doi.org/10.1080/01421590802208552.
126. Weight CJ, Sellon JL, Lessard-Anderson CR, Shanafelt TD, Olsen KD, Laskowski ER. Physical activity, quality of life, and burnout among physician trainees: the effect of a team-based, incentivized exercise program. Mayo Clin Proc. 2013;88(12):1435–42. https://doi.org/10.1016/j.mayocp.2013.09.010.
127. Moody K, Kramer D, Santizo RO, et al. Helping the helpers: mindfulness training for burnout in pediatric oncology-a pilot program. J Pediatr Oncol Nurs. 2013;30(5):275–84. https://doi.org/10.1177/1043454213504497.
128. Linzer M, Poplau S, Grossman E, et al. A cluster randomized trial of interventions to improve work conditions and clinician burnout in primary care: results from the healthy work place (HWP) study. J Gen Intern Med. 2015;30(8):1105–11. https://doi.org/10.1007/s11606-015-3235-4.
129. Ripp JA, Fallar R, Korenstein D. A randomized controlled trial to decrease job burnout in first-year internal medicine residents using a facilitated discussion group intervention. J Grad Med Educ. 2016;8(2):256–9. https://doi.org/10.4300/JGME-D-15-00120.1.
130. Riall TS, Teiman J, Chang M, et al. Maintaining the fire but avoiding burnout: implementation and evaluation of a resident well-being program. J Am Coll Surg. 2018;226(4):369–79. https://doi.org/10.1016/j.jamcollsurg.2017.12.017.
131. Dewa CS, Jacobs P, Thanh NX, Loong D. An estimate of the cost of burnout on early retirement and reduction in clinical hours of practicing physicians in Canada. BMC Health Serv Res. 2014;14(1):254. https://doi.org/10.1186/1472-6963-14-254.
132. Williams ES, Manwell LB, Konrad TR, Linzer M. The relationship of organizational culture, stress, satisfaction, and burnout with physician-reported error and suboptimal patient care. Health Care Manag Rev. 32(3):203–12.
133. Shanafelt TD, Bradley KA, Wipf JE, Back AL. Burnout and self-reported patient care in an internal medicine residency program. Ann Intern Med. 2002;136(5):358.
134. Shanafelt T, Sloan J, Satele D, Balch C. Why do surgeons consider leaving practice?. J Am Coll Surg. 2011;212(3):421–2.
135. Shanafelt TD, Mungo M, Schmitgen J, et al. Longitudinal study evaluating the association between physician burnout and changes in professional work effort. Mayo Clin Proc. 2016;91(4):422–31.
136. Shanafelt TD, Dyrbye LN, West CP, Sinsky CA. Potential impact of burnout on the US physician workforce. Mayo Clin Proc. 2016;91(11):1667–8.
137. Oreskovich MR. Prevalence of alcohol use disorders among American surgeons. Arch Surg. 2012;147(2):168–74. https://doi.org/10.1001/archsurg.2011.1481.

Chapter 19
Evaluating Organizational Structures and Institutional Policy for Wellbeing

Yue-Yung Hu and Karl Bilimoria

19.1 Introduction

Physician burnout has been linked to poor physical health, depression, alcoholism, and suicide. Because burned out and/or dissatisfied physicians have less satisfied and less compliant patients, make more errors, and are more frequently subject to litigation, poor physician wellbeing also detracts from patients' experiences and the quality of their care. Finally, as affected physicians reduce their professional efforts, turn over more rapidly, and leave medicine, wellbeing impacts the workforce and healthcare system [1, 2]. Given these costs, a business case for the organizational prioritization of physician wellness has been made [3].

Much of the focus on physician wellbeing has focused on the individual, with proposed strategies including training in resilience, coping strategies, emotional awareness/regulation, mindfulness, and stress reduction. In a recent meta-analysis of 52 physician burnout interventions, 32 were targeted at the individual and only 20 at the work environment. Yet, in studies that reported overall burnout as the outcome, structural or organizational interventions were more effective than those directed at the individual [4]. In keeping with these findings, the National Academy of Medicine has proposed a conceptual model (Fig. 19.1) in which 4 of the 7 factors

Y.-Y. Hu (✉)
Surgical Outcomes and Quality Improvement Center (SOQIC), Department of Surgery and Center for Healthcare Studies, Feinberg School of Medicine, Northwestern University, Chicago, IL, USA

Division of Pediatric Surgery, Ann & Robert H. Lurie Children's Hospital, Feinberg School of Medicine, Northwestern University, Chicago, IL, USA
e-mail: yueyunghu@luriechildrens.org

K. Bilimoria
Surgical Outcomes and Quality Improvement Center (SOQIC), Department of Surgery and Center for Healthcare Studies, Feinberg School of Medicine, Northwestern University, Chicago, IL, USA
e-mail: kbilimoria@nm.org

© Springer Nature Switzerland AG 2020
E. Kim, B. Lindeman (eds.), *Wellbeing*, Success in Academic Surgery,
https://doi.org/10.1007/978-3-030-29470-0_19

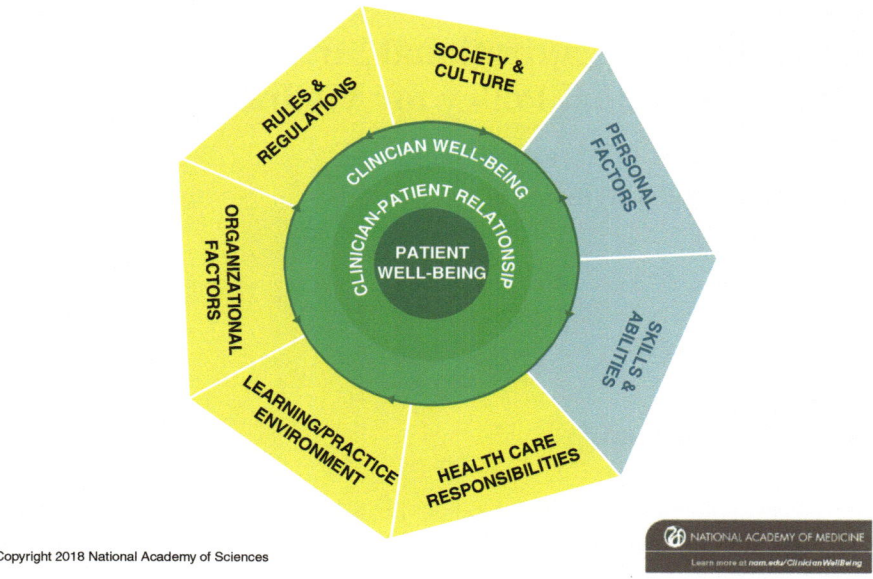

Fig. 19.1 National Academy of Medicine conceptual model

associated with clinician wellbeing are "external" (sociocultural, regulatory/business/payer environment, organizational, learning/practice environment), and only 3 "individual" (health care role, personal factors, skills & abilities) [5].

Our own ongoing qualitative studies of surgical resident wellbeing have corroborated this work. Poor wellbeing is multifactorial, and work/learning environments that are unsupportive or difficult to navigate heavily contribute. We've encountered resistance to the idea of individual training as a solution to a problem with environmental drivers. Individual training may increase the workload of already stressed physicians ("another checkbox") and may also further disillusion them by framing the problem as an inadequacy or weakness on their part ("if you were more resilient, you wouldn't be burned out"). Moreover, in failing to address structural or organizational factors that contribute to burnout, the opportunity to prevent it is missed. Evaluation at the organizational or environmental level is therefore critical to understanding individual wellbeing.

19.2 Content to Evaluate

19.2.1 Exposures

Of the 20 organizational/structural interventions in the meta-analysis, 11 involved a change in duty hours regulations [4]. However, duty hours are relevant only to residents, a small proportion of active clinicians. Moreover, after randomizing general

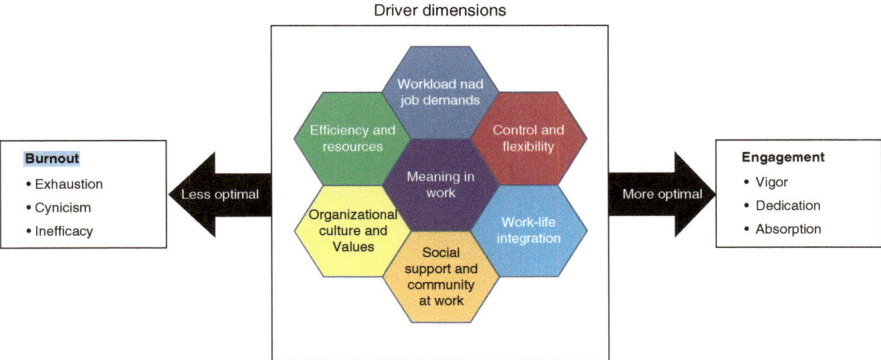

Fig. 19.2 Shanafelt Areas of Work-Life conceptual model

surgery residency programs to standard versus flexible duty hour restrictions for the Flexibility In Duty-hours Requirements for Surgical Trainees (FIRST) Trial, we found a substantial rate of burnout in both study arms with no significant difference between the two [6], indicating that even surgical resident wellbeing is more complex than the number of hours worked.

For the Surgical Education Culture Optimization using targeted interventions based on National Data (SECOND) Trial, we exhaustively reviewed existing conceptual models of wellbeing [7]. Ultimately, we found Shanafelt's Areas of Work-Life conceptual model (Fig. 19.2) [2] the most intuitive for gathering and feeding back data to institutions on their local drivers of wellbeing. In it, Workload & Job Demands is only one of seven domains—and duty hours are only one aspect among many (e.g., use of allied health professionals) within it. Other domains include Control & Flexibility (e.g., control over calendars), Work-Life Integration (e.g., expectations/role models, vacation policies, medical leave policies), Social Support & Community at Work (e.g., social gatherings, team structure, collegiality, physical configuration of work unit space), Organizational Culture & Values (e.g., equity/ fairness, organizational mission, behavior of senior leaders, communication/messaging), Efficiency & Resources (e.g., efficiency of electronic health record system), and Meaning in Work (e.g., opportunities for professional development). Based upon our FIRST follow-up work [8], we added Mistreatment (i.e., discrimination, sexual harassment, and/or abuse) as an eighth domain. As our work in this arena progresses, we may find additional determinants of physician wellbeing worthy of evaluation.

19.2.2   Outcomes

Although it is the most commonly published metric, burnout represents only one dimension of wellbeing. Shanafelt's model conceptualizes wellbeing as a spectrum, ranging from burnout to engagement; both likely need to be measured [2].

Institutions may also measure the downstream consequences of poor wellbeing. Residency programs, for example, may track their rates of attrition [9]. Hospitals may similarly assess their rates of turnover, as well as their productivity/revenue, patient satisfaction, and/or quality/safety [3].

19.3   Methods

19.3.1   *Measuring Exposures*

As with other evaluations of organizational performance, wellbeing may be studied both quantitatively and qualitatively. For the SECOND Trial, we are using both techniques. In this text, we will review methodologies that we have encountered and reviewed, as well as those we have implemented. For a more exhaustive review of organizational climate and culture theory and research, we direct readers to Schneider, Ehrhart, and Macey [10].

Survey is the most common means of gathering quantitative data on organizational drivers of wellbeing; institutions administer surveys to individual clinicians and analyze their results in aggregate to get an overall sense of their work environments and/or climates. Whenever possible, we select survey instruments that have been previously validated. However, because these instruments were not always developed specifically with residents, surgeons, or even clinicians in mind, modifications are sometimes necessary. When adaptations to existing instruments are made, we strongly recommend rigorous and iterative field testing prior to survey distribution, followed by confirmatory factor analysis of survey responses to ensure that the adapted or novel items accurately capture the intended questions [7].

No instrument currently exists that encompasses all domains described by either the National Academy of Medicine [5] or Shanafelt's Areas of Work-Life [2] model. Although the Areas of Worklife Survey [11] (AWS) shares a name with Shanafelt's conceptual model, it was developed by a different group for a much broader population; indeed, it was intended as a companion piece to the Maslach Burnout Inventory, described below under Measuring Outcomes. As with Shanafelt's conceptual model, the AWS seeks to describe the work environment and its contributions to employee engagement or burnout. It consists of either 18 (short version) or 28 (full length version) items that fall within 6 domains. Many overlap with Shanafelt's: Workload, Control, Community, and Values. The remaining two, Reward and Fairness, fall within Shanafelt's Organizational Culture and Values domain. Because the AWS was constructed for an audience that includes all types of employees, we found it necessary to modify some items for physician respondents. For example, we changed, "I have enough time to do what's important in my job," to, "I have enough time for direct patient care after completion of administrative tasks (e.g., notes, orders)," and, "My program effectively uses support staff (e.g., advance practice providers, social workers, patient transporters, etc.) to allow me to spend more time on patient care activities. To address the Shanafelt domains not captured by items in the AWS (i.e., Work-Life Integration, Efficiency & Resources, and Meaning in Work), we developed and exhaustively tested additional items, including many that address education specifically (e.g., "My program emphasizes learning from adverse events or complications rather than placing blame on residents," and, "My program protects educational time.").

We conceptualize mistreatment in several broad classes: bullying, discrimination, and harassment. To capture bullying, we adapted the Negative Acts Questionnaire, which, in its original form, lists 22 types of verbally/emotionally and/or physically abusive behaviors and has been used to survey surgeons [12]. Based on other work in trainee abuse [13, 14], we added an item for "being cursed or sworn at." The instruments that exist for discrimination or harassment are less universal; there are multiple survey studies published in the literature, each of which queries its respondents using a different list of behaviors. We therefore compiled items from multiple published articles for use [13–22].

Response bias should be considered when interpreting survey data; because affected individuals may be more willing to participate, data that derive from incomplete samples may overestimate the magnitude of organizational problems. Rigorous attempts to increase response rates should therefore be made. Many surveys published in the surgical literature are distributed in ways that preclude calculations of response rates (e.g., postings on open forum websites); a clear limitation in trying to characterize prevalence. We administer the SECOND Trial survey instrument at the time of the American Board of Surgery In-Training Examination (ABSITE). Because the ABSITE is mandatory for all residents training in Accreditation Council of Graduate Medical Education (ACGME)-accredited general surgery programs, we are able to reach the entirety of our population over a single brief period of time annually. Concerns have been expressed that measurement at the time of a national examination may overestimate distress, while our psychometricians have instead suspected that post-test elation underestimates it. We accept this uncertain bias as a tradeoff in order to obtain a near complete response rate. We further posit that individual residents are more likely to be similar to one another in terms of their external stressors at the time of the ABSITE than at other randomly selected times in the academic year.

When no comparable circumstance exists for a study population, incentives may be helpful. We administer another survey to program directors annually in order to inventory ongoing wellness initiatives at their institutions. To encourage participation, we tie survey completion to trial enrollment, and we allow participants to download their responses to submit to the ACGME as evidence of their work in wellbeing to maintain their own accreditation. We also multiply contact nonresponders to remind them to participate.

Finally, surveys are commonly criticized for capturing perception rather than observed "truth." We note that wellbeing in the workplace is dependent upon the perceptions of its suitability for the individuals working within it; psychological safety, for example, is by definition a perceived state. Hence, we believe that perception is not only the standard and most convenient, but also the most relevant metric in assessing organizational environments.

While useful for canvassing large populations, survey research is entirely dependent on preexisting hypotheses; concepts that are not directly addressed by survey items cannot be evaluated. Qualitative research fills this gap; it allows novel, previously unexplored themes to come to the fore. It also provides a nuanced understanding of the environment that may inform future survey development and/or refinement. Indeed, FIRST Trial survey data inspired qualitative work that subsequently informed the SECOND Trial: because we noticed a gender difference in burnout rates on the ABSITE survey, we performed qualitative interviews to explore the cause [23]. That data led us to add questions about mistreatment on the 2018 ABSITE, and we found that after controlling for these experiences, the gender difference became insignificant [8]. The SECOND Trial now seeks to characterize residents' work and learning environments more broadly than just mistreatment; we hope to better understand culture and how it is enacted and/or reinforced. To that end, we are currently visiting 20–30 surgical residency programs to collect various types of qualitative data.

Semi-structured interviews and focus groups are among the most common techniques for gathering qualitative data. Individual interviews may diminish anxiety about non-confidentiality and encourage people to speak more freely, while focus groups allow participants to react to one another's responses. We initiate our interviews and focus groups with questions based on pre-existing hypotheses, then explore the responses. Thus, each is conducted differently, and without the rigidity inherent to survey construction, we are able to follow where the data leads. Multiple viewpoints are important for triangulation. On each Program Tour, we perform individual interviews with program leadership, faculty, and residents, as well as separate focus groups for junior and senior residents. With all of these perspectives, we gain a complete understanding of the rationale behind a policy/intervention, the details of its implementation, and its impact. We record all interviews and focus groups and have them transcribed for later, iterative thematic analysis. Interviews and focus groups are continued until thematic saturation is reached, i.e., when no new themes emerge.

Interview/focus group participants may not be able to report all that the research team desires to understand. With our SECOND Trial Program Tours, we aim to compare and contrast different surgical residency programs, but because most of the residents with whom we interact have only had one training experience, they lack the context to directly answer that question. Ethnographic observations are an important complementary means of obtaining qualitative data: environments are visited, and *in vivo* interactions are observed directly by the research team. On our Program Tours, we visit resident workspaces (e.g., housestaff lounges/libraries, call rooms) and attend departmental and educational conferences. Tools may be developed and tested to structure the data capture from these observations. For Morbidity and Mortality conferences, we have developed an observation tool that captures aspects of the physical space (e.g., most attendees are unable to hear), the emphasis of the discussion (e.g., blame, learning), as well as the nature of the interactions (e.g., contentious, defensive, collegial) that may reflect each department's culture and values.

Finally, "artifacts," i.e., the "implements, notes, or materials," are another rich qualitative data source for understanding organizational culture. We request policies, procedures, and training materials at each Program Tour. Analysis of these articles provides information about codified values and existing infrastructure at each program.

19.3.2   Measuring Outcomes

The Maslach Burnout Inventory (MBI) is the standard instrument for measuring burnout. It consists of three domains, emotional exhaustion, depersonalization, and personal accomplishment. We use a clinician-focused version with three questions per domain. The response for each item is a Likert-type scale reflecting the experience with which that item is experienced. Because the longest frequency provided on the response scale is "a few times a year," the MBI is not intended for more than annual use. Since the ABSITE survey occurs annually, the MBI is appropriate for us. However, those seeking to track burnout more frequently (for example, those seeking to evaluate the impact of a month-long intervention) may find that the MBI is not sensitive enough to change. Moreover, despite having the strongest psychometrics of any instrument for measuring clinician wellbeing, interpretation and/or contextualization of the MBI is somewhat complex. It was originally intended to be used as a continuous scale, but many clinicians and researchers have found dichotomization more intuitive ("burned out" vs "not burned out"). Because no cutoff was established by Maslach, various criteria have been developed by different groups; currently there are 47 different ways to interpret the MBI published in the literature [1].

The Professional Fulfillment Index (PFI) is responsive to many criticisms of the MBI. It was designed to assess physicians specifically, and it measures professional fulfillment as well as burnout. Its items are anchored over the previous 2 weeks, allowing for more frequent assessments than the MBI [24]. Preliminary data indicate that its subscales (work exhaustion and interpersonal disengagement specifically pertaining to patient care) are more amenable to combining into a single "burnout" scale and therefore dichotomizing than the MBI [25]. However, because it is a relatively new instrument, the research experience with it is limited. Without published norms for their relevant subpopulations, organizations may find it difficult to contextualize their results.

Other instruments also exist. For a more exhaustive review, we refer readers to Rotenstein's JAMA article [1] and the National Academy of Medicine website [26]. Regardless of the instrument selected, organizations should note that wellbeing is a potentially sensitive topic and take care to preserve respondent confidentiality. To this end, we collect limited demographic variables, and we assure participants that, as an independent third-party conducting the survey and performing the analysis, we will not share their responses with their programs or the ACGME. Organizations should be prepared to act upon the results of these surveys, as physicians may become further disengaged if they report dissatisfaction and see that no action is taken as a result [27]. We plan to give SECOND Trial intervention arm programs personalized reports of their aggregated exposures and outcomes data (e.g., on the Areas of Work-Life questions, on the MBI), as well as access to a toolkit of wellbeing interventions built from what we've learned on our Program Tours. We intend for them to use this data to identify weaknesses in their learning environments then select interventions targeting those areas.

19.4 Future Directions

Although organizational culture/climate assessment [10] and physician wellbeing [1, 4] have been independently studied for decades, further research needs to be done to link the two concepts. We hope the SECOND Trial will begin to address this gap. After data and toolkit dissemination, annual reassessments (i.e., the ABSITE and program director surveys) will be conducted to identify the most impactful interventions to include in a final toolkit. Through organizational evaluation and intervention, we hope to make meaningful improvements in the education and wellbeing of our residents.

References

1. Rotenstein LS, Torre M, Ramos MA, et al. Prevalence of burnout among physicians: a systematic review. JAMA. 2018;320:1131–50.
2. Shanafelt TD, Noseworthy JH. Executive leadership and physician well-being: nine organizational strategies to promote engagement and reduce burnout. Mayo Clin Proc. 2017;92:129–46.
3. Shanafelt T, Goh J, Sinsky C. The business case for investing in physician well-being. JAMA Intern Med. 2017;177:1826–32.
4. West CP, Dyrbye LN, Erwin PJ, Shanafelt TD. Interventions to prevent and reduce physician burnout: a systematic review and meta-analysis. Lancet. 2016;388:2272–81.
5. Brigham T, Barden C, Dopp AL, et al. A journey to construct an all-encompassing conceptual model of factors affecting clinical well-being and resilience. Washington: National Academy of Medicine; 2018.
6. Bilimoria KY, Chung JW, Hedges LV, et al. National cluster-randomized trial of duty-hour flexibility in surgical training. N Engl J Med. 2016;374:713–27.
7. Zhang L, Cheung EOY, Ma M, et al. A conceptual model for understanding the learning environment and surgical resident wellbeing. (Abstract submitted to Surgical Education Week 2020).
8. Hu YY, Ellis RJ, Hewitt DB, et al. Discrimination, Abuse, Harassment, and Burnout in Surgical Residency Training. N Engl J Med. 2019;381:1741–52.
9. Ellis RJ, Holmstrom AL, Hewitt DB, et al. A comprehensive national survey on thoughts of leaving residency, alternative career paths, and reasons for staying in general surgery residency. Am J Surg 2019.

10. Schneider B, Ehrhart MG, Macey WH. Organizational climate and culture. Annu Rev Psychol. 2013;64:361–88.
11. Leiter MP, Maslach C. Areas of worklife survey manual and sampler set. Menlo Park: Mind Garden, Inc.; 2011.
12. Ling M, Young CJ, Shepherd HL, Mak C, Saw RP. Workplace bullying in surgery. World J Surg. 2016;40:2560–6.
13. Nagata-Kobayashi S, Maeno T, Yoshizu M, Shimbo T. Universal problems during residency: abuse and harassment. Med Educ. 2009;43:628–36.
14. Richman JA, Flaherty JA, Rospenda KM, Christensen ML. Mental health consequences and correlates of reported medical student abuse. JAMA. 1992;267:692–4.
15. Crebbin W, Campbell G, Hillis DA, Watters DA. Prevalence of bullying, discrimination and sexual harassment in surgery in Australasia. ANZ J Surg. 2015;85:905–9.
16. Rangel EL, Smink DS, Castillo-Angeles M, et al. Pregnancy and motherhood during surgical training. JAMA Surg. 2018;153(7):644–52.
17. Baldwin DC Jr, Daugherty SR, Rowley BD. Racial and ethnic discrimination during residency: results of a national survey. Acad Med. 1994;69:S19–21.
18. Carr PL, Ash AS, Friedman RH, et al. Faculty perceptions of gender discrimination and sexual harassment in academic medicine. Ann Intern Med. 2000;132:889–96.
19. Liebschutz JM, Darko GO, Finley EP, Cawse JM, Bharel M, Orlander JD. In the minority: black physicians in residency and their experiences. J Natl Med Assoc. 2006;98:1441–8.
20. Richman JA, Flaherty JA, Rospenda KM. Perceived workplace harassment experiences and problem drinking among physicians: broadening the stress/alienation paradigm. Addiction. 1996;91:391–403.
21. Cook DJ, Liutkus JF, Risdon CL, Griffith LE, Guyatt GH, Walter SD. Residents' experiences of abuse, discrimination and sexual harassment during residency training. McMaster University Residency Training Programs. CMAJ. 1996;154:1657–65.
22. Shinsako SA, Richman JA, Rospenda KM. Training-related harassment and drinking outcomes in medical residents versus graduate students. Subst Use Misuse. 2001;36:2043–63.
23. Dahlke AR, Johnson JK, Greenberg CC, et al. Gender differences in utilization of duty-hour regulations, aspects of burnout, and psychological well-being among general surgery residents in the United States. Ann Surg. 2018;268(2):204–11.
24. Trockel M, Bohman B, Lesure E, et al. A brief instrument to assess both burnout and professional fulfillment in physicians: reliability and validity, including correlation with self-reported medical errors, in a sample of resident and practicing physicians. Acad Psychiatr. 2018;42:11–24.
25. Trockel M. Personal communication. 2019.
26. Valid and reliable survey instruments to measure burnout, well-being, and other work-related dimensions. 2019. https://nam.edu/valid-reliable-survey-instruments-measure-burnout-well-work-related-dimensions/.
27. Dyrbye LN, Meyers D, Ripp J, Dalal N, Bird SB, Sen S. A pragmatic approach for organizations to measure health care professional well-being. Washington: National Academy of Medicine; 2018.

Chapter 20
Emerging Areas of Research

Robert Wright, Arghavan Salles, Dana Lin, and Claudia Mueller

Physician wellbeing has garnered widespread attention, from major organizations such as the National Academy of Medicine (NAM) and American Medical Association (AMA), to the popular press such as USA Today and Forbes. The attention is warranted; physician suicide rates are twice the national average [1]. As detailed in previous chapters of this encyclopedia, poor physician wellbeing has a far-reaching impact, extending beyond individual physicians to the patients [2] and health care systems [3, 4]. This chapter will focus on the empirical interventions aimed at improving physician wellbeing.

Research has shown wellbeing starts to worsen during medical school [5, 6], residency and early in careers [7]. The decline in wellbeing has not gone unnoticed by training programs. Most medical schools have dedicated programs focusing on medical student wellbeing. In addition, resident wellbeing has been addressed at the national level with the Accreditation Council for Graduate Medical Education (ACGME) duty hour restrictions [8] and the requirement that residency programs have a wellness curriculum.

In spite of the changes to residency training programs, wellbeing at every level continues to be an issue. The study of wellbeing within medical professionals has mainly focused on the reduction of burnout [9]. In research, burnout is mainly defined by its components: emotional exhaustion, depersonalization, and lack of personal accomplishment [10]. It is typically measured using a standardized outcome, the Maslach Burnout Inventory, previously described in Chap. 19, and is reliable and easy to administer for self-reporting [10].

R. Wright · D. Lin · C. Mueller (✉)
Department of Surgery, Stanford University, Stanford, CA, USA
e-mail: wrightr@stanford.edu; danalin@stanford.edu; ClMueller@stanfordchildrens.org

A. Salles
Stanford University School of Medicine, Stanford, CA, USA
e-mail: arghavan@alumni.stanford.edu

© Springer Nature Switzerland AG 2020
E. Kim, B. Lindeman (eds.), *Wellbeing*, Success in Academic Surgery,
https://doi.org/10.1007/978-3-030-29470-0_20

Broadly, wellbeing interventions are categorized by the level of their target: the organization or the individual [11, 12]. Organizational interventions focus on a systemic change and often involve changes in workflow. Individual interventions take a more traditional approach to focusing on the physician and not necessarily the system.

20.1 Organizational Interventions

An organizational intervention will most likely need the cooperation of many levels of the care team, including the administration. For example, an alteration in physician workflow also results in changes to ancillary staff workflow. In large organizations, changes require working with administration and potentially union heads to ensure alterations in workflow or work systems can be accommodated. Organizational interventions use workflow changes that are specific for the specialty, organization type, and the staff. It is important that the specific changes made in the interventions are designed for the individual organization, but the concepts and rationale for the changes are typically replicable to other organizations.

Involving physicians in the design of the organizational intervention is critical to successful improvements in wellbeing. One early intervention used a 5-year longitudinal multi-site study to reorganize three aspects of the institutional system to meet the desires of the physicians [13]. First, physicians were provided with greater control over their work environment, most specifically about the scheduling of clinical duties. Routine group meetings were held to help implement scheduling changes that were more in order with physician ideals. Second, focus was placed on improving order in clinic operations (e.g., through optimization of patient flow and medical assistant training). Third, the intervention created more meaning for the physicians in their work through changes such as highlighting clinical care rather than administrative tasks. Over the course of the study, physician wellbeing improved, as evidenced by a reduction in emotional and work-related exhaustion. This study provided an effective model and illustrates how changes to wellbeing can be made when physicians have an explicit voice in their planning and execution. Giving agency to the physicians allowed the intervention to be tailored to the needs of each site in the study, which led to improved outcomes.

Many organizational interventions also contain components of individual interventions. One randomized clinical trial tested small-group facilitation for physicians in a department of medicine [14]. The institution provided protected time for a group of physicians to participate in wellness sessions. The small-group meetings occurred for 1 h every other week and were led by a fellow physician who was trained in their conduct. At each session, a different wellbeing-related topic was highlighted. For instance, participants completed a wellbeing exercise (e.g., journaling), participated in a group discussion, and learned skills and solutions aimed at improving wellness. Another group of participants was randomly assigned to a control condition in which they were given a protected hour every 2 weeks to use at their discretion. The researchers also obtained the self-reported responses of physicians not enrolled in the study who took part in department surveys. The intervention lasted 9 months with self-reported measures assessed at 3, 6, 9, 12, and 21 months from the start date. Compared to the control group, the intervention group showed significant improvements in empowerment and engagement at work at 3 and 12 months post-intervention. Additionally, the intervention group had a large decrease in burnout, while the control group had a slight decrease in burnout compared to the physicians who completed department surveys over the same time period but did not participate in either condition.

An additional example of combining organizational and individual interventions, a pilot study tested a time-banking system and an integrated career-life planning intervention for physicians in clinical and basic sciences at a university hospital [15]. The interventions were designed based on qualitative work which found physicians often exchanged duties with friends and colleagues in order to meet all of the demands of their careers. The researchers aimed to formalize the exchange process and asked participants to log the time they spent on activities such as short notice coverage, teaching, and service. Participants were able to view their logs as well as their colleagues' logs to encourage accountability and fairness. The study set up two types of rewards for the banked time: home (e.g. meal delivery, errand outsourcing) and work (e.g. grant writing, academic support). The study found that the basic science physicians mainly used the work services while the clinical physicians mainly used the home services. Interestingly, the researchers focused on research productivity as a main outcome in this study. The researchers matched participants with other faculty with similar demographic and job standing variables. In the study's 2-year span, participants were awarded 1.3 more grants each compared to the controls, about $1.1 million more per person. Beyond the promising outcomes of the study, it was also cost effective, as it only cost about $3000 per year per participant. Such a time-banking system is very flexible and can be adapted to each institution or department. It may be tailored in both the activities which count toward the banking as well as the rewards. This allows for financial flexibility as well in that the rewards may be scaled down to lower the potential annual cost.

A multi-site study found tailored interventions help improve clinician wellbeing [16]. The study set up work teams at each of the 34 participating clinics to help identify specific issues. Participants were mainly physicians (90% intervention and 83% control). The intervention sites set up a combination of tasks meant to improve communication, alter current workflow, and develop quality improvement projects. These changes involved clinic administration staff assisting with coordinating changes to how standard procedures occur. This could be as simple as reassigning call schedules or hiring new staff to ensure each clinician has a dedicated medical assistant. The study showed that the interventions helped reduce clinician burnout and improve satisfaction. Further, they identified workflow modification as having the strongest effect, followed by communication improvement.

Not all effective interventions have been as complex as these. To investigate burnout in the ICU, researchers compared standard staffing, with a single intensivist covering for a week at a time, to shift staffing, with one intensivist during the day and another at night [17]. At the end of the study intensivists working shifts reported lower burnout than those in the standard staffing condition. Additionally, intensivists working shifts reported better work-home balance and less overload. Another similar intervention involved changing attending coverage of hospitalist services to 2 weeks at a time rather than four [18]. The researchers found that burnout was lower after the 2-week rotation compared to the 4-week. Additionally, there was no difference in patient outcomes between the two conditions, as measured by unplanned patient return visits in the month following discharge.

20.2   Physician Interventions

Many have tried to improve physician wellbeing by focusing on individuals. Certainly individual-level interventions are easier to design, test, and implement than those at the organizational level. For instance, counseling on an individual or group level has been identified as a potentially useful intervention at the physician level. A Norwegian study enrolled 227 doctors and provided them with individual or group counseling [19] for either 1 day or 1 week, respectively. Participants experienced reductions in burnout, mental distress, and job stress. One year later, these same physicians had lower burnout, mental distress, and job stress compared to the pre-intervention baseline. Those who had continued to see a therapist had even greater reduction in burnout than those who had not. These data suggest there may be long-term benefits to short-term interventions [20]. In a similar study, group counseling sessions that took place over the course of 6 weeks were associated with lowering of psychological distress and emotional exhaustion [21].

Mindfulness, the ability to be present and focus on current thoughts and situations, also has been targeted as a way to address decreased wellbeing in physicians [22]. One intervention consisted of mindfulness meditation for an intensive phase of 2.5 h/week for 8 weeks followed by a maintenance phase of 10 monthly 2.5-h sessions. Participants reported decreased burnout compared to prior to the course, an effect which persisted for 3 months after the last session. Other studies have shown similar benefits from mindfulness [22–25]. One study showed the effect on burnout persisted 10 months later. While many of the studies of mindfulness have required extensive training and effort, shorter training periods have also been assessed and been found to be effective [26]. Even a short course of mindfulness over 5 days was associated with less burnout, depression, anxiety, and stress after the intervention [27].

Physician coaching has garnered attention as a possible intervention for improving wellbeing. A recent pilot coaching program was tested which aimed at specifically improving wellbeing [28]. Physicians met with trained coaches: two pediatricians and a clinical psychologist. At the meetings, participants would initially discuss their core values for optimal health and wellbeing. The coaches would then work with the participants on a plan and motivation to make positive changes within the specific circumstances of each participant. Most participants (89%) completed between three and eight visits. A subset of physicians (39%) agreed to participate in semi-structured qualitative interviews after completing the coaching program. Three main topics emerged from the interviews: boundary setting, self-compassion/self-care, and increasing self-awareness. Overall, participants reported the coaching sessions helpful, particularly for being mindful of the main topics and developing plans to help improve wellbeing. In addition, the personalized coaching helped find specific coping strategies for the specific stressors facing each participant. The coaching programs have typically targeted residents or junior physicians, thus may not be as effective with more senior physicians [29].

Similar to many of the organizational interventions, most of the individual interventions presented have been intensive and required time and resources. There are simple interventions which have shown some promise, however. Researchers aiming to help reduce burnout in a group of surgical residents used a simple belonging intervention [30]. The researchers had a group of junior residents read anecdotes from senior residents about their struggles as early residents. A control condition read anecdotes about ethical dilemmas from senior residents. For junior residents, the simple act of reading stories about how senior residents struggling during their residency led to a reduction in burnout compared to those junior residents who read about ethical dilemmas.

20.3 Limitations

Although the studies reviewed in this chapter represent a potential way to address the wellbeing crisis facing physicians, there are some potential limitations to be addressed. First, these studies rely on volunteers and many were only successful in recruiting a small fraction of their target population. The benefits observed in the studies could be representative of the individuals who are actively trying to improve their wellbeing and not a reflection of all physicians. This seems to be true in studies that have tracked non-participants [22]. It is also difficult to tell what moderating variables and confounders might be at play. This is partially due to the small sample sizes in the studies. Understandably, it is difficult to conduct large scale studies on organizations or with large numbers of physicians.

There may also be a file drawer effect, where the studies being published are observing significant changes in burnout partially because the physicians were high in burnout to begin with, and the interventions reported in the literature captured a regression toward the mean. Additionally, a small study which used an intervention to train coping skills to pediatric house staff did not find a statistical improvement in burnout, yet qualitative follow-up revealed that many of the participants were already using the techniques the intervention aimed to teach [31]. Thus, it can be hard to know why interventions may or may not be found to be effective in the context of research without taking into account all relevant variables, including participants' ongoing, independent activities.

One major challenge to understanding physician wellbeing is that published studies often report different wellbeing measures, making comparisons difficult. However, there is evidence that this is changing. The NAM action collaborative on clinician wellbeing and resilience has provided standardized definitions for many of these concepts (Chap. 4). Many researchers have begun using standard measures in the field, such as the Maslach Burnout Inventory (MBI) (Chap. 19). However, how they define burnout—is it just emotional exhaustion? Is it depersonalization? Is it both? Does it have to include low personal accomplishment?—is still variable, again making comparisons difficult.

20.4   Implications for the Future

The interventions reviewed in this chapter represent several of the more promising empirical investigations available. Many more interventions are ongoing. The AMA offers many CME courses designed on improving wellbeing. The AMA also promotes programs like STEPS Forward, which utilizes learning modules designed by physicians to help care teams overcome common challenges [32]. Yale has turned to technology to help with physician wellbeing by improving systems that were meant to help improve patient care, [33] and have begun testing voice recognition software to help reduce electronic medical charting.

In spite of the discouraging low levels of wellbeing for physicians, there are paths to a promising future. The Mayo Clinic has recently reviewed the past 15 years of their Office of Staff Services (OSS) [34]. Much of the knowledge about physician wellbeing and the interventions presented in this chapter have derived from this program. The OSS is an organizational program aimed at helping individual physicians. It was originally a financial planning service provided to the physicians, but it was expanded to assist with other personal and professional needs. Each campus elected a medical director, along with a peer counsel. The counsel was designed to be diverse in specialty and other demographics in order to foster enhanced peer-to-peer interactions. While the financial services are accessed at a high rate (75% of eligible staff), the peer support services are used less (about 5–7% of eligible staff each year use them). Notably, the peer services can be used equally for personal and professional topics.

The high access rate for financial services helps provide cover for physicians who fear the stigma of seeking help from the peer support services [34]. It was in this light that the OSS ran a pilot study to test a check-up protocol. Participants were invited to schedule a meeting with a financial counselor. The intake questionnaire included financial topics the participant would like to discuss with the counselor (e.g. retirement planning, tax planning) as well as some wellbeing topics (e.g. work-life integration, self-care). The financial counselors in this pilot received specific training about the wellbeing resources the OSS offered in order to properly refer the individuals to those resources. After the visits, most participants reported that that check-ups should occur on an annual basis.

Changing a system or culture typically takes time and requires new people to achieve power to ensure the change endures. There is hope that the culture of burnout and poor wellbeing in medicine may change. Many medical schools and residency programs have incorporated wellness in their curriculum, including Stanford Healthcare's Balance in Life program described in detail in Chap. 17 [35].

Undoubtedly, understanding wellbeing in physicians is a challenging task [36], and the problem may not be solved by a single intervention. It will require a collaborative effort between organizations, physicians and researchers. The largest benefits from interventions seem to occur when the change is focused at the organizational level, [37, 38] yet there may still be benefit to interventions for individual physicians as well. Although these effects are generally small, they are still consistently beneficial to wellbeing and are typically low-cost. For their part, researchers need to continue to explore a larger number and variety of interventions. In doing so, looking to other fields may prove advantageous. For example, in psychology, the study of wellbeing looks at those who are thriving and investigates how they thrive [39]. In spite of the pressures faced by physicians, not all experience poor wellbeing. Researchers will benefit from understanding what makes some individuals thrive then designing interventions to target those factors.

20.5   Conclusion

Evidence suggests that wellbeing is declining among physicians. Fortunately, many recognize that this requires action. The interventions presented in this chapter, on the whole, have been shown to be beneficial. There is an obvious need to further research in this area to be able to better understand the factors that impact wellbeing. Organizational and individual interventions should continue to be implemented, although perhaps the focus should be more on the level of organizations than on individuals. As long as the systematic problems of the electronic health record, work compression, and insurance challenges persist, it will be difficult for physicians to thrive using mindfulness or other individual techniques. There must be a collaborative effort with the physicians and administration at each institution to identify the specific issues which impair wellbeing. From there, they can identify the interventions which best address those concerns and implement them.

References

1. Andrew LB, Brenner BE. Physician suicide. Medscape Drugs Dis. 2015.
2. Shanafelt TD, Balch CM, Bechamps G, Russell T, Dyrbye L, Satele D, et al. Burnout and medical errors among American surgeons. Ann Surg. 2010;251(6):995–1000.
3. Dewa CS, Loong D, Bonato S, Thanh NX, Jacobs P. How does burnout affect physician productivity? A systematic literature review. BMC Health Serv Res [Internet]. 2014;14(1). [cited 2019 Jan 10]. http://bmchealthservres.biomedcentral.com/articles/10.1186/1472-6963-14-325.

4. Wallace JE, Lemaire JB, Ghali WA. Physician wellness: a missing quality indicator. Lancet. 2009;374(9702):1714–21.

5. Dyrbye LN, Harper W, Durning SJ, Moutier C, Thomas MR, Massie FS, et al. Patterns of distress in US medical students. Med Teach. 2011;33(10):834–9.

6. Brazeau CMLR, Shanafelt T, Durning SJ, Massie FS, Eacker A, Moutier C, et al. Distress among matriculating medical students relative to the general population. Acad Med. 2014;89(11):1520–5.

7. Dyrbye LN, West CP, Satele D, Boone S, Tan L, Sloan J, et al. Burnout among U.S. medical students, residents, and early career physicians relative to the general U.S. population. Acad Med. 2014;89(3):443–51.

8. Vasilou E. ACGME task force on quality care and professionalism [internet]. ACGME; 2011. (ACGME 2011 duty hour standards: enhancing quality of care, supervision, and resident professional development). https://www.acgme.org/Portals/0/PDFs/jgme-monograph[1].pdf.

9. Shanafelt TD, Boone S, Tan L, Dyrbye LN, Sotile W, Satele D, et al. Burnout and satisfaction with work-life balance among US physicians relative to the general US population. Arch Intern Med. 2012;172(18):1377–85.

10. Maslach C, Jackson S, Leiter M, Schaufeli W, Schwab R. Maslach burnout inventory, vol. 21. Palo Alto: Consulting Psychologists Press; 1986.

11. Regehr C, Glancy D, Pitts A, LeBlanc VR. Interventions to reduce the consequences of stress in physicians: a review and meta-analysis. J Nerv Ment Dis. 2014;202(5):353–9.

12. Awa WL, Plaumann M, Walter U. Burnout prevention: a review of intervention programs. Patient Educ Couns. 2010;78(2):184–90.

13. Dunn PM, Arnetz BB, Christensen JF, Homer L. Meeting the imperative to improve physician well-being: assessment of an innovative program. J Gen Intern Med. 2007;22(11):1544–52.

14. West CP, Dyrbye LN, Rabatin JT, Call TG, Davidson JH, Multari A, et al. Intervention to promote physician well-being, job satisfaction, and professionalism: a randomized clinical trial. JAMA Intern Med. 2014;174(4):527–33.

15. Fassiotto M, Simard C, Sandborg C, Valantine H, Raymond J. An integrated career coaching and time-banking system promoting flexibility, wellness, and success: a pilot program at Stanford University School of Medicine. Acad Med J Assoc Am Med Coll. 2018;93(6):881–7.

16. Linzer M, Poplau S, Grossman E, Varkey A, Yale S, Williams E, et al. A cluster randomized trial of interventions to improve work conditions and clinician burnout in primary care: results from the healthy work place (HWP) study. J Gen Intern Med. 2015;30(8):1105–11.

17. Garland A, Roberts D, Graff L. Twenty-four–hour intensivist presence: a pilot study of effects on intensive care unit patients, families, doctors, and nurses. Am J Respir Crit Care Med. 2012;185(7):738–43.

18. Lucas BP, Trick WE, Evans AT, Mba B, Smith J, Das K, et al. Effects of 2- vs 4-week attending physician inpatient rotations on unplanned patient revisits, evaluations by trainees, and attending physician burnout: a randomized trial. JAMA. 2012;308(21):2199–207.

19. Ro KEI, Gude T, Tyssen R, Aasland OG. Counselling for burnout in Norwegian doctors: one year cohort study. BMJ. 2008;337(nov11 3):a2004.

20. Isaksson Ro KE, Tyssen R, Hoffart A, Sexton H, Aasland OG, Gude T. A three-year cohort study of the relationships between coping, job stress and burnout after a counselling intervention for help-seeking physicians. BMC Public Health [Internet]. 2010;10(1). [cited 2019 Jan 7]. http://bmcpublichealth.biomedcentral.com/articles/10.1186/1471-2458-10-213.

21. Winefield H, Farmer E, Denson L. Work stress management for women general practitioners: an evaluation. Psychol Health Med. 1998;3(2):163–70.

22. Krasner MS. Association of an educational program in mindful communication with burnout, empathy, and attitudes among primary care physicians. JAMA. 2009;302(12):1284–93.

23. Asuero AM, Queraltó JM, Pujol-Ribera E, Berenguera A, Rodriguez-Blanco T, Epstein RM. Effectiveness of a mindfulness education program in primary health care professionals: a pragmatic controlled trial. J Contin Educ Heal Prof. 2014;34(1):4–12.

24. Amutio A, Martínez-Taboada C, Delgado LC, Hermosilla D, Mozaz MJ. Acceptability and effectiveness of a long-term educational intervention to reduce physicians' stress-related conditions. J Contin Educ Heal Prof. 2015;35(4):255–60.
25. Amutio A, Martínez-Taboada C, Hermosilla D, Delgado LC. Enhancing relaxation states and positive emotions in physicians through a mindfulness training program: a one-year study. Psychol Health Med. 2015;20(6):720–31.
26. Fortney L, Luchterhand C, Zakletskaia L, Zgierska A, Rakel D. Abbreviated mindfulness intervention for job satisfaction, quality of life, and compassion in primary care clinicians: a pilot study. Ann Fam Med. 2013;11(5):412–20.
27. Gu J, Strauss C, Bond R, Cavanagh K. How do mindfulness-based cognitive therapy and mindfulness-based stress reduction improve mental health and wellbeing? A systematic review and meta-analysis of mediation studies. Clin Psychol Rev. 2015;37:1–12.
28. Schneider S, Kingsolver K, Rosdahl J. Physician coaching to enhance well-being: a qualitative analysis of a pilot intervention. Explore. 2014;10(6):372–9.
29. Lovell B. What do we know about coaching in medical education? A literature review. Med Educ. 2018;52(4):376–90.
30. Salles A, Nandagopal K, Walton G. Belonging: a simple, brief intervention decreases burnout. J Am Coll Surg. 2013;217(3):S116.
31. Milstein JM, Raingruber BJ, Bennett SH, Kon AA, Winn CA, Paterniti DA. Burnout assessment in house officers: evaluation of an intervention to reduce stress. Med Teach. 2009;31(4):338–41.
32. Implementing Team-Based Care [Internet]. [cited 2019 Jan 9]. https://edhub.ama-assn.org/steps-forward/module/2702513.
33. New Technologies Help Clinicians Spend More Time with Patients | Yale School of Medicine [Internet]. [cited 2019 Jan 9]. https://medicine.yale.edu/news/article.aspx?id=15493.
34. Shanafelt TD, Lightner DJ, Conley CR, Petrou SP, Richardson JW, Schroeder PJ, et al. An organization model to assist individual physicians, scientists, and senior health care administrators with personal and professional needs. Mayo Clin Proc. 2017;92(11):1688–96.
35. Salles A, Liebert CA, Esquivel M, Greco RS, Henry R, Mueller C. Perceived value of a program to promote surgical resident well-being. J Surg Educ. 2017;74(6):921–7.
36. West CP, Hauer KE. Reducing burnout in primary care: a step toward solutions. J Gen Intern Med. 2015;30(8):1056–7.
37. Panagioti M, Panagopoulou E, Bower P, Lewith G, Kontopantelis E, Chew-Graham C, et al. Controlled interventions to reduce burnout in physicians: a systematic review and meta-analysis. JAMA Intern Med. 2017;177(2):195–205.
38. West CP, Dyrbye LN, Erwin PJ, Shanafelt TD. Interventions to prevent and reduce physician burnout: a systematic review and meta-analysis. Lancet. 2016;388(10057):2272–81.
39. Sin NL, Lyubomirsky S. Enhancing well-being and alleviating depressive symptoms with positive psychology interventions: a practice-friendly meta-analysis. J Clin Psychol. 2009;65(5):467–87.

Index